The World of Food

Third Edition

The World of Food

Eva Medved

Professor, Food and Nutrition
Kent State University

Ginn and Company

Design/Production:
Blackbirch Graphics

Cover Design:
Richard Glassman/Blackbirch Graphics

Contents

Preface

The purposes of this introductory foods text are these: to encourage an interest in the importance of good nutrition throughout the life cycle; to develop an understanding and appreciation of all kinds of food; to strengthen decision making in the choice, storage, and preparation of foods of all types; to encourage good management practices in the kitchen which will lead to conservation of food, time, money, and energy; to provide ways in which cookery skills and techniques can be developed.

The world of food is exciting. It offers many opportunities for students in the home and outside in the business and professional world. This text offers knowledge, techniques, and understandings which will help students to develop the ability to

- know the richest food sources for each nutrient
- understand the purposes each of the nutrients serves in the body
- understand why good nutrition is important throughout the life cycle
- make choices of nutritional foods each day which will best support body needs

- identify, understand, and apply the basic principles of cookery
- evaluate the various forms of food and make the best selections for each situation
- use standard products for the comparative evaluation of other foods and convenience items
- understand cookery terms and their applications in the achievement of the best results in food preparation
- identify and use tools of cookery to promote efficiency, to take care of tools and equipment, and to avoid waste of resources
- use recipes and other directions accurately to produce products of high quality and to conserve food resources
- develop management techniques which will conserve time, energy, money, and food resources
- develop a creative interest in the selection and the preparation of all kinds of foods
- know and appreciate the wide range of job opportunities which are available in the food world today

The World of Food is a comprehensive foods text. There are six units: Unit 1, Tomorrow and Today; Unit 2, Tools of the Trade; Unit 3, The World of Cookery; Unit 4, The Language of Meals; Unit 5, The Conservation of Food; and Unit 6, Looking Ahead. These six units are organized into 32 chapters. Each chapter is concerned with a major concept which is basic in the study of food in all of its aspects. The concepts of nutrition are emphasized throughout all of the chapters with special attention to the best sources of each nutrient and the vital importance of having a balanced diet which supplies the correct amounts of protein, carbohydrates, vitamins, minerals, and fats which are essential for the maintenance of good health and well-being.

Recognizing that convenience foods in many different forms have become a part of today's living, caution is emphasized in the importance of making intelligent decisions about their use. These decisions call for careful attention to nutritional labeling, quality, cost, presence of additives, and the amount of energy required. Students are encouraged to be well informed before making decisions.

In the beginning of each chapter there is a list of important words and their definitions. These words are basic to the understanding of the chapter. Students are asked to learn to use the correct words and to know their meanings. Where there are specific techniques or skills to be developed, steps are carefully outlined to make it easy for students to follow directions successfully. These steps are strongly supported by photographs or illustrations. Appropriate photographs show finished products.

At the end of each chapter the main ideas of that chapter are summarized and highlighted for easy reference and review. Questions and activities reinforce the content and offer opportunities for further applications of the principles presented in the chapter.

At the back of the text there is a collection of basic recipes, including ones of foreign origin. These recipes emphasize the application of the principles and techniques of cookery which are presented throughout the entire book. The recipes are cross-referenced to the various sections of the text wherein the principles are discussed. Mastery of these recipes makes it possible to make application of the principles and techniques in other recipes. Students are in a position to select and evaluate new and more complicated recipes for their accuracy and quality of product.

The *Teacher's Guide* outlines activities which extend beyond the text and suggests additional resources which may be helpful. The objective tests for each of the chapters are reproducible.

For each chapter in the text, the *Teacher's Resource Book* offers pretests, worksheets, and word games. A large number of recipes, each of which can be prepared in a single class period, are also included. These recipes are student-tested. They are classified as foreign, convenience, and ones which are suitable for microwaving. Answer keys for all of the various word games and tests are provided.

Both the *Teacher's Guide* and the *Teacher's Resource Book* suggest a range of activities, games, and tests which have been planned to accommodate a range of student abilities. This is also the case in the activities and questions which are given at the ends of chapters in the text.

Many colorful photographs and illustrations reinforce the text and motivate students to pursue their interest in food and its importance to life.

This text and its teacher's guide and resource book will foster excellent teaching and enthusiasm for the study of nutrition and food. Students will catch the excitement of *The World of Food*.

Eva Medved

1 Tomorrow and Today

Chapter 7

A Common Concern

Words for Thought

Nutrient
a building block of food that furnishes nourishment.

Carbohydrate
a nutrient — a sugar or a starch — that supplies energy.

Protein
a nutrient essential for building and repairing cells and maintaining life. It is found in meat, milk, cheese, eggs, and some other foods.

Computer
a machine into which information is fed and processed to solve problems and give meaningful answers.

Processing
an intentional treatment given to a food until it is consumed.

Organic substance
a substance that contains carbon, can burn.

Fabricated food
new foods or imitations of regular foods synthesized from agricultural products.

Food is a common concern. A part of each day is spent in securing food in some manner. This may mean going to the garden and gathering vegetables or picking fruit from the trees in an orchard. Some people may make trips to the local supermarket or the neighborhood grocery store. Others may visit the roadside stand or the specialty food shop. Some will find their way to restaurants, fast food shops, or diners. Regardless of where one lives, there is the ever present need to have food to eat which will nourish the body with those nutrients which make it possible to survive.

2

The Beginning of Food

With each generation, people have learned ways to increase their food productivity. As a result, people have been able to settle and stay in one region or to move about as they choose. Their food productivity has led to our present diet of grains, meat, fish, poultry, tubers, vegetables, fruits, and milk. These foods provide the nutrients which support life and promote good health.

Food technology permits us to grow foods where they otherwise could not grow. Technology has given us our abundance of food and our knowledge about the preservation of food from one growing season to the next. Our food is nutritious, safe to eat, of high quality, and it is convenient.

Food for All of Us

Protein is basic to life. The world's diet is built around grains, cassava, potatoes, yams, and other carbohydrate-rich foods. These foods contain only 1 to 12 percent protein. Therefore, any diet based primarily on these foods will be deficient in protein. An increased consumption of these low-protein foods can lead to overweight but will not eliminate malnutrition. The human body must have protein in sufficient amounts for health and well-being.

New Sources of Protein

All nutrients of the diet are important and needed, but adequate protein will be the most difficult to obtain as the number of people in the world increases. Animal products are the rich sources of high-quality protein—the meats, fish, poultry, milk, cheese, and eggs. If present sources become scarce in the future, people will have to find new sources or find ways to increase the sources being used at present.

Beans, peas, and other legumes are 25 to 40 percent protein. The green vegetables and immature flowers of these are considered sources of protein. These foods contain indigestible fiber. Consequently, people who eat these foods may be getting only 3 to 4 grams of protein a day.

Methods are being developed to process the oilseed cakes or residues of cottonseed, soy, sunflower, and groundnuts

3

A variety of sources of protein for human consumption.

A worker harvesting kelp which is to be used as a source of food.

which remain after the oil has been removed. For example, soy and cottonseed flours make acceptable food products which contain 40 to 50 percent protein. The green leaves from plants and coconuts are sources of protein. However, because they do contain so much fiber, they yield only 2 or 3 grams of protein when eaten.

Algae, bacteria, fungi, and yeast are other possible sources of protein. Research has shown that microorganisms can be grown on petroleum waste products. Some of these unconventional food sources are being used now for animal feeding. All of these sources offer some promise for increasing the food supply of people for the future.

Small fish can be converted into fish flour (fish protein concentrate—FPC) which can be blended or added to other flours in order to increase their protein content. Products such as spaghetti and breads which are enriched with fish flour are being well accepted now. Fish protein concentrate has been approved by the Food and Drug Administration for limited use by humans. No doubt more sea life will be looked at seriously as a source of animal protein in years to come.

The use of unfamiliar animals, oilseed cakes, leaf and microbial-protein products will probably contribute to the dietary protein needs as the need is felt.

Technologists continue to study and plan appropriate diets and educational techniques to encourage people to eat these diets. The overall aim is for every person in the world to have a diet that permits maximal health and well-being.

Organic Nature of Food

All foods are chemicals. They are organic, basically composed of carbon, hydrogen, oxygen, and nitrogen. All foods

4

are organic or natural. However, the terms organic or natural are used by some to identify foods that are not processed in any way. They are identified as organic or natural foods which are grown on soils which have no chemical fertilizers and are not sprayed for pest destruction. These organic foods usually spoil or deteriorate more quickly than do regular foods since they have not been processed. They are sold in special stores or in special sections in markets.

The organic or natural foods have no miraculous qualities, are not richer sources of nutrients than regular foods, and range in quality from good to poor. The usual deteriorative changes occur in all food, organic or ordinary (regular), unless the food is processed in some way to slow these changes. Refrigeration, for example, slows the growth of microorganisms and enzymes which are responsible for the deterioration of fresh fruits and vegetables.

You should be aware that some promoters of organic foods change existing facts to suit their purpose. You should remember that vitamins in organic foods are not any different from synthetic vitamins. They are not any more plentiful than in regular foods. In addition, organic foods are usually more expensive than regular foods.

Health Food Stores

You will find most health food stores are similar to supermarkets. They, however, concentrate on the promotion of special foods. The salespersons are likely to offer you free medical advice and prescribe one of their products. They often promote natural food diets which may be very unbalanced nutritionally and can be dangerous. Remember that it will be your own intelligent choices of foods that will determine the nutrient adequacy of your diet.

Processing

Processing refers to any intentional treatment given to the food until it is consumed. Foods are processed to preserve perishable food for future use. Food as it comes from the farm, or center of production, spoils or deteriorates quickly. Spoilage is caused by microorganisms. Deterioration is due to enzymes, physical damage, or to the influence of light, temperature, or oxygen which cause changes within the food. Food preservation controls these factors and makes foods available throughout the year.

The chief methods of food preservation use heat, refrigeration or freezing, fermentation, dehydration or drying, or additives. Sugar, salt, and vinegar were among the first food additives to be used. Some additives improve the color, texture, flavor, nutritional value, and prevent the growth of undesirable microorganisms. See the discussion on pages 14-17.

The Advantages and Disadvantages

Processing changes agricultural products into other forms which are more suitable and acceptable to us, the consumers. Processing makes available certain components or parts of foods such as flour, starch, sugar, and oil which are not readily available from food.

Processed foods are not inferior foods. They are nutritionally valuable foods even though some nutrient loss may occur with processing. When nutrient loss does occur during processing it may be in place of, rather than in addition to, that which occurs during home cooking. It is generally believed that nutrient loss during controlled, modern processing and storage is less than that which occurs during home food preparation. Nutrients are less likely to be lost under controlled conditions than with home conditions.

Any possible nutrient loss through processing must always be weighed against the advantages gained. For example, pasteurization decreases the ascorbic acid content of milk (milk is a poor source of ascorbic acid) while it makes milk safe for consumption. Heat processing destroys harmful or undesirable substances in some foods (cereals, seafood) and makes other foods more digestible. Food processing generally improves the acceptability and digestibility of food. It leads to a more varied diet.

Processing also permits the intentional addition of nutrients to improve the quality of the diet. For example, there are the enrichment of refined cereals and flour and the addition of vitamin D to milk. An expert panel of food technologists conclude that the techniques for food preservation used today do not cause major nutrient loss in foods. The advantages of processed foods far outweigh any disadvantages they may have.

It is also possible to provide more people with food in various countries of the world where there is great need.

Fabricated – Engineered Foods

Food scientists and technologists have developed and used various processing methods to create fabricated or engineered foods. These new foods are prepared from agricultural products. They may or may not have minerals and/or vitamins added. They are blended to look and taste very much like the actual foods they represent. For example, meat-like products (beef, ham, bacon, poultry) are made from soy proteins.

These substitute food products contain one or more ingredients from nonconventional agricultural products. Margarine, nondairy coffee creamers, whipped toppings, and meatless meats are examples of substitute foods. These substitutions permit the replacement of animal fat and cholesterol with vegetable fats. The meatless meats may be consumed by vegetarians and other groups which, as part of their belief, forbid the eating of meat.

Synthetic and Substitute Foods

Synthetic and substitute foods include at least one major ingredient from nonfarm sources. These synthetic ingredients enhance the color, flavor, texture, or viscosity of food products. Fruit drinks and fruit juice powders (concentrates) are examples of synthetic products.

Some foods are designed to serve only as snack items. They usually have few nutrients, much fat, and many calories. However, there are nutritionally sound snacks, too.

Packaging

You may have noticed that each type of food is packaged in a very specific way, but you may not have realized why this is done. As a new food is developed, technology also develops the appropriate packaging material to maintain quality and safety. Packaging protects the food from contamination and physical damage during transportation and handling. Packaging is also designed to protect foods from oxygen, light, moisture, and heat. These elements can cause the food to lose crispness, color, and flavor. Appropriate packaging and storage delay these changes in food products.

You may have seen the use of perforated film bags for fresh fruits and vegetables; a shrink film for poultry and cheese;

7

opaque film for cured meats which keeps oxygen out; vacuum and nitrogen back-fill packages for luncheon meats; and vapor-proof packaging for frozen foods to prevent drying. These special packaging materials add to the cost of the food. Packaging materials also carry labels which inform you about the food and its use.

Universal Product Code

You are able to select your foods from hundreds of items in a supermarket. Available for purchase are the original foods which are much the same as they were when they came from the farm, processed foods, and convenience foods. Whether you purchase food in a supermarket, specialty food store, or a convenience food store, many items will show a Universal Product Code for computerized checkout.

Some markets may have computerized checkout systems now. Others, no doubt, will eventually have such systems. Computerized checkout reduces pricing errors and is fast.

Here is how the system works. The items which you purchase are tabulated by means of the Universal Product Code symbol as they pass an electronic optical scanner. The computer prints the name and the price of each item on a screen at the checkout counter and prints the information on your sales receipt.

If the computerized checkout system is in use, you will find the price displayed on the shelves which display the items which have been coded. You will still have decisions to make about what you buy.

Why Cook Food

Other than some fruits and vegetables, most foods are eaten cooked. Foods are cooked to (1) improve palatability; (2) develop, enhance, or alter flavor; (3) improve digestibility; (4) improve or enhance color; (5) and to destroy pathogenic organisms and harmful substances that may be found in or on raw food. Water-soluble nutrients are conserved when small quantities of water are used in cooking food. Nutrients are also conserved when recommended temperatures are used and the food is not overcooked.

Foods that look good, whether raw or cooked, are more likely to appeal to people.

Browning

Short periods of cooking (boiling, broiling) will maintain the original palatability of food, while long periods (roasting, baking, simmering) can enhance palatability.

Almost everyone enjoys the distinct flavor of browned food. When you want to blend the flavors of ingredients in a combination dish (casserole, soup) to develop a new taste, you should use a long, slow-cooking process. When foods are overcooked, volatile substances and flavor are lost. Cooking in water or steam does not allow browning. When you want food to brown, use dry heat (roast, broil).

Cooking to Change Texture

You may cook foods to change their texture. Cooking usually softens the texture. The method you use and the length of cooking time determine the degree of softness that will be developed. Overcooking causes undesirable changes in flavor, color, and texture. The cooking method you choose and the time the food is cooked will help you control the results.

Food and Ecology

In the age of ecology researchers are looking for better use of existing food sources as well as new sources of food. The challenge is to continue to use our technology and, at the same time, develop ways that will not waste or pollute our natural resources. The world's resources are limited and must be conserved and used carefully. The care we take of our environment affects food as well as air, water, and land. By controlling our food and environment we may be able to survive.

Management—The Key

All of our resources should be used and protected to avoid waste and pollution. Good management is the key to efficient use of time, energy, money, equipment, and all resources in the production of high-quality food products. Management includes all of the decision making and planning of work activity to complete a task. When you are responsible for meals you are the meal manager. You will see that you will have to consider your goals (aims, objectives) and values (ideals, attitudes) and those of your family when you make decisions and plans. Skillful management of all resources helps you prepare and serve meals or to complete other tasks with a minimum of time and energy.

There is usually more than one way to complete a task. When you consider what, why, when, and how the task is to be done, you can select the best and quickest way to complete the task satisfactorily.

Conserving Resources

As a meal manager you will want to conserve all resources as well as food resources. Food conservation means no waste of food before or after the meal.

1. You will buy only quantities of food that can be used without spoilage or staling.

2. You will shop carefully in sanitary markets and select quality products.

3. You will quickly transport the bought food from store to home properly, to avoid loss of quality and spoilage.

4. You will not leave perishable foods on the kitchen counter even for a short time.

5. You will store all foods properly so that you will thereby control waste and keep foods safe for eating.

Home kitchens are often the sources of food-borne illnesses. Bacteria are present everywhere, even on foods, and are the causes of such illnesses. When the supply of food is more abundant than can be used immediately, preserve it for future use by canning or freezing.

You will also conserve food when you use basic (standardized) recipes, such as those listed on pages 518–563. You will learn about the selection, language, and use of recipes on pages 48–67. Recipes will help you to use time and energy well, avoid waste, and produce quality products. Remember that any recipe is only as good as the measurements you make.

Every profession or trade has its own set of tools as does food preparation. Tools are as basic to cookery as is the food. You will learn about cookery tools and their uses on pages 28-46.

Knowing which tool is best for each job is essential. You should know how to handle each tool and the cooking process for which it is suited.

Energy Conservation

The conservation of energy is one of the most important matters today. There are a number of very practical ways in which to use or conserve energy as it relates to the preparation of food. A number of these are listed below.

Types of pans. Whether you cook with electricity, gas, wood, coal, or any other fuel, the need to conserve energy is always there. You conserve energy when you cook foods on top of the range; if you adjust the heat level of the unit (gas, electric) to provide only enough heat to cook at the desired temperature. Use only pans that fit the unit. Too large or too small pans waste heat, and therefore, waste energy. You use much less energy when you select pans with straight sides, a slight curve between the sides and bottom, and with tight-fitting lids.

Cooking time. Cook foods only to the desired doneness to save energy. Electric units may be turned off shortly before the food completes its cooking. You use less energy when using the oven by following these suggestions.

1. Preheat the oven only when necessary.

2. Use the full capacity of the oven.

3. Set oven 25 degrees lower when baking in glass, ceramic, or stainless steel utensils.

4. Open oven door only when necessary.

5. Turn oven off shortly before cooking is completed.

Refrigerating foods. You can use less energy in the use of the refrigerator by practicing these rules.

1. Open the door only when necessary.

2. Fill to the recommended capacity.

3. Cover all foods to avoid loss of liquid which is drawn into the air from uncovered food. Thus the refrigerator is not forced to work longer than is necessary.

4. Space the items in a refrigerator to permit circulation of the cold air. The refrigerator and freezer operate most efficiently when properly filled.

Use of dishwasher. The dishwasher uses energy in three ways (1) to heat water; (2) to operate the motor; and (3) to elevate the air temperature during the drying cycle. Operate the dishwasher only when filled to capacity.

At any time heat or cold is produced, a motor operates and energy is used. You can conserve considerable energy each day through skillful management of food preparation and service activities in your home. Remember this as you are working in the kitchen.

Main Ideas

The use of different sources of meat, oilseed residues, leaf and microbial-protein products will contribute to the human dietary protein needs of the future. All foods are organic in nature. Foods that are termed as organic or natural are no more nutritious than regular foods. Processing refers to any intentional treatment which is given to food before it is consumed. Processing preserves food, enhances the nutrient and quality characteristics of food, increases food variety, and provides food convenience.

The Universal Product Code permits computerized checkout. Foods are cooked to improve palatability; develop, enhance, or alter flavor; improve digestibility and color; and destroy pathogenic organisms and harmful substances in food.

The challenge is to use technology to develop ways that will not pollute or destroy natural resources. Skillful management of all resources will help to conserve them. This means careful consideration of goals and values, and wise decision making and planning.

Activities

1. Examine the meat-like products in your supermarket. Of what ingredients are they made? How would you use them?

2. Examine the processed foods available in your supermarket. Identify the values they contribute by listing them under these headings.
preserved food
saved preparation time
added nutritional value
improved quality
improved safety of food

3. Observe food preparation and service activities in your school laboratory and list all of the ways in which the conservation of resources could be improved. Observe food preparation and service activities in your home and list the ways in which resources conservation could be improved.

4. Find a current article in your library dealing with foods in the future. Report your findings to the class.

5. Check your newspaper or current news magazines for articles about energy and its use. What are the concerns most often written about? Collect suggestions about energy conservation. Share them with the class. After discussion decide what our priorities for energy are.

Questions

1. Why are scientists looking for new sources of food?

2. What reasons can you give for food shortages throughout the world?

3. What is the value grains contribute to the human diet? What nutrient do they lack?

4. What are some unconventional future sources of protein?

5. Which foods are the richest sources of protein for humans?

6. Why are all foods organic in nature?

7. What is processing? Of what value is it?

8. What are fabricated or engineered foods? Give examples. How do fabricated foods differ from regular foods?

9. What are substitute foods? Give examples.

10. What is the Universal Product Code? How is it used? What are the advantages of the product code?

11. What is the meaning of ecology as it is used today?

12. Define management. How is management used in food preparation and service?

13. What resources are used in food preparation and service? Give ways to conserve resources during food preparation and service. Consider all of the resources involved.

Chapter 2

Convenience

Words for Thought

Processed foods

partially or fully prepared products which eliminate some of the preliminary preparation required for cooking.

Mix

a premeasured blend of ingredients, usually in the dry form, from which food products can be prepared quickly.

Convenience foods

foods which have been prepared so that part of the assembling, measuring, and mixing has been done in preparation for cooking, and part or all of the cooking may have been done.

Nutritious food

supplies substantial amounts of one or more essential nutrients and is relatively low in kilocalories.

Food additive

any substance added intentionally for a specific purpose during food preparation, processing, or packaging.

Cookery principles

the special rules, based upon science or chemistry, which are followed when foods are prepared and cooked.

A century ago, most Americans ate foods that were grown at home. The products from nearby fields usually came straight into the kitchen except for an occasional brief stop in the cellar or pantry. Today, most foods come from farms often thousands of miles away. They reach the family table only after passing through a food processing plant and then being brought by truck, plane, or train.

Technology has widened the number of food choices that are available on the market today.

Our Food

Although foods in jars, cans, bottles, and boxes are common sights on the supermarket shelves, they are often filled with new and improved food products. The many prepared and semiprepared food products have revolutionized the task of preparing the daily meals. The idea of convenience was introduced into foods gradually when the first foods were canned, the first bread sliced, and the first ready-to-eat cereals packaged. A chain of events began which led to cake and pastry mixes, TV dinners, and instantized foods.

Foods today can be purchased in a variety of forms: fresh, canned, frozen, dehydrated, partially prepared, ready-to-serve, and as packaged dry mixes. These foods are often called convenience foods; they have been processed or prepared to eliminate part of the preparation required for cooking or when part of the cooking has already been done.

Food Additives

Many of the new foods were made possible through the use of food additives which may be added to foods during preparation, processing, or packaging. They improve or protect flavor, color, and texture, and retain the nutritional values of our foods. Without additives many of our foods would not exist and others would lose their quality or storage life. Through animal studies, the safety of the additives must be established by the food producer before they may be used in foods.

Additives may be natural or manufactured. Natural ones such as salt, sugar, spices, and vanilla are used to improve flavor of foods while sugar, salt, and vinegar may be used as preservatives. Many additives created in the laboratory are identical to those found in food. For example, lecithin acts as an emulsifier and is chiefly derived from soybeans. Calcium and sodium propionate are found naturally in food and can be produced in the laboratory. The propionates act as mold inhibitors in baked products. Your body cannot distinguish between the laboratory-prepared additive and the natural additive.

All additives are used in very small amounts (100th of the amount actually proven to be safe) for a specific purpose. The use of the additive is declared in the ingredient list along with other ingredients in descending order by weight. The ingredient listed first is present in the largest amount and the one listed last in the smallest amount.

Additives serve special needs. Some are identical to the substances found in nature. For example, synthetic vitamins are the same as those found in foods and are used by your body in the same way. Vitamins and minerals are added to foods to improve the nutrient value and to replace those which have been lost in processing.

Antioxidants prevent undesirable color and flavor changes in vegetables and meat products. Ascorbic acid and vitamin E are natural food antioxidants. The BHA (butylated dehydroxyanisole) and BHT (butylated hydroxytoluene) on labels identify common antioxidants.

Bleaching agents such as chlorine dioxide and nitrosyl chloride reduce the time required for aging flour to improve its baking quality.

Natural and synthetic coloring agents are used to improve acceptability and appearance of foods such as carbonated beverages, dairy products, and some meats. The 1960 Color Additive Amendment to the Federal Food, Drug, and Cosmetic Act controls the certification and listing of color which may be used in foods, drugs, and cosmetics.

A number of preservatives are used to extend the shelf life of food products. Sometimes they are identified as antioxidants, inhibitors, and fungicides. Some commonly used stabilizers and thickening agents include gelatin, pectins, and vegetable gums (carrageenan). These additives promote the smoothness of confectionery products and frozen desserts and add body (viscosity) to beverages.

You can recognize that most of the foods which are necessary for good health are highly perishable—meat-milk-fruit-vegetable—unless they are frozen, dehydrated, or preserved by some technique.

16

You need to recognize that some of our foods contain natural substances which would be toxic if consumed in large quantities. For example, the solanine in potatoes, hydrogen cyanide in lima beans, nitrate in lettuce, myristicin in nutmeg are toxic substances placed in food by nature. All of these are healthful foods and need not be feared. You do not eat only one food and nothing else; instead, you eat a variety of foods, each with its own toxin, and without harm.

Federal, local, state, and city governments exert considerable effort to protect our food supply. Some of the federal agencies are the Food and Drug Administration (FDA), the United States Department of Agriculture (USDA), the Federal Trade Commission (FTC), and the United States Public Health Service. All of these agencies play an important role in maintaining the safety of our food supply. In addition, state and local governments also promote the safety of food sold in their areas.

The body is made up of the same chemicals which are found in food. Any food or chemical can be harmful when it is improperly used. It is for this reason that government regulations and standards protect the safety of our food supply.

Convenience Foods

Convenience foods are means of shortcuts in food preparation. Some may need the addition of other ingredients to complete the preparation of the product. Although the popularity of prepared mixes is relatively recent, the prepared mix was introduced in 1849, when a self-rising flour was placed on the market. Since then, increasing numbers of convenience foods have been introduced. The convenience mixes available include puddings, gelatins, soups, salads, cakes, frostings, breads, cookies, casseroles, salad dressings, and others.

Several points need to be considered when you are deciding to use a convenience food or a similar homemade product. Convenience foods generally require less time and energy, but you should also consider the cost, quality, nutritive value, and your skill in food preparation.

Canned Foods

Canned foods are convenience foods. Vegetables, fruits, juices, soups, meats, fish, chicken, and relishes are canned foods frequently purchased. There are canned puddings, breads, chow mein, spaghetti, meat balls, stews, and many other main-dish foods. When foods are canned, most of the work of preparation has been done during the canning processes. For example, the cleaning, peeling, slicing, and cooking has been done. Canned foods are completely cooked and are ready to serve or heat with very little effort. They can be used alone or in combinations with other foods. The undiluted canned soups can be used as cream sauces in casseroles, or over vegetables or meats. Canned vegetables are used in salads, soups, and stews, and canned or carbonated juices are ready to use directly from the can.

Frozen Foods

Frozen foods differ from canned foods in that many require cooking. Foods may be frozen raw for later cooking, or frozen after they are partially or completely cooked. Meats, fish, and poultry are often frozen raw and need to be cooked before eating. Most vegetables are partially cooked before freezing. If foods are frozen after cooking, only heating to serving temperature is required. Soups, whole dinners, meats, poultry, and fish are examples of cooked frozen foods which require only heating before serving. Frozen foods such as fruits need only defrosting and frozen juices require dilution with water.

The efficiency of the time and energy gained by using frozen foods instead of one of the other forms of the same food depends on the kind of food and the form it replaces. For example, a considerable amount of preparation time and effort is saved by using frozen mixed fruits instead of preparing a similar fruit mix from fresh fruits. The frozen fruit is ready to serve after thawing while the fresh fruit requires washing, peeling, pitting, and cutting. Thus, by using frozen foods less cleanup time as well as preparation time is required.

The time required for defrosting foods should be considered and included in the planning for a meal so that there will be no time wasted in waiting for the food to thaw. Try to allow time for thawing before you are ready to begin cooking. In this way, cooking time will be no longer than the cooking time needed for a fresh product.

Frozen foods make available a year-round supply of fruits, vegetables, meats, fish, and seafoods. Frozen, ready-prepared dishes provide a variety of foods which includes appetizers and desserts as well as main dishes.

Ready-to-serve Foods

The ready-to-serve foods may require less time and effort. They can be eaten as they are or added to other foods. Included in the ready-to-serve foods are breads, crackers, breakfast cereals, sliced cold meats and cheeses, a variety of jams, jellies, pickles, and bakery products.

Ready-to-use Foods

Ready-to-use foods are those in which all of the preliminary preparation has been done. They require only cooking or heating and are then ready to serve. Foods of this type include instant coffee, tea, cocoa, prepared stuffing, brown-and-serve rolls, instant potatoes, chopped meat, washed spinach, canned foods, some frozen foods, shredded cabbage, and chopped vegetables for both salads and stews.

Cost of Convenience

The price of convenience foods includes the cost of the food plus the cost of processing, packaging, labor and management, shipping, and marketing. For some prepared mixes, packaging costs may be just as high or higher than the cost of the ingredients themselves. It is difficult to compare the cost of home-prepared foods with commercial mixes, since similar products may contain different proportions of ingredients. The cost of a rich, homemade cake may be higher when compared with the cost of a plain cake mix. It is also important to consider the number of servings from a packaged mix and the cost of ingredients such as eggs, milk, or nuts which may have been added to the mix. Convenience foods may cost the same or more than home-prepared foods. However, the difference in cost may be made up by the smaller amount of time used in the kitchen. To the working person, this convenience may be worth the extra cost.[1]

Ingredients in Convenience Foods

Because the ingredients in convenience foods may not be of the same kind and in the same proportion as those in homemade products, there can be a difference in nutritive values.

1. M. H. Morison, "Ready Mix for Chocolate Cake," *Journal of Home Economics,* 49:283-5, 1957.

For example, the flour in a mix may or may not have been enriched; a minimum of egg, milk, or fat may have been used in an effort to reduce cost. The commercial mix makes use of the highly stabilized fats which do not contain vitamin A. It is important to read the labels on all convenience products so that you know their contents.

However, it is possible that some convenience items can be higher in nutritive value than the fresh products. For example, frozen foods can be more nutritous than fresh foods stored for several days before use.

Many of the convenience foods that are on the market today are those known as dry mixes. Any of those ingredients which can be converted to a dry form are suitable to be used in the making of mixes. For example, the common dry ingredients which are used in cake mixes include flour, leavening agent, some type of shortening, sugar, milk solids, salt, and powdered vanilla.[2]

Packaging of Convenience Foods

The packages in which convenience foods are sold are designed to protect them from contamination and prevent deterioration caused by contact with air, light, or heat. The most serious problem with convenience foods is prolonged storage which tends to reduce quality. High temperature and humidity also hasten the rate of deterioration.

Convenience foods, as all other packaged foods, must meet the general requirements of the United States Food and Drug Administration for all foods shipped across state lines. Therefore, convenience foods must be prepared from wholesome foods and must be fit to eat. Each label must list the name of the product, the net contents of the package, the ingredients used, the nutrient content, the name of the manufacturer or distributor, and the place of manufacture.

Cookery Principles

Mixes and other convenience foods are often better than a homemade product prepared by an inexperienced person. But a product prepared by one who understands the principles involved in the preparation of the food can be superior to the mix or convenience item.

2. C. H. Matthews et al, *Home Economics Research Report No. 22,* Washington, D.C.: United States Department of Agriculture, 1963.

The convenience foods created by science and technology have been developed within the framework of the basic principles of food preparation. It may be easy to heat and stir a product, but the way in which the product is stirred and the temperature to which it is heated are very important to having a finished product of good quality. In order for convenience foods to give the greatest satisfaction, basic cookery principles must be learned, understood, and followed. Convenience foods save the time of assembling, measuring, and mixing ingredients, however, they have not eliminated the need for learning the basic principles and the correct techniques and basic skills of cookery.

If products made from convenience foods are to be successful, the directions must be followed carefully. Better products can be prepared when one understands why specific directions are given. For example, you will make more satisfactory pastry from mixes when you understand that overmixing or handling can develop too much gluten and result in a poor-quality, tough product.

Use of Convenience Foods

Today's meals are a combination of traditional, prepared-from-ingredients foods and convenience products. It is important to know how and when to use convenience foods and how and when to begin with ingredients. It will be easier to know how and when to use convenience foods or the homemade foods if careful consideration is given to the quality desired in the product, your preparation ability, time available, cost, nutritive value, the equipment needed, and supplies or ingredients required. The foods from which to choose will be almost unlimited. Planning ahead and shopping carefully are bigger jobs than ever before and more exciting.

Convenience foods tend to eliminate the individual errors in ingredient selection and measurement, but they do not eliminate the possibility of failure due to lack of understanding of principles. Nor do they eliminate the possibility of failure due to one's inability to follow directions accurately.

Similar convenience products made by various manufacturers have different recipes or formulas. Therefore, it is necessary to use the convenience products and other ingredients that are suggested in the directions provided by the manufacturers if you expect the best results.

Convenience Foods as an Ingredient

Many mixes are valuable not only for their original, intended purpose of reducing preparation time and effort, but also are valuable as ingredients for creating new dishes. Soup mixes can go into dips and casseroles or flavor meats and enhance sauces. A packaged casserole may be a ready-made meal in itself, or it can be a ready-mixed basis for a gourmet meal of your own creation. A gelatin mix may be used alone for a simple, light dessert. Or you may add fruits or vegetables to make a salad.

Packaged croutons can be a crunchy addition to a mixed vegetable salad. When crushed they become a topping for a casserole or a coating for poultry. Canned or dehydrated soups can be used as the bases for gravies or the sauce for baked dishes. Or they can be added to vegetable loaves or croquettes. Frozen cherries or berries can become the chief ingredients in cobblers, pies, or tarts. Precooked rice may replace the potato as an accompaniment to meat, poultry, or other vegetable. Packages or dried vegetables, when reconstituted and added to broth, become a quick soup.

Homemade Convenience

Home-prepared products can also be convenience foods. Homemade breads, cookies, cakes, casseroles, etc. can be stored in the freezer for later use. The basic ingredients of flour, leavening, salt, and shortening can be made into a dry mix, refrigerated, and used later in making muffins, biscuits, pastry, and cookies. The quality of any of the products made from homemade convenience mixes can be equal to that of those that are made by conventional methods.

Creating Variety

Because convenience foods are mass-produced, they often lack variety, but creativity can solve this problem. However, before one can be creative with convenience foods, basic cookery principles must be mastered. Creativity through variations in mixes is possible only when the proportions of basic ingredients are not changed. Variety in convenience foods can be achieved in several ways. Different garnishes or ingredients appropriate to the convenience food can be added such as raisins, nuts, spices, herbs, cheese, or bacon. The convenience item can be used as an ingredient in a homemade product such as a pie made with a homemade pastry and a convenience filling. A change in the size and shape or the arrangement of the food will also give some variation and reveal your personality and creative ability. The widespread use of convenience products will present a challenge to create new food combinations to satisfy the need for variety in eating.

Foods with built-in service do make for more efficient use of time and effort in the kitchen. However, if their flavor, texture, and quality do not suit, the cook can prepare the food from ingredients. Your job in the fabulous world of food is to make the best food attractive and to create a desire for a healthful balance of varied and nutritious foods. Using time and effort advantageously, and having the security of knowing your convenience product is acceptable can be satisfying. Convenience foods are widely used but there is still personal satisfaction in making some dishes from ingredients.

Putting It All Together for You

Modern technology gives you the opportunity to make selections from the greatest variety of foods ever available. The world of food is surrounded by the world of management which involves goals, values, decisions, and actions. You are your own meal manager. You decide what foods your body will receive. The variety of foods available forces you to make choices among them. You as the meal manager must make many decisions—what to serve, when and where to shop, how to prepare, and how and when to serve the foods. Your food intake involves the resources of money, time, energy, personal effort and skills, and your abilities to plan, purchase, prepare, and serve food.

You will make decisions and take actions in terms of your goals and values for meals, for good nutrition, cost, personal satisfaction, time, and energy both personal and mechanical. Food choices are influenced by your early experiences, traditions, positive and negative food associations, and food availability. It is your responsibility to make good choices since they affect your entire lifetime.

When the food groups set the pattern for your food intake (see Chapters 25 and 26), your food choices can contribute adequate nutrients without an excess of kilocalories. Depending upon which foods you select and how you prepare them, the food groups can contribute about 1000 to 1400 kilocalories. Active young adults require more kilocalories than the food group recommendations provide. Some of the kilocalories yet needed could come from larger servings, margarine, salad dressing, sugar, and desserts. Another choice is to use any spare kilocalories for iron-rich and other nutrient-rich foods. At any time more kilocalories are needed than the basic food group choices provide, they should come through the choices you carefully make rather than unintentionally through high-calorie foods.

When fewer calories are desired, select lean meats, skim or low-fat milk, and hard cheeses. Avoid adding sugar, fat, salad dressing, gravy, or alcohol. Consume fresh fruits and vegetables to satisfy your appetite. You add variety to your meals when you select different foods each day. The meal patterns in Chapter 25 make it easy for you to arrange your food choices into meals.

Whatever the source of food, it is the individual who determines the nutrient adequacy of any diet. You have the opportunity to be well nourished. Whether this goal is reached is a matter of choice and knowledge. The information or knowledge you will need is given in the chapters which follow. The choice is yours.

Main Ideas

There are more convenience food items in the world of cookery than ever before. The degree of convenience varies with the product and the forms in which it is available. Convenience products come ready-to-serve, partially prepared, or requiring certain ingredients to be added. All convenience items are designed to save the user some degree of time. The choice of any convenience item is influenced by its time-saving factor, cost, and the quality of the final product. The cost of convenience products increases in proportion to the work saved. Even with convenience foods, which may reduce the work in food preparation, it is still necessary to understand basic cookery principles. Since many convenience items lack variety, a degree of creativity is essential to replace some of the desirable homemade quality which may have been lost in the mass production of the items.

Additives make new and convenience foods possible. They improve or protect flavor, color, and texture, and retain or enhance the nutritional value of food. Food selections involve goals, values, decisions, and actions. Individual food choices determine the nutrient adequacy of the diet.

Activities

1. Read the food sections of magazines and newspapers and note suggestions given for creativity with mixes. What suggestions do you have for using mixes and convenience items?

2. Select several different brands of the same mix that is a cake, cookie, pastry, etc., and compare the ingredients listed, the directions given, kind of packaging used, weight of contents, and cost per serving.

3. Why may it be difficult to compare prepared mixes with homemade products?

4. Visit a neighborhood store and a supermarket.

a. Compare the convenience foods and mixes offered.

b. What proportion of the store's space was devoted to convenience items and to prepared dry mixes?

c. Which store had the greater variety of mixes?

d. What foods offered for sale were new to you?

5. What do you think makes a food a convenience item?

6. Keep a list of foods prepared from ingredients and those prepared from mixes in your home. Why are some foods prepared from ingredients and others from mixes?

7. Prepare two different brands of the same mix. Which was better? Why?

8. Ask the manager of a grocery store or supermarket to recall some new food products that were on the market recently, but are no longer available. Why were these products a market failure?

9. Read the labels on a variety of foods and make a list of food additives you find. Why were the additives used?

Questions

1. Define each form of food.

  a. convenience

  b. canned

  c. frozen

  d. ready-to-use

  e. home-prepared

2. What determines the amount of preparation a food will require?

3. Why is it necessary to know basic cookery principles when mixes are readily available?

4. In what ways do canned foods, frozen foods, and mixes differ?

5. How do the ingredients used in a mix differ from those used in a homemade product?

6. What will help you to decide whether to use a mix or a home-prepared product?

7. What are additives? Why are they used? How is their safety controlled?

8. What factors influence individual food choices? What is meant by good food choices? Why are food choices important to you?

2 Tools of the Trade

Tools of Cookery

Words for Thought

Tool
a device or instrument used to perform a specific task or job.

Strain
to remove liquid from solid food by placing it into a sieve or colander.

Sift
to force dry ingredients through a sifter or sieve.

Stir
to mix with a circular motion.

Blend
to combine two or more ingredients thoroughly.

Chop
to cut into small pieces, usually with a knife.

Bake
to cook in a large or small oven. Container may be covered or uncovered.

Beat
to mix with vigorous over-and-over motion with spoon or beater to make smooth or to incorporate air.

Mince
to cut into very small pieces with a sharp knife.

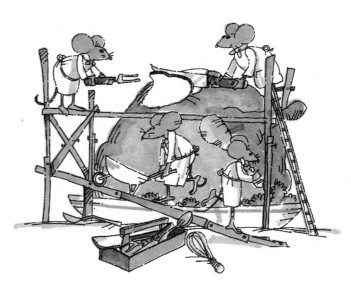

Tools are the mark of a trade. There are specific tools for each job and each vocation. Just as everyone who sews must have certain tools for making a garment or a carpenter for building a house, every cook needs the proper tools for the art of cookery. The proper handling of food materials alone will not insure good food products. The right kitchen tools must also be available for stirring, mixing, beating, cutting, draining, baking, top-range cooking, measuring, and for all of the various procedures of cookery. The right tool for the job is a must if the best results are to be realized.

Importance of Tools

It is important to know which is the best tool for a particular job. Using a wooden spoon instead of a fork to stir pastry may cause a poor product; baking cookies in a cake pan instead of on a cookie sheet may cause poorly shaped cookies that will not brown evenly. Each piece of equipment has its own specific use. It is important to know how to use each tool correctly and to know when it should be used. Proper use of cookery tools affects use of time and energy, and results in good food products. The tools of cookery recommended for specific cookery procedures are listed in the following groups.

For stirring, lifting, dipping, turning

Wooden spoon (graduated sizes)

creaming shortening and sugar, stirring hot foods or foods being cooked and sauces, etc.

Tablespoon

spooning ingredients into cup and many uses

Slotted spoon

lifting food out of liquid

Basting spoon

spooning liquid or fat over food during cooking

Kitchen fork

many uses

Ladle

serving soups

2-tined fork

lifting, turning large foods

Tongs

lifting vegetables, meats, etc. out of liquid or pan; turning meats without piercing

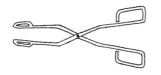

Pancake turner

lifting and turning pancakes, etc.

For beating and whipping

Rotary beater

beating icings, eggs; whipping cream, etc.

Wire whisk

beating air into egg whites

Electric mixer

mixing cakes, cookies, etc.; beating eggs, icings

For cutting, chopping, mashing

French or chef's knife

mincing and cutting nuts, celery, onion, etc.

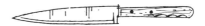

Meat slicer

slicing meat

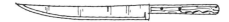

Bread knife (saw-tooth edge)

slicing bread

Paring knife

paring, cutting vegetables, fruits, etc.

Kitchen shears

trimming pastry, cutting dried fruits, etc.

Peeler (swivel blade)

scraping, peeling vegetables and fruits

Cutting board

protecting table top or counter when cutting

Potato masher

mashing potatoes and other foods

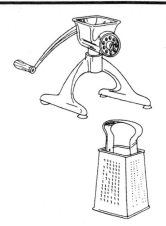

Crank-type food grinder

grinding meats, nuts, vegetables, etc.

Grater

grating cheese, vegetables, etc. to varying degrees of fineness

For draining, straining, sifting

Strainers, large and small

straining foods and beverages

Colander

straining coarse foods or puréeing vegetables and fruits

Flour sifter

sifting and aerating white flour and other dry ingredients

Food mill

puréeing vegetables and fruits

For measuring

Measuring spoons

measuring less than 60 milliliters (¼ cup) of all ingredients

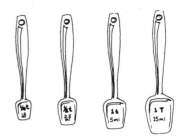

Liquid measuring cups 250 milliliters, 500 milliliters, 1 liter (1-, 2-, 4-cup) sizes

measuring liquids (usually made of glass)

Nested or graduated dry measuring cups 60 milliliters, 80 milliliters, 125 milliliters, 250 milliliters (¼-, ⅓-, ½-, 1-cup) sizes

measuring dry and solid ingredients

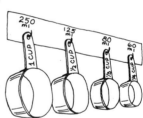

A balance

weighing dry and solid ingredients

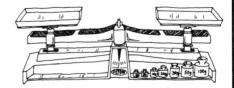

Straight-edged spatula (large and small)

leveling ingredients being measured

Kitchen spoon

spooning ingredients into cup

Rubber scraper

to scrape out cups

For cake and pastry making

Pastry blender

cutting shortening into dry ingredients

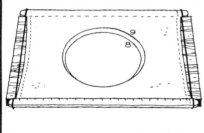

Pastry board; pastry cloth

kneading dough, rolling out cookies, pastry, etc.

Pastry brush

greasing pans, brushing dough with melted butter

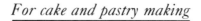

Rolling pin & cover

rolling dough and pastry

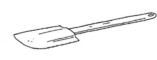

Rubber scraper

cleaning sides of bowls, etc.

Mixing bowls (0.48 liter (1 pint), 0.96 liter (1 quart), 1.9 liter (2 quarts))

mixing ingredients

Cutters of various shapes and sizes

cutting cookies, biscuits, doughnuts, etc.

For baking and oven cooking

Square cake pan (20 centimeters × 20 centimeters
(8 inches × 8 inches), 22.5 centimeters × 22.5 centimeters
(9 inches × 9 inches))

baking cakes, bar cookies

Roasting pan with rack

roasting meats and poultry

Wire cooling rack

cooling cakes, cookies, etc.

Cake pan (20 or 22.5 centimeters (8 or 9 inches) round)

baking layer cakes

Pie pan, metal or glass (20 or 22.5 centimeters (8 or 9 inches))

baking pies

Cookie sheet

baking cookies, etc.

Muffin pan (6-, 9-, or 12-muffin size)

baking muffins, rolls

Angel food pan

baking angel food, sponge, chiffon cakes

Baking dishes or casseroles

baking food combinations of vegetable, meat, noodles, etc.

For top-of-range cooking

Dutch oven

pot-roasting

Double boiler

cooking custards, sauces, icings

Steamer

cooking steamed puddings, vegetables

Deep-fat frying basket to fit large pan

cooking french fried potatoes, fritters, etc.

Griddle

cooking pancakes, grilled sandwiches

Skillets (large and small)

frying and pan-broiling foods

Saucepans (0.96 liters (1 quart), 1.44 liters (1½ quarts), 1.92 liters (2 quarts), 2.88 liters (3 quarts))

cooking foods in liquid

For cleanup

Vegetable brush

washing vegetables

Scouring pad or brush

cleaning stubborn food soil from pans

Bottle brush

cleaning bottles

Dishpan

washing dishes and utensils

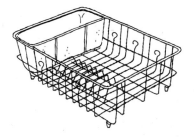

Dish drainer

draining washed dishes and utensils

Miscellaneous food preparation tools

Funnel

filling bottles or jars with liquid

Grapefruit knife

freeing citrus fruit sections

Apple corer

removing cores from fruit

Nut cracker

cracking nuts

Teapot

brewing and serving tea

Coffee makers (drip, percolator, filter)

brewing coffee

Meat thermometer

determining doneness of roasts

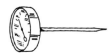

Deep-fat thermometer

measuring temperature of deep fat

Candy thermometer

measuring temperature of sugar syrup

Bottle opener

opening bottles

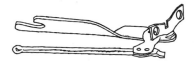

Can opener

opening canned foods

Melon-ball cutter

cutting melon, potato, butter balls, etc.

Jelly-roll pan

baking jelly roll, bar cookies, etc.

Individual custard cups

cooking custards and individual servings of many foods

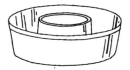

Ring mold

forming puddings, fancy desserts, salads

For cooking foods—Essential

Ranges (electric, wood, coal, or gas)

all types of cooking—surface cooking, roasting, broiling, baking

For cooking foods—Not essential, but handy

Fry pan

all types of frying, also for baking—custards, etc., vegetable cookery

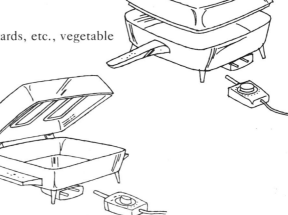

Broiler-fry pan

frying, broiling, baking

Roaster oven

baking, broiling

Microwave

cookery by high-frequency radiowaves

Ceramic cooking surface

a metal pan over heating coil under ceramic surface creates magnetic field to heat pan and food

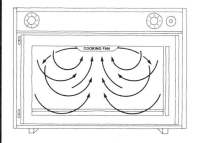

Convection oven

A fan in top of the oven circulates heated air evenly around the food in the cooling chamber. Foods do not require turning or shifting when roasting, broiling, or baking for even browning.

Rotisserie

roasting, barbecuing

Coffee maker

making coffee

Toaster

toasting bread, frozen waffles, pancakes, etc.

Waffle baker/Grill

baking waffles; grilling sandwiches; etc.

Burger cooker

convenient for preparation of one or two burgers

For food preparation—Not essential, but handy

Can opener (electric)

opening all cans except No. 10, (some have attachments for grinding and sharpening knives)

Standard mixer

mixing cake and cookie batters, and doughs

Blender

blending, whipping, mixing, chopping, puréeing

Hand mixer

whipping and mixing cake batters, icings, etc.

Food processor with attachments

beating, mixing, blending, whipping, slicing, grating, and puréeing

For food storage—Essential

Refrigerator

storing meats, vegetables, dairy products, prepared and cooked foods, eggs, frozen foods, ice cubes

For food storage—Not essential, but handy

Bread box

storing breads, rolls, etc.

Cake saver

storing cakes, pies, etc.

Cookie jar

storing cookies, rolls, etc.

Canister set

storing sugar, flour, coffee, tea

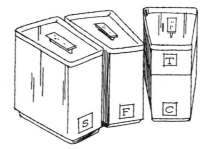

Refrigerator dishes

multiple uses for storing many foods

Cookery Tool Groups

The tools of cookery have been grouped according to the purpose they serve best. The food preparation tools have been classified as those needed for stirring, lifting, dipping, turning; for beating and whipping; for cutting, chopping, mashing; for draining, straining, sifting; for measuring; for cake and pastry; for baking and oven cooking; for top-of-range cooking; for cleanup; and for miscellaneous uses. In addition to the preparation tools, the tools which are needed for cooking and storing foods have been listed. Learn the tools and how they are to be used in preparing foods.

Cookery Tool Selection

A wide variety of cookery tools are noted; some of these are necessities while others are not. When selecting any type of cookery tool it is good to consider the following points: (1) What purpose will the tool serve? (2) How will it be used? (3) Can it be handled easily? (4) Will it be easy to clean and store? (5) How much does it cost? (6) Do I really need this tool? (7) Will this tool have more than one use? (8) Do I have a place to store it?

Any tool which is worth purchasing deserves to be used and cared for as directed by the manufacturer. With proper use and care, cookery tools can last for years.

Main Ideas

Proper tools and their handling are as basic to cookery as the food is itself. Quality tools may be initially expensive, but if properly cared for will last a lifetime. Essential tools are a first consideration; less essential ones may be added gradually over a period of time.

It is not a matter of having many different tools. But rather having ones with which you can do each job efficiently. Some tools can serve more than one purpose.

Activities

1. Identify the small equipment in the laboratory by name.

2. List the small equipment and give uses for each.

3. Read instruction booklets for the electrical appliances in the laboratory and outline the special instructions for their use.

4. Arrange an exhibit of cookery tools made from different materials such as glass, enamel, aluminum, steel, wood, etc. How does the material influence use, care, and appearance of the item?

5. Which food preparation tools are essential? Which tools of cookery make food preparation easier but are not absolutely necessary?

6. Examine the various small cookery tools in your home. List those that seem to be especially helpful as time and energy savers. Which tools are seldom used? Why are some tools more useful than others?

Questions

1. Why is it important to know the correct use of each tool and the cooking processes for which it is best suited?

2. What points should be considered when selecting cookery tools?

3. The next time you are in a department store, look in the household equipment section and see what other kinds of cookery tools you can find. How is each tool to be used?

4. List the cookery tools recommended for each of the following preparation procedures.

a. stirring sauces and creaming sugar and shortening

b. beating egg whites

c. mincing and cutting celery, onions, etc.

d. measuring liquid

e. cleaning sides of bowls and mixing spoons

f. cutting in solid shortening

g. cooking food in liquid

h. cleaning bottles

i. removing cores from fruit

j. determining doneness of roasts

The Recipe

Words for Thought

Recipe
directions for preparing a food.

Ingredients
a food item required for a specific task or job.

Equipment
all of the tools required for a specific task or job.

Measure
to determine the exact quantity of a food using a standard measuring spoon or cup.

Techniques of cooking
the methods and skills of preparing foods.

Equivalent
of the same value, measure, or quality as item replaced.

Metric measure
a decimal system of weights and measures (grams, liters, meters).

Substitute
to put or use in place of something.

In addition to the tools required for specific cookery procedures (as listed in Chapter 3) another important tool of cookery is the recipe. The recipe is a blueprint or a pattern to follow in preparing foods. It will tell you which ingredients to use and how to put them together. Each recipe has two important parts: (1) a list of ingredients used; and (2) directions for combining them to make a specific food product. Most foods undergo some kind of preparation for the table. There are as many different recipes as there are ways to prepare food, some complicated and some simple.

Recipes

Recipes are important to gaining good results in cookery. They are especially important for the beginning cook.

Recipes Follow Special Rules

The ingredients used and the directions given in a recipe for a particular product follow special rules or principles which are based upon science. From science we learn what nutrients are in food and how these nutrients will react to certain cooking procedures. Science tells us that protein will coagulate or become firm when heated, and at high temperatures it will toughen due to loss of water. We also learn that eggs contain protein. By applying this information to egg cookery, we know that heat will cause egg protein to become firm, and that low temperatures should be used to prevent toughening of egg protein. All good recipes are based on sound cookery principles. Since foods are made of ingredients which have a variety of nutrients, cookery is based upon scientific principles.

Standardized Recipes

For good results in preparing foods, it is best to select tested or standardized recipes. A tested or standardized recipe is one in which the proportion of ingredients has been carefully adjusted and the directions for making the food follow the rules of science. By following a standardized recipe carefully, you can produce a high-quality product every time. Tested recipes are given in this book and in most cookbooks, in government publications, in manufacturers' and food processors' booklets, and in newspapers and magazines.

Selecting Recipes

When there are many recipes for the same product, which one should you choose? Recipes which are selected with the following points in mind will be most satisfactory. Be sure that the selected recipe: (1) fits into your needs for the menu planned; (2) gives complete directions which are easily understood; (3) uses ingredients and equipment which are available; (4) is within the food budget; (5) can be made in the time available; (6) gives, if needed, temperature, time of baking or cooking; and (7) uses standard measurements. .

Other Recipe Information

Factors other than the proportion of ingredients and method of mixing that can influence the success or failure of a product are: the size of pan or utensil, temperature, and cooking or baking time. Good, standardized recipes also provide additional information such as: (1) size of pan or utensil such as 20-centimeters (8-inch) square, 1.89-liter (2-quart) casserole, or 22.5-centimeters (9-inch) cake pan; (2) preparation of pan (such as greasing, flouring, or lining with paper); (3) baking or cooking temperature, for example, medium heat or a specific temperature such as 180°C (350°F); (4) baking or cooking time (such as 20 to 25 minutes); (5) description of food when baking or cooking is completed as "fork tender" for vegetables, or "metal knife comes out clean" for custards; and (6) number of servings or yield (such as 4 to 5 servings, or 2½ dozen rolls). Each recipe has its own special directions.

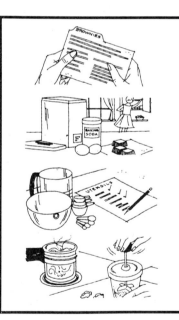

For Perfect Results

Read the recipe carefully! Every word of it.

Check to see that you have the ingredients you need.

Check to see that you have the utensils you need to prepare the recipe.

Complete preparation of ingredients such as chopping nuts, melting chocolate.

Carefully selected recipes can help you use time and energy to the best advantage and avoid food waste. Recipes usually list all of the dry ingredients first and then the liquid ingredients. This order will reduce the number of measuring utensils needed. It may be possible to use the same utensil for measuring more than one ingredient. Therefore, fewer utensils are needed.

Using Recipes

Carelessly used recipes can result in failure and waste of time, effort, food, and money. These steps will help you use a recipe so that the results will be good. First, read the recipe through. This will give you a complete picture of what has to be done and how. If you are confused, reread the recipe until every step is clear, every cookery term completely understood. Assemble the needed ingredients and equipment. Measure the ingredients carefully.

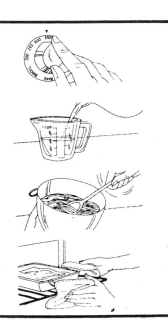

If oven is needed, set at desired temperature so that it can be preheated to proper temperature.

Measure as exactly as a druggist would measure.

Mix carefully, following every direction exactly.

Bake or cook as directed for perfect results.

Measurements in Cookery

Most of our recipes customarily specify cup and spoon measurements. However, in the next few years the United States will probably adopt the metric system and then liquids will come in liters instead of quarts and dry ingredients such as flour and sugar will come in kilograms instead of pounds. We now use metric measurements in research, clinics, pharmacies, and even in sports. In food preparation, you will be concerned with four metric units; *gram* for weight; *liter* for volume; *meter* for length; degrees of temperature in Celsius.

The metric system uses multiples of ten just as we do in our monetary system. The multiples of ten are identified by six prefixes that are added to the basic unit. You will use milli-, centi-, deci-, and kilo- most often.

51

Prefix				for Weight	for Volume	for Length
milli-	is	0.001	basic unit or	milligram	milliliter	millimeter
centi-	is	0.01	basic unit or	centigram	centiliter	centimeter
deci-	is	0.1	basic unit or	decigram	deciliter	decimeter
deka-	is	10	basic units or	dekagram	dekaliter	dekameter
hecto-	is	100	basic units or	hectogram	hectoliter	hectometer
kilo-	is	1000	basic units or	kilogram		kilometer

Customary measuring cup

Metric measuring cup

Our cup is based on the quart while the metric cup is based on the liter. Some measuring cups show our customary measure on one side and the metric measure on the other side. Both cups have a similar volume so that the difference in measurement with either cup falls within the tolerance permitted variance of plus or minus 5 percent set by the American Standard Association Institute for household measuring cups. The difference in position of markings on the two cups is very little. Look for these markings on the cups shown here. The next time your recipe calls for cup measurements use the metric measure.

250 milliliters   = 1 cup + 1 tablespoon
(¼ liter)   (8 ounces)
(2.5 deciliters)

Measurements must be made accurately to insure good results every time. All ingredients, whether liquid or dry, require special measuring techniques. The recommended measuring techniques are listed below and should be followed if one is to have food products which turn out successfully.

Standard measuring equipment

Graduated dry measuring cups 250 milliliters, 125 milliliters, 80 milliliters, 60 milliliters (1 cup, ½ cup, ⅓ cup, ¼ cup) sizes

Use for whole cups or fractions of cups of any dry ingredients or shortening.

Liquid measuring cup

Use for measuring any liquid ingredients. Note rim above top measuring line to prevent spilling.

Measuring spoons 15 milliliters, 5 milliliters, 2.5 milliliters, 1.2 milliliters (1 tablespoon, 1 teaspoon, ½ teaspoon, ¼ teaspoon)

Use for less than 60 milliliters (¼ cup) of any ingredient.

How to Measure Flour

Flour will pack on standing. For measuring, flour should be sifted once and then lightly spooned into a dry measuring cup to overflowing. The excess is leveled with a straight-edged spatula. The cup should never be tapped to level the flour; tapping packs down the flour and results in more than the required amount.

1. Sift flour onto paper before measuring.

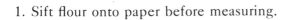

2. Spoon sifted flour lightly into dry measuring cup to overflowing.

3. Level cup with straight-edged spatula.

Presifted, no-sift, or instantized flours were developed to eliminate the need to sift flour. It was found that some adjustment in the amount of flour must be made when the presifted flour is used for regular recipes. The weight of a cup of unsifted, spooned flour can be adjusted to the approximate weight of a cup of sifted flour by removing 30 milliliters (2 level tablespoons) from each cup.[1]

1. O. Batcher and R. H. Matthews, "Sifted Versus Unsifted Flour," *Journal of Home Economics*, 55:123-4, 1963.

When your recipe calls for flour, not sifted flour, you may use the following spooning method to measure flour:

1. Spoon flour into a graduated "dry" measuring cup to overflowing.

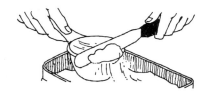

2. Level cup with a straight-edged spatula.

Note: Recipes calling for sifted flour will usually give you the best results time after time.

How to Measure Sugar

Sugar does not require sifting before measuring unless it is lumpy. White sugar is spooned into a dry measuring cup and made level with a straight-edged spatula. If brown sugar is lumpy, crush lumps with a rolling pin or press through a coarse sieve. Brown sugar free of lumps should be packed firmly into a dry measuring cup so that it will retain the shape of the cup when it is turned out. Use a straight-edged spatula to make the brown sugar measure level.

Confectioners' sugar tends to lump and may require sifting before measuring. It is lightly spooned into a dry measuring cup without tapping, and the measure is made level with a straight-edged spatula.

1. **White granulated sugar.** Sift if lumpy, spoon lightly into cup without tapping. Level with straight-edged spatula.

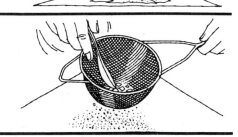

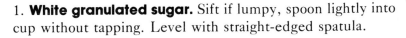

2. **Brown sugar.** Remove lumps by crushing with a rolling pin or pressing through sieve. Pack into "dry" measure until sugar holds shape. Level with spatula.

3. **Confectioners' sugar.** Sift to remove lumps. Spoon lightly into "dry" measure. Do not shake cup. Level with spatula.

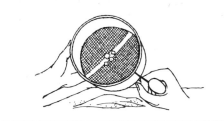

How to Measure Shortening

Shortening should be at room temperature when measured. Solid shortenings are pressed firmly into a dry measuring cup so that air spaces will be avoided. The measure is made level with a straight-edged spatula. Remove the shortening carefully from the cup so that none is left clinging to the sides.

Shortenings such as butter, margarine, or lard are often sold in 454 grams (1 pound) packages; butter and margarine are often packed four sticks to a pound. For approximate measures, a stick (114 grams (¼ pound)) of solid shortening is equal to 125 milliliters (½ cup). Butter and margarine wrappers are often marked with tablespoon or fractional cup measures. When approximate measures of butter or margarine are required (to use in a white sauce or to season vegetables, for example), the portion may be cut through the wrapper. Liquid shortenings such as salad oil or cooking oils are poured directly into the liquid measuring cup up to the desired level.

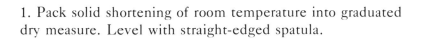

1. Pack solid shortening of room temperature into graduated dry measure. Level with straight-edged spatula.

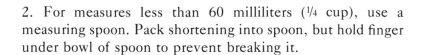

2. For measures less than 60 milliliters (¼ cup), use a measuring spoon. Pack shortening into spoon, but hold finger under bowl of spoon to prevent breaking it.

3. For approximate measure of butter or margarine, cut at desired mark on wrapper.
4 sticks (454 grams, 1 lb) = 500 milliliters (2 cups)
1 stick (114 grams, ¼ lb) = 125 milliliters (½ cup)
½ stick (57 grams, ⅛ lb) = 60 milliliters (¼ cup)

How to Measure Liquid

Liquid ingredients are measured in a standard liquid cup with a rim above the top measuring line. The cup is set on a level surface before pouring the liquid. Be sure to check the measuring line at eye level.

Place standard liquid measuring cup on level surface and fill to mark. Bend or stoop to check measurement at eye level.

How to Measure Dry Ingredients

Dry ingredients such as baking powder, soda, salt, cornstarch, cream of tartar, and spices are stirred first to break up lumps. With the standard measuring spoon, dip up an overflowing spoonful and level it with a straight-edged spatula.

Stir; then fill measuring spoon. Level off with straight-edged spatula.

How to Measure Eggs

Eggs vary in size from small to large; because of this some recipes call for milliliter or cup measurement of egg. Eggs are then measured in a liquid measuring cup and only the quantity called for should be used. Other recipes give the number of eggs required; in this case, medium-sized eggs are preferred. If large eggs were used the amount would be too great, or if small eggs were used the amount would be too little.

1. The eggs should be beaten with a fork or a wire whisk until the white and yolk are blended.

2. Then pour the beaten eggs into a liquid measuring cup to the desired mark. Remember to look at the cup at eye level.

2 medium = 80 milliliters = 1/3 cup
2 large = 125 milliliters = 1/2 cup
3 medium = 125 milliliters = 1/2 cup
3 large = 160 milliliters = 2/3 cup

How to Measure Other Ingredients

Ingredients such as shredded coconut, nuts, chopped dried fruits, and soft bread crumbs are lightly pressed into a dry measuring cup until level with the top of the desired graduated dry measure.

Lightly press coconut, nuts, chopped dried fruits, and soft bread crumbs into graduated dry measure of desired size until level with top.

How to Weigh Ingredients

Two scales, grams-kilograms and pounds-ounces are used to weigh all dry ingredients and solid fats. To weigh a small amount (grams or ounces) of food, waxed paper may be placed on the scale. The food is placed directly on the paper until the desired weight is attained.

Large amounts (kilograms or pounds) of foods are often weighed in a lightweight container. You should: (1) weigh the container, (2) add the desired weight of food to the container weight, (3) place the food in the container until the desired combined weight of the food and the container is reached. Foods to be weighed do not require sifting or packing as for cup measurement.

Language of the Recipe

Tested recipes and good measuring techniques alone do not insure good results with food products. The terms used in the recipe must also be understood. Many cookery terms are used in recipes. Each term has its own special meaning. It is important that you become familiar with the terms used in recipes for they, too, are tools of cookery. One must understand the meaning of such terms as cut in, fold, blend, beat, and others. They tell you what to do with ingredients. Some of the common terms used in recipes which refer to the techniques of mixing, cutting, and cooking are listed here with their definitions. The following chapters will include other terms of cookery which you should also know.

57

Terms Used — Techniques of Mixing

Beat

To mix with an over-and-over motion using a spoon, rotary or electric beater.

Blend

To thoroughly combine two or more ingredients.

Combine

To mix together, usually by stirring, two or more ingredients.

Cream

To soften and blend until smooth and light by mixing with a spoon or electric mixer.

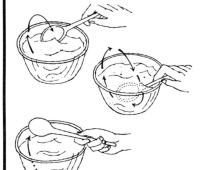

Fold in

To insert the edge of a spoon vertically down through the middle of the mixture, slide the spoon across the bottom of the bowl, bring it up with some of the mixture and fold over on top of the rest. Continue until all is evenly mixed. Used to combine a delicate mixture such as beaten egg white or whipped cream with a more solid material.

Mix

To combine two or more ingredients, usually by stirring.

Sift

To put dry ingredients through a sifter or a fine sieve to aerate.

Stir

To mix with circular motion of spoon or other utensil.

Whip

To beat rapidly with a rotary beater, an electric mixer, or wire whisk; to incorporate air and make light and fluffy as whipped cream or egg white.

Terms Used – Techniques of Cutting

Chop

To cut into small pieces with a knife or other cutting device.

Cube

To cut into small squares.

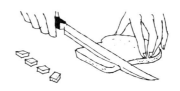

Cut

To divide foods into small pieces with a knife or with scissors.

Dice

To cut into very small cubes.

Grate

To rub food such as lemon or orange peel against a grater to obtain fine particles.

Grind

To cut by putting food through a food chopper or grinder.

Mince

To cut into very small pieces with a sharp knife.

Shred

To tear or cut into thin pieces or strips.

Sliver

To cut in long, thin pieces.

Terms Used — Techniques of Cooking

Bake

To cook in an oven or oven-type appliance in a covered or uncovered pan. The term "roasting" is used for meats cooked in an uncovered pan.

Barbecue

To cook meat or poultry slowly over coals on a spit or in the oven, basting it often with a highly seasoned sauce.

Boil

To cook in liquid, usually water, in which bubbles rise constantly and break on the surface.

Braise

To cook meat slowly in a covered utensil in a small amount of liquid or steam. Meats are often browned before braising.

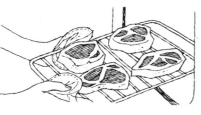

Broil

To cook under direct heat or over coals.

Brown

To make the surface of the food brown in color by frying, broiling, baking in oven, or toasting.

Deep-fat fry

To cook in deep fat which completely covers the food. Sometimes referred to as french fried.

Fry

To cook in hot fat.

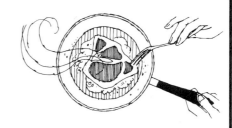

Pan-broil

To cook uncovered in an ungreased or lightly greased skillet, pouring off excess fat as it accumulates.

Pan-fry

To cook in an uncovered skillet with a small amount of fat.

Poach

To cook gently in a hot liquid below the boiling point.

Roast

To cook by dry heat, uncovered, usually in the oven.

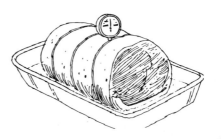

Sauté

To cook uncovered in a small amount of fat.

Scald

To heat a liquid to just below the boiling point. Also to pour boiling water over food or to dip food briefly into boiling water.

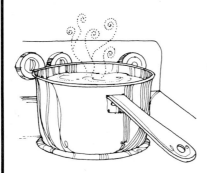

Simmer

Cook in liquid just below boiling point, 85-99°C (185-210°F).

Steam

To cook over steam rising from boiling water.

Steep

To cover with boiling water and let stand without additional heating until flavor and color are extracted as for tea.

Stew

To cook long and slowly in liquid.

Toast

To brown by direct heat in a toaster or in the oven.

Abbreviations in Cookery

Some units of measure used in cookery, at times, are abbreviated. In order to accurately read and understand recipes, it will be necessary to learn the accepted abbreviations and metric symbols as listed in the table below.

Abbreviations and Symbols in Cookery

few grains—f. g.

teaspoon—tsp or t

tablespoon—tbsp or T

cup—c

pint—pt

quart—qt

gallon—gal

ounce—oz

pound—lb

dozen—doz

square—sq

hour—hr

minute—min

inch—in

gram—g

kilogram—kg

milligram—mg

liter—L

milliliter—mL

deciliter—dL

centimeter—cm

millimeter—mm

Equivalent Measures

An understanding of the quantity relationship represented by the various measures used in food preparation is useful when making adjustments in recipe size and when calculating quantities of ingredients needed. Some important equivalent measures are included in the following tables.

Dry and Liquid Measures

15 milliliters = 3 teaspoons = 1 tablespoon
60 milliliters = 4 tablespoons = ¼ cup
125 milliliters = 8 tablespoons = ½ cup
185 milliliters = 12 tablespoons = ¾ cup
250 milliliters = 16 tablespoons = 1 cup
few grains, dash, or a pinch = less than 0.6 milliliters or ⅛ teaspoon

Liquid Measures

30 milliliters = 2 tablespoons = 1 fluid ounce
250 milliliters = 1 cup = 8 fluid ounces
0.48 liter or .5 L = 2 cups = 16 fluid ounces = 1 pint
0.96 liter or 1 L = 4 cups = 32 fluid ounces = 1 quart
1000 milliliters = 2 pints = 1 quart
3.8 liters or 4 L = 4 quarts = 1 gallon

Dry Measures

454 grams = 0.45 kilogram = 16 ounces = 1 pound
7.6 liters = 8 quarts = 1 peck
30.4 liters = 4 pecks = 1 bushel

Metric Measures

You will be able to convert cup, pound, and inch measures to the metric units by using the following tables:

Dry Measures

28.35 grams (28 g) = 1 oz
454 grams or 0.45 kilogram = 1 lb
(1000 grams = 1 kilogram)

Liquid Measures

1000 milliliters (1000 mL) = 1 quart
250 milliliters (250 mL) = 1 cup
14.8 milliliters (15 mL) = 1 tablespoon
4.9 milliliters (5 mL) = 1 teaspoon
(1000 milliliters = 1 liter or 1 L)

Length Measure

2.5 centimeters (cm) = 1 inch

Increasing or Decreasing Recipes

When it comes to quantity or size, most recipes provide enough food for six to eight servings. Because of this, it may be difficult to find recipes that will give the exact number of servings needed. If there were only two persons, you would not use a recipe serving six or eight. When friends come for dinner or the size of the family increases, the recipe may be too small. What can be done in these situations? If you are good with multiplication or division, you can reduce or increase the size of the recipe to meet your needs.

To make a half recipe, use exactly one-half the amount of each ingredient. To do this, you will need to know the equivalent measures listed above. Also, the food equivalents listed in the table on page 516 may help in dividing or multiplying ingredients.

If divided recipes call for less than one egg, beat up a whole egg and measure with a measuring spoon into two equal parts.

The leftover egg may be used in making scrambled eggs, sauces, batter coating, and french toast for example.

Baking pans used for half recipes of cakes or pies, for example, should measure about half the area or size of those which would be used for the whole recipe. The approximate baking time and oven temperature will be the same.

To double a recipe, use exactly twice the amount of each ingredient. For cakes, an extra minute of beating is necessary. The increased recipe may call for uneven amounts of ingredients. The following table may be helpful.

160 milliliters = ⅔ cup = ½ cup plus 2⅔ tablespoons
155 milliliters = ⅝ cup = ½ cup plus 2 tablespoons
215 milliliters = ⅞ cup = ¾ cup plus 2 tablespoons

You will need to use twice as many pans of the same size as called for in the original recipe, or a pan double in area, so that the batter will be of the same depth. The baking temperature and the time will remain constant.

Food Equivalents

Food equivalency tables help to determine the quantity of foods in terms of cups. The cup measures are often used in recipes, but kilograms and grams (pounds, ounces), and units (such as loaf of bread or box of crackers) are used when foods are purchased. Suppose you wish to make peanut cookies and the recipe calls for 250 milliliters (1 cup) of peanuts; how many peanuts would you need to buy? The *Table of Equivalents* on page 516 shows that 140 grams (5 ounces) of peanuts will measure 250 milliliters (1 cup), the amount indicated in the recipe. Use this table as a reference.

Substitutions

There may be times when the ingredients listed in a recipe may not be in your kitchen. This time, suppose that you wish to make brownies, but you have no chocolate. You could substitute cocoa for chocolate if you knew how to make the substitution. The *Table of Substitutions* on page 517 shows that instead of one square of chocolate you could use 45 milliliters (3 tablespoons) of cocoa plus 15 milliliters (1 tablespoon) of shortening. This table of substitutions is helpful in meeting emergencies, but it is best to use the ingredients listed in the recipe when possible. You can substitute one ingredient for another but the results may not be perfect.

Main Ideas

A recipe will explain how a product is made, but knowing how to use the recipe, how to interpret its symbols and terms, will insure the success of the product. Knowledge and understanding of cookery principles and techniques are also essential. A recipe, like any other tool, can be a great help, but only if one knows how to use it correctly.

Activities

1. Examine cookbooks, magazines, newspapers, and other publications that feature recipes. How do the styles of writing recipes differ? What other information is included besides ingredients and mixing method? What cookery terms are used?

2. What cookery terms appear in meat, bread, cake, and milk recipes? Which cookery terms appeared in two or more of the different food recipes?

3. What ingredients and what large and small tools of cookery would be required to make and bake a cake? To prepare and cook a vegetable? To make a beef pot roast?

4. Practice measuring flour, shortening, sugar, and liquid using the recommended measuring techniques. (Measure 250 milliliters (1 cup), 125 milliliters (½ cup), and 15 milliliters (1 tablespoon) of each.) If metric measures are available, measure sugar and flour in grams and deciliters and liquids in milliliters and deciliters.

Questions

1. What points should be considered when selecting a recipe?

2. List, in the proper order, the steps to follow when using a recipe.

3. Explain two methods for measuring egg.

4. Describe how to measure lumpy brown sugar.

5. Explain how you can use the markings on the wrappers of margarine and butter to measure these ingredients. Will this measurement be completely accurate?

6. Identify these techniques with the proper term used in recipes.

   a. to mix with over-and-over motion using spoon

   b. to combine a delicate mixture with a more solid substance

   c. to mix with a circular motion of the spoon

   d. to tear or cut into thin pieces

   e. to cut into very small cubes

   f. to cook under direct heat

   g. to cook uncovered in small amount of fat

   h. to cook slowly for a long time in liquid

   i. to cover with boiling water to extract flavor, color, etc.

7. Supply the following equivalents.

   a. teaspoons in a standard tablespoon

   b. tablespoons in a fluid ounce

   c. tablespoons in a standard cup

   d. grams in a pound

   e. milliliters in a cup

Chapter
5

Your Workshop

Words for Thought

Staples
foods which are used often and which are stored at room temperature, such as flour, sugar, salt, and rice.

Perishables
foods which require refrigerator storage such as milk, eggs, fresh vegetables, and fruits.

Work plan
a detailed listing of steps necessary to perform a job or task.

Sanitation
methods used to prevent and control spread of bacteria and other microorganisms.

Pretreatment
the manner or way of preparing a substance or material or surface for use or cleansing.

Conserve
to avoid waste, save, or preserve.

Safety
freedom from injury, damage, or danger.

Care
attention, cleansing, watchfulness given to an object.

The kitchen becomes your workshop as you prepare foods to create meals; it has all the tools and necessary materials. As you work here, you will use utensils (bowls and pans), large and small appliances (range and refrigerator, mixer and toaster), food, and recipes. Much of the work will center around the range, refrigerator, and sink. The activities you will perform include storing foods and supplies, preparing and cooking foods, serving meals, and cleaning up. At times you may use your kitchen to plan menus, prepare grocery orders, and set up meal preparation plans.

As the cook, you become the director of your kitchen. The activity which takes place, how it is performed, and when it is to be completed will all be determined by you. You, as the director, will want to look the part. Professionals who work with food such as bakers, chefs, and dietitians all wear clothing especially suited for their work, and are often recognized by the clothes they wear. The white uniform and high, white hat, for example, are symbolic of the baker and chef.

You, too, will want to wear suitable clothing when you work in the kitchen. Washable garments with short sleeves are comfortable and are easily kept clean. You will also want to wear an apron, uniform, or smock to protect your clothing while you work so that when you go to your other classes your clothing will be kept fresh and clean.

Your hair should be confined so it will not disturb you as you work and so there will be no chance of any loose hair garnishing your food!

You, your hands, and fingernails should be clean. Avoid wearing any garments or accessories which could become caught in kitchen utensils or equipment and cause accidents. Wear a comfortable pair of shoes with low heels and maintain a good posture since you will probably stand as you do most of your work in the kitchen. You ought to work at a surface which is of the proper height, one at which you can hold your body straight. When the work surface is too high, you will need to raise your shoulders; when the work surface is too low, you will have to bend your back. In both cases your muscles will be strained and you will become tired easily.

In addition to maintaining an attractive and neat appearance, you will need to organize your kitchen work in a logical order.

Food service workers dress in uniforms for their jobs.

Good posture is essential while working in the kitchen.

Procedure for Working

Before you begin to work in the kitchen, you need to arrange your work for preparing a single dish or a meal into a time-work plan. When you study Chapter 27, you will learn more about making meal preparation schedules. The steps in food preparation are to: (1) decide which foods you wish to make; (2) find the recipes; (3) check your supplies; (4) prepare a grocery list; and (5) establish a time-work plan.

The recipe is your guide for preparing foods. Read it carefully and make sure that you understand all the terms used. You may wish to review Chapter 4 on the use of recipes and to

Time-Work Plan

Foods to Prepare: Cocoa Drop Cookies

Food Supplies Needed:

All-purpose flour	435 mL (1¾ c)	Shortening	125 mL (½ c)
Soda	2.5 mL (½ t)	Sugar	250 mL (1 c)
Salt	2.5 mL (½ t)	Egg	1 egg
Cocoa	1.25 mL (½ c)	Buttermilk	185 mL (¾ c)
		Vanilla	5 mL (1 t)

Utensils Needed:

Set graduated measuring cups	Medium mixing bowl
Glass measuring cup	Wooden mixing spoon
Set measuring spoons	Metal spoon to lift flour and pack shortening
Flour sifter	Teaspoon to drop cookies
Spatula and rubber scraper	2 cookie sheets
2 sheets paper for sifting	2 racks to cool cookies
	Container to store cookies

Order of Work: Time in Minutes

1. Assemble utensils and ingredients.   3

2. Measure all ingredients.   5

3. Set oven at 200° C (400 °F), check rack position.   1

4. Mix cookies   5
   a. Soften shortening in bowl with wooden spoon.
   b. Add sugar and egg and beat thoroughly.
   c. Add milk and vanilla and stir.
   d. Sift flour, soda, salt, cocoa into bowl with shortening and stir to blend.

5. Bake cookies   25
   a. Drop rounded teaspoonfuls of dough on cookie sheet 5 centimeters (2 inches) apart. Bake 8 to 10 minutes.
   b. As cookies bake drop dough on second cookie sheet and begin to clean up.
   c. Bake second sheet of cookies. Remove baked cookies to cooling rack. Continue cleanup.
   d. After cooling, store baked cookies in covered jar or container.

Approximate Yield: 50 cookies   **Total time: 39 minutes**

check the meanings of recipe terms. You are now ready to prepare a time-work plan. See the sample above.

On your time-work plan, list the foods you wish to prepare, the food supplies needed, the steps or activities in preparing the foods, the utensils and equipment needed, the order in which you will perform the activities and the time required to do them. You may use the preceding sample time-work plan as a guide for preparing other plans of your own.

Pretreatment of Pans and Dishes

The pretreatment (rinsing or soaking before washing) you give to pots and pans or dishes will depend upon the type of soil and the kind of pan. See the chart on page 72.

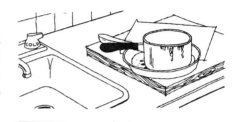

1. You should allow all pans which are very hot to cool for a short while before adding water so that you will not be burned by the steam formed. Any sudden changes in temperature can cause glass to break, enamel to chip, and thin metal pans to warp so the bottom of the pan will no longer be flat.

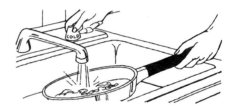

2. Use cold water to soak pans or rinse dishes which contained egg, milk, flour, starch, or cereal mixtures. Hot water will cook on these foods and they will be more difficult to remove.

3. For dishes which held sugar or syrup, use hot water to dissolve any remaining traces.

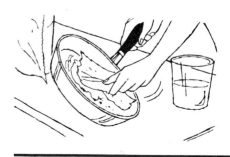

4. When the pans have contained greasy food, first pour off the remaining fat while the pan is warm, wipe out the pan with paper, then add a small amount of detergent and fill the pan with hot water.

When you use pans properly (control heat) and clean them well after each use, very few stains will develop. However, the following chart gives you suggestions for cleaning pans which have become stained. Notice that the kind of treatment necessary to remove the stain depends upon the type of pan.

Stain Treatment for Pans

Kind of pan

Aluminum To remove discoloration due to water or alkali: Use 10 milliliters (2 teaspoons) of cream of tartar for each quart of water and simmer until stain disappears (about 10 minutes). Vinegar and acid foods such as tomato will also brighten aluminum.

Enamel To remove burned food: Use 5 milliliters (1 teaspoon) baking soda for each liter (quart) of water and boil until food is loosened.

Glass To remove burned food: Soak in concentrated baking soda solution made with 15 milliliters (3 tablespoons) of baking soda for each liter (quart) of water.

Iron To remove burned food: Use 5 milliliters (1 teaspoon) baking soda for each liter (quart) of water and heat to a boil.

Stainless Steel To remove burned food: Soak in hot water with soap or detergent added. Scour if necessary with household cleanser. Brown spots caused by overheating pans cannot be removed; they are permanent.

Teflon To remove stains: Mix 10 milliliters (2 tablespoons) of baking soda and 125 milliliters (½ cup) of liquid household bleach with 250 milliliters (1 cup) of water. Boil this solution for five minutes in the stained utensil. *Wash thoroughly*, rinse, and dry; then wipe teflon surface with salad oil before using.

Tin To remove burned food: Soak in a solution of 5 milliliters (1 teaspoon) baking soda for each quart of water. Do not scour. This will remove the tin coating.

Cleanup at the End of a Meal

Every good cook leaves the kitchen clean. When you do not let foods harden or dry out on utensils or plates, dishwashing is much easier. Cleanup after meals will also be easier if you wash utensils and dishes and return them to their storage space as you are cooking. In this way, your kitchen will be clean and orderly rather than cluttered and crowded when you serve the meal. You will have more counter space for arranging serving dishes and platters which you are planning to use on the dining table. You will also have counter and sink space for those dishes which have been removed from the table during the service of the meal.

Your kitchen will also be neater at mealtime when you rinse and dispose of any empty jars or cans, waste paper, and garbage. Foods which remain in discarded containers attract flies and rodents and produce bad odors.

1. When the meal has ended, clear the table and take the soiled dishes to the sink area. Store leftover foods immediately to protect their eating qualities and nutrient values. They should be covered or wrapped to prevent drying out and to reduce flavor loss. Be sure to cool all hot foods before you store them in the refrigerator.

2. Scrape food from dishes and rinse under running water.

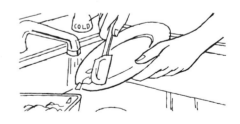

3. Then, stack the dishes to be washed on one side of the sink (side most convenient for you) in the order they are to be washed: glasses, flatware, cups and saucers, plates, serving dishes, utensils. The general rule is to wash the least soiled items first and then follow in order of soil to the most difficult to clean and greasy items which are washed last.

4. If you use a dishwasher, follow the manufacturer's directions for loading it.

5. When you wash dishes by hand, add a measured amount of detergent or soap (to avoid waste) and fill the sink about one-third full of hot water. Hold the dish near the level of the dish water as you wash it. Place the washed item into the drainer and rinse with scalding hot water. Be sure to rinse both the inside and outside of the cups, glasses, and bowls, and both sides of plates. Dishes which are scalded dry quickly and do not require drying with a cloth.

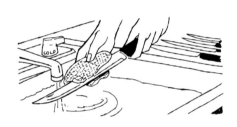

6. Wash and dry wooden items and items with wooden handles quickly so that they do not absorb water and become warped. Pick up sharp knives one by one and wash them carefully. Place them apart from the other items so that you will not cut yourself. Wash the remaining pots and pans last.

7. After the items are dry, return them to their proper storage space. In this way, you will be able to locate any item quickly when you wish to use it again.

8. Use a damp cloth to wipe the counter top, surface of range, and refrigerator. Empty the wastebasket and garbage (unless you have a garbage disposal) before washing the dishes.

9. Leave the sink clean and dry, especially stainless steel sinks which will water spot.

Make sure that all cupboards are closed and that the range is turned off. As the final touch, you may need to dry mop the kitchen floor. Also, when you use the dining room, make sure that the table is clean, that chairs are placed properly, and the room is vacuumed if necessary. Your kitchen and dining area are now in order. You, as the good cook, will always leave them this way, ready for the next meal.

Kitchen Sanitation

All the activities involved in preparing foods and the cleaning at the end of the meal can contribute to kitchen sanitation. However, the degree of sanitation in your kitchen will depend upon you and your personal standards of cleanliness.

Your first step to sanitation in handling food is to work with clean hands. Keep your hands away from your hair. As soon as you handle items not related to food (such as a handkerchief), you will need to wash your hands again.

Always use a separate spoon when you are tasting foods and when you are stirring.

Do not hang the dish towel over your shoulder or use it to wipe your hands. When flatware, utensils, or the dish towel fall to the floor, do not use them until they are washed. Your habits and personal cleanliness greatly influence sanitation in the kitchen. Foods are easily contaminated by careless handling and needless exposure to germs.

You are now aware that sanitation in the kitchen not only involves cleanliness of work areas, all appliances, and the entire kitchen including walls and floor, but also you and your personal habits.

Conserving Your Resources

As you work in the kitchen, you will want to learn how to use time and energy efficiently, and avoid food and fuel waste. As you know, the three chief activities in a kitchen are food storage and preparation, cleaning up, and cooking and serving food. When both large and small equipment are arranged so that these activities can proceed without wasting steps and motions, you will be able to avoid wasting time and energy. You will also avoid becoming tired.

Using Time in the Kitchen

The equipment which you have and the way you arrange it will influence considerably the amount of time and energy you will spend in the kitchen. Think of the kitchen as having three major work areas or centers; that is, one area in which to do each of the three major activities of storage-preparation, cleanup, and cooking-serving. What large pieces of equipment are required in each area?

In the storage-preparation center you will need cupboards to store staple foods (flour, sugar, canned foods, etc.) and a refrigerator for perishables such as milk, eggs, meats, and fresh vegetables. The more counter space you have, the easier it will be to work.

You will need a sink in the cleaning center and storage for supplies (soap, cleanser, paper towels, etc.) and utensils.

For the cooking-serving center, you will need a range and serving area on which to put food after it is cooked and while it is being arranged for serving. You also need storage space for utensils and dishes used in this area.

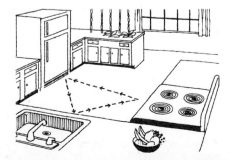

Food preparation usually begins in the storage-preparation area (refrigerator, cupboards), moves to the cleanup area (sink, cupboards), and to the cooking-serving area (range, serving center). In some kitchens as you move from the refrigerator to the sink and to the range, your steps will form a continuous unbroken line in the shape of a triangle. This arrangement helps to avoid wasted steps and motions.

Since you will carry out a particular kind of activity at each of the three centers, you will need certain supplies and utensils placed where they can be most conveniently used. The items which you will use most often in each area should be within easy reach, that is, bent-elbow reach or extended-arm reach. You should not need to reach above your head or down to the floor for these items. Store items which you use occasionally on shelves near the top of the cupboard or those near the floor. You should be able to perform each activity completely without crossing over to another area for a needed utensil or supply.

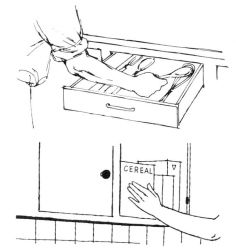

When an item may be used at more than one center, store it at the center where it is first used. For the small items which are frequently used at more than one center, as paring knives or salt, you may wish to have a duplicate at each center. This will help you to avoid crisscrossing from one center to another for the needed items.

The time-work plan which you learned to prepare earlier in this chapter will help you use time and energy well by helping you to follow a logical order for preparing foods. You will not use time trying to decide what should be done next, or retracing your steps to do an activity which you forgot to do.

You will also use time and energy advantageously in the kitchen when you understand a recipe so that you can work without hesitation.

When you work carefully and use equipment properly, you will avoid accidents and spattering or spilling foods. When you operate the range properly and time foods while they cook, you will avoid boil-over and scorched pans, both of which are time-consuming to clean up. Remember that messes you do not create do not need to be cleaned up.

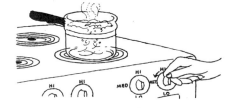

Utensils, equipment, work surfaces, and floors which can be cleaned easily require less time to care for. Checking your supply of staples and making sure needed foods will be on hand when you begin to cook will also save time.

Using Fuel in the Kitchen

You will use less fuel by using the proper heat setting for range surface burners or units and ovens and by turning them off as soon as foods are cooked. Fuel can be conserved by preparing an entire meal in one area—top burners, broiler, or oven—instead of using all of them. Set the oven for the temperature you intend to use. Do not preheat the oven too far in advance. Do not preheat for casseroles, meats, or similar foods.

Learn to cook vegetables in as little water as possible. Using more water than needed wastes fuel as well as water, time, and some nutrients. After the water boils, turn the control to "simmer" or "low" to maintain boiling temperature and use less fuel. Remember, slightly boiling water is the same temperature as rapidly boiling water. Use pots and pans with flat, undented bottoms and tight-fitting lids. Foods will cook quickly, evenly, and economically. You will work more efficiently and conserve fuel.

Safety in Your Kitchen

Safety in the kitchen means accident and fire prevention. When you know the possible causes of accidents and fires you can do a better job of preventing them. Burns, cuts, and falls are the kinds of accidents that can frequently occur in the kitchen.

To avoid burns, use pot holders when handling hot pans.

Tilt the lids of pots and pans toward you so that the steam will not burn your hand or face as you remove the lid.

Always keep the handles of pans turned away from the outer edges of the range so there will be no danger of pulling or pushing them to the floor as you move about the range.

Store sharp objects and knives separately; this will prevent cuts and, at the same time, the blades of your knives will remain sharp longer. As you work with knives, keep them apart from other equipment; and do not place them in the dish water but wash each separately.

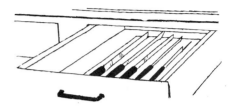

Keep kitchen floors clean and dry to avoid any accidents by slipping.

Use a sturdy stool when you reach for objects that you cannot reach from the floor. Also, keep the cupboard doors closed so that you will not bump into them.

Learn to use all equipment (electrical and nonelectrical) properly and only for the intended purpose. When equipment is misused accidents are more likely to occur and the equipment also wears out more quickly. You will recall that dangling jewelry and some types of clothing are potential causes of accidents and should not be worn in the kitchen.

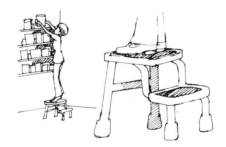

You should know how to avoid fires as well as other accidents. Strike matches away from yourself and hold them upright so that the flame burns more slowly. Make sure the match is out by running cold water over the tip of it before discarding it.

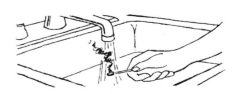

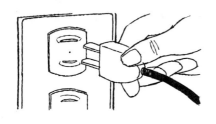
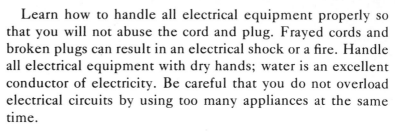

Learn how to handle all electrical equipment properly so that you will not abuse the cord and plug. Frayed cords and broken plugs can result in an electrical shock or a fire. Handle all electrical equipment with dry hands; water is an excellent conductor of electricity. Be careful that you do not overload electrical circuits by using too many appliances at the same time.

You will avoid an electrical fire when you check cords for breaks or frayed edges. Do not overload the electrical outlet, and keep water away from cords which are not waterproof. For an electrical fire, you will need a chemical fire extinguisher, but first be sure you turn off the electric current.

Keep your range clean so that grease does not accumulate. Do not use water for fat and oil fires; this will only spread the fire. Use a dry powder such as baking soda or salt to keep the flame from spreading. Carbon dioxide released by the soda consumes some of the oxygen required for the fat to burn. Use water to put out paper, wood, or fabric fires.

Care of Appliances

The range and refrigerator are essential appliances to every kitchen. All parts of the range require cleaning: the cooking surface, oven, and broiler unit. With proper care you will retain the beauty of your range even though you use it daily.

As you recall, controlling the heat-setting of surface burners and units will help you to avoid boil-overs; but, should they occur, wipe them up immediately. Acid foods such as tomato and lemon will cause the enamel to become dull. Since the surface of your range is actually glass fused onto metal (enamel), use a dry cloth to wipe spills when the range is hot, and warm soapy water when it is cold.

The surface units including the drip trays should be cleaned daily. The chromium trim (same as on your automobile) needs only to be cleaned with soap and water. Avoid using steel wool or soap pads on chromium or enamel for abrasiveness of these materials will scratch the surface.

80

Clean the broiler pan after each use. Allow the pan to cool for a few minutes after the food is removed, pour out the fat from the drip tray, and wipe it with absorbent paper.

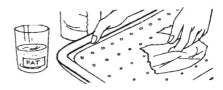

Place soap or detergent into drip tray and add hot water. Any hardened drippings will soften while you are at the table and while you wash other dishes from the table. The bottom of the broiler may be lined with foil to make cleaning easy.

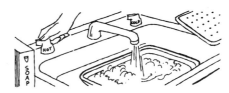

Electric surface units are self-cleaning. As you turn the unit on, the food will burn off. You need only to clean the drip pan by washing it in soapy water. Follow the directions given with your particular gas range for cleaning gas burners.

If you wipe the oven after each time you use it and when it is cool, you will avoid the difficult task of removing baked-on food, vapors, and grease. You may use a piece of aluminum foil (slightly larger than the pan or dish) under a dish, such as a cherry pie, that is likely to run over while baking.

The refrigerator, like the range, will be easy to keep clean with daily care. Make sure your hands are clean when you open and close the refrigerator, keep foods covered, and try to avoid spills. By doing this, your refrigerator will require little daily care. To clean the outer surface of the refrigerator, wipe it with a damp cloth whenever necessary.

If your refrigerator is self-defrosting, the interior will need occasional cleaning with baking soda solution: (5 milliliters (1 teaspoon) soda for 1 liter (1 quart) of water). Defrost refrigerators which do not defrost automatically when frost is about 6.25 millimeters (¼ inch) thick.

Turn the control to off or defrost. Remove frozen foods and wrap them in several sheets of newspaper to prevent thawing. You may place pans (not ice trays) of hot water into the freezer compartment for quicker defrosting.

Remove all food from the refrigerator and clean the interior and the freezer with a baking soda solution.

Turn the control to normal setting and replace the food. Wash the ice trays and the outside of the refrigerator with warm water and a mild detergent or soap. The instruction booklet for your refrigerator will give you complete instructions.

In addition to large appliances, kitchen equipment includes small electrical appliances. The booklet which comes with each appliance is your best guide for its use and care.

Handle small appliances gently and avoid dropping them. Always connect or disconnect an appliance by grasping the plug and not by pulling the cord. Connect the appliance by plugging the cord into the appliance first; then into the electrical outlet. Remove the plug from the outlet before you remove the cord from the appliance.

Heating units of appliances are never placed into water unless they are water sealed. Small appliances such as coffeemakers and mixers should be cleaned after each use. The inside of the coffeemaker is washed with soapy water and the outside should be wiped unless it has an immersible unit (one that is sealed). Beaters and bowls of electric mixers are washed in hot soapy water. The power unit or motor needs only to be wiped with a damp cloth.

Main Ideas

In any cooking situation, the cook, kitchen, and all equipment to be used must be clean and organized, so that the cooking can be done with the least effort and confusion. A definite plan or schedule of kitchen activities promotes efficiency while working. Because the kitchen with all its equipment can be a potential safety and fire hazard, the proper care and the use of appliances and equipment are absolutely necessary.

Activities

1. Look in magazines for kitchen storage ideas. Bring these to class. Can you apply any of them?

2. Read the directions for the use and care of a small appliance available in your school laboratory and demonstrate the appliance.

3. For each of three work centers (storage and preparation, cleanup, and cooking-serving), list the equipment which should be within bent-elbow reach. Is your school equipment arranged in this way?

4. Find pans in your school laboratory which are discolored. Use the recommended method for removing the stains.

5. Develop what you think is an efficient plan for dishwashing, then wash dishes according to it. What changes did you make in your plan which were different from the usual method of washing dishes? Was your plan an improvement? Why?

6. On graph paper draw to scale the kitchen in your home. Mark the path you would travel to prepare the recipe listed on page 70 and to clean up afterward. Did your path form a triangle? Did your path cross over at any of the centers? Did you retrace any of your steps? If so, how could this be avoided?

7. Observe your kitchen at home during meal preparation. Did you notice any possible fire or accident hazards? Have you observed any of these hazards in your school kitchen? How could the hazards both at home and school be eliminated?

8. With permission, select one of the three major work areas in your home kitchen and check the equipment arrangement. Would you make any changes for the items that are stored within bent-elbow reach? Within extended-arm reach? Discuss these changes before you rearrange the equipment. What kinds of changes did you propose to make? Were the changes actually made?

9. Select a recipe for which a comparable convenience product is available such as cake, muffins, or casserole. Read the directions (recipe) for preparing the product you selected with ingredients and with a mix. In what ways are the directions for the making of the product similar and different? Explain the reasons for the similarities or for the differences.

Questions

1. What are the three major work areas in a kitchen and what kinds of activities are performed in each?

2. Why is good grooming important when you prepare food?

3. Why are recipes essential to food preparation?

4. What are the advantages of a time-work plan for preparing food?

5. What pretreatment is required for food preparation?

6. What methods can be used to remove stains from cooking utensils?

7. In what ways can cleanup after meals be made easy?

8. Describe the logical procedure to follow when you are doing cleanup in the kitchen.

9. How can you use time and energy in the kitchen efficiently? Fuel and food?

10. What causes electrical fires?

11. How can kitchen fires be controlled?

12. How can kitchen accidents be prevented?

13. How can sanitation be observed in the kitchen?

14. What care is required by the range? Refrigerator?

15. What is a surface unit? Surface burner?

16. How could you reduce the amount of time required to clean a refrigerator? Range?

17. What care is required by small electrical appliances?

18. What is your best guide to the care of equipment?

19. How should foods be stored in the refrigerator? Why?

20. Why should you clean a self-defrosting refrigerator?

3 The World of Cookery

Words for Thought

Vitamin

a nutrient essential for growth and normal functioning of the body required in very small amounts.

Ascorbic acid

the chemical name for vitamin C.

Scurvy

a disease of joints, teeth, and blood vessels caused by a severe lack of vitamin C.

Collagen

a cement-like substance which binds or holds the cells together.

Carotene

a yellow to orange plant pigment that can be converted to vitamin A by the body.

Enzyme

a substance which causes a chemical reaction to take place. There are many kinds of enzymes; some cause fruits to ripen, while others split large food molecules into smaller particles during digestion.

Fruit

a product of a tree or plant containing the seed, used for food.

Protective food

serves to maintain health and growth by providing nutrients.

Canned

preserved by heating and sealing in a can or glass jar.

Storage

placing foods or objects in a container or space to protect them.

Chapter
6
Fruits

Ever since Eden and the forbidden apple fruit has played an important part in the lives of people. Fruit has even helped people to endure the seas. During long voyages, a disease called scurvy developed among the sailors. James Lind, surgeon to the British Navy, performed an experiment in 1747 in which he chose twelve sailors who showed similar symptoms of scurvy and grouped them into six pairs. These men ate the same food prepared in the ship's kitchen but were given different remedies to cure them of scurvy. Every day, two of these sailors drank a quart of cider; two others received twenty-five drops of dilute sulfuric acid three times a day; a third pair drank two spoonfuls of vinegar three times a day; a fourth pair drank sea water; a fifth pair ate a nutmeg three times a day; and a sixth pair ate two oranges and a lemon daily.

The sailors who ate the oranges and lemons were the only ones who showed improvement and, by the sixth day, were able to report for duty. Forty-eight years later, the British Navy began the practice of giving a small amount of lime juice each day to every sailor so that scurvy could be prevented. Because of this practice, the British sailors were nicknamed "limeys." The substance in oranges, lemons, and limes which prevented the sailors from contracting scurvy was vitamin C, or ascorbic acid.

This experiment of Lind's and those of his successors in the twentieth century have established the protective value of fruits. Because fruits contribute vitamins, minerals, and cellulose (bulk), they are called "protective" foods.

Because of their varied sizes and shapes, colors, flavors, and aroma, fruits add joy to eating. Modern transportation, packaging, and refrigeration make it possible to have fresh fruits the year round.

Fruit Groups

The many varieties of fruits can be divided into groups or classes according to their shape, structure, and botanical nature. One such grouping includes the following: pomes, drupes, berries, citrus fruit, melons, and tropical fruits.

Pomes

The pomes are characterized by a smooth skin covering an enlarged fleshy area surrounding the core.

Apples range in color from green to yellow to red. They have many uses and an excellent keeping quality.

Pears range in color from green-yellow, yellow with red blush to brown. They are eaten raw, canned, pickled, or dried.

Quince is creamy yellow in color, has a hard texture, and a tart flavor. It is used primarily for jellies and preserves.

Kiwi fruit is a fuzzy, brown pear from New Zealand. The fuzz is rubbed off and the fruit is peeled. It has a sweet lime-like flavor.

Drupes

Drupes contain a single seed, surrounded by a fleshy, juicy, edible portion. They are used fresh, frozen, canned, and in jellies.

Peaches are white or yellow in color with a fuzzy skin. They are spherical in shape with a groove on one side.

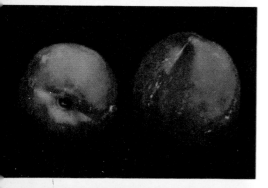

Nectarines have a smooth yellow skin with a red blush. They are similar in flavor and shape to a peach.

Apricots are yellow-orange in color. They are juicy with a sweet flavor. They have a smooth skin and are smaller than a peach.

Sweet cherries range in color from pale yellow with a red blush to dark red or purple. Their flesh is firm. Sour cherries are red with a soft flesh.

Plums are red, yellow, green, or blue to purple in color.

Berries

Berries are pulpy and succulent, with tiny seeds imbedded in the flesh. They have a fragile cell structure.

Blackberries are dark in color and are used mainly for desserts, jams, jellies, and juices.

Blueberries have a smooth skin, and are blue-black in color. They may be frozen or canned. They are used for desserts, jams, and jellies.

Cranberries are bright red. They are used for sauces, jellies, and juices.

Strawberries are a deep, bright red color and range in size from very small to over an inch in diameter. They are a popular dessert berry and are also used in jams, syrups, ice cream, and confections.

Grapes are berries with fairly tough skins which grow in bunches. They range in color from green to red and purple. They are used for desserts, juices, jams, conserves, and jellies.

Citrus Fruit

Grapefruits have a smooth yellow skin. Their flesh is white, pink, or red and may or may not have seeds.

The citron resembles a large avocado. It is not eaten raw. The fleshy portion is used as candied citron peel.

The kumquat is a bright orange, oval, small fruit. The rind and the pulp can be eaten. It is used to make preserves and is candied.

Ugli fruit, grown in Jamaica, is one of the latest additions to the citrus family. It is thought to be a cross between a tangerine, an orange, and a grapefruit.

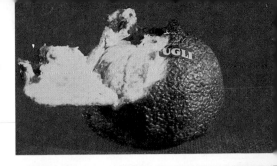

The tangerine has a very loose skin and segments that separate very easily. It is a dessert fruit.

The tangelo is a tangerine crossed with a grapefruit. It is juicy, thick-skinned, and easy to peel.

The Mandarin orange is grown in China and Japan and is usually available in the canned form. It is used in desserts and salads.

The navel orange has an umbilical mark on the blossom end of the fruit. It has a thick skin and is seedless. It is grown mainly in California and is used as a dessert.

The Valencia orange is known as the juice orange because of its thin skin and high juice content.

The Temple orange is a cross between a sweet orange and a tangerine. It is used as a dessert fruit.

The lemon has a yellow, smooth skin and a very tart flavor. It is used as an ingredient in beverages, baked products, jams, jellies, and candies.

The lime is smaller than a lemon and has a green skin. It has a tart flavor and is used in beverages and desserts and as a garnish for other foods.

Melons

The muskmelon has a grooved, netted outer surface and orange flesh.

The Casaba melon has yellowish-white flesh.

The Persian melon is similar to a cantaloupe but has a thicker flesh.

The Casaba and Persian melons were crossed to produce the Cranshaw melon which has a rich flavor and salmon color.

The cantaloupe has a netted outer surface and dark yellow to orange flesh.

The honeydew has a smooth, hard outer surface. The flesh is greenish-white.

The watermelon has a smooth green or green-striped skin. It is large and elliptical in shape and has red to pink flesh. Some varieties may have yellow flesh.

Tropical Fruits

The banana is yellow in color and has a finger-like shape. It is imported from Central and South America.

Plantain is a tropical fruit twice the size of a regular banana. It is not eaten raw but is boiled, baked, or fried.

The mango is a large, heavy, pear-shaped fruit grown in limited areas of Florida. It is similar to a peach in flavor and has deep yellow flesh. It is used fresh, canned, and as juice.

The pomegranate is valued for its dark red seed. Juice is extracted from the seed and is used in fruit beverages. The seeds are an attractive addition to fruit combinations.

Papaya has green to yellow smooth skin and is pear-shaped. It has smooth yellow flesh and is grown in Hawaii and Florida.

The avocado is pear-shaped with green or purplish skin. It has a large seed and flesh with a smooth texture. It is grown in California, Florida, Central America, and Mexico.

The pineapple has a cylindrical shape crowned with a tuft of stiff leaves. It is grown in Hawaii, Puerto Rico, Cuba, South America, and Florida. It is used fresh, canned, frozen, and as juice and in preserves.

The date is a dessert fruit and is used as an ingredient in baked products. It is grown in the North African countries and in California and Arizona.

Figs are pear-shaped and very sweet. They are dried, canned, preserved, and used in confections. They are grown in the United States and the Mediterranean countries.

95

Forms of Fruit

Not only are there many varieties of fruits from which to choose, but many fruits are usually available in several forms: fresh, frozen, canned, and dried. Fresh fruits spoil or deteriorate rapidly and must be used shortly after purchase. Frozen, canned, and dried fruits, specially treated, keep longer.

Fresh Fruit

Usually, only ripe fruit is good for use. Ripening enhances the overall eating quality of the fruit. Several changes take place during ripening: the fruit develops to its full size, the edible tissue becomes soft, the color changes, the flavor becomes mildly sweet, and the characteristic aroma of the fruit develops. These changes are brought about by enzymes found in the fruit tissue. The enzyme will continue to function even after the fruit is ripened, and will cause eventual spoilage and an undesirable texture and flavor. The softening of fruit can be slowed down by proper refrigeration.

Late in the season, some valencia oranges tend to turn from a bright orange to a greenish color. This color change affects only the outer skin. The oranges are fully ripe inside and may have certified food color added to the skin to improve its appearance. Oranges so treated must be marked "color added." This color treatment has no influence on the interior.

Some fresh fruits are packaged in plastic bags. The prepackaging cuts down on loss of moisture from the fruit and reduces contamination by dirt and insects. The plastic bags have small holes to prevent softening of the fruit due to an accumulation of carbon dioxide.

Large fruit is generally more expensive than average-size fruit of the same variety. The largest fruit is not necessarily the best; its flavor and texture could be less desirable than that of the smaller fruit. The color and size of fruit rather than its flavor and quality tend to determine its cost and salability.

It is no longer necessary to live in the tropics to have fresh fruit the year round. Even though some fruits tend to be seasonal and other fruits are grown only in certain areas, some variety of fresh fruit can be purchased the year round. Improved transportation, refrigeration, storage, and packaging have made available a constant supply of fruits from the many areas of our country and from distant lands. However, the fresh fruits which are grown locally may be somewhat lower in price and may be fresher.

Processed Fruit

For longer periods of storage, fruits are processed by freezing, canning, and drying. These foods are readily available regardless of season. The basic purpose in all three methods of processing is to control the action of spoilage organisms and enzymes.

Many kinds of *frozen fruits* are available. Small whole fruits such as cherries, raspberries, strawberries, and sliced or cut large fruits such as peaches, apples, and pineapple are frozen. There are also frozen mixed fruits and fruit juices. Most fruits are sweetened and then frozen quickly at a very low temperature. The low temperature prevents the action of spoilage organisms. The color, flavor, and nutritive value of frozen fruits tend to be like that of the fresh fruit.

Most common fruits are available in the *canned* form. Fruits may be canned whole, in halves, sliced, cubed, as a sauce or juice. Fruits are usually sweetened before canning. During canning, the fruits in containers are exposed to high temperatures which destroy spoilage organisms and enzymes so that the fruits will not spoil.

Fruits which are commonly *dried* include plums (prunes), apricots, dates, figs, grapes (raisins), currants, and mixed fruits. As a result of drying, a large portion of the water is removed from the fruit and the keeping quality of the fruit is extended considerably.

Selection of Fruit

Most cultivated fruits are available in many varieties. One variety may be especially valued for its flavor such as the red or yellow Delicious apples, while another may have better cooking qualities, for example, the Rome Beauty or McIntosh apples. When it comes to oranges, the two most common varieties are the navel which is seedless and best suited for eating raw, and the Valencia orange which is known as the juice orange and may contain seeds.

When purchasing fruit, it is important to consider the intended use. Fruits which will be cut, sliced, or cubed in preparation for the table need not be the largest in size. Small-size fruits such as apples, peaches, etc. are excellent for stewing and pastry. The medium to large-size fruits may be more attractive to serve whole. They may also be cut into slices or chunks and served in salads.

Selecting Fresh Fruits

The United States Department of Agriculture has established grades for fresh fruits but these do not always appear on the fresh fruit labels. When they are used, grades are a good guide for purchasing fruits. The grades used for fresh fruit are the premium grades, U.S. Extra Fancy, U.S. Fancy, U.S. Extra No. 1, and the basic trading grades, U.S. No. 1 and U.S. No. 2.[1]

Fruit prices are not a reliable guide to the quality and nutritive value of fruits. Fruit in season is generally cheaper and of better quality than fruit sold out of season. When poor growing conditions limit the supply of fruit, it may be of inferior quality yet high in price.

Since fresh fruits deteriorate rapidly after they have ripened, buy only the quantity which can be used before spoilage sets in. Color is an excellent indication of ripeness in many fruits. Most fruits lose their green color as they ripen; peaches and apricots turn yellow; cherries turn pink or red. A characteristic fruit fragrance can also be a guide to the selection of ripe cantaloupes and pineapples.

Some fruits are sold by the pound such as apples, pears, grapes, peaches, plums; berries are sold by the pint or quart; others are sold by units such as one avocado, lemon, or melon; oranges are usually sold by the dozen.

Because fresh fruits are perishable, it is necessary to be able to recognize good quality when buying them. Good quality fruits are sound (free from blemishes and bruises, mold, etc.), crisp (not wilted or limp), and firm (not overripe or soft). When looking for any fruit, the words sound, crisp, and firm are the keys to freshness.

Selecting Frozen Fruits

Even though the United States Department of Agriculture has established some standards and grades for frozen foods, these seldom appear on the labels. One must rely on the brand name as a guide in selection of frozen fruits. After you have used a brand you will know its quality. Avoid buying frozen fruits in packages that are stained or not hard frozen. These signs indicate that defrosting and deterioration have taken place and quality is spoiled.

1. "Shoppers Guide to U.S. Grades for Food," *Home and Garden Bulletin 58* (Washington, D.C., United States Department of Agriculture).

Selecting Canned Fruits

Canned fruits and fruit juices are packed in cans and jars of different sizes. Knowing the can sizes and number of servings in each can will help you to avoid waste. The following chart shows some of the popular can sizes for fruits.

8 ounce	227 g	8 oz	2 servings	fruits
No. 303	454 g	1 lb	4 servings	fruits
No 2½	822 g	1 lb 13 oz	7 servings	fruits
No. 3 or 46 oz	1.3 kg	3 lb 3 oz	10-12 servings	juices

Most fruits are canned in a sugar syrup but some are packed in fruit juice or water. The label gives information about the quality and contents of the can. Every label should include name of food, net contents in weight or fluid ounces, and name and address of the processor. It may include a letter grade or a descriptive word, or both, to indicate quality: Grade A or Fancy, Grade B or Choice, Grade C or Standard.

The largest and most perfect of each kind of fruit is Grade A. Grade B is used for good fruit not so large as Grade A, and Grade C for good fruit less uniform in size and shape. Graded canned fruits are packed under the supervision and inspection of a government official.

Packers may set their own standards of quality for fruit and may use their own brand names. Each grade would have a different brand name. Choose the grade that is satisfactory for your use. Avoid cans with dents or bulging ends. These are signs of a broken seal or spoilage.

Canned fruits are available in small, handy sizes.

Selecting Dried Fruits

Dried fruits come in handy protective cartons and in clear bags. Quality grades are not usually listed on packages of dried fruit, but their labels give valuable information about the contents. Some fruits are packed according to size. The common dried fruits and their package sizes are listed in the table given on page 100.

Storage of Fruit

In order to preserve and protect the quality, nutrient value, color, flavor, and its general appearance, fruit should be stored properly.

Some fresh fruits are washed and then refrigerated.

Usual Dried Fruit Package Sizes

Raisins: 42.5 g (1½ oz) Snac-Paks
425 g (15 oz) pkg = 3 c (approx.)
454 g (1 lb) transparent bag = 3¼ c (approx.)

Prunes: Prunes are graded and sold according to size in 454 and 900 g (1 and 2 lb) cartons and transparent bags.

Usual sizes are:

Jumbo Imperial . . . . 26 to 30 per lb

Extra Large . . . . 38 to 43 per lb

Large . . . . 48 to 53 per lb

Medium . . . . 62 to 67 per lb

Breakfast . . . . 75 to 85 per lb

Also sold vacuum-packed in 454 g (1 lb) jars and cans

Apricots: Sold in 312 g (11 oz) cartons and 227 and 340 g (8 and 12 oz) transparent bags. Medium and large size fruits.

Peaches: Sold in 312 g (11 oz) cartons and 340 g (12 oz) transparent bags. Medium and large size fruits.

Mixed Fruits: Assorted prunes, apricots, peaches, and pears. Sold in 312 g (11 oz) cartons and 340 g (12 oz) transparent bags.

Adapted from *Your Guide to Buying, Storing, Cooking, Dried Fruits and Raisins* Leaflet by Del Monte Foods, San Francisco.

Fresh Fruit Storage

Ripe fruits are perishable and should be stored in the special fruit and vegetable drawer of the refrigerator which prevents rapid loss of moisture. Fruits may be washed before storage except berries in which water encourages spoilage. Fruits should be handled gently to avoid bruising. If fruits such as peaches, pears, plums, and bananas are slightly green, they may be ripened at room temperature and then stored in the refrigerator. The skin of banana may darken but the flesh will remain flavorful and firm. Fruits with strong aromas such as pineapples, cantaloupes, or apples should be carefully wrapped before they are stored so that their fragrance will not be absorbed by any of the other foods in the refrigerator.

Frozen Fruit Storage

Frozen fruits should be stored immediately in the freezer. They should not be thawed until they are to be used. Once the fruit has been thawed it should not be refrozen.

Many fruits are packed so that they can be easily stored in a freezer.

Canned Fruit Storage

Canned fruits should be stored in a cool, dry place. After the can has been opened, the fruit becomes perishable and should be stored covered in the refrigerator.

Leftover canned fruits should be placed in a covered container and refrigerated.

Dried Fruit Storage

Dried fruits are stored in a cool, dry place in their original sealed carton or clear bag. After opening, close the box tightly, or fold the bag tightly. Cooked dried fruits are perishable and should be covered and refrigerated.

Dried fruits are stored on a shelf after opening. They should be in a tight container or secure package.

Fruits can add much to the pleasure of eating when properly stored. Proper storage of all fruits will preserve color, texture, flavor, aroma, and nutrient values. It is because of their nutrient values that fruits are important protective foods.

Nutrient Contributions

The nutrients are the building blocks of food, and the same building blocks that make up food are used to make up your body. These nutrients are divided into six groups: carbohydrates, fats, protein, vitamins, minerals, and water. Your need for each of the nutrient groups will be studied along with the foods in which they are found most abundantly. Most foods are made of more than one nutrient. Fruits, for example, are made chiefly of vitamins, minerals, water, and carbohydrates.

Vitamins in Fruits

Most fruits contain generous amounts of vitamins, but all vitamins are not present in the same amounts in all fruits. Fruits are the best sources of vitamin C (ascorbic acid); they are good sources of vitamin A; and they provide moderate amounts of the B vitamins.

The citrus fruits—oranges, grapefruits, lemons, limes—as well as cantaloupes and strawberries, supply *vitamin C* in the largest amounts. The citrus fruits are our most dependable common food sources of vitamin C. Oranges in some form, fresh, frozen, or canned, usually give more vitamin C per dollar spent than other foods. Most fruits contain vitamin C, some in abundance as in citrus fruits, cantaloupes, and strawberries, and others in lesser amounts as in pears and apples.

The high levels of vitamin C in pills, advocated by some, have no special curative powers, and could be harmful. Food can supply your body with all the vitamin C it needs.

Although scurvy is not a problem for us today, many people do not get as much vitamin C as they need for good health. Many students have diets that are low in vitamin C. Does your diet measure up to your vitamin C needs? It probably does if you include one serving of citrus fruit with the other fruits and vegetables in your daily food intake.

Your body needs vitamin C to form a cement-like material called collagen which holds the cells together in much the same way mortar holds bricks together. When vitamin C is lacking, collagen cannot be formed and then several things happen: (1) the bones become fragile and break easily; (2) gums become soft and can bleed easily; (3) walls of blood vessels and muscle cells become weak, less elastic, and frequently rupture causing small pinpoint hemorrhages; and (4) wounds and broken bones do not heal properly.

When vitamin C is adequate, the blood vessels are more elastic, gums are firmer, bones are stronger. The body is made of many types of cells, and all of these cells require vitamin C to form the collagen which binds them together. You will need vitamin C, or ascorbic acid, as long as you live.

Your body cannot store or manufacture vitamin C so your supply of it will need to come from the food you eat each day. Therefore, it is important to include in your daily diet at least one food which is high in vitamin C.

Along with vitamin C, some fruits, recognized by their yellow to red color, can also contribute vitamin A to your diet. A yellow pigment in plants (fruits and vegetables) is called carotene. This pigment can be converted by the body into vitamin A. The yellow melons, pineapple, apricots, and peaches are special sources of vitamin A because they contain carotene. Most fruits supply some vitamin A, but the fruits which are deeper yellow supply more carotene than those which are pale yellow or white. You will learn more about the foods which contain vitamin A in the milk and vegetable chapters.

Vitamin A is important for good vision. In other areas of the world where diets are low in vitamin A, severe eye disease is a problem. In our country, most of us get enough vitamin A to prevent a serious eye disease. How quickly do your eyes adjust when you go from a well-lighted lobby into a dark theater? Vitamin A helps your eyes adjust quickly from light to dark. It prevents "night blindness" so that your eyes can adjust to the dark. You also need vitamin A for good growth, skin, and hair. When vitamin A is missing from the diet, hair becomes dry and coarse, and growth decreases. Foods which contain vitamin A should be included in your diet each day.

In addition to vitamins A and C, most fruits contain the B group of vitamins. Although fruits are not as important sources of these vitamins as are other foods such as milk and cereals, which will be discussed in the chapters to come.

Minerals in Fruits

In addition to vitamins, fruits supply an added bonus by contributing minerals to the diet. Two minerals, *iron* and *calcium*, are found in fruits in important amounts. Fruits such as oranges, strawberries, cantaloupe, and the dried fruits such as figs, dates, raisins, prunes, and apricots are good sources of iron and calcium. You need iron for red blood and calcium for strong bones and teeth.

Other Nutrients in Fruits

Sugar and *cellulose* are carbohydrates found in fruits. Ripe fruits contain more sugar which gives a pleasant sweet flavor to fruits. Fruit sugar supplies the body with energy. The skin and pulp of fruits contain cellulose which the body cannot digest, but which serves as a natural laxative and helps to maintain body regularity.

Fruits, as a group, contain very little protein and fat. These nutrients are provided by other foods. Fruits make their most important contribution to the diet through their generous supply of vitamins, minerals, and cellulose.

Preparation of Fruits

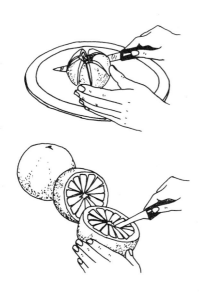

Most ripe fruits are delicious and enjoyable when eaten raw and require very little preparation. Raw fruits need only a thorough washing to remove any dirt or remaining spray before eating. Fresh fruit may be served whole, cut, or sliced, or as a combination of several cut fruits. Fruits are popularly served for breakfast, but they can and should be included at other meals. Fresh fruits served as appetizers, salads, and desserts give a pleasing contrast in firmness to the other soft foods of the meal.

Most raw fruit is more palatable and has a higher nutritive value than the cooked or processed fruits. Cut raw fruits such as banana, apple, and pear, which have a low acid content, turn dark on exposure to air. This discoloration can be prevented by sprinkling the cut surface with an acid fruit juice such as lemon or orange.

Principles of Fruit Preparation

Fruits may be cooked to increase variety in eating and to soften the cellulose of hard fruits. Fruit cookery involves two important principles: (1) a change in texture, form, or consistency of the fruit due to cooking; and (2) the preservation of nutrients or food values.

The method of cooking will determine the *texture* of the cooked fruit, that is, whether the fruit will break apart or retain its shape. When fruits are cooked in moist heat, the cellulose becomes soft and the fruit breaks apart. This is desirable when fruits are used for making sauces such as apple or rhubarb sauce. When fruits are cooked with sugar, they will retain their shape because sugar strengthens the cellulose structure and keeps the fruit from coming apart. When preparing cinnamon apple rings or stewed apples or peaches, the fruit is cooked with sugar or in a syrup. Fruits cooked in a sugar syrup will retain their shape and firm texture, while fruits cooked without sugar will soften and break apart. The texture desired in the cooked fruit product will determine whether sugar is to be added before or after cooking.

Another principle of fruit cookery and preparation involves the *preservation of the food values or nutrients*. Some vitamins, especially vitamin C, can be destroyed by exposure to the oxygen in the air. If fruits and fruit juices are prepared just before serving, vitamin loss due to air can be reduced. Cooked fruits and canned fruits after opening should be stored in a covered container in the refrigerator. Use the proper size jar for leftover fruits and juices so that oxygen will have less chance to destroy vitamins. Also, when fruits are cut, more surface is exposed to air and vitamin loss will be greater. When preparing fruit juices, do not strain them because this brings the juice into greater contact with air and results in greater destruction of vitamin C.

Fruits should be cooked in as little water as possible so that vitamins and minerals will be preserved. Some vitamins, like vitamin C for which fruits are important, can dissolve in water as sugar does. The amount of water used to cook fruit depends on its cellulose and water content. Juicy fruits such as berries and rhubarb contain less cellulose and more juice or water; they can be cooked in their own juice without adding water. Other fruits such as apples and peaches may require a very small amount of water. The liquid in which fruits are cooked will contain dissolved vitamins and minerals and it should be served with the fruit.

In many fruits, vitamins and minerals are concentrated just under the skin. You will have the advantage of all of the nutrient values when fruits are used with their skins. For example, unpeeled apples in Waldorf salad will not only retain the nutrients, but will add color appeal as well. When you wish to remove the skins from fruit, peel thinly so that nutrient loss will not be great. Also, large whole fruits, such as apples, pears, and apricots, can be cooked in their skins. The skin preserves the shape of the fruit and helps to retain more of the vitamins and minerals.

Special care is required to protect the nutrients in fruits. Vitamin C is the most easily destroyed of all vitamins. To avoid unnecessary loss of vitamin C, remember that it is easily destroyed by oxygen and heat, and it dissolves in water.

Methods of Cooking Fruits

To provide interest and variety in the use of fresh fruit, the fruit may be cooked. The appearance, texture, and flavor will be changed by cooking. Fruits are most often cooked by *simmering, stewing,* and by *baking.* To simmer, fruits are cooked covered in their own juices or in a small amount of added water. Simmered fruits are often mashed to give a fruit sauce of uniform consistency as in applesauce, for example. Stewing is another way to cook fruit. Stewed fruit is usually cooked in a small amount of liquid with added sugar, and each piece of fruit retains most of its original shape. Fruits with heavy skins are good for baking because the skin serves as a cover and holds in the steam needed to soften the cellulose and protects the nutrients and fruit flavors. Other fruits such as peaches, plums, rhubarb, and bananas may be baked in a covered baking dish.

Many people enjoy eating dried fruits without cooking them; others prefer the plump, soft texture of cooked dried fruits. Much of the moisture lost when fruits are dried is replaced during cooking. Dried fruits may be soaked in hot water for a short time and then cooked in the same water. The fruit is cooked at a *simmering temperature (below boiling) in a covered pan.* However, most dried fruits do not require soaking before cooking. If sugar is used, add it near the end of the cooking period, after the fruit is plump and soft. Sugar can interfere with the absorption of water by the fruit and keep the cell walls from softening.

Fruits may be used in a variety of other ways. Occasionally fruits are used to make *fritters.* Fruit fritters are made from such fruits as apples, bananas, and pineapple. The cut or dried fruit is dipped into a batter, deep-fat fried until golden brown, and served hot with powdered sugar or syrup.

Some *baked products* are made with fruit. Date, orange, cranberry, and blueberry quick breads are popular. These special breads may use canned, frozen, fresh, mashed, or candied fruits.

Pies to please every taste can be made from fresh, canned, frozen, or dried fruits. Cream pies often include a layer of fruit such as banana, peach, or strawberry. Fruit-flavored sherbets and ice creams are always popular. The variety of fruit desserts is almost endless and ranges from an exotic cherries jubilee to a gourmet fruit soufflé!

Convenience in Fruits

The canned, frozen, and dried fruits offer a convenience. First, they have been processed so that the fruit can be kept without spoilage long after the growing season ends. Preparation procedures such as washing, peeling, and cutting are done by the packer, and even sugar is added to most fruits except the dried fruits. All of the forms of fruit can be served directly from the package except for the partial thawing of frozen fruits.

Canned and frozen fruits are prepared in the same forms— whole, half, sliced, sauce, or juice—as are commonly used for fresh fruits. Fruit pie fillings are available and are ready for the pastry as soon as the can is opened. Juices which have been frozen, canned, or packed as a dry mix eliminate the need to squeeze the fruit. Canned juices need only to be chilled before serving; frozen juices and powdered fruit concentrates require only dilution with water for serving.

All of these convenience items have been designed to use time, effort, and energy well. However, these convenience items have not eliminated the need to make decisions. Because of the wide variety of fruit products available, decision making has become more complicated. The decision is yours when it is time to select which item to use. Will it be fresh, frozen, dried, or canned peaches? What will help you make the decision? Will your consider time available, quality of food, and cost? How will the color, flavor, size and shape, texture, and nutrient value of the prepared food product fit into your meals? Will the convenience fruit item add interest, contrast, and attractiveness to your meal? If the food is not packed in glass, how will you learn what quality and kind of food is in the package?

Your answers to these many questions can help you decide which food product is best for your meals. In deciding which fruit product to purchase you should also consider your values and standards. Products which measure up to your values and standards will provide greater eating pleasure and satisfaction for you. You will be pleased with your accomplishments.

Main Ideas

Fruits are said to be "protective" foods because of their abundance of vitamins and minerals. Citrus fruits are especially important because of their vitamin C content. The full nutritive and esthetic values of fruits can be realized only through careful selection and proper storage and preparation. Fruits are available in tremendous variety in fresh, frozen, dried, freeze-dried, and canned forms.

Activities

1. Visit a local grocery store and note the variety of convenience fruit products available. What should you consider when buying them?

2. Examine labels on several fruit products. What information do they supply? In what ways do the labels differ?

3. Indicate some ways to introduce variety into meals with fruits.

4. Suggest several ways to serve fruit for breakfast, lunch, and dinner.

5. Calculate the cost of one serving of the same fruit in the different forms of canned, frozen, fresh, dried.

6. Choose several of your favorite fruits and compare their price, color, texture, and nutritive value.

7. Prepare applesauce and stewed apples. Note the difference in texture, appearance, and flavor. What causes the difference?

8. What convenience fruit products are used in your home? Why were they selected?

9. Prepare a display of the various containers in which fruits and juices can be purchased. Of what materials are they made? How many servings are available from each? Which size containers do you recommend for one person? For two-person families? Why?

10. Explain the statement "Fruits are protective foods."

11. What vitamin is found in abundance in citrus fruits?

12. Why should fresh fruits be carefully selected according to the use to which they will be put? Give examples.

13. List some of the advantages of canned, dried, and frozen fruit products.

Questions

1. What important nutrients are contributed by fruits? Can these be supplied by other foods?

2. What happens when vitamin C is lacking in the diet? How can this be avoided?

3. Why is it better to serve raw fruits often rather than cooked fruit?

4. What are signs of quality in fresh fruit.

5. How can the nutrients of fruit be saved when fruits are cooked?

6. Why are the largest fruits not always best?

7. How can you identify a juice orange a dessert orange?

8. Why are fruit prices not a reliable guide to quality?

9. Why do fruits deteriorate after ripening?

10. How can cooked fruits be kept from breaking apart?

11. What size can of peaches would serve four persons? Seven persons?

12. How would you store fresh, canned, frozen, and dried peaches? Leftover canned peaches? Cooked dried peaches?

13. Can convenience foods eliminate making decisions? Why?

Chapter 7

Grains

Words for Thought

Beriberi
a disease caused by the lack of vitamin B_1 or thiamin.

Enriched
a term used to identify bread and flour to which thiamin, riboflavin, niacin, and iron have been added.

Restores
a term which means the total replacement of certain nutrients lost during processing.

Thiamin
the chemical name for vitamin B_1.

Riboflavin
the chemical name for vitamin B_2.

Amino acids
the building blocks of protein.

Grain
edible seeds of grasses.

Cereal
a grain product prepared for human use such as breakfast cereal.

Cereal, the common name for grains, refers to the Roman goddess Ceres who ruled over grains. The grains are the edible seeds produced by certain plants of the grass family. The principal grains include rice, oats, barley, rye, corn, buckwheat, as well as wheat. In the United States, wheat is the chief grain. Wheat is called "the staff of life" because it is available for food in nearly every place where people live. Wheat, the most important of the grains, provides nourishment for more nations of the world than any other food. Some form of grain is grown in every area of the world. Wheat is basic to the diets of Europe, Africa, North and South America, Australia, and a part of Asia, while rice is still the common food in many parts of the Orient and India. Because of their good keeping quality, high energy value, and relatively low cost, grains and their products are staple foods for all people. In some underdeveloped countries, 80 to 90 percent of the food calories are supplied by only one kind of grain.

Grains

Many kinds of breakfast cereals, pastas (macaroni products), and flour are prepared from grains. Wheat is used mainly for flour, but smaller amounts are used in wheat breakfast cereals. Durum wheat is used for the manufacture of macaroni products.

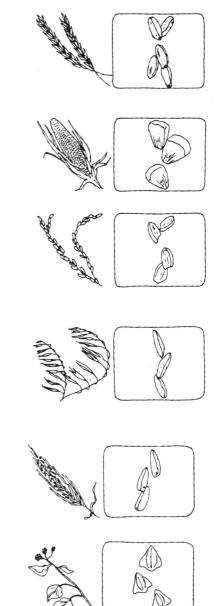

Next to wheat, corn is the grain most used in the United States. Corn is made into breakfast cereals, grits, or hominy. It is also used as a vegetable.

Rice is an important food in Asia and the Far East. It is used in a variety of breakfast cereals and as an accompaniment to meats instead of potato, as an ingredient in main dishes such as Spanish rice, and as a dessert pudding. Rice is grown in California, Louisiana, Missouri, Texas, and Arkansas.

Oats are used mainly in breakfast cereals, as an ingredient in baked products, and in some desserts. Breakfast cereals from oats are usually made of the whole grain with only the outer husk removed. These cereals are rich in nutrients because the whole grain is often used.

Rye is used mainly for bread, while barley is used in soups, and barley flour is used in baby foods, and for the production of malt. Malt syrups are used for malted milk.

Buckwheat is used mainly for the manufacture of pancake flour. Some buckwheat groats are used as a breakfast cereal.

111

Parts of Grains

Each grain has three basic parts: bran, endosperm, and germ. The bran is the outside covering of the grain and consists of several layers. It protects the grain kernel until it is planted or milled. The endosperm is the white, inner portion. The germ is found at one end of the kernel and is the part from which the new part sprouts. The grain kernel illustration shows the location of the three parts of a grain.

The bran and germ may be separated from the endosperm in the milling process, leaving only the white endosperm for use as flour or as refined cereals.

Whole grain flour and cereals contain the finely ground bran, germ, and endosperm of the whole kernel. Whole grain products have a distinctive flavor and coarser texture than those made from white flour. Because of the higher fat content of the germ, whole grain flour is more difficult to keep and sometimes develops an unpleasant flavor under poor storage conditions.

Nutrient Contributions

The grain kernel is a storehouse of nutrients needed and used by people since civilization began. The nutrients provided by cereals include carbohydrates, vitamins, minerals, fat, and protein. The nutrients are not equally distributed throughout the three parts of the grain. The bran and germ are rich sources of minerals, vitamins, and cellulose; the endosperm is a rich source of starch but lacks vitamins, minerals, and cellulose.

Note the proportions of bran, endosperm, and germ in each of the four types of grain shown.

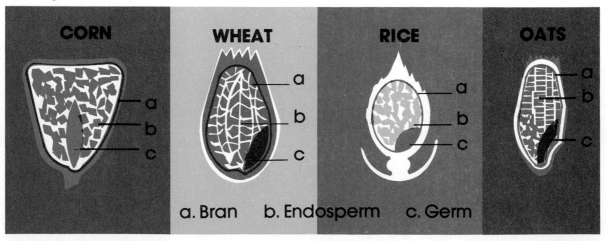

CORN   WHEAT   RICE   OATS

a. Bran   b. Endosperm   c. Germ

All cereals and grain products are rich sources of energy, but their vitamin and mineral values will depend upon which parts of the grain are used. Cereals and breads which have high vitamin and mineral value are those which contain all three parts of the grain. The refined cereal products are made from the endosperm which is rich in starch but which lacks vitamins and minerals.

Carbohydrates

The nutrients supplied by grains serve many functions in the body. Two forms of carbohydrates are found in grains: *starch* for body energy and *cellulose* for regularity. Three-fourths of the grain is made up of starch, and is an excellent source of energy. Cellulose is found abundantly in the bran, and although it cannot be digested by the body, it supplies roughage, bulk or fiber. Because cellulose is not digested, it acts as a natural laxative and sometimes is called the "scrub brush" for the intestine, helping to keep the body regular.

Fiber

The bran of whole grains is a concentrated source of fiber in your diet. For this reason, fiber from whole grains is a more effective laxative than that from fruits and vegetables. The fiber of whole grains absorbs water and thus enlarges in bulk and keeps fecal materials soft. If your diet includes little fiber-rich foods, an increased intake of whole grain products, fruits, and vegetables could overcome most constipation problems. The skin, peelings, and pulp of fruits and vegetables and the hulls (bran) of grains will furnish the fiber you need.

Some recent research also suggests low-fiber diets may contribute to an increase in diseases of the intestinal tract such as constipation and diverticulosis. Some native Africans consume an unrefined diet and take in six times more fiber than people of developed Western countries. They do not develop intestinal diseases.

High-fiber diets are now used to relieve the pain and bowel irregularity associated with diverticulosis (pouches or sacs in intestinal membrane). Liberal intake of fiber-rich foods will help you avoid constipation as well as diverticular disease.

It is generally believed that dietary fiber increases fecal bulk. Although some have proposed other benefits for dietary fiber, at this time, no other general agreement has been reached concerning the role of fiber for humans. Some speculate dietary fiber causes fecal substances to move quickly through the intestinal tract before bacterial decomposition of intestinal materials occurs. Others speculate that dietary fiber may combine with some possibly harmful substances and prevent their absorption into the body.

Although dietary fiber serves an important function in contributing to bowel regularity, in excess, it can reduce the digestibility of other food constituents. Fiber in your diet should come from the generous use of fruits, vegetables, and whole grains rather than from high-fiber breads or other purchased fiber supplements. An excessive intake of fiber can interfere with absorption of calcium and trace elements such as zinc.

Whole grains, fruits, vegetables, nuts, and legumes (peas, beans) are fiber-rich foods. Wheat bran is the richest source of fiber; refined grains (breads, cereals, pastas) have considerably less fiber than do whole grains; while fish, poultry, meat, eggs, sugars, and fats lack fiber.

Fiber is a necessary part of the diet as are the nutrients which you studied. Foods can provide all of the fiber you need when you include liberal amounts of fiber-rich foods daily.

Vitamins

The loss of Japanese sailors because of the disease beriberi led to the discovery of another vitamin, *vitamin B_1, or thiamin.* This disease was so common among Japanese sailors that three out of every ten were likely to have beriberi, and some died from it.

Takaki, a Japanese navy physician, believed that the disease was due to diet. He sent two shiploads of men on a nine-month voyage. On one ship, the regular diet of white rice was served; on the other ship, the diet included meat, fish, and vegetables in addition to white rice. On the first ship the sailors developed beriberi, while the sailors on the second ship did not.

Dr. Eijkman, a Dutch physician, fed two groups of birds. To one group he gave white polished rice; the other group ate brown rice. The birds on white rice developed beriberi. It was several years later that vitamin B_1 was discovered as the nutrient that prevented beriberi.

Grains are important food sources of the vitamin B group which is also known as the B complex. Whole grain cereals are important sources of several of the B vitamins—B_1, B_2, and

B Vitamins

Name	Purpose	Deficiency
B₁(thiamin)	Thiamin is needed for growth, good appetite, healthy nerves, good body coordination. It helps the body release energy from carbohydrates.	*Beriberi* *Symptoms:* polyneuritis, fatigue problems, and lameness of the legs.
B₂(riboflavin)	Riboflavin is needed for growth, nerve tissue, the digestive tract, and health. It helps the body to release energy from carbohydrates, fats, and protein.	*Ariboflavinosis* *Symptoms:* Cheilosis cracks at corners of mouth, lips become inflamed Glossitis—smooth, purple-red tongue
niacin	Niacin is needed for oxidation of carbohydrates in body cells. It is needed by all living cells to release energy from carbohydrate, fat, and protein.	*Pellagra* *Symptoms:* red rash on face and hands, scaly and dark pigmentation of skin exposed to sun, nervousness, irritability.

niacin. The chemical name for vitamin B_1 is thiamin, and for vitamin B_2, riboflavin. Your body needs vitamin B_1 for growth, good appetite, healthy nerves, good body coordination, and to help the body release energy from carbohydrates. Vitamin B_1 prevents the disease beriberi. Some of the symptoms of beriberi are: fatigue, dizziness, digestive problems, and lameness of the legs.

Riboflavin or B_2 is needed for growth, nerve tissue, the digestive tract, and health. It helps the body oxidize or "burn" sugars and starches to release energy.

Niacin is required for oxidation of carbohydrates in body cells and it prevents pellagra. Niacin is required by all living cells to release energy from food.

The B vitamins, like vitamin C, are soluble in water and cannot be stored in the body. You need a new supply of these vitamins each day; therefore, it becomes important to include grains and grain products in your daily meals. Your body has a very special need for each of the B vitamins, since they cannot replace each other.

Minerals

In addition to carbohydrates, and the B vitamins, whole grain and enriched grain products contribute minerals to your diet. The minerals *iron* and *phosphorus* are found in important amounts in grain or cereal products. You will recall that iron is needed for good red blood, and phosphorus for strong bones and teeth.

Protein

Grains supply proteins, but some of the protein in grain products or in cereals lacks essential *amino acids*. The amino acids are the building blocks from which protein is made. The proteins which lack some of the essential amino acids are called incomplete proteins because they are unable to adequately meet the needs of your body for protein. However, the proteins of cereals do make a valuable contribution to the total amount of protein in your diet. Cereals are usually served with milk and, in this way, the milk protein will supplement the cereal proteins. The milk protein contains the amino acids lacking in cereal, and the two foods, milk and cereal together, supply valuable proteins to meet the needs of your body.

Enrichment of Grain Products

Whole grain or enriched products add important nutrients to the diet. Grains which have been refined contribute only calories and incomplete proteins, since vitamins, minerals, and cellulose are removed in the refining process.

Many people prefer white bread to whole grain bread products. To offset the loss of nutritional value, a bread enrichment program was initiated in 1943. The nutrients thiamin (B_1), riboflavin (B_2), niacin, and iron, lost in the refining process, were put back into the bread product. This bread is called enriched bread. These same nutrients are also added to some cereals and other grain products which are labeled restored or enriched. Many bakers and producers voluntarily enrich their bread and cereal products.

Today, more than 85 percent of cereals are fortified. Some cereals are fortified to provide greater than whole-grain amounts of vitamins and minerals including iron. Some cereals are fortified to provide more protein than the original grains. Most ready-to-eat cereals are fortified with B vitamins (B_1, B_2, and niacin) and usually iron. A 30 grams (1 ounce) serving of these cereals before the addition of milk provides about 20 percent of your minimum daily requirement for these vitamins. The whole grain cereals and bread products contain *all* the nutrients, both known and unknown, while enriched products include only those that have been restored after refinement.

White rice in which nutrients have been preserved is known as "converted" rice. Before polishing, the brown rice is soaked and steamed under pressure and then dried. This parboiling treatment draws the vitamins into the endosperm where they will be retained during milling. No added nutrients are necessary since the natural vitamins of the rice are preserved.

Uses of Grains

The term cereal can mean any breakfast food made from grain, or it can mean any grain that is used as food. However, the term cereal often refers to specially prepared grain products used as breakfast cereals. Grain products can be used in a variety of ways in our meals. For convenience, their uses can be grouped into three general classes: the breakfast cereals, the pastas (macaroni products), and flour.

Breakfast Cereals

Breakfast cereals appear in many shapes and forms. They can be grouped into two major types: the ready-to-eat cereals which have been cooked and are ready for the table, and the cereals which require cooking before serving.

Common uncooked cereals are made from corn, oats, and wheat and are purchased as cornmeal, rolled oats, and cream of wheat. Many of the uncooked cereals are available in a form for quick cooking such as quick rolled oats.

The variety of ready-to-eat cereals is almost endless. Ready-to-eat cereals are precooked and then rolled, flaked,

Among the great variety of ready-to-eat cereals available in the market today, many are presweetened.

Cooked cereals may need only a minute or two of cooking.

117

Cereal can be used in combination with main-dish foods and snacks as well as for breakfast.

puffed, or shredded. They are often made from corn, oats, wheat, and rice.

All forms of cereals served with milk are popular for breakfast. The combination of cereal, milk, and some fruit is an excellent source of food nutrients, and is a good way to begin the day.

In addition to their service as breakfast main dishes, cereals have other uses. The ready-to-eat cereals may be used as topping on casseroles, or may be rolled into crumbs and used for breading meats, poultry, and fish. They are used as an ingredient in cookies, quick breads, and special desserts. The uncooked cereal may replace part of the flour in cookies and quick breads. Rolled oats may replace part of the flour in oatmeal cookies or bread; cornmeal may replace part of the flour in muffins and pancakes. Whenever whole grain or enriched cereals are used as an ingredient, they increase the nutritional value of the product.

Pastas or Macaroni Products

Pastas or macaroni products include spaghetti, vermicelli, and noodles along with macaroni. They are made of a special durum wheat which is high in gluten, a protein. Noodles are a macaroni product to which egg has been added.

Macaroni products are made in many different shapes and sizes such as tubes, solid rods, ribbon shapes, alphabet, sea shells, spirals, and others. They can be used as a main dish (macaroni and cheese, chicken and noodles), as an accompaniment to meat instead of potato (spaghetti or noodles), and as an ingredient in a main dish, soup, or salad.

Because of their variety of shapes, macaroni products add eye appeal to many everyday meals.

Flour

Another grain product, flour, is used as the chief ingredient in many baked products. The various kinds of flour will be discussed in the chapters dealing with quick and yeast breads.

Starch as a Thickener

Starch, obtained from grains in the form of cornstarch and flour, is used to thicken gravies, sauces, puddings, and pie fillings. When starch in the form of cornstarch, flour, or tapioca is heated in water or another liquid such as milk or fruit juice, the starch granules will absorb water and swell. The swollen particles of starch require more space and crowd together making the product thicker. The thickness of the product is determined by the amount of starch or flour used.

The starch particles in flour and cornstarch are very fine and lump together easily. Lumping can be prevented by separating the starch in one of the following methods.

The flour or starch may be mixed with a small amount of cold water or liquid.

The flour may be mixed with a small amount of melted or liquid fat before the liquid is added. This method is used when making gravy or white sauce.

The starch or flour may be mixed with sugar. This method is used for puddings and pie fillings.

After the starch grains are separated, the flour or starch mixture is combined with the remaining liquid or ingredients of the recipe. The mixture is usually cooked, with constant but gentle stirring, until the mixture thickens and becomes clear. Properly cooked starch loses its milky appearance and becomes clear.

Principles of Grain Cookery

Grain and cereal products come in a variety of forms; many require cooking and others, such as ready-to-eat cereals, are ready for the table when purchased, while "instant" cereals require only the addition of boiling water. The objectives of grain cookery are to improve flavor, soften the cellulose, gelatinize the starch, and produce a product free of lumps. The most abundant nutrient in grains is starch which makes up three-fourths of the grain. It is the starch which determines the cookery procedures used for grains.

Breakfast Cereals

In all cereals, the goal is to avoid lumps. Cereal granules must be separated from each other so that lumps will not form. Two methods are used to separate cereal granules.

Cereals may be added slowly to rapidly boiling water while stirring.

Fine cereals such as cream of wheat and cornmeal may be mixed with a small amount of cold water before they are stirred into boiling water.

When cereal grains are placed in boiling water, the outer surface becomes sticky. To prevent the granules from sticking, continue stirring slowly until the water boils again. Several things happen when starch is cooked: (1) the starch absorbs water; (2) with heat and excess of water starch swells enormously; (3) with continued heating starch becomes translucent; (4) thickness develops.

The term gelatinization refers to the thickening or soft gel which forms when starches are cooked. A proper amount of water and heat are required to produce gelatinization. Some cereals, such as cream of wheat, are able to absorb more water than others, such as rolled oats. The various cereal grains will use different amounts of water to form a gel of the right stiffness or consistency. Gelatinization, the thickening or formation of a starch gel, takes place quickly at the boiling temperature. Well-prepared cereals will have a pleasing flavor, will be free of lumps, will form a soft gel, and will not be pasty.

Other Cereals and Pastas

Regardless of the type of raw cereal product, the goal is to gelatinize starch without the formation of lumps. The basic principles of starch cookery, separation of cereal particles with cold water, and application of heat to swell the starch grains, apply to all cereal products.

The whole cereal grains such as rice, and pastas such as macaroni, spaghetti, and noodles are larger pieces than cereal granules and are more easily separated when stirred into water. The starch which they contain will swell during cooking. The granules will double in size (125 milliliters (½ cup) of raw macaroni = 250 milliliters (1 cup) cooked). The starch will gelatinize and the rice or macaroni product will become tender and easy to chew without breaking apart.

Cereal products are cleaned before packaging and do not require washing before use. Whole grain or enriched cereal products contain the water-soluble B vitamins and minerals. Excess water should not be used to cook cereal products so that dissolved nutrients will not be discarded with the excess water. The amount of water and cooking time will vary with the different cereal products.

Each cereal package provides recipes and instructions for the best use of a cereal product. The suggested amount of water is usually two to two and one-half times that of the cereal product. With this amount of water, none will remain to be discarded.

The practice of rinsing cooked cereal products such as spaghetti or rice with boiling water tends to prevent sticking of the cooked product, but it also tends to rinse away some of the water-soluble nutrients.

Buying Grain Products

Cereals and grain products are an economical source of energy. They are among the most widely used foods and can contribute important vitamins and minerals. The vitamin and mineral content of grain products is determined by the parts of the cereal grain used. Whole grain cereals and breads include the bran, germ, and endosperm and will provide the most nutrients for the money spent. The "enriched," "restored," or "converted" grain products may provide more than whole-grain amounts of some nutrients. You will get the least nutrients

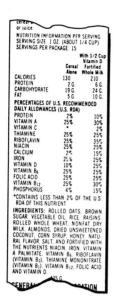

Informative labels are on cereal packages of all sizes.

for your money from refined grain products such as plain white bread or flour. Some kind of grain product usually appears in most every meal, therefore, the nutrient values of these products should be considered when they are purchased. Read the label on all grain products before buying. The label will indicate whether the cereal is whole grain or enriched and tell you the percentage of the RDA for the nutrients in each serving. Whole grain and enriched grain products can contribute valuable nutrients to all diets, especially when money is limited.

It is better to buy cereal products by weight and not by size of package or size of loaf. Puffed cereals may be in a box several times larger than a compact cereal, yet the small box may be greater in weight and provide more servings. Some big boxes may be only partly filled. Some of the cost of the cereal may be due to the prizes or toys included. The cost of cereal is best compared by determining the cost per serving or weight. Look for unit pricing, the cost per pound or unit of weight, to determine which product is the best buy. Ready-to-eat cereals are more expensive weight for weight than cereals which require cooking. Presugared cereals, individual multipacks of cereal, and instant cereals prepared directly in the serving bowl are the most expensive usually.

Check the label to note what other ingredients were used in bread, macaroni, and noodle products. The yellow of noodles is due to food color as well as egg yolk. The food color itself has no nutrient values, but the eggs are a rich source of nutrients. Bread products made with milk or milk solids will provide more nutrients than those which do not include milk.

All forms of grain products are made by several different food processors and are sold under different brand names. The personal experience that you gain through using different brands along with the information on the labels will help you select those which meet your needs best.

Storage of Grain Products

The eating quality and nutrients can be preserved in grain products by proper storage. The cereal should be stored in a closed container which is kept in a cool, dry place. The boxes or packages in which cereals are purchased are suitable for storage. The opened package should be closed tightly so that the cereal will not absorb moisture from the air and lose its crispness. You can restore the crispness of ready-to-eat cereals by placing them in a preheated oven for a short period. Cereal and grain products properly stored have excellent keeping quality. However, whole grain products stored for long periods of time may acquire a rancid flavor due to a chemical change in the fat contained in the germ.

Sweetened Cereals

Cereal manufacturers recognized the consumer practice of adding sugar to cereals before consuming them. They, therefore, developed presweetened cereals. The manufacturer fortifies the ready-to-eat presweetened cereal in the same way as the unsweetened cereal. Both the sweetened and unsweetened cereals contain exactly the same amounts of added vitamins and iron. You, as the consumer, have a choice between presweetened or unsweetened cereals. Sugar added to cereals at home or by the manufacturer contributes four calories per gram. Learning to eat cereals without sugar would be a painless way to begin a needed decrease in your caloric intake (15 milliliters (1 tablespoon sugar) = 46 calories).

The starch in cereals is digested by your body into glucose, a simple sugar, and in this way contributes to your body's energy need. The chemical name for table sugar is sucrose. Two simple sugars, glucose and fructose, combine to form sucrose—the most common sugar in foods of plant origin. The sugar you use to sweeten foods and as an ingredient in food products was extracted from sugar cane and sugar beets. Fruits, some vegetables, and milk contribute small quantities of sugar.

Most of us consume about 45 kilograms (100 pounds) of sugar each year as a sweetener and as in ingredient in food preparation. This amount of sugar as sucrose contributes about 12 percent of our total daily caloric intake. Your body cannot distinguish between the sugar that comes from the sugar bowl or the sugar present in fruits and vegetables.

Some bacteria in the mouth can ferment sugar and lead to tooth decay. Sticky foods and frequent consumption of sweets between meals increase the risk of caries (cavities) formation. Diabetes is a metabolic disorder which prevents the normal use of all carbohydrates not just sugar. In addition, excess calories from all of the various kinds of food sources also contribute to problems of weight control.

The Food and Drug Administration ordered an extensive review of the scientific literature on sucrose by a group of recognized authorities. These authorities found sugar to be a safe food in the quantities presently used of 15 or 20 percent of total calories. Other than tooth decay, this intake of sugar was not associated with any disease as many popular myths would have us believe.

A healthful diet provides a balanced and varied selection of nutrient-rich foods and enhances your well-being. You should remember that sugar in any form (white, brown, honey, and all other forms) is nutrient poor but calorie rich. Regardless of the form of sugar you prefer, use it to enhance taste appeal, but do not go the extreme of eating large amounts of any sweetener. Sugar easily satisfies your appetite and, in this way, keeps you from eating other nutritious foods. You can handle the calories provided by sugar as long as your total energy intake meets your energy expenditure.

Any nutrient you consume in excessive amounts, including sugar, leads to a dietary imbalance and should be avoided. Sugar is a normal constituent of fresh fruits, vegetables, and milk—all nutrient-rich foods. The food groups continue to be very reliable guides to your dietary balance.

Convenience in Grains

There was a time when cereal grains were grown in fields surrounding the home, and when the small hard kernels of cereal were pounded between stones to crack and pulverize the grain. Grains are no longer soaked in water and boiled to soften the kernels. Today, the growing, processing, milling, and even some of the cooking has been completed before the cereal products reach the home. Cereal may be flaked, puffed, shredded, or sugar-coated, and it can go directly from the package into the cereal bowl. It may be precooked so that only a few minutes cooking time is required, or it may be instantized so that it can be placed directly into the cereal bowl, requiring only the addition of boiling water or milk.

The milling and packaging of grains signaled the first step in convenience which led to today's just-add-boiling-water-and-stir cereals. All of the convenience cereal items were designed to use time and energy to the best advantage.

When it comes to selection, you are confronted with an almost unlimited choice. Which will you select: whole grain, enriched, or refined? Will it be ready-to-eat, instantized, or precooked? Will it be wheat, oats, corn, or rice? With sugar or without? Will it be with or without added fruit? Will your decision consider nutrient values, palatability, cost, your personal values, as well as saving time and energy? Your decision is most important because it will not only influence you and your food needs, but it could influence others.

Convenience also tends toward a built-in monotony because of the sameness and exactness with which each product is produced. It is only with your creativity and imagination that this monotony can be overcome. Convenience items make it possible to use time and energy to advantage, but their use demands creativity and increased cost per serving.

Main Ideas

Grain products are economical staples which furnish a tremendous amount of energy, especially whole grain or enriched products which provide vitamins, minerals, and iron in particular. Grain products come in many convenience forms which can be used alone or in creative ways in many different recipes.

Activities

1. Calculate the cost of 28 grams (1 ounce) of a ready-to-eat cereal, of a cereal to be cooked, and of an instant cereal from the same grain. Prepare each cereal according to package directions and compare their flavor, texture, and nutritive values as well as cost. Which did you prefer? Why?

2. Visit a local grocery store and note the kinds of cereals which are offered for sale. How would you group them? What information is found on the labels? Which cereal provides the highest percentage of the RDA for vitamins and minerals? Which cereals are presweetened? Read the nutritional label and compare with that of the unsweetened cereal of the same kind. What differences or similarities did you find?

3. Which macaroni and spaghetti products were available?

4. In what ways could cereal and grain products be served for lunch or dinner?

5. Suggest ways to be creative with cereals.

6. Keep a record of your meals for two days. What nutrients did you receive from the cereal and grain products? What portion of your total calories came from cereals and grains?

7. Cook a fine-grained cereal such as cream of wheat and a coarse cereal such as rolled oats using the two methods recommended for preventing lumping. Evaluate the methods with regard to ease of preparation and lump-free product. Which method do you recommend for each cereal?

8. Cook 250 milliliters (1 cup) of macaroni. Remeasure it after cooking. How much cooked macaroni did you have? Select a recipe for using the cooked macaroni in a prepared dish to be served either for lunch or supper, and explain why you liked or disliked it.

9. Recall the food you ate yesterday. Identify the fiber-rich foods. What is the value of dietary fiber?

Questions

1. What important nutrients are contributed by grains? Can they be supplied by other foods?

2. Explain what is meant when a label reads enriched cereal.

3. What are the parts of a cereal grain? How do their nutrient values differ?

4. Why is cereal and milk a good food combination?

5. What are the uses of grains other than as a breakfast food?

6. Why does starch thicken a cornstarch pudding?

7. How is lumping prevented in cereals to be cooked?

8. What is beriberi? How is it prevented?

9. Why is excess water not recommended for grain cookery?

10. What points should be considered when cereals are purchased?

11. How should grains be stored?

12. What are the disadvantages of convenience grain products?

13. List some guides for the most effective use and selection of convenience grain products.

Chapter 8

Milk

Words for Thought

Lactose
the sugar (carbohydrate) in milk.

Coagulation
the settling out of protein due to action of acid, heat, or an enzyme.

Homogenization
process by which fats are broken into very small particles and then permanently distributed throughout a food.

Pasteurization
process of heating milk to destroy harmful bacteria.

Nutrient
a component (building block) of food that promotes growth and health.

Minerals
the chemical components of foods which remain after the organic (carbon-containing) material of which they were a part burns (oxidizes).

Fortified
a food product with added nutrients such as vitamins or minerals.

Curdling
to thicken into a curd or clot and separate from the liquid portion.

Ferment
to change the sugar in a food to an acid by means of bacteria or yeast and give a sour flavor to the food.

Milk is one of our best and most popular foods and has been used as a food for centuries. The Bible makes numerous references to milk. Milk, cheese, and butter were used by the Egyptians, Greeks, and Romans; and the Spanish brought cattle to the new world.

Milk and milk products are so diverse that a wide variety of them can be easily included in any meal or between-meal snack. It is used as a daily beverage by all age groups, and it is used as the liquid ingredient in many recipes. Milk is a food for which there is no substitute.

Nutrient Contributions

Milk is one of the best foods for promoting and maintaining the health of all people. The main reason is that it contains so many different nutrients which are needed by people of all ages. Milk is an excellent source of minerals, vitamins, and proteins.

Minerals

Minerals are vital for life and health and for the regulation of all body processes. Milk is an abundant source of *calcium*, and calcium is present in the body in larger amounts than any other mineral. Most of this calcium is in the bones, a smaller part is in the teeth, and a very small amount is in the blood serum. Bones and teeth, like other body tissues, are living structures which are constantly changing. Although the amount of calcium in blood is small compared with that in the bones, it is necessary for normal bodily functions.

Calcium is needed by every body cell as it helps to: (1) build strong bones and teeth; (2) give strength or firmness to body cells; (3) aid in clotting of blood; (4) regulate contraction and relaxation of muscles; (5) assist in regulating the action of the heart muscle; and (6) maintain normal nerve function. Because of its many functions in the body, calcium is important to adults and adolescents as well as growing children.

What happens when the food you eat does not supply the calcium your body needs? The body can draw calcium from the bones whenever the diet is deficient in this mineral because the bones are a storehouse for calcium. At the same time, calcium strengthens the bones. A continuous loss of calcium from the bones will affect the soundness of teeth and bones. A calcium-poor diet will not permit you to grow to your full height. In fact, nutrition studies with animals show that the animals on a low-calcium diet do not grow well and remain much smaller than those on a calcium-rich diet. A calcium-poor diet can cause fragile bones and teeth, poor posture, and can interfere with normal nerve function, blood clotting, muscle contraction, and heart beat. Milk is an important daily source of calcium. Without milk, it is difficult for both children and adults to meet the body's need for calcium.

In addition to calcium, milk contains a high level of *phosphorus*. Phosphorus is needed for every body cell and it combines with calcium to make bones and teeth. Phosphorus

Milk is an excellent source of calcium, a mineral which is important to every body cell.

influences the oxidation of foods in the body cells to release energy to the body. Most of the compounds which release energy to the body from food contain phosphorus. From 80 to 85 percent of the phosphorus in your body is present in the bones, with smaller amounts in muscles and in body fluids.

Milk and milk products are excellent sources of phosphorus. Phosphorus is more widely distributed in foods than calcium. Whole grain cereals, meats, poultry, and eggs are also good sources of phosphorus.

Vitamins

Vitamins aid the body in growth, maintenance, and repair. Because they keep the body operating in an efficient and orderly way, vitamins are often referred to as body protectors and regulators. Vitamin A is found in the fat portion, or cream, of milk, and the B complex vitamins are in the nonfat or liquid portion of milk.

Milk is the best food source of *vitamin B₂, or riboflavin*. It helps all of the cells use oxygen so that the carbohydrates, the sugars, and starches which you eat can release energy for all your activities. Vitamin B_2 keeps the skin, eyes, and tongue in good condition and also promotes growth. It is needed for good health, vigor, and healthy appearance. It is also necessary for proper function of nerve tissues and the digestive tract. A common sign of vitamin B_2 deficiency is cracking of the lips, especially in the corners of the mouth.

Milk provides vitamin B_2. This is the vitamin which is necessary for a vigorous and healthy appearance.

Riboflavin is very easily destroyed by light, and that is why paper milk cartons or brown bottles, which light cannot penetrate, are used to help protect the milk against loss of vitamin B_2. All forms of milk are rich sources of riboflavin, or vitamin B_2.

Thiamin and *niacin* along with riboflavin belong to the B complex or B group of vitamins. Thiamin and niacin are found in milk in fair quantities. You will remember that the B vitamins were found in whole grain cereal products discussed in Chapter 7. You will also recall that these vitamins assist in maintaining a normal appetite, a good digestive system, and proper nerve function. They help in releasing food energy for use by the body.

Most of the B complex vitamins are found in milk; some are in large amounts such as riboflavin, others in moderate amounts such as thiamin, and others, such as niacin, are in only fair amounts.

Comparison of Nutrient Values of Milk with Other Foods
Contribution to U.S. Recommended Daily Allowances

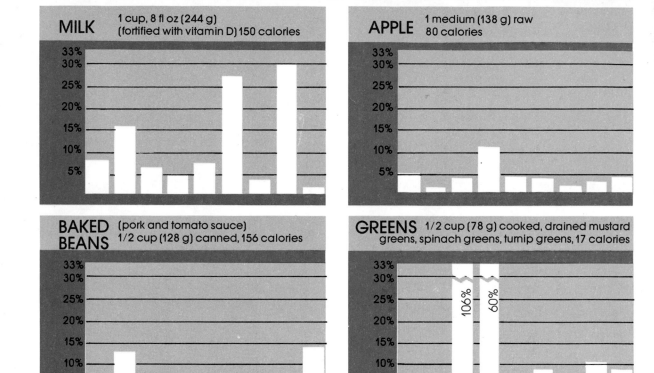

MILK — 1 cup, 8 fl oz (244 g) (fortified with vitamin D) 150 calories

APPLE — 1 medium (138 g) raw 80 calories

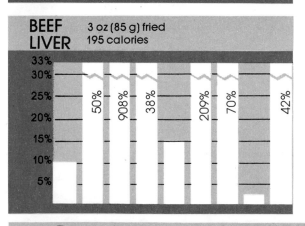

BAKED BEANS — (pork and tomato sauce) 1/2 cup (128 g) canned, 156 calories

GREENS — 1/2 cup (78 g) cooked, drained mustard greens, spinach greens, turnip greens, 17 calories

106% 60%

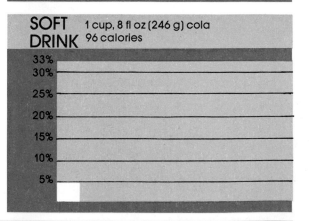

BEEF LIVER — 3 oz (85 g) fried 195 calories

50% 908% 38% 209% 70% 42%

SOFT DRINK — 1 cup, 8 fl oz (246 g) cola 96 calories

The percentage bars in each of the graphs above represent the following nutrients, from left to right: calories, protein, vitamin A, vitamin C, thiamin (B₁) riboflavin (B₂) niacin, calcium, and iron.

Courtesy of National Dairy Council. Used by permission.

Whole milk is also a good source of *vitamin A*. When skim milk is made, this fat-soluble vitamin is removed with the cream. However, today it is possible to buy skim milk with vitamin A added. You will remember that vitamin A in the form of carotene is found in fruits. Vitamin A is important for vision, mucous membranes, and growth.

Another fat-soluble vitamin in milk is *vitamin D*. Whole milk does not contain very large amounts of vitamin D, but this vitamin is often added to milk to make it a rich source of vitamin D. It helps your body to use the minerals calcium and phosphorus in a way that builds sound bones and teeth. When vitamin D is lacking a disease called rickets develops. Rickets is a disease of defective bone formation. The bones are weak and remain soft. The legs will bow because the bones are not rigid enough to support the weight of the body. Most milk is fortified with vitamin D and is a reliable source of this vitamin.

Protein

Along with vitamins and minerals, milk contains high-quality protein. You need protein to help you grow, to make muscles and build your body, and to repair worn or broken tissues.

Carbohydrates

Lactose or milk sugar is the carbohydrate found in milk. Lactose, like all carbohydrates, provides energy. When milk becomes sour, the lactic-acid bacteria change lactose into lactic acid, giving sour milk its characteristic flavor.

Fats

Fats also supply energy for your body. The fat in milk is referred to as cream or butterfat. Milk fat is very special because it contains the fat-soluble vitamin A in large amounts and vitamin D in smaller amounts. Remember that whole milk and lowfat milk contain fat. Skim milk and nonfat milk do not contain fat. Because nearly all the fat has been removed from skim milk and nonfat dry milk, they provide fewer calories and can be used when necessary to reduce calories.

Whole milk does contain minerals, vitamins, protein, carbohydrate, fat, and water. Because milk contains important amounts of most nutrients, it has been called the most perfect food. However, milk with all its goodness is very low in iron and vitamin C, or ascorbic acid, and is rather low in niacin. Milk is especially important in your meals because of its abundant supply of calcium, riboflavin, and protein. By including a generous supply of milk in your meals each day, you can eat well, look good, and feel good.

Lactose Intolerance

Lactose, the sugar in milk, lacks sweetness and is found only in milk. Some healthy individuals, both children and adults, are unable to use lactose because their bodies cannot break the lactose down into the simple sugars (glucose and galactose) of which it is composed. This is because a sugar-splitting enzyme, lactase, is lacking in the small intestine. Such individuals are unable to use lactose and, therefore, are identified as being lactose-intolerant. Lactose remains undigested in their intestinal tract and contributes to abdominal pain, diarrhea, and flatulence (gas). These individuals can usually tolerate fermented dairy products such as buttermilk, cottage cheese, and yogurt and milk to which lactase has been added.

Lactose intolerance is usually found among Black Africans; Black Americans; Chinese; some South Americans; Alaskan, Canadian, and American Indians; and among Eskimos and Mexicans. Lactose intolerance begins early in life and may become more prevalent with age. Research studies show lactose-intolerant individuals have sufficient lactase to digest small quantities of milk (250 milliliters (l cup)).

Should you be lactose-intolerant, include small quantities of regular milk and/or fermented milk products to be sure that your body has an ample supply of calcium. You will recall milk is the best food source for calcium which serves many functions in the body.

Processing of Milk

Milk which is sold must be free of harmful bacteria, and therefore the production and sale of milk is controlled by local health departments. There are regulations designed to produce milk with a low bacterial count, good flavor, satisfactory keeping quality, and high nutritive value. Thus, people are assured milk that is safe to use.

Pasteurization

To insure safety, most milk is pasteurized. Louis Pasteur, a French scientist after whom the process of pasteurization is named, is credited with developing the heat treatment of milk. Pasteurized milk has been heated at a temperature below boiling to destroy harmful organisms. Two methods are used to pasteurize milk: the flash method and the holding method. In the flash method, the milk is brought to 71°C (160°F) for a minimum of fifteen seconds. In the holding method, the milk is brought to a temperature no lower than 62°C (143°F) and is held for thirty minutes, and then cooled rapidly.

Homogenized Milk

Most whole milk today is homogenized to reduce the size of fat particles. The milk under pressure is forced through small openings to break the fat particles so small that they will remain uniformly distributed throughout the milk and will not rise to the top. Because of homogenization, the protein of milk forms a soft curd and is more easily digested. (See illustration above.)

Fortified Milk

The amount of vitamin D in fresh whole milk is small and variable. Most whole milk being sold is now fortified by adding vitamin D. Each quart (liter) of fortified milk contains 400 I.U. (International Units) or 10 micrograms (new unit for measurement of vitamin D level) of vitamin D. This amount of vitamin D will supply your body's need for this vitamin. Milk is fortified by exposing it to ultraviolet light (irradiation) which changes some of the fat components in milk to vitamin D or by adding a vitamin D concentrate to milk prior to pasteurization.

Most of the milk sold today is pasteurized, homogenized, and fortified. In addition to fresh whole milk several other kinds of milk and milk products are available.

Forms of Milk

Milk is available in a number of different forms. Each has special qualities.

After milk is pasteurized in these huge vats, it flows along the pipe into the homogenizer which can process 3800 liters (1000 gallons) per hour.

133

Pasteurized Milk

Milk heated to destroy harmful organisms.

Certified Milk

Milk produced under very strict sanitary conditions. Used on doctor's orders in cases of infant and invalid feeding.

Skim Milk

Milk from which the fat has been removed. It will have fewer calories than whole milk because fat is removed. Skim milk is a good source of calcium, riboflavin, and protein. The fat-soluble vitamins A and D are removed along with the fat, but can be replaced when the milk is processed.

Low-fat Milk

Milk from which some of the fat has been removed. Low-fat milks contain between 0.5 and 2.0 percent milk fat and are usually fortified with 2000 I.U. of vitamin A (or 400 R.E.) and 400 I.U. or 10 micrograms of vitamin D per liter (quart), and milk solids are added. The label indicates the percent of fat and other nutrients present. Low-fat milk has a nutrient value comparable to whole milk, but with fewer calories. Low-fat milks are suitable for fat-controlled and/or calorie-restricted diets.

Chocolate Milk

Whole milk to which chocolate flavor has been added.

Chocolate Drink

Skim milk to which chocolate flavor has been added.

Homogenized Milk

Pasteurized milk forced through very small openings which reduce the fat globules to very small particles evenly distributed throughout the milk and not rising to the surface.

Vitamin D Milk

Usually homogenized and pasteurized milk to which vitamin D has been added.

Concentrated Milk

Fresh fluid milk has a large water content. Reducing the water content concentrates the milk so that it has less bulk.

Evaporated milk is canned milk from which about 60 percent of the water is evaporated. It is sealed in a can and heat treated so that it will not spoil. Undiluted evaporated milk, chilled until ice crystals form, may be whipped. It can be reconstituted with an equal amount of water and used as whole milk.

Sweetened condensed milk is canned milk made from sweetened whole milk and from which about 60 percent of water has been removed and about 45 percent sugar added.

Dry whole milk is whole milk from which the water has been removed. It does not keep well because the fat it contains easily develops an unpleasant flavor.

Nonfat dry milk is skim milk from which water has been removed. Nonfat dry milk will keep for a long time and it is economical. It can be reconstituted with water and used in the same manner as fresh milk. Dried skim milk which has been only partially reconstituted to liquid milk can be whipped to provide a low-calorie whipped topping.

Fermented Milk

Fermented milks have a sour flavor due to breakdown of lactose (milk sugar) to lactic acid by bacterial action.

Most buttermilk today is cultured buttermilk made chiefly from pasteurized skim milk which has been treated with lactic-acid bacteria. Buttermilk is also available in the dried powder form. Cultured buttermilk is mild in flavor.

Sour milk, whole or skim, is soured by lactic-acid bacteria.

Sweet acidophilus milk is a new cultured milk. Fresh milk is inoculated with a pure culture of acidophilus bacteria. When the milk is drunk, these bacteria enter into the intestine where they may retard the decomposition of organic material.

Yogurt is a coagulated milk product with a custard-like consistency. It is made by fermenting partially skimmed milk with a special acid-forming bacteria. Its nutritive values are similar to those of the milk from which it is made.

Cream

This is the fat of milk. Creams vary in fat content.

Whipping cream or heavy cream contains a minimum of 36 percent fat, and generally averages 36 to 40 percent fat.

Coffee cream or light cream contains 18 to 20 percent fat.

Half-and-half, a milk/cream blend, has 10 to 12 percent fat.

Sour cream is cream, with 18 percent fat, which has been soured by lactic-acid bacteria.

Milk is graded according to how clean and free of contamination it is.

Milk is such a versatile beverage that it can be combined with many flavors and ingredients to make hot or cold drinks for all occasions.

Grades of Milk

The bacterial count of milk is the basis for its grading. The highest grade, *Grade A*, has the lowest bacterial count and is the grade sold in retail stores. *Grades B and C* are safe and wholesome; however, in some areas only one grade may be available. The grade is usually indicated on the bottle cap or on the side of the milk carton. The grade of milk does not indicate its richness, but applies only to its degree of sanitation. Butterfat content is usually indicated as a percentage on the bottle cap or on the side of the carton, for example, "Standardized 3.5% B.F."

Uses of Milk

Milk has two general and most popular uses. It is used as a beverage and as an ingredient in recipes. Either way it is wholesome and filling.

Milk as a Beverage

If milk is to be used as a beverage, it requires no preparation other than chilling. Because milk has a mild taste, it can be blended with a number of flavors. Flavored milk drinks, milk shakes, and eggnog are available in an endless variety to suit everyone's taste. Select your flavor choice from chocolate, fruit flavors, malt, syrups, spices, ice creams, vanilla, and others. Milk and milk beverages can be served hot or cold with meals, as snacks, and as party foods.

Milk as an Ingredient

Milk contributes to the nutritive value, flavor, texture, consistency, and browning quality of food products. Milk in all forms can be used as an ingredient in a variety of recipes. It can be used in cream soups, chowders, sauces, gravies, casseroles, custards, puddings, breads, and cakes. As an ingredient, milk is used with a variety of foods such as vegetables, meat, fish, poultry, fruits, and cereals.

Milk will greatly improve the nutritional value of any food or recipe with which it is used. It also promotes the browning quality of baked foods. A nice golden brown in certain foods and baked products adds a special taste and appearance which most people associate with attractive meals.

Evaporated milk may be used to replace fresh milk in a recipe. For general use in cookery, evaporated milk is diluted with an equal amount of water (125 milliliters (½ cup) evaporated milk plus 125 milliliters (½ cup) water = 250 milliliters (1 cup) fresh whole milk) and can be used as a substitute for fresh whole milk. Only recipes developed for evaporated milk use this milk right from the can. For all other recipes, evaporated milk must be diluted with an equal volume of water.

Condensed milk contains added sugar and, therefore, requires special recipes for its use in food preparation.

Whole or nonfat dry milk reconstituted with water can be used as a substitute for fresh milk in most recipes. Reconstituted dry milk is used as a beverage and as an ingredient in soups, custards, and sauces. For baked products, the dry milk solids may usually be sifted with the other dry ingredients and then water is added instead of the fluid milk.

Principles of Milk Cookery

Milk is an important protein food. It is the protein of milk that influences the principles of milk cookery. The objectives of milk cookery are to prevent: (1) film or scum formation; (2) boiling over; (3) scorching; and (4) curdling.

A thin film or scum may form when milk is heated at a low temperature. As the temperature is increased, a tough film forms; as soon as the film is removed, another will form. The protein in milk is chiefly responsible for the scum or film.

Prevention of Milk Film

One of the objectives in milk cookery is to prevent the formation of the film or scum. Formation of the film on the milk surface can be prevented by using a covered container, by stirring the milk during heating, or by beating the mixture with a rotary beater to form a layer of foam on the surface. Hot cocoa, for example, is often beaten to form a layer of foam so that a film will not develop on the surface.

Boiling-over

The formation of the film on boiled milk is the principal reason for the boiling over of milk. A pressure develops under the scum which forces the milk to break through the film and boil over the sides of the pan.

Scorching of Milk

When milk is heated, some of its protein tends to settle out (coagulate) on the sides and bottom of the pan and can scorch easily unless the milk is heated on a very low heat. Stirring the milk while it heats helps to thin out the film, but a low temperature must be used to prevent scorching. The milk sugar, lactose, with protein also forms a brownish film on the pan when milk is heated. Milk can be heated over hot water to avoid scorching; however, with controlled low-heat settings on ranges, the use of water is not essential. Heating milk on low heat will take longer, but it will avoid scorching.

Curdling of Milk

Another objective of milk cookery is to prevent curdling. When acid is added to milk, the protein settles out in white clumps or curds and separates from the liquid. The milk is then said to be curdled. This can easily happen when, for example, cream of tomato soup is prepared. The acids in tomato and other vegetables can cause the milk protein to separate. Curdling of milk can be prevented in two ways: (1) by thickening the milk or the food to be added with starch before combining them; or (2) by using a low temperature for cooking the food. For example, curdling of tomato soup can be prevented by first thickening the milk with flour and then adding the tomato; or the tomato could be thickened and the milk added.

The tendency to curdle is reduced by the use of low or moderate temperatures. For example, scalloped potatoes will show less curdling if a low temperature is used than they will when a high temperature is used.

Milk which is less sweet will curdle when heated. Acid can develop in milk which has not been properly stored or has been stored for too long a time. The lactic-acid bacteria normally found in milk can change the milk sugar, lactose, into lactic acid which will result in curdling. The curd is the separated protein and is a white solid; the remaining greenish-yellow liquid is the whey. Milk with a high acid content will curdle when heated.

To prevent curdling of milk in cookery: (1) use fresh milk; (2) thicken the milk or the acid food; and (3) use a low temperature. Low-temperature cookery will also help to prevent scorching, reduce scum formation, and avoid boiling over.

138

Storage of Milk

Proper storage of milk will protect its flavor and nutritive value. Milk storage involves cleanliness, cold temperature, and prevention of contamination.

Fresh Milk Storage

The care of milk begins as soon as it is delivered to the home. The first step is to wash or wipe off the outside of the milk container. This will prevent bringing any dirt and germs into the refrigerator. Milk is a very perishable food and should be kept in the coldest part of the refrigerator, that is, beside or below the cooling unit. It should always be stored in a covered container to protect it from absorbing undesirable flavors and odors.

Allowing milk to stand on the doorstep or in a warm kitchen causes rapid growth of bacteria and hastens spoilage. Permitting milk to stand exposed to light destroys vitamin B_2, or riboflavin.

Milk should be refrigerated at once and kept covered.

Dry Milk Storage

Dry milk can be stored at ordinary room temperature in an air-tight container. Once the package has been opened, it should be closed tightly and kept in a cool place. Since the fat has been removed from nonfat dry milk, it has a better keeping quality than dried whole milk. When dried whole milk is exposed to air and moisture it develops an undesirable flavor. To avoid flavor changes, the dry whole milk package can be placed in a container with a tight-fitting cover.

Reconstituted dry milk has a high water content and will spoil in the same way as fresh whole milk. Dry milk should be refrigerated as soon as it is reconstituted if it is not used immediately.

Evaporated and Condensed Milk Storage

Unopened cans of evaporated and condensed milk may be stored at room temperature. The cans should be kept in a dry, well-ventilated place to prevent rusting of the can. Once the can is opened, the remaining milk in the can must be stored in the refrigerator.

Milk Substitutes

Several imitation milk products are available on the market. Some of these are found on shelves near regular milk products and others are found in frozen food cases. An imitation milk product is made to resemble fluid whole milk by substituting a nondairy ingredient for one or more of the nutrients found in milk products. This product is not permitted for sale in all states. Nondairy ingredients included in the imitation dairy products are coconut oil, vegetable oils, monoglycerides, corn syrup solids, soy protein, and others.

The nutrient values of imitation products can be quite different from those found in milk. Milk and milk products represent one of the best food sources of nutrients in the best proportion required for optimum health and body maintenance. Earlier in this chapter, milk was designated as the best food source of calcium, and rich in complete proteins and vitamins A, D, and B complex. The amounts of protein, vitamins, and minerals can be quite variable in imitation products. The nondairy foods are imitations of milk but not necessarily a substitute for milk. They do not provide the same nutrients found in milk.

The nutrient content of nondairy products should be listed on the carton or package. The nutrient content of these products should be considered carefully before purchase since the nutrient content of nondairy foods and milk are not the same.

With such a variety of milk and nondairy products from which to choose, selection becomes the major problem. It is important to select the products which best meet your needs and nutritional requirements.

Milk as a Convenience Food

The milk bottle has replaced the family cow as a source of milk. Milk in a bottle or carton is a convenience in itself which cannot be appreciated unless one has experienced the work involved in obtaining milk directly from the cow. Milk in a bottle is ready to be used as a food or as an ingredient in a recipe without further preparation.

Convenience in the use and storage of milk has been increased by processing. Nonfat dried milk and unopened cans of evaporated and condensed milk do not require refrigeration, which makes storage easy. Because they do not require refrigeration, an extra supply of milk can be on hand so that the milk supply will never run out, even in an emergency.

Both dried and evaporated milks can be easily reconstituted with water, and can replace whole milk in recipes. The dry or instant form of milk can also be combined directly with the dry ingredients without first being reconstituted. Then, only water is added as the liquid to provide the needed moisture. In this way, the milk becomes automatically reconstituted as the liquid (water) is added to the dry ingredients of the recipe. Nonfat dry milk can also be added to foods such as breads, gravies, soups, and beverages to supplement their food value.

Nonfat dry milk and evaporated milk can be whipped. Equal amounts of nonfat dry milk and cold water are beaten until soft peaks form. Evaporated milk is first chilled until fine ice crystals are formed and then it is whipped. The foams formed by both milks make an acceptable topping.

Sweetened condensed milk adds to the convenience of dairy products. This milk is useful in desserts because it will thicken to the consistency of a pudding when an acid such as lemon juice is added to it. Heating the milk will also cause thickening. Many special recipes which can be made quickly and easily use condensed milk.

Cream combined with sugar, stabilizers, emulsifiers, and an appropriate gas is available in pressurized cans. This is a convenience form of whipped cream. In addition, many whipped-cream substitutes are now being marketed. These products generally have a protein base, vegetable fat, and stabilizers, but some are made without any dairy products. They may come as powders to whip with water, in pressurized cans, or prewhipped in containers. Because of their lack of fat, these items have fewer calories than whipped cream. For example, one tablespoon pressurized whipped topping provides 10 kilocalories, while whipped cream provides 15 kilocalories.

Main Ideas

Milk is a complex, nutritious food available in a variety of forms. Each brings its special qualities to food preparation. Milk is a protein food which affects the ways it is used in foods when heat, acid, or certain enzymes are present. Milk can be treated to improve and insure its nutritive value and quality. Its convenience forms have, in some cases, eliminated the need for refrigeration, and have made storage easy.

Activities

1. Keep a three-day record of all the milk, in any form, that you include in your meals or snacks, and the cheese and ice cream you eat.

a. Does your diet measure up to your body's need for milk?

b. What was your average daily intake of milk?

c. Do you need to improve your intake of milk? How can this be done if you are not getting enough milk?

d. What nutrients will be low in your diet when milk intake is inadequate?

2. Suggest five different milk snacks that you can prepare. Why is milk a better snack than soft drinks or candy?

3. Collect an exhibit of cartons or containers used for milk and milk products. Are some of these cartons from imitation milk products? What information is on the labels? How many of the listed ingredients were new to you? Were any of these products labeled as "low-fat"? Compare the fat and nutrient content of regular milk products with that of low-fat milk products. What differences in nutrient content did you find? When would you use the low-fat milk products?

4. Prepare 250 milliliters (1 cup) of nonfat dry milk. Heat half of it in a pan on high heat and the other half on low heat. What differences did you observe in the milk and on the pan surface? Was there any change in flavor? Which heat do you recommend and why?

5. Prepare foams from nonfat dry milk and evaporated milk. Serve these as toppings to replace whipped cream. Compare the flavor, texture, foam stability, and cost of each, and compare both to whipped cream. Which of the milk toppings were acceptable?

6. Find a recipe for cream of tomato soup. Is the milk or the tomato thickened before combining? Prepare the soup. Were you able to prevent curdling? Describe ways in which curdling can be prevented.

7. Find a recipe for cocoa. Prepare the beverage so that film formation is minimal. What technique did you use? Did it work well?

8. What kind of milk do you purchase at home? What are some ways in which you mght be able to spend less money than you now do when purchasing milk?

142

Questions

1. Why is milk sometimes called the perfect food?

2. Which vitamins are not found in skim milk?

3. What is the carbohydrate in milk?

4. What is the basis for grading milk? Is Grade A milk the only milk safe for drinking? Give reasons for your answers.

5. How is milk fortified? Why is it fortified?

6. Define cream, buttermilk, condensed milk, and evaporated milk.

7. What are the advantages of using milk in recipes?

8. How can milk boil-over be prevented?

9. Why is scorching a problem with milk cookery? How is it prevented?

10. What causes milk to curdle?

11. How is milk used as a beverage? As an ingredient?

12. Describe storage of fresh whole milk, nonfat dry milk, canned condensed milk, and reconstituted evaporated milk.

13. In what ways do milk substitutes differ from cow's milk?

14. In what ways is milk a convenience food?

15. What is lactose intolerance?

Chapter
9

Cheese

Words for Thought

Curd
the protein-rich solid part of coagulated milk

Whey
the liquid remaining after milk has formed curds.

Kilocalorie
a unit used to measure the energy value of food. A unit of 1000 calories.

Casein
the chief protein of milk.

Process cheese
a mixture or blend of two or more cheeses.

The making of cheese is an ancient art. Although the origin of cheese making is unknown, many legends concerning its origin have been handed down through the centuries. One of these legends concerns a person who, setting off on a long journey, took milk in a calfskin container. According to the story, he ripped open the bag and carefully tasted the solidified mass inside, found it had a pleasant flavor, and ate the rest of it.

The art of cheese making was brought to this country by European immigrants. In making cheese, the first step is to warm the milk slightly, and then add a starter of lactic-acid-

144

producing bacteria. When the milk becomes slightly acid, rennin, an enzyme which causes milk protein to settle out, is added. The casein, milk protein, will coagulate and the curd that has formed is cut to separate the whey, a clear liquid that contains some of the water-soluble substances in milk. After the curd is cut and stirred to remove the whey, it is mixed with salt and packed into cheesecloth-lined hoops. At this stage the cheese is called "green cheese." The pressed green cheese is dried for several days and is then coated with hot paraffin to prevent moisture loss during curing. The cheese is placed in a ventilated room at a controlled temperature, about 10°C (50°F), to develop the desired flavor.

The ripening or curing causes desirable changes in the texture and flavor of cheese. Some cheese becomes softer and more tender so that it can be blended easily or mixed into other foods. The changes in texture will vary with the different types of cheese. During ripening some cheeses become very soft, others become harder and even crumbly, and others become porous or develop holes. In addition, a distinctive flavor is developed in each kind of cheese.

Kinds of Cheese

Cheeses are available in many varieties. They are made from cow's milk, goat's milk, reindeer milk and many other sources. They can be conveniently classified according to their degree of hardness.

Hard Cheeses

Hard cheeses are made principally from partially skimmed cow's milk. Parmesan is a very hard cheese of Italian origin which is usually used as a grated cheese. Swiss cheese is identified by the large holes which develop during ripening when special bacteria produce a gas. Edam and Gouda are hard cheeses recognized by their bright red wax coatings. A very popular hard cheese is Cheddar or American cheese. Food coloring is added to give some Cheddar cheese a yellow color.

Semisoft Cheeses

Brick, Roquefort, and Muenster are examples of semisoft cheeses. Brick cheese is a popular semisoft cheese. It derives

Since many hard cheeses have a mild flavor, they are perhaps the most popular and versatile.

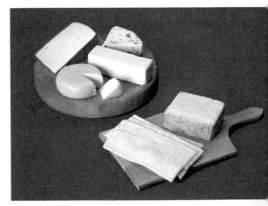

Many of the semisoft cheeses have a distinctly strong flavor and pungent odor.

145

its name from its shape. Roquefort, Gorgonzola, and Blue cheese have a characteristic blue-green color and a pronounced flavor which is caused by a special mold which develops during the ripening of the cheese. Gorgonzola and Blue cheese are made from cow's milk while Roquefort is produced from sheep's milk. Muenster cheese that is sold in the United States is mild in flavor while that sold in Europe has a sharper flavor. This distinctive flavor is due to longer ripening. Other cheeses are described in the chart below and on the next page.

Some Common Cheeses and Their Uses*

Name	Color, texture, flavor	Use
Muenster	Creamy white, semi-soft with tiny holes. Pungent flavor.	Appetizers; sandwiches.
Romano	Yellow-white; hard, granular. Piquant.	Grated for seasoning.
Parmesan	Yellow-white, hard. Sharp flavor.	Grated on soups, breads, spaghetti; in cooked foods.
Mozzarella, Pizza	Nonripened soft; white, stretchy. When served hot becomes chewy.	Sliced; in cooked foods.
Provolone	Light yellow, semi-soft, smooth and somewhat plastic. Mellow smoky flavor.	Appetizers; sandwiches; in cooked foods; desserts.
Ricotta	White, sweet, cottage-type; nonripened soft.	Appetizers; salads; in cooked foods; desserts.
Camembert	Creamy with edible white crust; soft, surface ripened.	On crackers or with fruit; for appetizers or desserts.

*American Dairy Association.

Soft Cheeses

Soft cheeses are made from skim milk or whole milk. Two popular soft cheeses are cottage cheese and cream cheese. The action of rennin and acid causes curds to form in the milk. The soft unripened curds are sold as dry cottage cheese or with added cream as creamed cottage cheese. Cream cheese is a soft, uncured, smooth cheese made from whole milk to which cream has been added. Neufchatel is made with less cream and is similar to cream cheese.

Because these cheeses are bland and soft they make an excellent base for unusual party dips.

Name	Color, texture, flavor	Use
Cheddar	White to orange; hard. Mild to sharp flavor. America's most popular.	Appetizers; sandwiches; salads; in cooked foods; desserts.
Blue	Blue-veined, crumbly; semi-soft to hard. Sharp, salty flavor.	Appetizers; salads; salad dressings; cooked foods; desserts.
Swiss	Light yellow, large holes; hard. Nutlike sweet flavor.	Appetizers; sandwiches; salads; in cooked foods.
Brick	Creamy yellow; semi-soft with small holes. Mild to sharp.	Appetizers; sandwiches; salads; desserts.
Cream	White, nonripened, soft and smooth. Mild, delicate flavor.	Appetizers; sandwiches; salads; cooked foods; desserts.
Gouda	Red wax on surface, creamy yellow interior; semisoft. Nutlike.	Appetizers; salads; in cooked foods; sliced; desserts.
Edam	Red wax outer surface, yellow interior; soft to hard. Nutlike.	Appetizers; salads; in cooked foods; desserts.

Process Cheeses

Process cheeses are produced from a blend of cheeses to develop a different texture and flavor. Process cheeses are made from selected cheeses with the desired flavor and texture characteristics. The cheeses are shredded and mixed together and an emulsifier is added such as sodium citrate or disodium phosphate. The mixture is stirred and heated until the cheese becomes soft and well blended. This heating of process cheese stops bacterial and enzyme action so that no additional ripening can occur. Because of this heat treatment this cheese may be labeled "pasteurized process cheese." Process cheeses have a mild, bland flavor and an excellent keeping quality. They do not become stringy or tough during cooking. They blend easily.

Process Cheese Foods

Pasteurized process cheese foods are similar to process cheese but contain less fat and milk solids and more moisture. In making cheese food, cream, milk, skim milk, or whey can be added to the cheese. They blend easily with other ingredients.

Grades of Cheese

To assure a quality product, the United States Department of Agriculture (USDA) has defined quality standards for some varieties of cheese (Swiss, Cheddar). The USDA inspection shield means the product was produced under sanitary conditions and is of good quality. The USDA grades are based on flavor, texture, appearance, and color. Cheese and cheese products not covered by a United States grade standard may be inspected and bear the USDA "Quality Approved" inspection shield on the container.

Nutrient Contributions

Cheese is a concentrated form of milk. A piece of cheese weighing 454 grams (1 pound) contains the protein and fat of approximately 3.8 liters (1 gallon) of milk. Cheese is a highly nourishing food containing protein and important amounts of several of the vitamins and minerals. It is an excellent source of calcium.

Protein

Cheese is an excellent source of complete protein which is required for growth and body building. The milk protein, casein, is found abundantly in cheese.

Vitamins

The cheese made from whole milk is an excellent source of *vitamin A*. You will recall from Chapter 8 that vitamin A is a fat-soluble vitamin found in the fat of milk, the cream. Further, from Chapter 6, you learned that vitamin A is needed for good vision, proper growth, and healthy mucous membranes. Cheese is one of the foods which provides your diet with important amounts of vitamin A.

Cheese can add to your intake of the B group of vitamins but not in as great quantities as milk. Since these vitamins are water-soluble, there is some loss of them in the whey which is pressed out from the curd in making cheese. Therefore, cheese is a fair source of the B vitamins, *thiamin* and *riboflavin*. In Chapter 7, you learned that these vitamins are needed for growth, nerves, and to help the body cells oxidize food for the release of energy.

Minerals

The minerals in cheese are those found in milk and, like milk, cheese is an important source of *calcium* and *phosphorus*. Do you recall your body's need for them? Calcium and phosphorus are needed for strong bones and teeth. In addition, calcium is required for blood clotting, muscle contraction, and nerve function; while phosphorus is also involved in the oxidation of foods to release energy to the body.

Fats

Cheese will vary in fat content depending upon the type of milk used to make it. Cheese made from skim milk, such as cottage cheese, will be low in fat, while cream cheese made from whole milk and added cream will be high in fat. Most other cheeses are made from whole milk and, therefore, are a rich source of fat.

Fats provide energy for play and work and also for basic body functions such as breathing and heartbeat. Fats provide a very concentrated source of energy. They contribute two and one-fourth times as much energy value as carbohydrates and proteins do.

The energy value of foods is measured in kilocalories. A kilocalorie is the unit used to measure the energy value of foods in much the same way that a centimeter or an inch is used to measure a small object. Since fat contains more than twice as much energy as carbohydrates and proteins, it will also provide more than twice as many kilocalories. Each gram of fat yields 9 kilocalories and each gram of carbohydrate and protein will yield only 4 kilocalories.

Besides energy, fats serve other important functions in your body. They are needed for the attractive appearance of your hair and skin. Too little fat in your diet may cause eczema and dry, rough skin. Fat cushions or protects vital body organs against shock of movement, and insulates the body against changes in temperature. Some foods such as cream, egg yolk, and butter, which contain fats, bring to your diet the fat-soluble vitamins A and D. Fats are found in all foods which are greasy such as cheese, butter, nuts, meats, and oils.

Cheese and other foods which contain fats are popular foods. Because fats are an abundant source of energy and calories, it is easy to eat them in amounts greater than your body requires for energy. When energy supplied to the body exceeds the energy need, a gain in weight will occur. If you have a tendency toward overweight, avoid selecting too many foods that are rich sources of fats. You will learn more about fats in Chapter 20.

Carbohydrates

The carbohydrate in milk is *lactose,* a sugar. Lactose is a water-soluble nutrient which tends to be lost in the whey when cheese is manufactured. Therefore, cheese is not a source of carbohydrate. Cheese, however, is a good source of many other nutrients already mentioned and should be included in a good diet.

Principles of Cheese Cookery

Cheese has a high protein content, and it is the protein that influences the principles of cheese cookery. Cheese protein, like the milk from which it is made, coagulates when heated and becomes tough and rubbery when overcooked. The principles or rules of cheese cookery are: (1) cook at a low temperature to avoid a rubbery, tough consistency; (2) cook for a short time to avoid toughness; (3) when added to other ingredients, cut into small pieces so that it will melt quickly and blend with other foods; and (4) use ripened cheese in cookery because unripened cheese may not blend with the other ingredients.

A high temperature and extensive cooking of cheese not only cause the cheese to become tough and stringy, but also may cause the fat to separate and drain from the cheese. Overcooking can be caused by cooking at too high a temperature as well as cooking for too long.

Cheese as an Ingredient

When cheese is combined with other foods, the temperature should be low, and you should take care not to cook it any longer than necessary so that the cheese will remain soft and tender. For foods which require a hot oven temperature, such as pizza, the cheese may be covered with a sauce to protect it from the high temperature.

In some foods the cheese is protected from the heat of cooking. Cheese in the center of a grilled sandwich is protected and will remain soft and tender, while the cheese in an open-face sandwich may become tough. Cheese can also be protected by the ingredients with which it is combined. Cheese added to pastry and biscuits is protected by the dough during baking. Cheese dishes are served hot and immediately after the cooking is completed.

Cheese which has ripened or aged will blend easily with the ingredients in a recipe. Ripened Cheddars or process cheeses are popularly used in cooked cheese dishes because they do not form strings. However, all cheeses must be cooked carefully as they can become tough and rubbery if cooking temperature is too high or cooking time is too long.

A variety of cheeses decoratively arranged on a tray make attractive and nutritious appetizers.

Uses of Cheese

Cheese adds variety and pleasure to any meal. It can be eaten alone, combined with foods, the chief ingredient in a dish, or grated and sprinkled only on the top of a main dish.

Cheese is a favorite for sandwiches but is also popular on crackers. Crackers spread with cheese are pleasing accompaniments served with soups and salads. Canapés (small pieces of bread), cheese dips, raw vegetables and crackers spread with cheese are served as appetizers and are party foods as well as before-meal taste-tempters.

Slices of cheese over grilled vegetables or hamburgers, or on top of individual casseroles add flavor, variety, and nutrients. Bits of cheese can be added to cream sauces and soups for a flavor accent.

Cheese used in a main dish may be of a bland or sharp variety, depending on your own tastes. Nippy or strong flavored cheeses are used in smaller amounts than bland cheeses. Mild cheeses are popular for sandwiches.

Cheese sauces are easily made by adding shredded cheese to a medium white sauce. Cheese sauces are excellent additions to vegetables. Foods cooked in a cheese sauce or sprinkled with grated cheese are listed as "au gratin" on restaurant menus. Cheese sauces are also used with pastas in main dish foods such as Lasagna and Moussaka.

Cheese may be used to improve the nutritional value of foods. When cheese is added to vegetables, pastas, and legumes, it improves the protein value of these foods so that they can be used as substitutes for meats. Cheese, like eggs and meats, is rich in complete protein and in fat. For this reason cheese is best used to replace meat and eggs in meals rather than in addition to them. Cheese and foods containing cheese are low-cost replacements for meats.

Cheese can be combined with fruits and vegetables and made into salads. Cheese may be the major ingredient in a salad such as cottage cheese on pineapple or a peach; as one of the ingredients of a salad such as cheese cut into strips or cubes in a tossed or garden salad; as a grated topping for fruit and meat salads; or as a salad dressing ingredient as in Roquefort or Blue cheese dressing. Hearty cheese salads are used as the main dish of a meal, while lighter cheese salads are used as accompaniments to the meat or other main course.

Cheese pies, cakes, and fancy frozen or gelatin desserts are choice endings for meals. Cheese pies and cakes are made from soft cheeses such as cottage or cream cheese. Fruit and cheese trays are a popular Continental dessert custom. Because cheese is a concentrated food, a fruit-cheese tray should be served as a dessert for a light meal. Cheese is also a favorite accompaniment to a fruit pie such as apple.

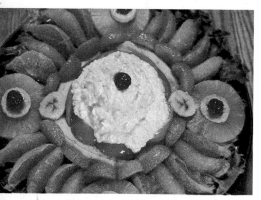

Cheese and fruit salads are popular main dishes because of their low cost and high protein value.

152

Storage of Cheese

All cheeses should be tightly covered or wrapped and stored in the refrigerator. Soft cheeses (cream, cottage) spoil more quickly than hard and semihard cheeses (Swiss, Parmesan, Brick). Cheese and cheese products such as spreads and dips are usually purchased in a protective package or container. Once the container has been opened, it should be closed carefully and refrigerated so that the product will not dry out and deteriorate.

The flavors of strong cheeses can be picked up by other foods, and cheese can readily absorb flavor from other foods. This is another very good reason for keeping cheeses tightly covered.

Cheese improperly stored or stored for too long a time may have mold growing on its surface. Cheese should be purchased in amounts which can be used conveniently without prolonged storage.

Convenience with Cheese

Convenience began with the availability of store cheeses which took the art of cheese making out of the home and put it into the factory. Store cheese is available in many varieties and forms and is packaged in many different containers. Sliced cheese comes in packages in which the slices can be separated for use or where each slice comes individually wrapped. You may purchase cheese in a piece, grated, shredded, cubed, in pressurized cans, as spreads and dips in many flavors, and as a ball rolled in nuts. These convenience forms usually cost more than the same weight of cheese in a solid piece.

Cottage cheese comes in several varieties. It can be purchased as dry cottage cheese (no cream added) or creamed cottage cheese, with added fruits, fresh garden vegetables, or chives.

Canned cheese soup or cheese sauces are available. The canned cheese soup is a ready-made cheese sauce for au gratin vegetables, casseroles, meats, and pastas.

With so much variety and convenience, you are forced to make your selection from among many. Will you select an unripened, ripened, or process cheese; will it be soft, semihard, or hard; a mild or a strong flavor; sliced, grated, a spread or a dip; or a canned cheese sauce? To complicate matters even more, in addition to the true cheeses, there are many food products containing cheese on the market. These foods resemble process cheese but are not regular cheese foods. These products may be labeled "pasteurized process cheese food" or "pasteurized process cheese spread." They differ from the true cheese foods in fat content and moisture, and in other added ingredients such as milk solids and *stabilizers*.[1] Each product is identified by its label and ingredients used; it is important to read this label in order to get exactly what you want.

Main Ideas

Cheese is a product of milk and therefore a protein food. Like milk, it provides essential minerals and vitamins. The great variety of flavors and textures determined by the source of the cheese and length of ripening time make cheese an extremely versatile product. Cheeses are available in many different convenience forms.

Activities

1. Visit a supermarket and make a list of cheeses and cheese products available. What other foods were near them and how were they stored?

2. Check through magazines and cookbooks for pictures of cheese dishes used as salads, desserts, and main dishes. Bring to class.

3. Make a display of cheeses using labels or cartons from cheese. Group them as soft, semihard, and hard cheeses. Give suggestions for their use.

4. Arrange the cheeses you displayed for Activity 3 into low-fat and high-fat cheeses. Were any of these labeled cheese food? In what ways do cheese foods differ from regular cheese? When would you use each product? When is cottage cheese low in fat, high in fat?

5. Prepare a cheese sauce for use in macaroni and cheese. Which cheese did you select and why? Divide the mixture into two small casseroles. Bake one at 180°C (350°F) and the other at 200°C (400°F) for thirty minutes or until lightly browned.

1. *Stabilizer*—This is an ingredient which is added to preserve the texture of a food or an ingredient which prevents changes in the texture of a food.

Compare the texture and flavor. Which did you prefer and why?

6. Suggest three cheese dishes which would be substitutes for meat and prepare and serve one of them to your family. Were you pleased with the results?

Questions

1. What is the difference between the curd and the whey? How do their nutrient values differ?

2. What cheeses are best for cooking? Why?

3. Why is cheese important in the diet?

4. What are the values of fats in the diet? In what kinds of food are they found in abundance?

5. What are the principles of cheese cookery? In what ways are they similar to those of milk cookery?

6. In what ways is cheese used as an ingredient? What does cheese contribute to the foods with which it is combined in a recipe?

7. Why can cheese be a replacement for meat? Why is it often used this way?

8. In what ways is cheese used as an ingredient? What does cheese contribute to the foods with which it is combined in a recipe?

9. What is the best way to protect the flavor and texture of cheese?

10. What is the difference between a true cheese and a cheese-containing food?

11. List all of the factors to be considered when selecting cheeses.

12. What kind of convenience is associated with cheese?

Words for Thought

Emulsion

a thin film of a substance surrounding tiny droplets of a liquid so that they do not separate.

Albumen

the white portion of an egg.

Yolk

the yellow portion of an egg.

Poach

to cook in a hot liquid so that the shape of the food is preserved.

Bloom

a thin film which helps to seal the pores of the eggshell and protect the egg from contamination.

Candling

a method of grading eggs for freshness by placing them in front of a strong light beam.

Shirred

eggs baked in a shallow dish.

Omelet

beaten eggs, often with added ingredients, browned in a pan without stirring.

Custard

a baked or cooked egg-and-milk mixture which forms a gel.

Foam

formation of air bubbles in a viscous liquid by beating.

Meringue

stiffly beaten egg whites with sugar.

Chapter 10

Eggs

Eggs are significant for many cultures and religions. They are symbolic of Easter for many, and possibly symbolic of a tradition handed down from earlier religious festivals. The Hindus believe eggs to be the source of all life and therefore do not eat them. In the Jewish Passover Feast, the egg symbolizes the deliverance from bondage. These religious celebrations offer some explanation for eggs at Eastertime. Eggs have also symbolized life for many throughout history. This may be related to the fact that an egg, properly incubated, can develop into a chick in twenty days.

Structure of the Egg

You know that the egg is contained in a shell and consists of a white (albumen) and a yellow portion (yolk). In addition eggs have several other parts, and, according to the nursery rhyme, "all the King's horses and all the King's men couldn't put Humpty Dumpty (an egg) together again."

The shell of the egg is porous and permits moisture and gases to pass through. On the outside of the shell there is a thin film called the bloom which helps to seal the pores and protect the egg from contamination. The color of the shell will vary from white to brown depending upon which breed of chicken laid the egg. The color of the egg does not affect its cooking or eating quality, or nutrient value.

Between the shell and the egg white there are two membranes, the inner and outer, which protect the quality of the egg. The white of the egg consists of the thin and the thick white. Fresh eggs will contain more thick white than older eggs. The thick white gives a high, rounded appearance to the egg when it is removed from the shell. Such an egg is more attractive when cooked than one in which the white spreads.

The yolk membrane (the vitelline membrane) separates the yolk from the white. Attached to the yolk membrane on each side is a rope or cord called the chalaza which holds the yolk near the center of the egg. There is a light spot on the yolk known as the germ spot. This spot, on a fertilized and incubated egg, can develop into a baby chick. The yolk supplies the food for the growing embryo. The color of the yolk depends upon the food the hen eats. In a fresh egg, the yolk is high, rounded, and centered in the thick white. The air cell is at the blunt end of the egg; its size increases as the egg ages.

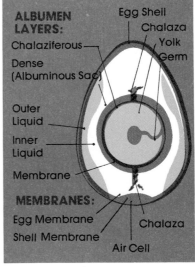

The yolk, the albumen, and the shell are not the only components of an egg.

Grade and Size

Most eggs sold are graded for freshness and size. The standards for grading eggs were set up by the United States Department of Agriculture. The freshness of an egg is graded by candling, which is placing the egg in front of a strong light beam in a darkened room. Twirling the egg in front of the light makes it possible to judge the thickness of the white, the size and position of the yolk, and the size of the air space. The freshest egg has a thick white which supports the rounded, firm yolk and a small air space.

The freshness of an egg refers to its quality and not its size. The freshest eggs are *Grade AA*, followed by *Grade A* and *Grade B*. From the pictures on page 159 you will observe that the difference in grade is the firmness of the white and the yolk. The color of the shell has no influence on egg quality. Eggs are classified according to size and weight.

When eggs are graded for freshness and size, the carton has a label which indicates the grade (freshness) and size of the egg. Although quality and size are both marked on the carton, one is not related to the other. That is, the largest eggs are not necessarily of the best quality. Eggs of any size may be in any of the three grades. For example, Peewee eggs can be Grade AA and Jumbo eggs can be Grade B.

Nutrient Contributions

The nutrients in eggs are so well balanced that they can be rated with milk as a nutrient-rich food. Eggs make important contributions to the needs of your body. The yolk, rather than the white, is a rich source of nutrients, and contains more vitamins and minerals than the white and also contains some fat. However, the yolk and white are most often used together so that the nutrient values are usually considered for the whole egg, and not for the yolk or the white alone.

Protein

The egg contains a high-quality protein and can be used as a substitute for meat. Eggs, like milk, contain a complete protein which is needed for growth and replacement of worn body tissues.

Vitamins

The yolk contains most of the vitamins found in the egg. The egg white contains only *riboflavin;* the yolk contains *vitamins A and D,* is a good source of B_2 (riboflavin), a fair source of B_1 (thiamin), and contains only a trace of niacin.

Eggs are also important sources of *vitamin D* because most other common foods do not provide this vitamin. The fish liver oils are the richest sources of vitamin D, but they are not usually eaten as food. Vitamin D was first found in cod-liver oil and then later in egg yolk and the cream of milk.

KNOW THE EGGS YOU BUY

consider SIZE

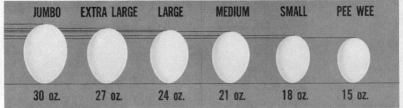

JUMBO	EXTRA LARGE	LARGE	MEDIUM	SMALL	PEE WEE
30 oz.	27 oz.	24 oz.	21 oz.	18 oz.	15 oz.

U.S. WEIGHT CLASSES   Showing Minimum Weight Per Dozen

consider QUALITY

 **U. S. Grade AA** (or Fresh Fancy) Egg covers small area; white is thick, stands high; yolk is firm and high.

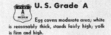 **U. S. Grade A** Egg covers moderate area; white is reasonably thick, stands fairly high; yolk is firm and high.

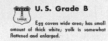 **U. S. Grade B** Egg covers wide area; has small amount of thick white; yolk is somewhat flattened and enlarged.

UNCOOKED

 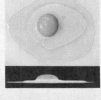 

FRIED

 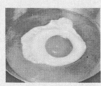 

POACHED

EGGS ARE GRADED FOR BOTH SIZE AND QUALITY

POULTRY DIVISION, CONSUMER AND MARKETING SERVICE, U.S. DEPARTMENT OF AGRICULTURE

USDA

C & MS-62

The largest size eggs are called "Jumbo," and weigh 850 grams (30 ounces) to the carton or per dozen; the smallest eggs are called "Peewee," and weigh 425 grams (15 ounces) per dozen. An inspection stamp such as the one shown in the center indicates both the size and quality of the eggs.

The sun can change some of the skin oils into vitamin D, and it is for this reason that vitamin D is called the "sunshine" vitamin. The sun must shine directly on the skin to convert skin oils into vitamin D. Window glass, clothing, and clouds prevent the ultraviolet rays of the sun from reaching the skin and prevent vitamin D formation. Therefore, in cold climates and in areas where the sun isn't visible each day, very little vitamin D will be produced.

From your study of milk, you learned that vitamin D is added to milk and that vitamin D prevents a disease of the bones called rickets. Rickets is a disease caused by too little vitamin D in the diet or too little exposure to sunshine. Children who were living in sunny climates did not develop rickets while those who were living in other climates did develop rickets. Vitamin D is needed for the growth and maintenance of bones and teeth. It helps the body absorb calcium and make use of that calcium to build it into strong bones and teeth. The use of eggs in your meals will help you meet your body's need for vitamin D. Milk which has been fortified with vitamin D also helps to meet this need.

Minerals

The most important minerals provided by eggs are *iron* and *phosphorus*, found only in the yolk. Iron is not widely distributed in foods, but it is found in meats and green leafy vegetables.

Iron is essential for the formation of hemoglobin, the red pigment of the blood. Hemoglobin carries oxygen to body cells and carries carbon dioxide away to be discarded from the body. When there are too few red blood cells, a condition called anemia develops. Since eggs are such an important source of iron and hemoglobin, they help prevent anemia. You will learn about another source of iron when you study about meats in the next chapter.

Fat

Only the yolk of the egg contains fat. The vitamins A and D, because they are fat-soluble, are dissolved in the fat. The fat in egg yolk will also help to provide some of the body's energy need. Any excess of these vitamins is stored by the body for future use.

Egg Substitutes

The nutrient contribution of eggs makes them a valued food even though some individuals must carefully control the kind and amount of fat they consume. The high cholesterol content of egg yolks is of concern to those who are on cholesterol- or fat-restricted diets. Especially for these individuals, food technologists developed egg substitutes. These products differ from eggs in that they are lower in fat, cholesterol, and calories. Several of these products are available in liquid, frozen, or dried forms.

The complete-egg and partial-egg substitutes are both available, although the partial-egg substitute appears to be preferred. The complete-egg substitute is made from soy or milk proteins. The partial-egg substitute retains the egg white but not the egg yolk. These egg substitutes have about one-half of the calories and fat of regular eggs and contain less sodium. The fat of eggs is replaced with vegetable oil (usually corn oil), giving the egg substitute a higher ratio of polyunsaturated fat to saturated fat. Unopened containers of egg substitute can be stored for ten weeks in the refrigerator and for two weeks after they have been opened.

The flavor of egg substitutes is different from that of regular eggs and can be blended with that of other ingredients in cooked food products. You can make acceptable omelets or scrambled eggs from these products. They may be substituted for eggs in recipes which call for whole eggs. Egg substitutes made of milk proteins do not have the thickening power of eggs and are not suitable in recipes which use the egg as a thickener, in custard, for example. Milk proteins do not coagulate (thicken) when heated as do egg proteins.

Products prepared with egg substitute are acceptable but you may rate them somewhat lower than the product that you make with whole eggs. For example, the volume of cakes made with egg substitute may be less than that of those which contain the whole egg. Egg substitutes are suitable for individuals who are on low-cholesterol or low-calorie diets.

Principles of Egg Cookery

The principles of egg cookery are very much influenced by the egg's high protein content. As with all protein, high temperatures and overcooking cause toughening. Whether eggs are cooked alone or combined with other foods, the principles to observe are: (1) use low temperatures to prevent toughening, curdling, and discoloration; and (2) cook only until desired firmness is achieved. Overcooking also causes toughening, curdling, and discoloration.

Functions of Eggs in Cookery

Eggs serve many important functions in cookery and are used in a variety of foods. Because of their color, flavor, viscosity, and ability to coagulate, eggs are valuable in various cookery processes. The functions of eggs in cookery are: (1) to add nutrients; (2) to improve color, flavor, and texture of food products; (3) to thicken liquids; (4) to bind foods together or coat foods for frying; (5) to act as a leavening agent; and (6) to act as an emulsifying agent.

Because of their nutrient content, one of the most important functions of eggs is *to contribute nutrients*. They may be prepared alone or combined with other foods. Whether eggs are used alone or as a part of another food combination, they will add to the nutrient values of the prepared food and the meal.

The *color* and *flavor* of most foods are improved when eggs are added. Eggs used in puddings, custards, and ice creams improve their color, flavor, and texture. In baked foods, eggs will improve the browning quality of the outer crust and can give a creamy or yellow color to the interior.

The protein in both the egg white and the yolk is a *thickening agent*. Because of the ability of protein in both egg white and yolk to coagulate, or clot, when heated, eggs can be used to thicken food mixtures. The coagulated egg will be firm. The coagulation of the egg protein will thicken custards; help to form the outer shell of cream puffs and the cell walls of cakes; bind together the ingredients of meat loaves; and hold crumbs together for a coating on breaded foods.

When eggs are heated the protein will coagulate and become firm with a tender texture. However, if the heating is continued too long or if the temperature is too high, the protein will overcoagulate and become tough and rubbery. All protein, whether from cheese, meat, milk, or egg will become toughened when permitted to overcoagulate.

The *leavening action* of eggs is due to the air which can be beaten into them. Beaten egg white can hold a large quantity of air and form a foam. The air bubbles in the foam are surrounded by a film of egg white. When the foam is heated, the air bubbles expand and the egg white stretches, and then the egg coagulates to give a light, porous structure to the product. The yolk forms only a small amount of foam and is not used for leavening.

The egg yolk acts as an *emulsifying agent* because the proteins which it contains can surround tiny globules of oil and keep them from separating. Eggs act as an emulsifying agent in many foods including cakes, popovers, and mayonnaise.

Preparation and Uses of Eggs in Cookery

During cooking, eggs coagulate, and the degree of coagulation depends upon the cooking temperature and length of cooking time. Sometimes eggs coagulate only slightly, as in soft-cooked eggs and, at other times, more completely, as in hard-cooked eggs.

Eggs may be cooked in the shell or out of the shell such as fried or poached, and they are used as an ingredient in many dishes. When cooking eggs alone or in combination with other foods, the best results are obtained when cooking temperatures are low and when cooking time is carefully controlled to give the desired degree of firmness.

When eggs are used alone or are the principal ingredient, it is important to use eggs of high quality. For your protection, use only clean eggs with no cracks in shells.

Eggs Cooked in the Shell

Eggs cooked in the shell are correctly referred to as hard-cooked or soft-cooked rather than the more popular terms of hard-boiled or soft-boiled, since they are heated only to a simmering temperature. Boiling water causes overcoagulation and toughness. Eggs in the shell may be cooked by immersing them either in cold or hot water. The water should be heated only to simmering, which means that the water is just below the boiling point. The length of time eggs are cooked in the shell will determine the degree of coagulation or firmness. Eggs which are cold, as taken directly from the refrigerator, require a longer time to reach the simmering temperature than eggs at room temperature.

Sometimes the yolk of a hard-cooked egg may develop a dark green ring on the outer surface. This discoloration is due to a combining of the iron and the sulfur of the egg. The greenish color occurs when eggs have been overcooked or allowed to cook in boiling water. Cooling eggs immediately after cooking helps prevent discoloration.

Eggs Cooked out of the Shell

Fried eggs are an American breakfast favorite. The shape of a fried egg depends upon the quality of the raw egg. A high-quality egg will result in the desired oval shape. Fried eggs are cooked in a small amount of fat over very low heat to the desired degree of firmness. To cook the top of the egg more quickly, the pan may be covered. If the fried egg is brown and the edges crisp, the pan and fat were too hot.

Poached eggs are another favorite. It is important to use eggs of high quality so that the poached egg will be rounded with a film of coagulated white over the yolk. The egg to be poached is broken into a cup and carefully slipped into enough simmering liquid (milk, water) to cover the egg. A little salt or acid (vinegar) may be added to the cooking liquid to hasten the coagulation of the egg and minimize spreading. The liquid must be below the boiling point so that the egg will not toughen. The length of cooking time will determine the degree of firmness of the poached egg.

Baked or *shirred* eggs are very similar to fried eggs. The egg is placed into a lightly greased baking cup and is cooked in the oven at a moderate temperature—160°C (325°F)—to the desired degree of firmness.

Since eggs are usually beaten to blend the yolk and the white for *scrambled* eggs, eggs of a quality lower than AA or A can be used. A small amount of milk is added to the blended egg to produce a more tender product. The mixture is cooked in a pan containing a small amount of melted fat. A low temperature is used and the eggs are stirred occasionally as they coagulate. Scrambled eggs should be tender, slightly moist, and in fairly large pieces.

Omelets may be either plain (French) or puffy. The plain or French omelet is made from beaten whole egg. For the puffy omelet, the yolk and white are beaten separately and then blended together by folding. Omelets, like scrambled eggs, are cooked on low heat in a skillet containing melted fat. The mixture is allowed to coagulate without stirring. Small areas of the coagulated portion are raised with a spatula to allow the uncoagulated egg to collect on the bottom of the pan. The omelet is a continuous disc of coagulated egg that is slightly moist on the upper surface. The disc or circle of egg is usually folded over when the omelet is served.

Eggs as an Ingredient

As an ingredient, eggs are versatile because of their ability to form foams and to coagulate. Custards are thickened by coagulation of the egg protein, while angel food cakes, soufflés, and meringues use egg foams.

A *custard* is a sweetened milk mixture thickened with egg. As the custard is cooked, the egg will coagulate, forming a protein network which can entrap liquids and cause the mixture to become a smooth, thickened product. Custards must be cooked at low temperatures so that the egg protein will not overcoagulate and squeeze out the trapped liquid to cause a watery or curdled custard.

The two types of custards are stirred or soft, and baked. The ingredients used and method of mixing are the same for both types of custard, only the method of cooking differs. The soft or stirred custard is cooked over hot water with constant stirring. It does not set firmly to form a gel like baked custard, but it is thick and velvety like a heavy cream. A baked custard is cooked in the oven without stirring and will hold its shape when removed from the baking dish.

To avoid overcoagulation, soft custards are cooked with constant stirring over water that is simmering and not boiling. Cooking is stopped when the custard coats a spoon. Baked custards are set in a pan of hot water and baked in a moderate oven—180°C (350°F)—until a knife inserted near the center of one of the custards comes out clean.

Cooking custards for too long a time overcoagulates the egg protein. An overcooked stirred custard will be curdled or watery; an overcooked baked custard will have bubbles which can be seen through a glass baking dish, will be porous, and liquid will separate when it is cut.

Custards can be used in a variety of ways. A soft custard can be served alone or as a sauce over fresh or canned fruit, cake, or gelatin. Floating island, a dessert, is a soft custard garnished with spoonfuls of meringue.

Baked custards, too, can be varied. Before baking, a variety of flavorings or extracts can be added or the top of the custard can be sprinkled with a favorite spice or coconut. Custard, pecan, coconut cream, and pumpkin pies are popular variations of baked custard.

Egg whites beaten to a soft-peak stage look like those shown above; the hard-peak stage is shown below.

Custard mixtures without sugar can serve as the basis for a main dish. Seasonings, grated cheese, corn, bread cubes, and other foods can be added and the mixture is cooked as a baked custard. These custards make unusual main dishes. *Quiche* is an unsweetened, open-faced custard pie flavored with cheese and served as an entreé or main dish. It often contains chopped vegetables, meat, poultry, or seafood.

A *foam* is formed when air is beaten into egg whites. The egg white surrounds the air bubbles in the foam. Egg white foams are used in puffy omelets, soufflés, meringues, angel cakes, and in other foods. These foods use the egg foam as a leavening agent. The air in egg white foams will expand when it is heated and cause the batter or omelet to increase in volume until the heat coagulates the egg protein which surrounds the air bubble. This will give a light, porous structure to the product. Low temperatures delay coagulation of the egg white so that it can stretch with the expanding air and increase in volume.

Several things can affect the amount of air that can be beaten into egg whites: (1) egg whites at room temperature beat more quickly than those at refrigerator temperature and give a larger volume; (2) fat from any source interferes with the whipping of egg whites. Fat from egg yolk, milk, or a greasy bowl or beater will reduce the air which egg whites can retain; and (3) a bowl with a small rounded bottom and sides that slope out to a wider top permits eggs to beat to a better volume. The beater should fit the bottom of the bowl and the size of the bowl should suit the amount of egg white.

For the best leavening action, the egg white should form a stable foam. A stable foam is one in which little liquid separates on standing. Some factors which influence the stability of the foam are: (1) cream of tartar added to egg white makes a more stable foam; (2) thick whites form more stable foams than thin whites; and (3) sugar increases stability but delays foam formation so that more beating will be required. It is usually best to beat the egg white to a soft-peak stage and then to add the sugar gradually.

The stiffness to which egg white is beaten is very important. After a little beating, the egg white looks frothy with large air bubbles on the surface. As beating is continued, the air cells become smaller, the foam becomes stiffer and is white in appearance. The bubbles will become increasingly smaller as beating continues. The egg whites are suitable for folding into mixtures when the peak will just bend over as the beater

166

is slowly lifted out of the foam. This soft-peak stage is also used for the beating of soft meringues which are to be spread on various kinds of cream pies.

Additional beating will cause the peak to stand up straight as the beater is lifted. A stiff foam is difficult to fold into other ingredients. Hard meringues are beaten to stiff-peak stage.

Further beating produces a dry foam that breaks into pieces or lumps and does not blend well into other ingredients. At this stage, the egg whites are not useful in food preparation.

Hard and *soft meringues* are egg white foam to which sugar is added. Soft meringues are used as toppings for pies and as an ingredient in fruit whips and other desserts. The foam for hard meringues is beaten to the stiff-peak stage and contains twice as much sugar as the soft meringues. Hard meringues may be shaped into meringue shells or cookies and baked at a low temperature—120°C (250°F). Meringue shells filled with ice cream and fruit are a very special treat.

Hard meringues, also known as Swiss meringues, are easily shaped into feather-light cookies.

Selecting Eggs

When buying eggs, the grade and classification standards set up for eggs are useful guides to egg quality and size. Along with grade and size, the use of the egg and cost should be considered.

In high grade eggs the white is thick and the yolk will stand up higher in the center of the egg than in low grade eggs. (See page 159 for egg grade chart.) Because of this, it is possible to have more attractive poached or fried eggs from Grade AA than Grade B eggs. However, the highest grade eggs need not be purchased for all uses. All grades of eggs have acceptable uses. When eggs are served out of the shell alone, Grades AA and A may have a more delicate flavor and attractive appearance; but when eggs are combined with other foods as in casseroles, salads, cookies, or muffins, Grade B may be used.

In addition to grade, eggs are sold on the basis of weight. You must consider both grade and weight in relation to the price of eggs. The highest grade and largest eggs are the most expensive. Grade and size are two separate factors; that is, Grade A eggs are of the same quality whether they are small or large. Generally, when there is less than seven cents difference between one size and the next smaller size of the same grade, the larger size will be more economical. Small eggs may cost less per dozen but not be a better buy in terms of weight and actual quantity of egg.

Then too, the color of the shell may influence cost. White-shell eggs may be in greater demand than brown-shell eggs and therefore cost more. You may save money by buying eggs with the shell color which is less in demand. The color of the eggshell does not influence nutrient value or eating quality of the yolk or white.

The size of eggs as well as quality should be considered in relation to the use. The fact that Jumbo eggs weigh twice as much per dozen as Peewee eggs points out why uniform results in baking cannot be expected if a specified number of eggs is used in a recipe unless the size is controlled. Most recipes were developed to use large or medium eggs rather than the Jumbo or Peewee sizes; some avoid variation in egg size by using a measured amount of egg—125 milliliters (½ cup).

Storage of Eggs

An egg begins to deteriorate immediately after it has been laid, but this process can be slowed down by proper storage. As eggs deteriorate in quality the white becomes thinner, the yolk flattens, and the air space increases in size. Purchase only eggs which are kept under refrigeration until they are sold. Place them immediately into the home refrigerator until you are ready to use them.

Because eggs can absorb odors through shell pores, they may be kept in the closed carton as purchased or in a covered container. Eggs are washed just before they are used rather than before they are stored. The protective coating on the shell helps to maintain egg quality during storage. Store eggs with the blunt end up to avoid movement of the yolk and the air cell. Leftover whites are stored in a tightly covered container; leftover yolks, if the quantity is small, may need to be covered with a thin layer of milk or water and then tightly covered.

Convenience and Eggs

Frozen and dried eggs are not usually sold in retail stores. However, frozen omelet mixtures and frozen cholesterol-free egg substitutes are available. Dehydrated egg products are used in some packaged mixes. For example, angel food cake mix contains dried egg whites and a custard mix contains egg yolk solids. The use of egg solids in packaged mixes eliminates the need to add fresh eggs at the time of mixing. Because of the fat content of egg yolk, dried whole egg or dried yolk powders deteriorate and consequently do not keep well over long periods of time.

Because of their high nutrient value, short cooking time, and versatility in cookery, eggs can be used as the main food for any meal.

Main Ideas

Eggs, another important source of animal protein, minerals, and vitamins, serve many different functions in food preparation. They are used to thicken, emulsify, leaven, and improve the taste, texture, and color of many products. Eggs, while not available in as many convenience forms as milk or cheese, are included in dehydrated form in many convenience mixes. Eggs require the same care in cooking as do other protein foods. The grading of eggs makes it possible to have a reliable indication of the quality of the eggs being sold. The retention of the fresh quality of eggs is directly related to proper handling and storage.

Activities

1. Visit a store and notice eggs offered for sale.

a. Record the grades, weights, sizes, prices.

b. What kinds of labels were used?

c. Which eggs are the best buy for breakfast? For use as an ingredient in general cooking? Why?

2. Using a table of food values, compare the nutrients in eggs with those in beef. How do they differ, and in what ways are they similar in nutrient content?

3. Look through cookbooks and list the recipes in which eggs are used for these functions: to emulsify, to leaven, to thicken, and to bind or coat.

4. Look through cookbooks and list the different ways eggs are prepared for breakfast. With which of these ways are you not familiar? In what ways are eggs served for lunch?

5. Examine an egg against a tube of light. Using the cardboard tube from a roll of waxed paper, place a flashlight at one end of the tube and an egg at the other; darken the room. Do you see the air space? The yolk? What grade would you assign to the egg? Why?

6. Break an egg on a plate (use the same one you candled). What grade would you assign to the broken egg? Why? Is the grade the same as you determined when you observed the egg with a light? How many parts of the egg in the dish can you identify?

7. Select a recipe calling for one egg and prepare it. Was the product pleasing to you?

8. Plan, prepare, and serve a lunch which includes a puffy omelet. Evaluate the results. How did your lunch menu differ from a breakfast menu that includes a puffy omelet?

9. What egg substitutes are available in your supermarket? Compare the nutrient value of these substitutes with that of regular eggs. When would you use egg substitutes?

Questions

1. What nutrients are supplied by eggs? Why do you need these nutrients?

2. What determines the color of the yolk? Of the egg shell?

3. How does a Grade A egg differ from a Grade B egg?

4. Why are eggs considered a substitute for meat?

5. What is the "sunshine" vitamin? Why is it so called?

6. What are the functions of eggs in cookery?

7. What are the results of high temperatures and over-cooking on eggs and foods containing eggs?

8. What causes a custard to curdle?

9. Which term is correct: hard-cooked or hard-boiled?

10. What causes the dark rings around cooked egg yolks?

11. What grade eggs are suitable for poaching? Cookies?

12. Describe a French omelet and a puffy omelet?

13. Decribe the soft-peak and stiff-peak stages for beating egg whites. When is each used?

14. What factors influence the amount of air beaten into egg white?

15. What should be considered when eggs are bought?

16. How are eggs stored? Leftover yolks and whites?

Chapter 11

Meats

Words for Thought

Amino acids
the building blocks from which proteins are made.

Essential amino acids
the amino acids which must come from food because they cannot be manufactured by the body.

Hemoglobin
the red pigment in blood which carries oxygen to a cell and carbon dioxide away from a cell.

Trichinosis
a disease of muscles, tendons, and intestines caused by a parasite which may be found in pork.

Collagen
a protein in white connective tissues which can be converted to gelatin by moist heat.

Meat analog
a product which has characteristics of another product it replaces.

Protein
a nitrogen-containing component of food essential for growth and health.

Since medieval times the great feasts have included meat. The people feasted on wild boar, fish, fowl, and deer. The American pioneers based their diet on meat and ate heartily of buffalo, turkey, deer, and bear.

The common ancestor of our modern beef animals was the aurochs, a fierce beast with long horns which was almost seven feet tall and grazed over the vast regions of Africa, Asia, and Europe. Archeologists know little of the early use of cattle. The first cattle to be tamed may have been the sacrificial animals, sacred to the goddess of the moon. Later, cattle may

171

have been harnessed to wagons used in religious processions, and still later slaughtered for food. By 5000 B.C., beef cattle were domesticated in parts of western Asia.

Meat has a satisfying flavor and a stick-to-the-ribs quality which wards off hunger. It is one of the most expensive items in a meal. Meat is usually the starting point for planning. Many people consider meat the star of the meal. Meat adds eating enjoyment to meals and is high in nutritional value.

Nutrient Contributions

Besides being a popular food, meat has outstanding nutritional value. It is an important source of complete protein, iron, and the B vitamins.

Protein

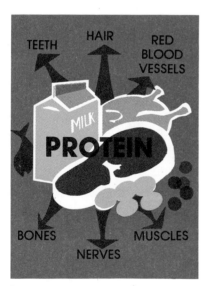

Protein is an essential nutrient for all body cells.

Protein is made of small units or building blocks called *amino acids*. Meat protein contains all of the esssential amino acids required by your body. When the diet does not contain enough complete protein, growth stops, muscles weaken.

Meat supplies a complete protein that is used by the body for growth and maintenance. Protein is needed by every body cell—muscles, red blood cells, skin, hair, teeth, bones, and nerves. You need protein for as long as you live to repair and replace worn tissues and cells.

The building blocks of protein are called amino acids. Each amino acid has its own special name and a particular job in building different tissues in your body. All amino acids need not be present in every food you eat. The body can make some of them if you eat the proper foods, but there are some which the body cannot make. The amino acids which the body cannot make are called the *essential* amino acids. They are found in foods from animal sources which supply complete proteins. Milk, cheese, eggs, fish, and poultry, in addition to meat, come from animals and are *complete protein foods*. Complete protein foods promote growth and maintain the body.

Different foods contain different amounts and different kinds of protein. Cereals, breads, and vegetables lack one or more of the essential amino acids; therefore, they are *partially incomplete protein* foods. The partially incomplete protein from these foods can repair your body, but it cannot support growth. The protein in animal foods balances or supplies the missing amino acids in the incomplete protein from plants when they are eaten in the same meal. This is why it is important for you to eat a variety of foods.

Minerals

Meats are important sources of the minerals iron, copper, and phosphorus. Minerals do not burn and do not give calories, but they are needed to repair and build cells and to maintain life processes.

Your body needs *iron* and *copper* to make red blood cells. *Iron which gives the blood its red color is needed to make hemoglobin. The hemoglobin in red blood cells transports oxygen from the lungs to all body cells and removes waste.* When the supply of iron is low, there will be too few red blood cells; this condition is known as anemia. In addition to fatigue, anemia may also cause lowered resistance to infection. Girls and women are more inclined to be anemic than men because of the loss of blood, and therefore iron, during the menstrual period.

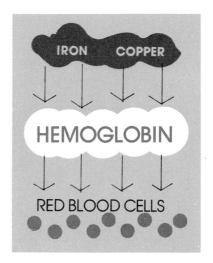

Iron is not widely distributed in common foods. Liver is the best food source. Lean meats, egg yolk, and green leafy vegetables are also important for their iron content. The iron and copper which meat contains help to build red blood cells.

Lean meats are also a good source of *phosphorus*. You will recall that phosphorus is needed to build bones and teeth and to help in the oxidation of foods (release of energy from food) in the body cells. Can you think of other foods that also contain phosphorus?

Vitamins

Lean meats are a good source of *thiamin, riboflavin, and niacin.* Lean pork is the richest source of thiamin. Because these B vitamins are water soluble, some will dissolve in the cooking liquid. However, the juices from meat may be used to make gravy or soup, and in this way the vitamins in the juices are not lost. Can you recall what these vitamins provide for you? In what other foods besides meat are they found?

Fat

The fat of meat does not provide vitamins, minerals, or protein. Fats as you recall are an abundant source of energy. Much of the fat in meat forms a thick layer around the meat

173

muscle and is often removed before cooking or at the table. The lean which remains will contain some fat. In addition to energy value, fat will contribute to the flavor and palatability of meat.

Meats do contribute important amounts of nutrients, but they are low in calcium and vitamins A and C. This will not throw your diet off balance if you include milk, cheese, fruits, and vegetables along with meats in your meals.

Types of Meat and Meat Cuts

Modern markets wrap retail meat cuts in transparent material and display them in open self-service, refrigerated cases. All animals supplying these meats are very similar in shape. The techniques of cutting meat are standardized so that similar cuts are generally available. Your knowledge of muscle and bone structure of animals in general will help you recognize specific cuts of meat from any animal. The shape of the retail cut from the same location on any animal will be the same; only the size of the piece and the color of the lean will vary.

All cuts of meat are composed of lean or muscle tissue, connective tissue, fat, and some cuts contain bone. A carcass too heavy to be easily handled will be cut into smaller pieces called *wholesale cuts.* The wholesale cuts will be divided by the butcher into smaller cuts called *retail cuts* which are offered for sale in display cases of markets. These cuts of meat come from beef, veal, pork, and lamb.

Meat from cattle over one year old is known as *beef.* It is bright red in color and has a white or cream-colored fat. The

Shown here, in order of size, are beef, veal, and lamb rib cuts.

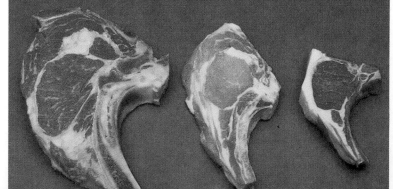

beef carcass is the largest of all animals used for food. It is first cut in half through the backbone to form two *sides* of beef. The side of beef is cut into two quarters and then into wholesale cuts which can be handled easily. Wholesale cuts are divided into retail cuts at each local store.

Only two wholesale cuts of beef, the rib and the loin, are tender; the other cuts are less tender. You will learn how to match the tenderness of meat cuts with cooking methods. The ability to recognize retail cuts is most helpful in selecting and cooking meat.

Veal is meat from cattle three to fourteen weeks old and is next in size to beef but much smaller. The term calf is used for meat from cattle fourteen weeks to one year old. Veal is fine grained, pink in color, lacks fat and marbling (flecks of fat in the meat), and has considerable connective tissue. The bones are pliable, porous, and red. It has a delicate flavor that blends well with other foods.

Because veal is from very young cattle, the cuts of veal differ somewhat from beef cuts. For example, the loin of veal and the rib section are used for chops instead of steaks as in the beef.

Pork comes from hogs or pigs usually not more than a year old. The color of young lean pork is grayish pink, changing to a rose color as the animal matures. The lean is well marbled and covered with a soft, white fat. The cut surface of the bone is red. All cuts of pork must be thoroughly cooked to avoid the risk of *trichinosis,* a disease caused by a harmful parasite sometimes found in pork.

Bacon is usually made from pork sides which are treated with salt, sugar, certain chemicals, and often wood smoke. Meats treated in this manner are known as *cured* meats. They have a better keeping quality than fresh meat. Good bacon has liberal streaks of a dark pink lean in a snowy-white fat.

Ham is a hind leg of a hog which has been cured and smoked. The ham is injected with a curing solution and then smoked. A picnic ham is a pork shoulder after curing and smoking. The permanent pink color of ham is a result of the curing process.

Lamb is the smallest animal used for meat; it is the flesh of sheep not more than fourteen months old. Mutton is the flesh of mature sheep. The lean of lamb is dark red and the fat is white and firm. Mutton has dark red flesh, firm bones, and creamy fat. The cuts of lamb are very similar to those of veal but smaller in size.

Beef Chart

Retail Cuts of Beef—Where They Come From and How to Cook Them

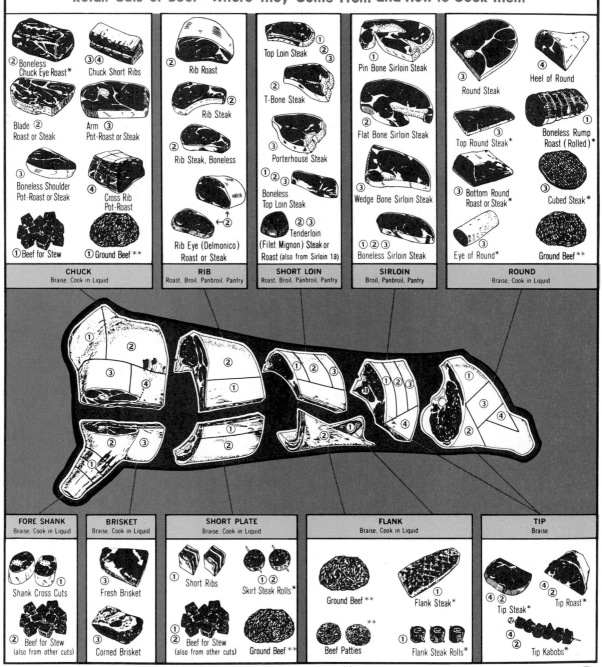

CHUCK
Braise, Cook in Liquid

- ② Boneless Chuck Eye Roast*
- ③④ Chuck Short Ribs
- ② Blade Roast or Steak
- ③ Arm Pot-Roast or Steak
- ③ Boneless Shoulder Pot-Roast or Steak
- ④ Cross Rib Pot-Roast
- ① Beef for Stew
- ① Ground Beef**

RIB
Roast, Broil, Panbroil, Panfry

- ② Rib Roast
- ② Rib Steak
- ② Rib Steak, Boneless
- ②
- Rib Eye (Delmonico) Roast or Steak

SHORT LOIN
Roast, Broil, Panbroil, Panfry

- ① ② ③ Top Loin Steak
- ② T-Bone Steak
- ③ Porterhouse Steak
- ① ② ③ Boneless Top Loin Steak
- ② ③ Tenderloin (Filet Mignon) Steak or Roast (also from Sirloin 1a)

SIRLOIN
Broil, Panbroil, Panfry

- ① Pin Bone Sirloin Steak
- Flat Bone Sirloin Steak
- Wedge Bone Sirloin Steak
- ① ② ③ Boneless Sirloin Steak

ROUND
Braise, Cook in Liquid

- ③ Round Steak
- ④ Heel of Round
- ③ Top Round Steak*
- ① Boneless Rump Roast (Rolled)*
- ③ Bottom Round Roast or Steak*
- ③ Cubed Steak*
- ③ Eye of Round*
- Ground Beef**

FORE SHANK
Braise, Cook in Liquid

- ① Shank Cross Cuts
- ② Beef for Stew (also from other cuts)

BRISKET
Braise, Cook in Liquid

- ③ Fresh Brisket
- ③ Corned Brisket

SHORT PLATE
Braise, Cook in Liquid

- ① Short Ribs
- ① ② Skirt Steak Rolls*
- ① ② Beef for Stew (also from other cuts)
- ② Ground Beef**

FLANK
Braise, Cook in Liquid

- ** Ground Beef**
- ① Flank Steak*
- ** Beef Patties
- ① Flank Steak Rolls*

TIP
Braise

- ④ ② Tip Steak*
- ④ ② Tip Roast*
- ④ ② Tip Kabobs*

*May be Roasted, Broiled, Panbroiled or Panfried from high quality beef.
**May be Roasted, (Baked), Broiled, Panbroiled or Panfried.

This Chart approved by
National Live Stock and Meat Board

© National Live Stock and Meat Board

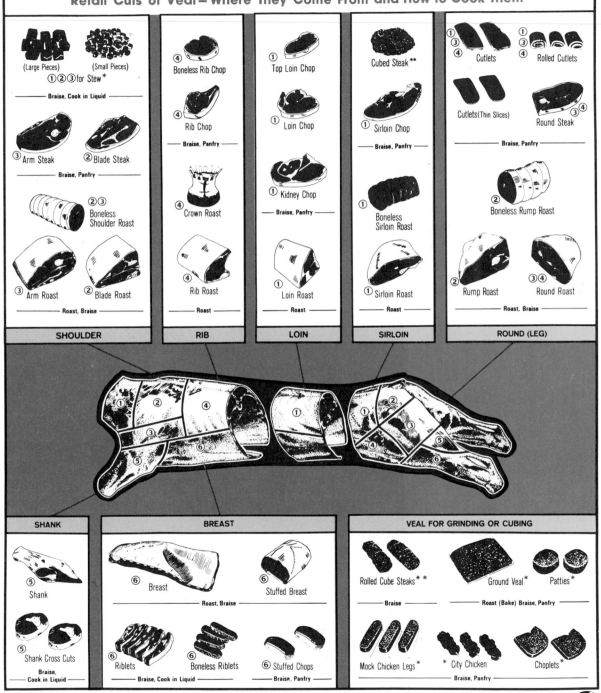

Veal Chart

Retail Cuts of Veal – Where They Come From and How to Cook Them

SHOULDER

(Large Pieces) (Small Pieces)
① ② ③ for Stew*
— Braise, Cook in Liquid —

③ Arm Steak   ② Blade Steak
— Braise, Panfry —

② ③ Boneless Shoulder Roast

③ Arm Roast   ② Blade Roast
— Roast, Braise —

RIB

④ Boneless Rib Chop

④ Rib Chop
— Braise, Panfry —

④ Crown Roast

④ Rib Roast
— Roast —

LOIN

① Top Loin Chop

① Loin Chop

① Kidney Chop
— Braise, Panfry —

① Loin Roast
— Roast —

SIRLOIN

Cubed Steak**

① Sirloin Chop
— Braise, Panfry —

① Boneless Sirloin Roast

① Sirloin Roast
— Roast —

ROUND (LEG)

① ③ ④ Cutlets   ① ③ ④ Rolled Cutlets

Cutlets (Thin Slices)   ③ ④ Round Steak
— Braise, Panfry —

② Boneless Rump Roast

② Rump Roast   ③ ④ Round Roast
— Roast, Braise —

SHANK

⑤ Shank

⑤ Shank Cross Cuts
— Braise, Cook in Liquid —

BREAST

⑥ Breast   ⑥ Stuffed Breast
— Roast, Braise —

⑥ Riblets   ⑥ Boneless Riblets   ⑥ Stuffed Chops
— Braise, Cook in Liquid —   — Braise, Panfry —

VEAL FOR GRINDING OR CUBING

Rolled Cube Steaks**   Ground Veal*   Patties*
— Braise —   — Roast (Bake) Braise, Panfry —

Mock Chicken Legs*   * City Chicken   Choplets*
— Braise, Panfry —

*Veal for stew or grinding may be made from any cut.

**Cube steaks may be made from any thick solid piece of boneless veal.

This chart approved by
National Live Stock and Meat board

© National Live Stock and Meat Board

177

Pork Chart

Retail Cuts of Pork—Where They Come From and How to Cook Them

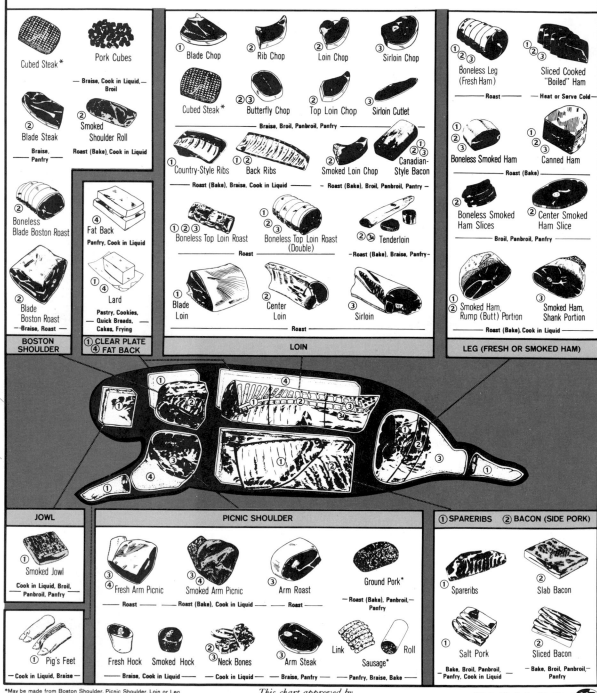

BOSTON SHOULDER

Cubed Steak*

Pork Cubes

— Braise, Cook in Liquid,—
Broil

Blade Steak

— Braise,
Panfry

② Smoked
Shoulder Roll

Roast (Bake), Cook in Liquid

② Boneless
Blade Boston Roast

② Blade
Boston Roast

— Braise, Roast —

① CLEAR PLATE ④ FAT BACK

④ Fat Back

Panfry, Cook in Liquid

① ④ Lard

Pastry, Cookies,
Quick Breads,
Cakes, Frying

LOIN

① Blade Chop

② Rib Chop

② Loin Chop

③ Sirloin Chop

② ③ Cubed Steak*

② ③ Butterfly Chop

② Top Loin Chop

③ Sirloin Cutlet

— Braise, Broil, Panbroil, Panfry —

① Country-Style Ribs

① ② Back Ribs

② Smoked Loin Chop

② ③ ① Canadian-Style Bacon

— Roast (Bake), Braise, Cook in Liquid —   — Roast (Bake), Broil, Panbroil, Pantry —

① ② ③ Boneless Top Loin Roast

① ② ③ Boneless Top Loin Roast (Double)

② ③④ Tenderloin

— Roast —   — Roast (Bake), Braise, Panfry —

① Blade Loin

② Center Loin

③ Sirloin

— Roast —

LEG (FRESH OR SMOKED HAM)

① ② ③ Boneless Leg (Fresh Ham)

① ② ③ Sliced Cooked "Boiled" Ham

— Roast —   — Heat or Serve Cold —

① ② ③ Boneless Smoked Ham

① ② ③ Canned Ham

— Roast (Bake) —

② Boneless Smoked Ham Slices

③ Center Smoked Ham Slice

— Broil, Panbroil, Panfry —

① ② Smoked Ham, Rump (Butt) Portion

③ Smoked Ham, Shank Portion

— Roast (Bake), Cook in Liquid —

JOWL

① Smoked Jowl

Cook in Liquid, Broil,
Panbroil, Panfry

① Pig's Feet

— Cook in Liquid, Braise —

PICNIC SHOULDER

③ ④ Fresh Arm Picnic

— Roast —

③ ④ Smoked Arm Picnic

— Roast (Bake), Cook in Liquid —

③ Arm Roast

— Roast —

Ground Pork*

— Roast (Bake), Panbroil,—
Panfry

Fresh Hock   Smoked Hock

— Braise, Cook in Liquid —

③ ② Neck Bones

— Cook in Liquid —

③ Arm Steak

— Braise, Panfry —

Link   Roll

Sausage*

— Panfry, Braise, Bake —

① SPARERIBS ② BACON (SIDE PORK)

① Spareribs

② Slab Bacon

① Salt Pork

② Sliced Bacon

— Bake, Broil, Panbroil,—
Panfry, Cook in Liquid

— Bake, Broil, Panbroil,—
Panfry

*May be made from Boston Shoulder, Picnic Shoulder, Loin or Leg.

This chart approved by
National Live Stock and Meat Board

© National Live Stock and Meat Board

Lamb Chart

Retail Cuts of Lamb — Where They Come From and How to Cook Them

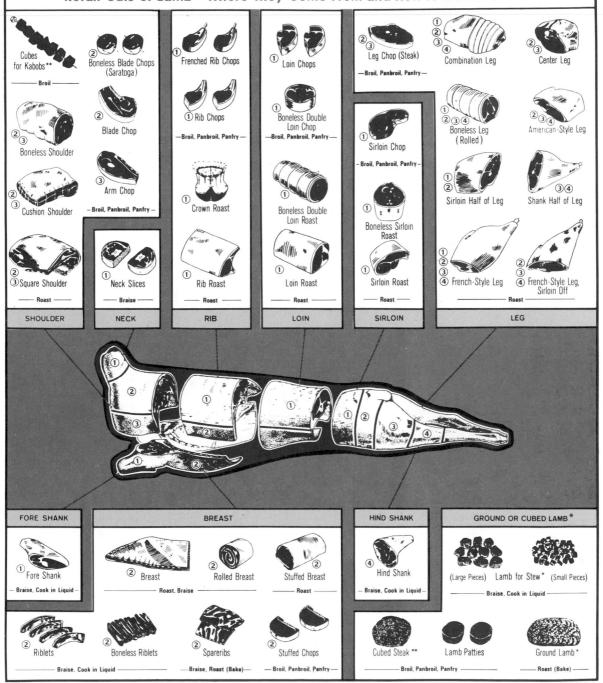

SHOULDER

Cubes for Kabobs**
— Broil —

② Boneless Blade Chops (Saratoga)

②③ Boneless Shoulder

②③ Cushion Shoulder

②③ Square Shoulder
— Roast —

② Blade Chop

③ Arm Chop
— Broil, Panbroil, Panfry —

NECK

① Neck Slices
— Braise —

RIB

① Frenched Rib Chops

① Rib Chops
— Broil, Panbroil, Panfry —

① Crown Roast

① Rib Roast
— Roast —

LOIN

① Loin Chops

① Boneless Double Loin Chop
— Broil, Panbroil, Panfry —

① Boneless Double Loin Roast

① Loin Roast
— Roast —

SIRLOIN

②③ Leg Chop (Steak)
— Broil, Panbroil, Panfry —

① Sirloin Chop
— Broil, Panbroil, Panfry —

① Boneless Sirloin Roast

① Sirloin Roast
— Roast —

LEG

②③④ Combination Leg

② Center Leg

②③④ Boneless Leg (Rolled)

②③④ American-Style Leg

①② Sirloin Half of Leg

③④ Shank Half of Leg

①②③④ French-Style Leg

②③④ French-Style Leg, Sirloin Off
— Roast —

FORE SHANK

① Fore Shank
— Braise, Cook in Liquid —

② Riblets
— Braise, Cook in Liquid —

BREAST

② Breast

② Rolled Breast

② Stuffed Breast
— Roast, Braise —   — Roast —

② Boneless Riblets

② Spareribs
— Braise, Roast (Bake) —

② Stuffed Chops
— Broil, Panbroil, Panfry —

HIND SHANK

④ Hind Shank
— Braise, Cook in Liquid —

Cubed Steak **
— Broil, Panbroil, Panfry —

GROUND OR CUBED LAMB*

(Large Pieces) Lamb for Stew* (Small Pieces)
— Braise, Cook in Liquid —

Lamb Patties

Ground Lamb*
— Roast (Bake) —

---

* Lamb for stew or grinding may be made from any cut.

** Kabobs or cube steaks may be made from any thick solid piece of boneless Lamb.

This chart approved by
National Live Stock and Meat Board

© National Live Stock and Meat Board

The organs of meat animals are known as *variety meats* and commonly include brains, liver, kidney, heart, tongue, sweetbreads (thymus gland of veal, lamb, young beef), and tripe (stomach lining of beef). Liver is one of the most popular variety meats. Many variety meats have a distinctive flavor and all are rich in nutrients.

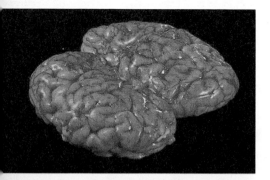

Brain

Beef, veal, pork, and lamb brains are all edible. When they are fresh, they are firm with a bright color.

Liver

Beef, pork, and lamb livers are usually sold in slices; chicken livers are usually sold whole. They are often sold frozen but this does not affect their eating quality.

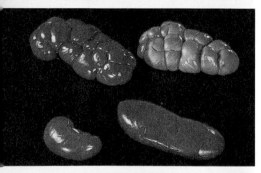

Kidney

Beef, lamb, and veal kidneys are used more in cookery than pork kidneys. All kidneys, however, must be light in color and firm. Soft, dark red kidneys are not fresh.

Heart

Hearts of beef, veal, pork, lamb, and poultry are used in cookery. Since hearts are not very tender, they are often sliced, diced, or ground.

180

Tongue

Tongue may be sold fresh, corned, pickled, or smoked. It is used as meat when taken from beef, veal, pork, and lamb.

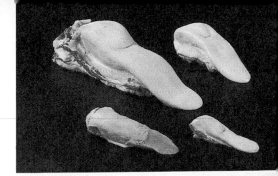

Sweetbreads

Thymus glands of lamb, veal, and young beef are known as sweetbreads. Lamb and veal sweetbreads are tender and white, while beef sweetbreads are red in color and less tender.

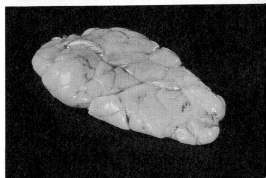

Tripe

The inner lining of the stomach of beef is called tripe. There are three varieties: honeycomb, pocket, and smooth.

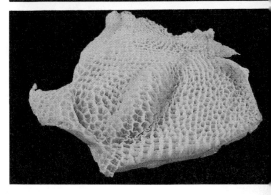

Forms of Meat

Canned, cured, and frozen meats, in addition to fresh meat, are available.

Fresh meat undergoes no special treatment except that it may be aged in cooling rooms for a short time so that it becomes more tender. During aging, enzymes in the meat tissue cause changes that contribute to the tenderness and flavor of the meat.

Canned meat, however, is usually fully cooked and sealed in containers for storage without refrigeration. Popular canned meats include ham, dried beef, corned beef, and others. Meats are also often canned in combination with other foods such as stews, or spaghetti and meat balls.

Frozen meats may be either raw or cooked. Roasts and other large cuts are usually frozen raw. Smaller cuts such as chops and steaks may be either cooked or uncooked when frozen. There are many combination dishes made with frozen meat.

The package label indicates the contents and includes the cooking directions.

Fresh meats which have been treated with a mixture of salt, sugar, and spices, and are often smoked, are called *cured meats*. Ham, sausages, lunch meats, bacon, Canadian bacon, and dried beef are examples.

Inspection and Grading

The purpose of meat inspection is to protect the consumer. According to federal law, meat sold between states subject to interstate commerce regulations must be inspected. This service is an assurance that the meat is from healthy animals slaughtered under sanitary conditions and is safe for consumption at the time of inspection.

Inspection Stamp

Inspected meat is identified with a round, purple, federal *inspection stamp*. The stamping is done with a safe purple vegetable dye on each wholesale cut. Because of the mechanized method of stamping, the stamp may not appear on all retail cuts. It is not necessary to cut the stamp off before cooking as the vegetable dye is harmless.

The Meat Inspection Act covers processed meats and canned meats in addition to fresh meats. The inspection stamp is found on the containers of processed meats. The ingredients used must be wholesome and listed on the label along with the net weight, and the name and address of the processor. The grade of meat may also be listed.

This stamp is found on all federally inspected meat.

Grading

The grading of meat is not required by law, but most meat packers prefer to sell graded meat. The United States Department of Agriculture has set standards for different grades of meat. The meat grades indicate the quality of the meat while inspection indicates its wholesomeness.

Beef is graded for two factors; quality and cutability. Quality refers to the proportion of meat to bone, degree of marbling in the lean, firmness in texture, and normal color. Cutability refers to the proportion of edible meat: a greater amount of muscle in relation to a smaller layer of external fat. Beef which is graded for quality and cutability helps you select high-quality beef without excess fat.

Although there are several grades of beef, only the higher grades are found in the retail store. The top grade, known as *Prime*, makes up only a small portion of beef and is usually purchased by restaurants. *Choice*, the second grade, and *Good*, the third grade, are usually available in markets. The lower grades, *Standard*, *Commercial*, and *Utility* are not found in most markets. These grades are usually used in processed meats.

The packers who wish to sell graded meat hire government graders to grade their meat. However, some packers use their own grading system using such terms as premium, select, and others instead of the grades of the United States Department of Agriculture. The grade is marked on the meat with a roller stamp that leaves an imprint of the grade (again, harmless) which can be seen on most retail cuts.

Beef of high quality comes from a young animal. The lean is well-marbled, fine in texture, and normal in color (red). The texture becomes coarser and the color darker as the animal ages. The United States Department of Agriculture quality grades for beef are described below.

Grades of Beef

Prime beef is bright cherry red, well-marbled and fine-textured, with an outside layer of creamy-white fat. It is the juiciest and most tender.

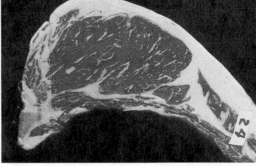

Choice beef is bright to deep red, has smooth texture, is moderately marbled, with a moderate layer of white to creamy-white fat. It is a very popular consumer grade.

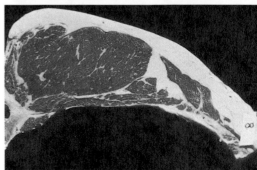

Good beef is light to dark red, has moderately smooth texture and some marbling, with a thin outer layer of creamy fat.

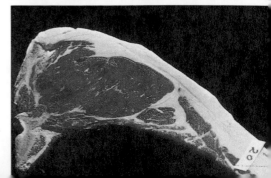

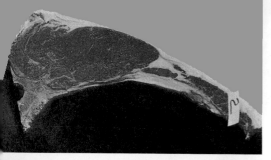

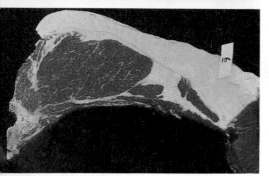

Standard beef is dark red, has uneven, coarse texture and little marbling, with a thin layer of slightly yellow fat.

Commercial beef is light to dark red, has very little marbling and coarse texture, and may be somewhat soft and watery, with a very thin covering of yellowed fat.

Utility beef is light to dark red, has coarse texture and lacks marbling, with a very thin layer of grayish-white to yellow fat.

The United States Department of Agriculture grades of *veal* are: *Prime, Choice, Good, Standard, Utility,* and *Cull.* High-quality veal is rosy pink, fine in texture and moist, with a very small amount of white fat. Poor-quality veal is dull pink, limp and very moist, and has no fat.

The United States Department of Agriculture grades of *lamb* are: *Prime, Choice, Good, Utility,* and *Cull.* Most of the lamb produced is either of Prime or Choice grade, and, therefore, may not be graded, but it is inspected for interstate commerce. High-quality lamb is bright deep red, firm and fine-textured, and has a covering of firm white fat.

Pork does not usually carry a federal grade stamp, but it is inspected for interstate commerce. However, federal grades are used by some states and some meat packers. The grades of *pork* are: *U.S. 1, 2, 3, Medium,* and *Cull.* The lean of high-quality pork is grayish-pink and firm, and has a fine texture. The fat is medium-soft and snowy white. Pork of poor quality is deep red and flabby and coarse.

Selection and Buying

Standard names have been developed for cuts of meat by The National Live Stock and Meat Board. You will find these names on meat labels, including both the name of the primal cut (wholesale cut) and the standard name for the retail cut. The bones and muscles which make up the meats are similar, making it easy to learn to identify cuts of meat by the bones and muscles they have.

A large proportion of the food dollar is spent on meat. You, as the buyer, will rely on your own ability to judge quality and select the meat best suited to your wants and needs. Your selection should be based on quality, intended use, time available for preparation, and cost.

Signs of Quality Meats

The first sign of quality is the official United States Department of Agriculture stamp on meat that assures you of wholesome, inspected meat. The next clue to quality is the grade stamp or label. Prime is the highest quality and the most expensive. U.S. Choice and Good grades are most frequently available in the meat case. Grade influences flavor, juiciness, and ease of cooking, not nutritive value.

Other signs of quality meats include color, marbling, and bone color. High-quality meats will have a fine texture and a good characteristic color for the kind of meat; that is, beef will be a bright red and pork a light or grayish pink. The color and firmness of the fat and the degree of marbling vary with the meat quality. A white to creamy-white fat which is firm to medium-firm, and liberal marbling throughout the lean are associated with high-quality meats. A coarse texture, very dark color in the lean, and a very yellow fat indicate poor-quality meat. The bone in meat indicates the age of the animal. The cut surface of the bone from a young animal is porous and pinkish in color, of an older animal, gray and flinty.

Meat Tenderness

The location of the meat cut on the animal is a clue to its tenderness. The muscles which are used least are the most tender. Muscles of the back, loin, and rib sections receive little exercise and are found in the tender steaks such as sirloin, porterhouse, T-bone, and club, and tender roasts such as rib and standing rib. Muscles of the legs and shoulders receive much exercise and are found in the less tender steaks and roasts such as round and chuck.

Higher grades of meat are usually more tender than the same cut of a lower grade. *The tenderness of meat is related to the degree of marbling; meats with more marbling are more tender and of a higher grade.*

Because beef comes from mature animals, all cuts of beef except the loin and rib sections are considered less tender. Even though veal is a young animal, it is considered as less tender because of the high proportion of connective tissue to muscle and because of the lack of fat. Lamb is slaughtered when young so that all cuts except the neck and shoulder are considered tender. Pork is generally classified as tender.

Bone shapes are also clues to tenderness. Cuts of meat that have either the rib, T-bone, or wedge bone are tender from all animals. The round bone indicates a tender cut from all aminals except beef where it indicates a less tender cut. The blade bone indicates the least tender cut in all animals. The chart on page 187 identifies these bone shapes.

Meat can be made more tender by treating it with *enzymes* that split proteins. Meat tenderizers contain protein-splitting enzymes and may be sprinkled over meat before cooking to increase tenderness. The most commonly used enzyme is *papain* from a fruit called papaya.

The protein-splitting enzymes can be injected into the veins of the animal a few minutes before slaughter. The enzyme is spread throughout the meat by the animal's circulatory system and causes tenderizing in all cuts. This meat is usually sold under special brand names.

Meat can be tenderized by using *mechanical methods* to break up the connective tissue. Methods such as grinding, pounding, cubing, or scoring are used to make meats more tender. Hamburger is made tender by grinding. Swiss steak is tenderized by pounding, cube steak by passing through a cubing machine, and flank steak by scoring.

Now that you know how to judge the quality and tenderness of meat, it is important to learn how much meat you should buy to serve specific numbers of people.

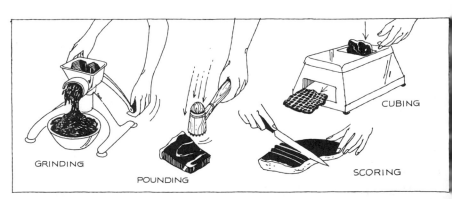

GRINDING

POUNDING

CUBING

SCORING

MEAT IDENTIFICATION GUIDE

	Tender Cuts To Cook With Dry Heat			Less Tender Cuts To Cook With Moist Heat	
these Bones					
called	T-BONE	RIB BONE	WEDGE BONE	ROUND BONE	BLADE BONE
identify these Beef cuts					
called	T-bone steak Porterhouse steak Strip loin* Tenderloin*	Rib steak Club steak Rib roast Rolled rib roast*	Sirloin steak Sirloin roast Top sirloin steak	Shoulder steak Round steak Chuck steak Chuck roast Rump roast*	Chuck steak Chuck roast
identify these Pork cuts					
called	FRESH Loin chop† *Tenderloin† Center cut loin roast (rib and T-bone)	FRESH Rib chop† Center cut loin roast (rib and T-bone) *Butterfly chop† Spareribs††	FRESH Loin end roast (wedge and T-bone) *Boneless loin	FRESH Ham Picnic Shoulder Shoulder steak† *Cutlets† SMOKED Ham Ham Slice Picnic Shoulder	FRESH Blade loin roast** Boston butt** Shoulder steak SMOKED *Daisy†† (Shoulder Butt)
identify these Lamb cuts					
called	Loin chop English chop Kidney chop Loin roast *Rolled loin roast	Rib (rack) roast Crown roast Rub chop French chop Riblets or Breast†	*Rolled sirloin roast Sirloin chop	Leg roast Leg steak Roundbone chop†† Square cut, *rolled or *cushion shoulder roast†† Shank†	Blade bone chop†† Square cut, *rolled or *cushion Shoulder roast†† Saratoga chop†

* Cuts will appear boneless in store
** Cook with dry heat

†Cook with moist heat
††Cook with moist or dry heat methods

Amount to Buy

Meats are sold by grams (pounds). You must know how many grams (pounds) are needed to serve a given number of people. You will need to consider the amount of bone present in the meat when estimating the amount to buy. When meat contains bone, you will need to buy more than when the meat is boneless. The following table considers the bone present and indicates the amount of meat needed for one serving.

113 g (¼ lb) of boneless meat = 1 serving
151 to 227 g (⅓ to ½ lb) of meat with small amount of bone (steak, roast) = 1 serving
302 to 339 g (⅔ to ¾ lb) of meat with large amount of bone (spare ribs, short ribs) = 1 serving

Multiply the quantity suggested for one serving by the number of servings desired to determine the amount that you should buy. However, with chops or slices of meat, you may only need to count the number of pieces needed.

Cost

The cut or type of meat that is the *best buy depends upon the cost per unit and upon the amount of waste in bone and fat.* The prices of various meats can be best compared by cost per serving. A unit of meat which provides four servings will usually be cheaper per serving than a unit which provides only two servings.

The cost of meat is influenced by supply and demand. The tender beef steaks and roasts are in demand and the supply is limited, therefore the price is high. The less tender cuts of meat are more plentiful and less in demand, therefore they cost less than the tender cuts. Similarly, lower grades of meat are less expensive than the higher grades. Lower grades contain less fat and thereby less waste which can mean more servings at a lower cost.

The size of a cut of meat can influence cost per unit. For example, a pork loin roast will cost less per unit than pork chops from the same meat cut.

Most cuts of meat which can be cooked quickly cost more than those which require longer cooking. Select the cut and grade best suited for the cooking method you plan to use.

Uses of Meat

Meat or a combination meat dish is the center of interest in a meal and the starting point for planning the rest of the meal. All other foods such as salad and vegetables are chosen to enhance and go with the meat selected.

For lunch or supper, meats are usually served in combination with other foods so that their flavor is extended. Other foods such as macaroni, noodles, spaghetti, rice, or vegetables can be combined with meat for main dishes. Meats are used in casseroles, creamed dishes, main-dish salads, and sandwiches. Meats are filling, but also add nutrients and variety to breakfast. Sausage, bacon, and ham are popular breakfast meats.

Because of their flavor, meats are used to enhance soups and to provide stock for soup-making. Meats such as bacon and ham are used to add flavor to green beans, scalloped potatoes, baked beans, salad greens, and other vegetables.

Principles of Meat Cookery

Meat is cooked to improve its flavor, change its color, make it more tender, and to destroy harmful organisms. As with milk and eggs, the principles of meat cookery are greatly influenced by the high protein content. When meat is cooked, the protein of the muscle, or the lean, coagulates and the protein of connective tissue is softened.

The long, tiny fibers of muscle tissue are held together by connective tissue. The connective tissue is made of a different protein from that in muscle tissue. A protein called *collagen* is tough and flexible and makes up the connective tissue that holds muscle fibers together. It can be softened by cooking. Another protein, *elastin*, makes up the connective tissue, but there is very little elastin in meat muscles. Some elastin is present in neck ligament. Elastin fibers stretch, are yellow in color in contrast to the pearly white of collagen.

Meats are classified into tender and less tender cuts. The tender cuts contain less connective tissue than the less tender cuts, which come from muscles frequently exercised.

The principles of meat cookery require the use of low temperatures. The low temperature will coagulate the meat protein and prevent toughening. Meats are cooked only until they are done. Overcooking as well as high temperatures will cause toughening due to overcoagulation. Meat cooked at low temperatures will be juicy and flavorful.

Moisture whether from the meat itself or added is needed along with heat to soften collagen. Because protein coagulates more slowly at low temperatures the muscle protein will not toughen before the collagen (connective tissue) can soften. For this reason, moist-heat methods are used to cook less tender cuts of meat. The tender cuts of meat contain little connective tissue and need to be cooked only long enough to coagulate the protein. Dry-heat methods are used to cook tender cuts of meat.

Methods to Cook Meat

The cut and tenderness of meat determine the cookery method. Study the meat charts in this chapter to learn which parts of the animal are most exercised and the cuts which you may buy from each section. When you know whether the cut of meat is tender or less tender you will be able to select the proper cooking method.

Meats are classified into two groups according to tenderness, and the cooking methods required to cook them are also classified into two groups. In general, meat is cooked by dry heat for tender cuts and moist heat for less tender cuts.

Dry-heat Methods

Roasting, broiling, and *pan-broiling* are the dry-heat methods for cooking meat. The meat is cooked by direct heat, requires no added water, and is not covered. Dry-heat methods are used to cook tender cuts because they contain little connective tissue.

Large tender cuts of meat are used for *roasting.* A shallow open pan with a rack is used. The meat is placed on the rack in the pan with the fat side up. The rack elevates the roast from the bottom of the pan so that heat can circulate around and under the roast.

A meat thermometer can be placed into the center of the thickest part of the roast, away from bone or fat. The thermometer shows the exact temperature at the center of the roast and in this way the exact doneness. A timetable for roasting meat (found in most cookbooks) can be used to estimate the cooking time required, but the meat thermometer is more accurate. The meat will continue to cook for a time after being removed from the oven.

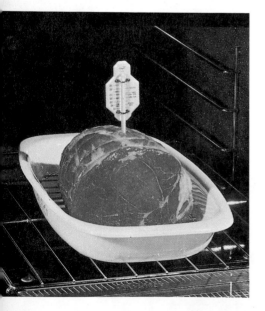

Low oven temperatures—150 to 180°C (300 to 350°F)—are used to cook the meat to the desired doneness. Beef can be cooked rare, medium, or well done. Veal, lamb, and pork are usually cooked until well done. Large, tender cuts of all meats may be roasted successfully. The following cuts of meat are suitable for roasting.

Beef Standing Rib Roast

This roast contains two or more ribs from which short ribs and backbone have been removed.

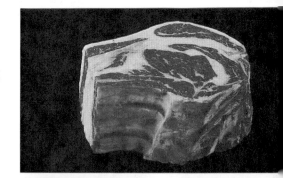

Rolled Rib Roast

This is the same cut of meat as the standing rib roast except that it has been boned and rolled.

Veal Loin Roast

Veal loin roast is cut from the short loin section and contains a T-bone. It is usually cut thick for roasting.

Veal Rib Roast

Veal rib roast contains two or more ribs. It has less fat than beef rib roast.

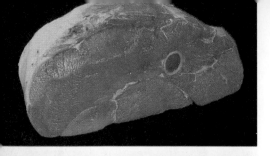

Veal Center Leg Roast

This is cut from the hind leg and contains top, bottom, and eye of round. It is usually about 5-7.5 centimeters (2-3 inches) thick.

Lamb Rolled Loin Roast

After the T-bone is removed, the roast is boned, rolled, and tied into a compact roll.

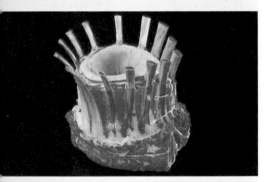

Lamb Crown Roast

This is cut from the rib section. The tips of the rib bones are trimmed of fat and lean and then fastened to form a crown.

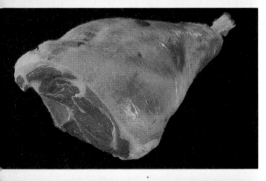

Frenched Leg of Lamb

For this cut, enough meat is removed to expose 2.5 centimeters (1 inch) or more of the lower end of the shank bone.

Pork Arm Roast

This roast is cut from the lower portion of the shoulder and contains a small, round bone.

Pork Fresh Picnic Shoulder

The picnic shoulder contains forearm and shank sections of the shoulder. It is similar to whole fresh ham but smaller.

Pork Blade Loin Roast

The blade loin roast is cut from the shoulder end of the loin and contains a portion of the blade and rib bones.

Pork Boston Butt

The Boston butt comes from the upper shoulder and contains a portion of the blade bone.

Broiling is cooking meat above or below the direct source of heat from an oven unit or glowing coals. Meats to be broiled should be tender or made tender by the use of tenderizers and should be about 2.5 centimeters (1 inch) thick.

The meat is placed on the broiler rack, and the rack is usually placed 7.5 to 15 centimeters (3 to 6 inches) away from the heat. A moderate temperature is maintained by regulating the distance of the meat from the source of heat. When the meat is half done (one side cooked), it is turned to cook the other side. Broiled meat is salted after it is cooked because salt retards browning.

Small, tender cuts of meat are suitable for broiling. Veal is not usually broiled because it lacks fat and will dry out. Fresh pork should not be broiled; instead it should be cooked well done to avoid possible trichinosis. Cured ham and sausage, lamb, and the tender cuts of beef may be broiled. The following cuts of meat are suitable for broiling.

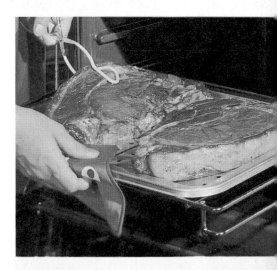

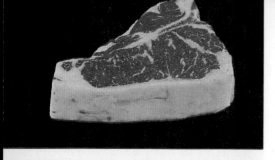

Beef T-Bone

This steak is also cut from the loin. It has a small portion of tenderloin and a T-bone for which it is named.

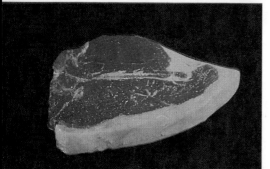

Beef Porterhouse Steak

Porterhouse steak is the largest steak in the short loin. It has more tenderloin than the T-bone steak. It also has a T-bone.

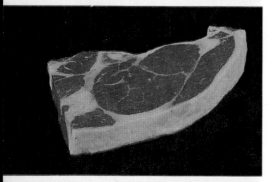

Beef Sirloin Steak

This cut contains part of the hip bone which varies in shape from wedge-shaped to oval. There is also variation in the muscle structure.

Beef Rib Steak

Beef rib has the tender rib eye and may have a rib bone. Without the bone, the steak is known as Delmonico, Spencer, or rib eye.

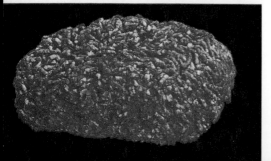

Beef Patty

This patty is made from less tender cuts of beef such as chuck, flank, brisket, and round. Grinding tenderizes the meat.

Lamb Loin Chops

Lamb loin chops contain loin and tenderloin and usually have a T-shaped bone separating them.

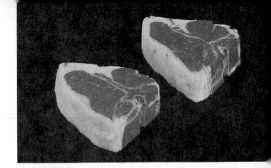

Lamb Rib Chops

These chops contain rib eye muscle. There is also a rib bone which is similar in shape to that in the veal rib chop but smaller.

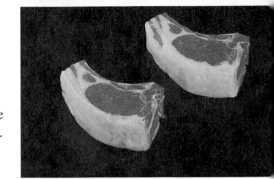

Lamb Patty

Any wholesale cut of lamb or its trimmings may be ground and shaped into patties.

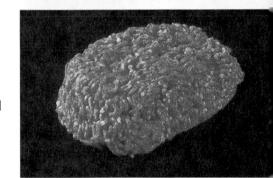

Pork Smoked Ham Slice

The ham slice is cut from the hind leg of the hog. It is oval with a small round bone and four separate muscles.

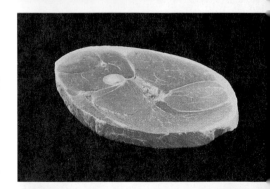

Bacon

Bacon is the trimmed breast and flank section of a side of pork which has been cured and smoked. It is sliced or in a slab.

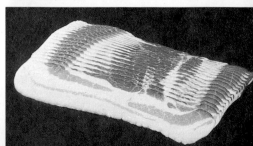

Canadian Bacon

Canadian-style bacon is made from the loin muscle which is rolled and cured. It is sold in large pieces or in slices.

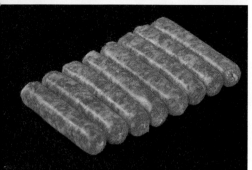

Pork Sausage

Pork sausage is made from ground pork to which seasonings are added. It is packed into casings and may or may not be smoked.

Pan-broiling is cooking meat in a skillet without added fat. As the fat melts from the meat, it is poured off. Cook the meat slowly over low heat until it is brown on one side and then turn. Never cover the meat or add water; to do so would be braising and not pan-broiling. Pan-broiling is used for small tender cuts. All cuts which can be broiled are also suitable for pan-broiling.

Moist-heat Methods

Moist-heat methods are used for the less tender cuts because of the large amounts of connective tissue in them. Moisture and heat are required to soften the protein of connective tissue. The moist-heat methods of cooking are *braising* and *cooking in liquid.*

Braising is using moisture from the meat itself (steam) or from added liquid. The meat may be browned, if desired, before liquid is added or before the pan is tightly covered.

196

As the meat cooks, juices will be released to provide moisture, or a small amount of liquid such as water, vegetable juice, or stock may be added. Cooking may be continued over low heat on a range or in an oven at 150 to 160°C (300 to 325°F) until the meat is tender. A large cut of meat cooked by braising is often referred to as a pot roast.

Braising is used for all less tender cuts of meat and it is used for the tender cuts of veal and pork. Both pork and veal should be cooked well done; pork to guard against trichinosis, and veal to develop flavor. These cuts are suitable for braising.

Beef Round Steak

This cut of meat usually contains a small round bone and three muscles: top round, bottom round, and eye of round.

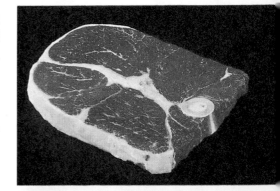

Beef Flank Steak

Beef flank steak is stripped from each side of the beef (one per side). It is boneless, thin, flat, and has coarse muscle fibers which run lengthwise.

Beef Chuck Blade Steak

This steak contains a portion of blade bone, backbone, and often rib bone. It is both economical and flavorful.

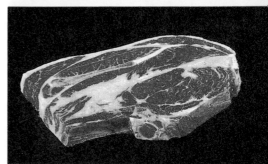

Beef Short Ribs

Short ribs contain alternating layers of lean and fat and usually a section of flat rib bone.

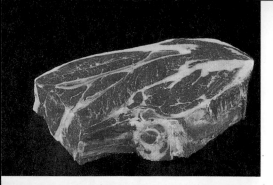

Beef Blade Chuck Roast

This chuck roast is cut from the rib end of the chuck and may or may not contain bone. It is commonly used for pot roasting.

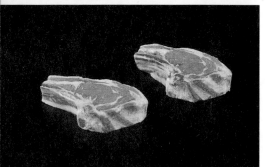

Veal Rib Chop

This chop is cut from the rib section and contains the rib bone.

Veal Loin Chop

Veal loin chops are similar to beef porterhouse steaks in that they have a T-bone and a good portion of lean.

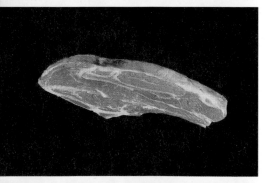

Veal Blade Steak

This is sliced from the shoulder. It contains a portion of the blade bone and is less expensive than veal rib or loin chops.

Veal Arm Steak

Veal arm steak is an oval-shaped steak. It contains the arm (round) bone and rib bones.

Veal Arm Roast

This roast is cut from the shoulder and contains the arm (round) bone and usually part of the rib bones.

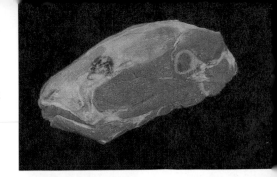

Smoked Pork Loin Chops

These are slices from the loin which have been cured. Like fresh chops, they contain a T-bone and tenderloin.

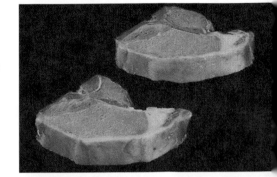

Pork Loin Chops

Pork loin chops contain loin and tenderloin muscles, and usually have a T-shaped bone separating them.

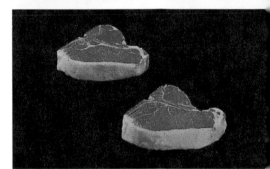

Pork Loin Rib Chops

These chops are cut from the rib end of the loin. They contain the rib bone but no tenderloin.

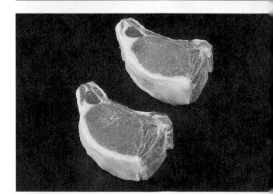

Pork Shoulder Arm Steak

Pork arm steak is cut from the lower shoulder, is slightly oval, and contains a small round (arm) bone.

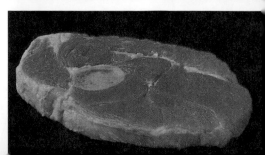

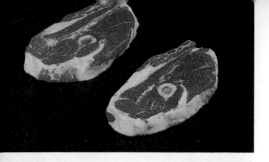

Lamb Shoulder Arm Chops

Lamb arm chops come from the shoulder of lamb and have a small, round bone.

Lamb Shoulder Blade Chops

Lamb blade chops come from the shoulder of lamb and have the blade bone.

Lamb Rolled Shoulder, Boneless

Lamb rolled shoulder is cut from the shoulder. When the bones are removed, the roast is rolled and tied into a compact roll.

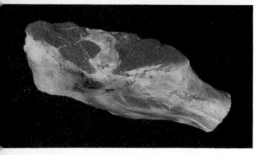

Lamb Fore Shank

This comes from the front leg and contains the round leg bone.

Meats which require long, slow cooking to soften the large amounts of connective tissue which they contain are cooked in liquid. *Simmering* and *stewing* refer to cooking in liquid. Simmering refers to cooking large pieces of meat in enough liquid to cover them. When small pieces of meat are almost covered with liquid and then cooked, the process is called stewing.

For both stewing and simmering, the heat must be low so that the liquid remains at the simmering temperature and does not boil. Boiling overcoagulates the protein and causes toughening. The following are some cuts of meat suitable for cooking in liquid.

Beef Plate

Beef plate contains part of the rib bone and has alternating layers of lean and fat.

Beef Short Ribs

Beef short ribs contain alternating layers of lean and fat and usually a section of flat rib bone.

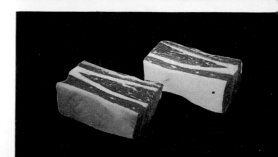

201

Beef Brisket

Beef brisket is cut from the breast portion near the front leg. It is flat and boneless.

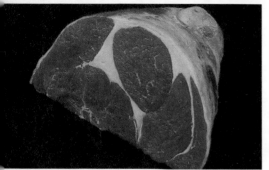

Beef Heel of Round

Heel of round is a wedge-shaped cut which is taken from the lower part of the round.

Beef Stew

Beef stew is usually cut from less tender pieces of beef and is often cut into small cubes.

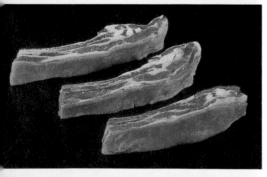

Veal Breast Riblets

These are rectangular strips of meat made by cutting between the ribs. They contain part of the rib bone.

Veal Breast

Veal breast is cut from the breast area under the rib section. It is a thin, flat cut which contains the breast bone, rib, and rib cartilage.

Veal Stew

This is usually made from the shank and shoulder cuts. The pieces are boneless and cut into varying sizes.

Veal Fore Shank

The fore shank contains the leg bone and a fair portion of lean.

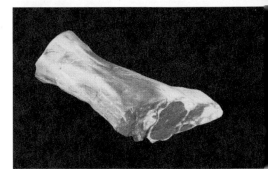

Pork Smoked Picnic Shoulder

The picnic shoulder is cut from the lower portion of the shoulder. It has been cured and smoked.

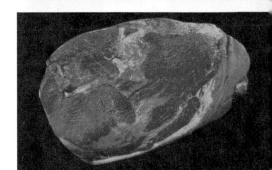

Pork Smoked Ham Shank

The ham shank is cut from the lower half of the ham. It is usually less expensive than the upper portion which is called the butt half.

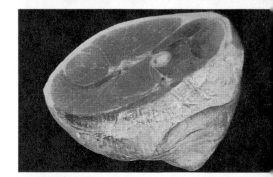

Pork Spare Ribs

Spare ribs are cut from the belly portion. They contain a large proportion of rib bone to lean.

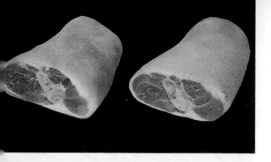

Pork Hocks

Fresh pork hocks, cut from the picnic shoulder, are round, tapering, skin-covered pieces containing shank bones.

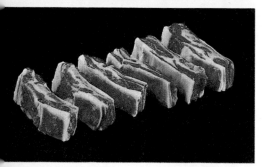

Lamb Riblets

These are cut from the breast section. They are rectangular in shape and contain part of the rib bone.

Cooking in Fat

Two methods are used for cooking in fat: *pan-frying* and *deep-fat frying*. Frying is a quick method of cooking and is best suited for thin pieces of tender meat which have been made tender by cubing, pounding, or grinding. The meat may be rolled in flour or dipped in egg and then crumbs before frying. This gives the meat an attractive brown coating, contributes to flavor, and may help to retain meat juices. Meat prepared in this way with crumbs is called breaded meat.

Pan-frying is cooking in a small amount of fat in an uncovered skillet.

Pan-frying differs from pan-broiling in that the fat is not poured off as it collects. Moderate temperatures are used and the meat is turned occasionally. High temperatures will cause the fat to smoke and to break down into an unpleasant-tasting substance. This method may be used for thin steaks and chops and ground and cubed meat. The following are some cuts of meat suitable for cooking in fat.

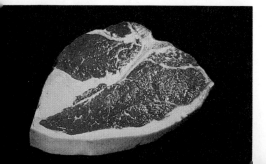

Beef T-Bone Steak

This steak is cut from the loin. It has a small portion of tenderloin and a T-bone for which it is named.

Beef Porterhouse Steak

Beef porterhouse steak is the largest steak in the short loin. It has more tenderloin than the T-bone steak, and also has a T-bone.

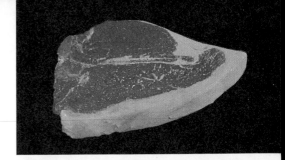

Beef Rib Steak

Beef rib has the tender rib eye and may have a rib bone. Without the bone, the steak is known as Delmonico, Spencer, or rib eye.

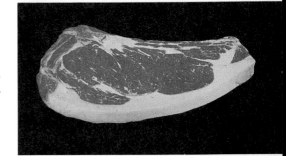

Beef Patty

A beef patty is made from less tender cuts of beef such as chuck, flank, brisket, and round. Grinding tenderizes the meat.

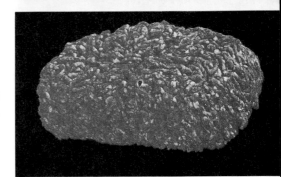

Beef Liver

Beef liver is the largest of the edible animal livers. It ranges from light to dark red in color; the lighter the color, the more tender the liver.

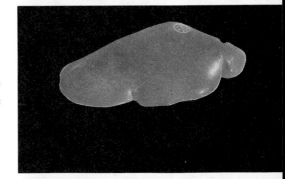

Veal Cube Steak

Veal cube steak is a mechanically tenderized lean cut which may be from the round, shoulder, or loin.

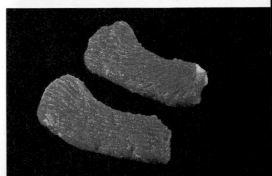

Veal Patty

Veal patties can be made from ground shoulder, neck, flank, breast, or leg meat.

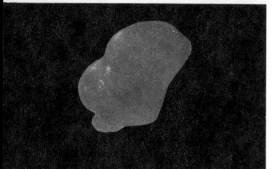

Veal Liver

Veal liver, more commonly known as calf's liver, is about half the size of beef liver. It is more tender than beef liver.

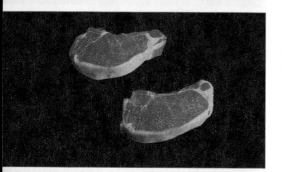

Pork Rib Chops

These chops are cut from the rib end of the loin. They contain the rib bone but no tenderloin.

Pork Arm Steak

Pork arm steak is cut from the lower shoulder, is slightly oval, and contains a small round (arm) bone.

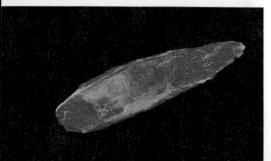

Pork Tenderloin

This cut is often sold in the form of patties which are made by slicing and flattening the round, tapering tenderloin muscle.

Pork Fresh Ham Slice

The ham slice is cut from the hind leg of the hog. It is oval with a small round bone and four separate muscles.

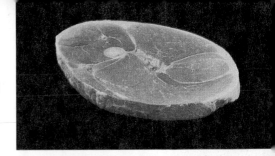

Canadian Bacon

Canadian-style bacon is made from the loin muscle which is rolled and cured. It is sold in large pieces or in slices.

Lamb Sirloin Chops

These chops are cut from the loin section. They contain a portion of the hip bone which varies in shape.

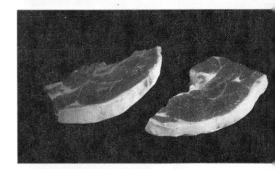

Lamb Loin Chops

Loin chops contain loin and tenderloin and usually have a T-shaped bone separating them.

Lamb Rib Chops

Lamb rib chops contain rib eye muscle. There is also a rib bone similar in shape but smaller than that in the veal rib chop.

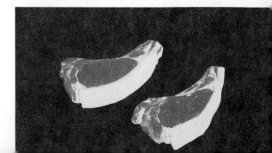

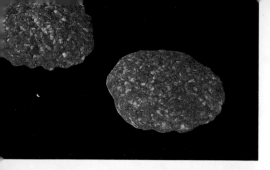

Lamb Patties

Any wholesale cut of lamb or its trimmings may be ground and shaped into patties.

For *deep-fat frying* enough fat is used to cover the food. Deep-fat frying is not considered a basic meat cookery method. It is best suited for meats that have been breaded or for cooked meat which has been combined with other foods and then breaded such as croquettes. The temperature for deep-fat frying is higher than the temperatures recommended for meat cookery. However, the coating or breading may help to protect the meat from the hot fat.

Cooking Frozen Meats

Commercially frozen products should be prepared according to the directions on the package. Frozen meat may be cooked satisfactorily either by defrosting before cooking or during cooking. When defrosting meat before cooking, the meat should be defrosted in its original wrapper either in the refrigerator or at room temperature. Once defrosted, it should be cooked in the same way as fresh meat. The tenderness of the cut will determine the appropriate method.

When meat is cooked from the frozen state, it is necessary to allow additional cooking time. Frozen roasts may require about one-third longer cooking time than defrosted roasts. However, completely defrosting large roasts before cooking will insure even cooking.

Cooking Variety Meats

Since variety meats are more perishable than other meats, they should be used soon after purchase. Liver is the most popular variety meat. You may braise or fry beef or pork liver; veal, lamb, and baby beef liver may be broiled, pan-broiled, or pan-fried.

The heart and tongue are less tender variety meats and may be braised or cooked in liquid. Tongue may be purchased fresh, pickled, corned, smoked, or canned. It requires long, slow cooking in liquid.

The kidney, brains, and sweetbreads are tender variety meats. The kidney is a delicacy and is served in several gourmet dishes. You may broil lamb and veal kidneys, but beef kidney is less tender and should be braised or cooked in liquid. Brains and sweetbreads have a delicate flavor. They may be broiled, fried, braised, or cooked in water.

A Reminder

In all meat cookery, low temperatures are required to protect the protein of meat and avoid toughening. To develop the browned meat flavor, meats may be browned in a small amount of fat before they are cooked by moist heat methods. At one time, meats were seared before roasting (browned quickly at high temperature) to keep in juices. We now know that searing does not prevent the escape of meat juices and there may actually be a greater loss of juices. A constant low oven temperature will give you the advantages of: (1) more evenly cooked meat; (2) less shrinkage of meat; (3) less spattering of fat; and (4) roaster pans that are easier to clean.

Proper cooking methods will retain the quality of the meat at the time of cooking, but the quality of the meat at the time of purchase can only be preserved by proper storage. Cooking cannot improve the quality of mistreated or poorly stored meats; it can only retain the quality present in the meat at the time. You will need to store meats properly to retain all of their flavor and quality.

Care and Storage of Meat

All kinds of meat including cooked meat spoil quickly. To reduce spoilage, meat should be properly stored as soon as possible after purchase. It is with proper storage that you can preserve the safety, nutritive value, and quality of meat.

Fresh Meat Storage

Fresh meat not to be frozen should be stored in the coldest part of the refrigerator or in the meat storage compartment. The meat should be loosely covered and storage should not exceed three days. Meat prepackaged for self-service may be stored in the original wrapping if used within two days. The wrapper may be loosened at both ends to permit circulation of air around the meat to preserve its red color. When meat surface is deprived of oxygen it will become dark.

Ground meats spoil very quickly because a larger area has been exposed to air and handling. If you plan to keep meat cuts and ground meat longer than two or three days, they should be wrapped for freezer storage. To prepare meats for freezer storage, first remove the original wrap and rewrap tightly in moisture-vapor-proof freezer wrap.

Cured and Ready-to-eat Meat Storage

Cured and ready-to-eat meats such as the variety of cold cuts, ham, bacon, and frankfurters should be wrapped tightly to prevent drying. You may store the sealed, prepackaged cold cuts in their original wrap. Once the package is opened, it may require an additional wrapping to prevent drying. The flavor and quality of ready-to-eat meats are best when they are used within a short time.

Frozen Meat Storage

You should store purchased frozen meats at -18°C (0°F) in their original wrapping. Prepackaged, self-serve, fresh meats should be over-wrapped or rewrapped with moisture-vapor-proof material for frozen storage, separating individual servings by a double layer of wrapping material. Keep meat frozen until you are ready to thaw or use it. Use thawed meat immediately, do not refreeze it.

Canned Meat and Leftover Meat Storage

Most canned meats can be stored in a cool, dry storage place except canned hams weighing over 681 grams (1½ pounds). Large canned hams are perishable because they have not been completely sterilized. They must be stored in the refrigerator in order to prevent spoilage. You should also notice how these hams have been stored when you buy them in the supermarket or in the neighborhood store or specialty shop.

All leftover meats both canned or cooked should be tightly wrapped or placed in a covered container and stored in the coldest part of the refrigerator. You should plan to use them within a short time.

Meatless Meats

Meatless meats (meat analogs) look very much like actual meats and are cooked in the same way as the meats they represent. These meatless products are prepared from textured soy proteins. The oil is first removed (pressed) from the soybeans. The protein is modified and extruded into fibers for use in meat-like products such as ham, ground beef, chicken, bacon, and sausage. You may combine textured soy protein (TSP) in granular form with ground meats and thus get more servings from each pound of meat.

Textured soy meat-like products contribute nutrient values similar to those in meats. They are good sources of protein, contain no cholesterol, and have less fat than meats. They add to the variety of foods acceptable to vegetarians as well as contribute essential nutrients.

Convenience in Meats

The cold cuts and canned meats were among the first convenience meat items. The variety and number of these items is steadily increasing. They may be canned, frozen, or refrigerated. Examples of canned meat products include beef stew, hash, ravioli, deviled ham, chili con carne, or spaghetti and meat sauce. Frozen meat products include meat pies, breaded chops, and frozen dinners. Meat products which require only refrigeration include lunch meats or cold cuts, wieners, and other sausages.

Many of the convenience meat items can be classified as meat products rather than as meat-alone products because they contain other ingredients in addition to meat. Examples of nonmeat items used in convenience products are cereal, starch, soya flour, and nonfat dry milk. Other convenience items, the add-to-meat variety, include a blend of seasonings and extenders (macaroni, noodles, rice) and granules of textured vegetable protein (TVP) to add to meats and meat combination dishes. When these products are added to meats, you get more servings than when the meat is prepared alone.

You may not realize it, but lunch meats often contain nonmeat products. Generally, the greater the amount of a nonmeat ingredient used, the lower the complete protein value of the food. The price of the lunch meat tends to be lower when nonmeat ingredients are used.

Some processed meats are relatively low in price and contain as much protein as higher priced fresh meats. For example, bologna usually has as much protein as an equal amount of fresh meat. Other processed meats may have only a little over half as much complete protein as meat.

With meats as with any other food item, it is necessary to read the labels. All ingredients including the nonmeat items must be stated on the label. Locally processed meats do not require federal inspection as do the processed meats sold in interstate commerce. If you select meat products with United States Department of Agriculture inspection labels, you can be assured that you are selecting a wholesome product with a limited amount of nonmeat ingredients.

Buying processed meat items whether canned, frozen, or refrigerated also requires a cost comparison based on the home-prepared product versus the convenience product. You may find that chili con carne costs about the same as the home-made or that a frozen dinner costs twice as much as a comparable dinner prepared at home.

In addition to the label and the United States Department of Agriculture inspection stamp, another guide to quality is who made it? Well-known manufacturers will protect their reputations. Brand names usually can be reliable guides for selecting convenience meat items.

Convenience items make meal preparation less complicated, but they make food selection more complicated. It becomes your challenge to select the best convenience items for your use. What guides and criteria will you use in the selection of convenience items?

After you have found the best convenience foods, how will you fit them into your plan? All of the convenience meat items have in common the factors of improving the use of time and work, the fact that they may or may not be more expensive, and that they may or may not provide the same food value as the home-prepared product. You should think of them as assistants and use them creatively.

Gelatin: A Meat Product

Gelatin is a product manufactured by the meat industry. It is formed from collagen, a protein in the connective tissue of animals. You will remember that cooking softens the connective tissue of meats by changing collagen into gelatin. Perhaps you have observed homemade soup or broth which cooled to a jelly-like consistency in the refrigerator because gelatin was formed from collagen in the soup meat or bones. Gelatin is manufactured from bones and hides.

Nutrient Contributions

As you recall, meats provide complete protein but gelatin is an incomplete protein. It is the only incomplete animal protein. It is not an important protein in the diet because it is used in small quantities and because it is lacking in some essential amino acids. Gelatin desserts and salads are easily digested, bland in flavor, and popular with many people. They derive their food value from the other ingredients used. You may use gelatin in several ways in your meals.

Uses of Gelatin

The principal use of gelatin is to change a liquid into a jelly-like solid. It is used as the base for a wide variety of salads and desserts that add sparkle and color to a meal. Gelatin used in candies and frozen desserts insures a smooth texture.

Preparation of Gelatin

Granulated, unflavored gelatin is usually packaged in envelopes that contain 15 milliliters (1 tablespoon), enough to gel 500 milliliters (2 cups) of liquid. The liquid may be water, fruit or vegetable juices, milk, or broth. The gelatin is mixed with a small amount of cold liquid to soften it. It is then dissolved in hot liquid. If a recipe includes sugar, the dry, granular gelatin may be mixed with the sugar and then added directly to the hot liquid, instead of first being softened in cold water. However, the gelatin softened in cold liquid disperses more uniformly in hot liquid and particles of gelatin do not remain on the spoon or pan. Directions on most packages of flavored gelatin omit the softening of gelatin in cold liquid before adding it to the hot liquid. The gelatin mixture is cooled until slightly thickened and is then placed into molds and allowed to set (become firm) in the refrigerator.

Convenience and Gelatin

Flavored gelatin or gelatin dessert mixes are a familiar convenience item. A gelatin mix usually includes sugar, gelatin,

213

and some artificial flavoring and coloring. Gelatin mixes are available in both fruit and vegetable flavors. A gelatin-like product extracted from algae (seaweed) instead of from meat is a very recent substitute for gelatin. It can be dissolved in cold water instead of hot water and becomes firm very quickly. Prepared gelatin salads and desserts, ready for the table, can be purchased in some food specialty stores.

Main Ideas

Meat, one of the most nutritious foods eaten, is a source of complete protein, iron, and B vitamins. Government inspection of meat safeguards the consumer. The inspection stamp is an indication that the meat is from disease-free animals and has met certain standards of quality enforced by the United States Department of Agriculture. Knowledge of meat cuts, standards, and signs of quality makes it possible to distinguish between high-quality and low-quality cuts to make the best choice for whatever purpose intended. The appearance, texture, flavor, and tenderness of meat depend on its physical structure and compositon. When meat is cooked the lean tissue becomes toughened at high internal temperatures, while the connective tissue becomes softened with long heating. Cuts with much connective tissue require long heating times.

The method chosen to cook any meat depends on the kind, the cut and its size, the time available for cooking, and the degree of doneness preferred. Tough cuts of meat can be made more tender by changing the character of the meat by mechanical and chemical methods. In any cut of meat, the tenderness after cooking is dependent upon the relationship between the temperature and the length of the cooking period.

Meat has many convenience forms. The most perishable ones are those that are fresh, cured, or ready-to-eat. These must be eaten quickly or stored properly in the refrigerator until used. Canned and frozen meats are less perishable. Freeze-dried meat products have a longer storage life and require no refrigeration. Since meat represents an important nutrient source and one of the most expensive items in your budget, careful selection, preparation, and handling are of utmost importance.

Activities

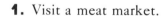

1. Visit a meat market.

 a. Observe the inspection stamp and grades.

 b. Which meats are most expensive?

 c. How does the price vary with different grades? Which grades were you able to find?

 d. How do prices of different cuts vary?

 e. What is on the label of packaged meat?

2. Visit the canned meat department of a supermarket. What items are for sale? How are they labeled? Did you find the United States Department of Agriculture stamp?

3. Study the frozen meat counter in a supermarket. What meat items are available? How are they packaged and labeled? How can you determine the quality of these items?

4. Suggest several retail cuts suitable for each of these methods: broiling, braising, roasting, and simmering.

5. Plan a menu using an inexpensive cut of meat. Prepare and serve it to your family. How did you prepare the meat? Were you pleased with the results? What comment did your family offer?

6. Use two meat patties of the same weight; pan-broil one at a high temperature and the other at a low temperature. Compare their weight, size, tenderness, and moistness. What were the results? Which method do you recommend? Why?

7. Select and prepare a variety meat as liver, kidney, or heart. What did you consider when selecting the variety meat? Describe the preparation method. Evaluate the result.

8. Visit your favorite supermarket and make a list of the textured soy meat-like products (meatless meats) available. Compare their nutrient values and prices with those of the actual meat products they represent. When would you use meat analogs? How would you prepare them?

Questions

1. In what ways does meat contribute to your health and well-being?

2. How does veal differ from beef?

3. In what ways do meat inspection and grading differ? Of what value are they?

4. What should be considered when meat is selected?

5. Why are some cuts of meat tender and others not?

6. What methods are used to tenderize meats?

7. How will you determine how much meat to buy?

8. What are the principles of meat cookery?

9. What are the advantages of low-temperature meat cookery?

10. What cuts of meat can be cooked by dry heat? Why cannot all meat be cooked in this way?

11. How is collagen related to meat cookery? Gelatin? How is gelatin used?

12. How does pan-frying differ from pan-broiling? Can the same cut be used?

13. How are fresh meats stored in the home? Leftover cooked meats?

14. What is gelatin?

15. In what ways are some meats considered a convenience?

16. How would you judge the quality of processed meats?

17. In what ways can convenience meats be used as an "assistant" in cookery?

Chapter
12

Poultry

Giblets

edible organs of poultry: liver, heart, and gizzard.

Capon

a full-breasted, desexed male bird, weight from 1.8–3.6 kg (4–8 lb), with high proportion of white meat.

Braise

to brown meat and cook slowly in a covered utensil in a small amount of liquid or in steam.

Fricassee

a term often used in poultry cookery which means the same as braise. The meat is usually cut into pieces.

Simmer

to cook in a liquid just below the boiling point—85 to 99°C (185 to 210°F). Bubbles collapse below the water surface.

Truss

to tie poultry or meat so that it will hold its shape.

Trussing

in preparation for roasting, the wings are turned back on the shoulders and the drumsticks are tied to the tail to prevent overbrowning.

Stew

to cook slowly in a small amount of liquid.

Chicken has been a symbol of pleasurable eating and still is associated with many memorable occasions. What pleasant memories does chicken help you recall? Roast chicken, turkey, goose, or duck are the center of interest for many feasts, holidays, family get-togethers, and company meals. Chicken and turkey were once a Sunday and holiday treat, but now they are served any day of the week either alone or in combination with other foods.

Today, chicken is a relatively low-cost, high-quality food. The low cost is a result of the development of new and better

In addition to chicken and turkey, there are less common types of fowl which make delicious and unusual dishes.

breeds of chicken and the use of improved feeds. Because of these improvements it is possible to grow chicken to market size with less feed in a shorter period of time. Chicken is an inexpensive source of protein as compared with most other meats.

The term poultry not only refers to chicken and turkey but also includes duck, geese, guinea and Cornish hens, squab, and pigeons. Of this group, chicken and turkey are most commonly used, and chicken is the most popular and plentiful. Which of the birds above have you seen? Which ones have you eaten?

Classes of Poultry

There are several classes of poultry. Each kind of poultry is classified or grouped according to age, weight, and sex. Because poultry becomes less tender with age, these groupings are related to tenderness and to the suitable cooking method. The chart on page 219 lists the common forms of poultry, their weight and age, and some suggested methods for cooking.

Ducklings, Cornish hens, and geese are delicacies. Ducklings are young ducks nine to twelve weeks of age weighing from 1.59–2.27 kilograms (3½–5 pounds). They contain more fat than chickens. Cornish hens weigh about 454 grams (1 pound) and are usually sold frozen and ready-to-cook. Chilled or frozen ready-to-cook young geese weigh about 2.72–5.45 kilograms (6–12 pounds).

Kinds of Poultry

Type	Description	Age	Weight	Cooking Method
Chicken **Broiler or Fryer**	Very young, either sex, smooth thin skin, tender, small amount of fat	9–12 wks	0.68–1.1 kg (1½–2½ lb)	Broil Fry
Roaster	Fully developed, either sex, young, tender, smooth skin with layer of fat	3–5 mos	1.1–2.04 kg (2½–4½ lb)	Roast
Capon	Young, desexed male bird, very meaty, juicy flesh	less than 8 mos	1.8–3.6 kg (4–8 lb)	Roast
Stewing chicken or Fowl	Mature bird, coarse skin, less tender, well-developed muscle	more than 10 mos	1.8–2.7 kg (4–6 lb)	Braise Simmer Stew
Turkey **Fryer or Roaster**	Young, tender	15–17 wks	1.8–2.7 kg (4–6 lb)	Broil Fry Roast
Roaster	Young, tender	5–6 mos	hen 2.7–6.4 kg (6–14 lb) Tom 4–10.9 kg (9–24 lb)	Roast

Market Forms of Poultry

Most poultry is sold ready-to-cook either whole or in parts and is sold fresh, frozen, or canned in most markets. The class name on poultry suggests the cooking method and helps you make the right choice for the use you have in mind.

Fresh Poultry

Dressed and ready-to-cook poultry is sold fresh chilled or as cold storage poultry. Dressed poultry has been bled and has only the feathers, head, and feet removed and has been drawn (internal organs removed). The liver, heart, and gizzard, known as giblets, are washed, wrapped, and placed inside the body cavity. The bird can be sold whole, in half, or in pieces such as breasts, legs, and thighs. You will find that the already cooked bird—barbecued, roasted, or fried—is sold in some markets and specialty stores.

Frozen Poultry

Poultry is frozen for your convenience and for safety during shipment and comes ready-to-cook. Turkeys and Cornish hens that are stuffed are sold frozen. Some poultry is frozen after it has been cooked and you will need only to heat it for serving.

Canned Poultry

You can make your selection from a variety of canned poultry. The bird may be whole, cut into pieces, or boned and canned. The canned poultry items include chicken, turkey, and specialty foods such as chicken chow mein or turkey à la king. As with meats, there are quality signs or clues which will aid you in making the best choice from among the many classes and forms of poultry.

Selection of Poultry

Look for inspection and grade labels when selecting poultry; they are your clues to quality. Poultry sold in interstate commerce must be government inspected; this will assure you that the poultry comes from healthy birds, is processed in sanitary surroundings, and labeled accurately. Inspection labels indicate that the poultry is wholesome.

Poultry which has passed the federal inspection for wholesomeness may be graded for quality and assigned a U.S. Grade A, B, or C. Grade A poultry is well-finished, full-fleshed and meaty. Grade B indicates a good quality poultry which is slightly less meaty, and Grade C poultry has less flesh and fat.

Quality poultry has meaty breasts and legs, well-distributed fat, and skin with few blemishes or pinfeathers.

You will recognize the best quality poultry by these characteristics: full-fleshed, meaty breast and legs; well-distributed fat; skin with few blemishes or pinfeathers.

Federal inspection stamps such as those shown are assurance that you are buying quality poultry.

Nutrient Contributions

Like meats, poultry of all kinds contains proteins, fats, minerals, and vitamins. Poultry contains a high-quality (complete) protein and is a good source of iron, phosphorus, and the B complex vitamins, thiamin, riboflavin, and niacin. The fat varies with the kind and age of the bird. Ducks and geese have more fat than do chickens and turkeys. Old birds contain more fat than the young birds. The dark meat is slightly higher in fat content than the white meat.

Principles of Poultry Cookery

Like meat, poultry contains an abundance of protein, and therefore you may apply the same general cooking rules as those used for meat. The first rule is the same as for all protein foods: cook at a low temperature. You will recall that high temperatures toughen protein while low temperatures keep the protein tender. You should not roast poultry in a very hot oven as this will cause shrinkage and toughening as well as the loss of juices and flavor. Nor should you use hot fat for frying or browning poultry because this, too, will toughen the protein. When using moist heat as in braising and cooking in liquid, a low temperature is maintained by letting the liquid simmer rather than boil.

The second rule to remember is that the tenderness of the poultry determines the suitable cookery method. The tenderness of poultry is influenced by age; young birds are tender, older birds less tender. For young birds, broiling, roasting, and rotisserie cooking are good methods. For older, less tender birds, braising and cooking in liquid are most suitable.

Methods of Cooking

Poultry is cooked by the same methods used for meats: the tender cuts by dry heat such as roasting and broiling, and the less tender cuts by moist heat such as stewing and braising.

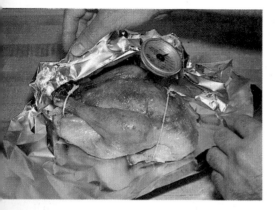

Most all of the poultry you purchase is ready-to-cook. You should inspect it before cooking to make sure all the pinfeathers and hair have been removed. Rinse the cut pieces in cold water. If the bird is whole, let cold water run into the cavity and remove any viscera that may remain. Dry the washed poultry, including the interior cavity of the whole bird, with paper toweling.

If you are using frozen poultry, thaw it before cooking so that it will cook uniformly. Leave the bird in its wrapping and thaw in the refrigerator for about twenty-four hours.

Dry-heat Methods

Roasting is the same for poultry as for meats. Tender poultry such as chicken, turkey, and duck can be roasted on a rack in a shallow pan in a 160°C (325°F) oven. Do not cover or add water. Overbrowning of the breast of a large bird can be prevented by placing a loose tent of aluminum foil over the breast when the bird is half-done. If you wish to stuff poultry, the stuffing should be lightly placed inside the bird just before roasting. The stuffing and the bird may be prepared a day in advance but must be refrigerated separately to avoid the possibility of food poisoning.

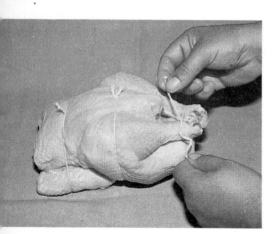

The bird is usually trussed for *roasting;* that is, the wing tips are turned back on the shoulders and the drumsticks are tied to the tail. This prevents the wings and legs from becoming too brown and dry.

If the bird is lacking in fat you may brush it with soft fat or oil to prevent drying of the skin. You may cover the turkey loosely with a sheet of foil or a piece of thin cloth dipped in melted fat to avoid overbrowning of the breast.

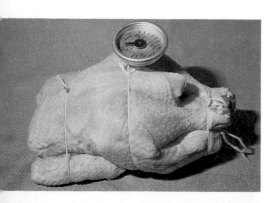

A meat thermometer is your best guide to doneness and should be inserted so that the bulb is 1.2 to 2.5 centimeters (½ to 1 inch) deep in the thickest part of the breast or the center of the inner thigh muscle. The thermometer will register 85 to 90°C (185 to 190°F) when a roasting chicken is well done. You may also use this test for doneness: press the thickest part of the drumstick between two fingers (protected with cloth) and move the leg. If the leg moves easily and is soft, the bird has been cooked sufficiently.

222

The broiler-fryers are used for *broiling*. Depending upon their size, these chickens are split in half lengthwise or quartered. The wing tip is folded back on the shoulder and the pieces are placed on a broiler rack skin side down. You may brush the chicken with melted fat and place it 10 to 12.5 centimeters (4 to 5 inches) from the source of heat for about fifteen minutes. Turn the pieces with tongs as they are browned and cook for another 15 minutes.

Young, tender chicken which has been cut into the desired pieces may be prepared for *frying* in several ways. You may roll it in flour, in egg and bread crumbs, or dip it into a batter. The prepared chicken is browned in about 1.2 centimeters (½ inch) of fat. The pieces are turned with tongs as they brown.

After the chicken is browned, you may continue to cook it slowly until tender in one of three ways: (1) continue the cooking over low heat in the skillet; or (2) continue cooking in the oven; or (3) cover the skillet to complete the cooking. However, if you cover the chicken after browning, the method then becomes braising rather than frying.

Moist-heat Methods

The term *fricassee* is often used in poultry cookery although it means the same as *braised*. To braise, brown the chicken in fat as if for frying; add 30 to 45 milliliters (2 or 3 tablespoons) of water; cover the pan. The cooking may continue over low heat on top of the range or in the oven at 160°C (325°F) until the chicken is tender (45 minutes to 1 hour). Remove the cover for the last ten minutes to make the chicken crisp.

Cook old and mature poultry by *simmering* or *stewing*. The water should be below boiling, that is, simmering. Steam will come from the water surface but there will be no bubbling of the water.

When tender, the chicken is removed from the bone in large pieces and is used in a variety of chicken dishes as salads, casseroles, creamed chicken, and sandwiches. You may use the broth for soup, gravy, white sauce, and as the liquid for prepared chicken dishes.

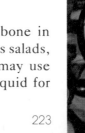

Turkey, served imaginatively, can look like this.

Uses of Poultry

Poultry provides the same nutrient values as meat and it can replace meat in your meals. It can be used as the main dish with vegetables and salad selected to complement it. It is used both in simple and fancy meals and as a snack or a party food. Cooked poultry can be used as an ingredient in a variety of ways ranging from salads and sandwiches to casseroles and croquettes. For delicious and attractive poultry dishes, select the bird that is suited for the dish you are planning.

Selecting and Buying Poultry

When buying poultry, select the birds that have been inspected and graded. Inspection is your key to wholesomeness and the grade is your key to quality poultry. Canned and frozen poultry have passed the inspection before processing and this is listed on the package labels.

Poultry which is not sold in interstate commerce may not be inspected. It is up to you to look for signs of quality such as meaty breast and legs, firm flesh, and thin, yellow skin which is free of any blemishes or bruises.

Brand names can be clues to quality, but first you will have to use the brand to decide whether its quality meets with your standards. When selecting frozen poultry, watch for freezer burn (dry, pale, frosty areas) that indicates long and improper storage. The wrapper should not be stained or broken.

Poultry is classified by age and weight and is listed in terms of appropriate use as broilers, fryers, roasting, and stewing birds. When you buy, you should have a specific recipe in mind.

Poultry contains more bone in proportion to muscle than red meat. The following general rules will help you determine the quantity of ready-to-cook poultry to buy.

Fryer   .35 to .45 kilogram (¾ to 1 pound) per serving
Roaster   .32 to .35 kilogram (½ to ¾ pound) per serving
Broiler   .45 kilogram (1 pound) or ½ chicken per serving
Stewing   .32 to .35 kilogram (½ to ¾ pound) per serving

When poultry is used as an ingredient, you may need to determine the quantity by milliliters (cups). You can figure on 250 milliliters (1 cup) cooked poultry meat from .45 kilogram (1 pound) of a stewing bird. After you have selected the poultry you will need to protect its freshness and quality by storing it properly.

Storage of Poultry

Poultry is a very perishable food. Poultry which has been cut up is more perishable than the whole bird. To store properly, remove poultry from the market wrap and rewrap loosely with waxed paper or a similar wrap and store in the coldest part of the refrigerator—2 to 3°C (35 to 38°F). The poultry should be used within two or three days.

Poultry may be stored for up to a year if wrapped in freezer wrap to seal out air and then put in the frozen food compartment. Poultry which you purchase frozen should be stored immediately in the freezer without rewrapping and should not be thawed until you are ready to use it. It will retain its freshness if it is stored at −18°C (0°F). Frozen poultry is clean and ready for cooking.

Canned poultry is stored in a cool dry place. Any opened canned, or leftover cooked poultry must be stored in the

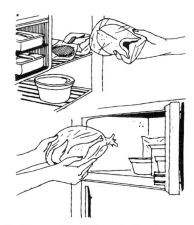

Poultry can be refrigerated or frozen safely.

225

coldest part of the refrigerator in a tightly covered container. Before storing it, remove the stuffing. You should use leftover poultry within two or three days. Properly stored, poultry is available for use when you need it and along with other poultry products can contribute to the convenience of meal preparation.

Convenience in Poultry

All ready-to-cook poultry is a convenience which allows you to use less time and effort than is usually required to dress and prepare poultry. Ready-to-cook poultry is sold as the whole bird, in halves, quarters, cut in pieces such as thighs, legs, breasts, or wings. Buying only the meaty parts such as breasts, thighs, and legs may be more economical in terms of cost per serving.

Most research studies which have compared home-prepared poultry products with similar convenience items indicate a higher cost for the convenience product. The greater the convenience provided for you, the higher the cost. For example, it has been found that breaded chicken ready for frying and frozen chicken dinners were much higher in cost (double or more) than similar home-prepared products. Canned prepared chicken products were also higher than comparable home-prepared items.

Other studies found that there can be a difference in nutritive values of convenience and home-prepared products. The convenience products tend to contain less poultry meat (which means less protein) than a similar home-prepared food.

A variety of convenience poultry products is available both canned and frozen. Some of the canned poultry items include the canned whole bird, cut pieces, boneless meat, sandwich spreads, soups, and prepared specialties such as turkey a la king. Dehydrated chicken soups are generally available.

Frozen convenience poultry items include birds stuffed with dressing, frozen pieces or parts, breaded cuts, and frozen specialties such as chicken pies, turkey rolls, and complete dinners. Frozen cooked poultry provides an extra convenience, since it only needs to be heated for serving. In some markets and specialty shops such items as barbecued chicken, duck, roasted chicken, and fried chicken are available and require no preparation, not even heating.

There are instances when it is wise to use less time and energy with the help of convenience foods. However, remember

226

that when you buy convenience foods you are paying for the work involved in its preparation. At times convenience foods may be a good buy, especially if they add to the quality of the meal you serve. How well these and other convenience products serve and meet your needs will be determined by your ability to judge their quality, to fit them into your plans, and to use them creatively to extend variety in your meals.

Main Ideas

Poultry, like meat, is a source of complete protein, B vitamins, and minerals. The inspection of poultry protects the consumer and helps to insure quality. Poultry is available in many different forms which make it possible to make choices best suited to specific purposes. Some poultry forms have limited keeping quality while others, in convenience forms, can be stored for future use with little difficulty.

Activities

1. Visit the poultry department of a supermarket. What kinds and forms of poultry were offered for sale? Look for federal inspection and grade stamps. What grades were available? Look for signs of quality in whole chicken.

2. From magazines and advertisements, collect recipes and pictures of poultry arranged for serving. Describe the garnishes used.

3. Calculate the cost per serving (using serving portions suggested in the chapter) of broilers, fryers, roasting chicken, capon, stewing chicken, roast turkey, and Cornish hen. Which form of poultry would you select for chicken salad, chicken and noodle casserole, or creamed chicken? Give reasons for your selections.

4. Give examples of similarities between the cooking of poultry and meat. Which cuts of meat and types of poultry should be used for moist-heat and dry-heat methods of cooking?

5. Plan, prepare, and serve a chicken dinner. In your report describe the menu, the food cost, the table setting, and the time schedule.

6. Find a recipe for a "new" way to prepare chicken. Plan a lunch or dinner menu to include this recipe. Prepare the new recipe. In your report describe the recipe and the menu, the food cost, and preparation schedule. Compare the new dish for flavor, texture, and eye appeal with two of your favorite chicken dishes. Would you use the recipe again?

7. Select poultry suitable for braising. Brown all of it as directed for braising. Place half of the browned chicken into a covered casserole or skillet; wrap the other half in aluminum foil, sealing the edges well. Place all of the chicken in an oven set at 160°C (325°F); cook until tender. Compare the two methods for flavor, tenderness, and amount of dripping.

8. Which convenience poultry items are used in your home? Why? Give suggestions for using them creatively to add variety to your meals.

9. Compare the nutrient value of poultry with that of meat. When would you use poultry rather than meat?

Questions

1. What meats are represented by the term poultry?

2. Name five market classifications of chicken. Give the characteristics of each and the recommended cooking methods.

3. What is meant by "cuts" of chicken? What are the advantages or disadvantages of buying chicken parts instead of the whole bird?

4. What forms of chicken are available in most supermarkets? What are the advantages of the different forms?

5. Explain the inspection and grading of poultry. Of what advantage is graded poultry to you as a consumer?

6. Compare the nutrient value of white and dark meat of chicken.

7. Compare the nutrient contribution of poultry and meat. Is it wise to substitute poultry for meat in menus?

8. Compare the principles of poultry and meat cookery.

9. Why should poultry not be stuffed the day before it is to be cooked?

10. Describe the methods for determining doneness of roast poultry. Which method is considered best? Why?

11. List several points to consider when buying poultry.

12. Describe the proper storage of fresh, frozen, and leftover poultry.

13. What conveniences are provided in poultry? How will you judge the quality of convenience poultry items?

14. Define: capon, freezer burn, duckling, giblet, fricassee.

Chapter
13

Fish

Words for Thought

Iodine
a mineral substance found in fish required for the proper function of the thyroid gland.

Thyroid
an important gland in the neck which produces thyroxine.

Thyroxine
a substance made by the thyroid gland which requires iodine along with other nutrients for its formation. It controls the rate at which cells use or burn food, and prevents goiter.

Goiter
an enlargement of the thyroid gland due to a lack of iodine.

Scallop
cut food covered or mixed with a sauce and baked.

You no longer need to live on the seashore to enjoy clams, lobster, crab, shrimp, and other seafoods. The wonders of the seas are within easy reach of your skillet. As those who fish will tell you, nothing has quite the flavor of fish caught, prepared, and eaten on the edge of a stream. However, through the achievements of quick freezing, the freshness and flavor of many favorite seafoods have been captured for your year-round enjoyment.

Fish is a unique source of food that is not dependent upon the cultivation of farm land. A large variety of fish comes from

229

oceans, seas, rivers, lakes, and streams. Since the supply of fish appears to replace itself, the supply seems to be almost endless although some varieties are becoming scarce.

Kinds of Fish

About two hundred different varieties of fish are sold in our markets. Most of them come from the oceans and some from lakes and rivers. They are classified into two general groups: finfish and shellfish. The finfish come from both salt and freshwater and have scales and fins. Some shellfish are enclosed in a hard shell such as oysters, clams, and scallops, while others have a crust-like shell and segmented bodies such as lobster, crab, and shrimp.

Fish are also classified as lean or fat according to the amount of fat they contain. However, fish contains much less fat than red meats. The flesh of fish with a high fat content is either yellow, pink, or grayish in color, while fish with white flesh is less fat. The fat fish include salmon, mackerel, and tuna; the lean fish include haddock, cod, and halibut. Most of the shellfish contain little fat and are lean.

Forms of Fish

Several forms of fish and seafoods are available for your selection. When you visit the market or a fish specialty store you will find fresh, frozen, canned, cured, and pickled fish. About half of the fish used in the United States is fresh or frozen and the remainder is canned. A very small amount of cured fish is used in this country, but it is very popular in the Scandinavian countries.

Shellfish are as various in flavor and texture as they are in shape.

230

Fresh Fish

The common forms of fresh fish which you will see in markets are: whole or round, drawn, dressed, steaks, and fillets.

Fish marketed just as it comes from the water is known as whole or round fish. The scales and entrails must be removed before the fish is cooked.

Drawn fish has only the entrails removed; the head, fins, and scales remain on the fish.

Dressed fish comes ready for cooking. The head, tail, fins, scales, and entrails are removed.

Fish steaks are cross-section slices of dressed fish. Large fish such as halibut and salmon are often sold as steaks. The backbone is usually the only bone in a fish steak.

A lengthwise cut away from the backbone is a fish fillet. A single fillet comes from one side of the fish; a double or butterfly fillet comes from both sides of the fish and is held together by uncut flesh and skin. You will find only a few and sometimes no bones in a fillet.

Frozen Fish

You may purchase several varieties of frozen fish all year round. Frozen fish can even be fresher than fresh fish since much of the freezing of fish takes place on the same boats where they are caught. Frozen fish is usually sold as fillets and steaks. Fish sticks, which are cut from fillets, may be breaded and partially cooked before freezing. Breaded uncooked fillets and shellfish are also frozen. The frozen fish which you select is ready for cooking without further preparation.

Canned Fish

Both finfish and shellfish are canned in a variety of forms. Popular canned finfish include salmon, tuna, and sardines. Among the canned shellfish are oysters, clams, lobsters, crab, scallops, and shrimp which are considered delicacies.

Cured Fish

Fish may be cured to preserve it and also to give it a distinctive flavor. Fish which has been salted, smoked, or pickled is referred to as cured fish. Examples of cured fish are salted cod, smoked mackerel, finnan haddie, and kippered herring.

Fish such as cod or herring is salted in dry salt or a brine and then dried. Mildly salted fish can be treated with smoke which gives it a special smokey flavor. Finnan haddie is haddock which has been cured in brine and then smoked. Kippers, salmon, and whitefish may also be cured.

Pickled fish is cured in a brine that contains vinegar and spices and, after processing, is packed into jars. The many kinds of fresh, frozen, canned, and cured fish can add variety and interest to your eating pleasure. There are several signs of quality that help you to select good fish and seafoods.

Selection of Fish

Unlike meat inspection, the inspection and grading of fish for wholesomeness is voluntary. The grading program is supervised by the United States Department of Interior. All inspected fish will be identified with an inspection stamp which indicates its quality. Some of the fish products which you buy may show an inspection stamp. The grading standards usually grade fish as U.S. Grade A, U.S. Grade B, and Substandard. When available, these grades will enable you to purchase a wholesome, good-quality, fresh product. Since inspection is not mandatory, it is important to purchase fish from reliable sources.

Inspected fish will have stamps like these.

Shellfish

Shellfish are sold live in the shell, shucked (shell removed), and cooked. The following characteristics will be your clues to the freshness of shellfish: (1) shucked oysters and clams are plump, creamy in color, and the liquid they are in is odorless and clear; (2) shells of live clams and oysters should be tightly closed or should close when touched; (3) the tail of a live lobster snaps back quickly after it is flattened out (both lobster and crab should be kept alive until they are cooked); (4) the fresh deep-sea scallop is white and the bay scallop is creamy white or pinkish in color; and (5) shrimp should be odorless and the thin shell covering it should be firmly attached.

Finfish

Here are several characteristics that will help you judge the freshness of finfish. The whole or round fish should have bulging, bright, clear eyes, bright red gills, and scales that cling tightly to the skin. The flesh of the fish should be firm, springy, and leave no dent when pressed. There should be no disagreeable odor.

Frozen and Canned Fish

Choose only fish that is solidly frozen and is in packages which show no sign of being thawed or refrozen. Like fresh fish, some frozen and processed fish may not have a government grade. The information on the label and the brand name are your only clues to quality.

Fish Buying Guide

Market Form	Description	Amount to buy per serving
Whole or Round	As it comes from the water. Must be scaled, cleaned; head, tail, fins must be removed.	454 g (1 lb)
Drawn	Cleaned only. Scales, head, tail, and fins must be removed.	454 g (1 lb)
Dressed	Scaled, cleaned, usually with head, tail, and fins removed. Ready for cooking.	227 g (½ lb)
Steaks	Cross-section slices of large dressed fish with a section of backbone.	151 g (⅓ lb)
Fillets	Sides of fish cut lengthwise from the backbone, boneless.	151 g (⅓ lb)
Sticks	Pieces of fish cut from blocks of frozen fillets into portions of uniform dimensions, usually 28 g (1 oz) portions. Usually covered with batter, breaded, and browned in deep fat.	75 g (3 1-oz sticks)

Amount to Buy

The amount you buy is determined by the form of fish. Canned and frozen fish are ready for cooking and therefore will have no waste. Fresh whole or drawn fish will have waste. There is less waste in dressed fish since the entrails, head, tail, fins, and scales have been removed. Fish steaks will have

234

Seafood Buying Guide

Market Form	Description	Amount to buy per serving
Live	Clams, Oysters	6
	Crabs	3
	Lobster	454 g (1 lb)
Shucked	Oysters, Clams	167 mL (1/3 pt)
	Scallops	151 g (1/3 lb)
Fresh or Frozen	Shrimp	117 g (1/4 lb)
	Lobster Tails	227 g (1/2 lb)
Cooked in the Shell	Crabs	3
	Lobster	454 g (1 lb)
Cooked, Shelled	Shrimp, Crab, Lobster	117 g (1/4 lb)

little waste and fillets of finfish will have no waste. The tables on these pages will help you determine how much fish you will need to buy. All of these forms of fish and seafoods will provide valuable nutrients for you.

Nutrient Contributions

In general, the nutrients contributed by fish are similar to those of meat. Fish and meat both contain protein, minerals, vitamins, and fat.

Protein

The protein of fish is complete and can be used in place of meat or poultry in your meals. An average serving of meat and fish will give you about the same amount of protein.

Minerals

The mineral content of the fish will vary somewhat with the kind of fish. However, fish in general will provide important amounts of *phosphorus* and a fair amount of *iron* and *calcium*. Meat is usually a better source of iron than fish. Fish makes its most important contribution to your diet through the mineral *iodine* which is not provided by meat. All foods other than seafoods are poor sources of iodine.

When iodine is lacking, a disease called *goiter* develops. Goiter is an enlargement of the thyroid gland. Some of the early scientists noticed that people who lived near the sea and regularly ate fish did not get goiter, while goiter was common among those who lived inland. Many years later, in 1917, a group of children in Akron, Ohio, were given 0.2 gram of sodium iodine each day for two weeks at the beginning and end of the school year. The children who received iodine were able to recover from the goiter.

Without iodine the thyroid gland cannot produce thyroxine. Thyroxine is needed to control the rate of food oxidation in your body cells. When seafoods are included in your meals regularly, they will supply the needed iodine. Today, you also have iodized salt (salt with iodine added) along with fish to help you meet your need for iodine.

Vitamins

The vitamin content of most fish is comparable to that of meat. The *B vitamins* (B_1, B_2, niacin) are found in fair amounts in fish. *Vitamins A and D* are present in fatty fish, especially in the oil of the fish liver.

Fats

Fish contains less fat than meat and the lean fish is especially low in fat. Because fish is lower in fat it will supply fewer calories. This can be an advantage for those who are on low-calorie or low-fat diets.

However, the fat content of cooked fish depends upon the amount of fat added in cooking. Fish is often rolled in bread crumbs, flour, or cornmeal during preparation for frying. This enhances flavor, but also increases fat content and calories.

Uses of Fish

Like meat, fish may be used as the main dish around which the rest of the meal is planned. It may be combined with other foods to make salads, casseroles, and croquettes which are main dishes around which meals can be planned. Fish chowders or oyster and lobster stews are favorite hearty soups used as lunch or supper main dishes.

Fish can be served as an appetizer. Fresh, frozen, or canned shrimp, lobster, and crab are served as seafood cocktails at the beginning of special meals. Pickled and smoked fish can also be served as part of the appetizer course.

Principles of Fish Cookery

Because fish is a food rich in protein it needs to be cooked at low temperatures to prevent toughening of the protein. Unlike meat, fish contains little connective tissue and cooks quickly. If you cook fish too long, it is apt to break apart. It is sufficiently cooked when it is easily flaked with a fork. Remember that overcooking as well as high temperatures can toughen fish.

Methods of Cooking Fish

You recall that the degree of tenderness of meat depends upon the cooking method. Fish differ from meats in that they are all tender. Swimming must be easy for fish because they have no tough muscles and there is no such thing as less tender fish! You may cook fish by moist- and dry-heat methods, but it will be the fat content of the fish rather than tenderness which will be your clue to the best method. Generally, the fatty fish are cooked by dry-heat methods and the lean fish by moist-heat methods.

When you learn which fish are fat and which are lean, you will be able to match the proper cooking method with the fish. The fat fish such as whitefish, mackerel, catfish, salmon, and trout are best broiled or baked. Their fat content keeps them from drying out during cooking. The lean fish include swordfish, red snapper, halibut, haddock, and flounder. They are usually fried, poached, and steamed. The lean fish may be broiled or baked if they are brushed with fat or cooked in a sauce to prevent drying.

Regardless of the cooking method you select, fish should be cooked at a low temperature in order to maintain the best quality. No fish should ever be overcooked.

The fish is ready to serve when you can easily separate firm flakes of flesh with a fork.

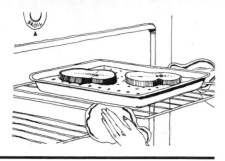

Which of the following methods for cooking fish would you like to try? Have you tried any of these before?

Broiling is the easiest and quickest method of cooking fatty fish.

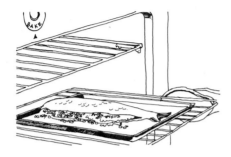

Baked fish which is stuffed not only has more flavor but also retains its shape.

When fish is to be fried, it is often first cut into fillets and breaded.

Fish which is poached should be tied in cheesecloth and simmered gently in salted water.

Fish may also be cooked in a chowder with your choice of liquid and vegetables.

The flavor of fish is retained by proper cooking; however, when you do not wish to cook fish immediately, protect its flavor by proper storage.

238

Care and Storage of Fish

You can preserve the quality, freshness, and flavor of the fish you select by storing it properly. All fish, except canned, is very perishable.

Fresh Fish

To store fresh fish wrap it tightly in waxed paper or foil and place it in a covered container in the coldest part of the refrigerator. If you are unable to use it within a day, wrap it tightly in moisture-vapor-proof paper and place it into the freezer, since fish odors can easily penetrate other foods.

Refrigerated or frozen fish must be tightly wrapped.

Frozen Fish

Commercially frozen fish is stored in its original package and should be placed into the freezer immediately after purchase. It should not be thawed until you are ready to use it. Thin or small pieces of frozen fish can be cooked without thawing. Large pieces of frozen fish are thawed in the original wrapping in the refrigerator. They will cook more evenly when thawed.

Fish which is purchased frozen may be stored in its original package.

Canned Fish

Canned fish keeps well at room temperature, but once the can is opened, it must be kept in a tightly covered container in the refrigerator. In addition to the fresh, frozen, and canned fish there are several convenience fish and seafood products that you should know about.

Convenience

You will find that there is a variety of convenience fish and seafood items. The convenience forms of frozen fish include frozen fillets, steaks, fish sticks, fish pies, chowders, and other processed fish products. These products may be breaded and ready-to-cook, or they may be precooked and require only heating before serving. Frozen steaks, fillets, and whole fish are ready to cook. Shrimp, oysters, scallops, and fillets may be breaded, or breaded and precooked. The breaded seafoods require cooking, while the precooked ones require only heating.

239

Frozen fish soups are another convenience item. Frozen fish dinners packaged in divided foil plates usually include vegetables and need only to be cooked in their containers before serving.

You may use canned fish as it comes from the can in salads and sandwiches or as an ingredient in any recipe that calls for cooked fish. Tuna, salmon, sardines, lobster, crab, and shrimp are popular canned items. In addition, smoked fish such as oysters, herring, and salmon are ready to eat without further cooking. You will also find boil-in-bag fish and seafoods which are vacuum-sealed to preserve their goodness.

The use of these convenience seafoods may permit you to serve more elaborate dishes and menus, to include more variety, to make up for your lack of experience and skill, as well as use less time. But, wherever there are advantages, there may also be disadvantages. Convenience items may deprive you of eating pleasure because flavor and quality may be inferior or may deprive you of the satisfaction of creating. They can also be a strain on your budget. You should evaluate their contributions in terms of your needs, abilities, and values.

Main Ideas

Fish is classified as either finfish or shellfish. It contributes protein, vitamins, and minerals, particularly iodine, to the diet. Fresh fish is highly perishable and has a short storage life. In frozen, freeze-dried, dried, salted, smoked, and canned forms a longer keeping period is possible.

Activities

1. Evaluate the contributions of convenience seafood items. List their advantages and disadvantages.

2. Visit a local fish market and note the varieties of fresh fish available. In what forms could you purchase fresh fish? Which of these fish are lean and which fat? How would you cook them?

3. Visit a supermarket and note the frozen and canned seafoods. What information was listed on the label? Did you find any seafood packages with government grades? What clues to quality did you find?

4. Prepare and present a report on the thyroid gland and goiter to the class.

5. Compare the cost per serving of fish: fresh, frozen, and canned. Which of these do you consider to be better protein sources? Cheaper protein sources? Why?

6. Find an inexpensive finfish in the fresh or frozen form. Prepare it by the method you think is best and serve it to your family. Were you pleased with it? Why?

7. What convenience seafood items have you used?

8. Collect recipes and pictures of fish dishes from magazines and advertisements. Arrange and garnish a platter of fish which you prepared. Describe your arrangement. What comments did your family make?

9. Demonstrate wrapping fish for refrigerator storage. Plan to use the fish later and note the flavor, odor, and texture. How long was it stored? How was it wrapped?

10. Compare the nutrient value of fish with that of meat. When would it be preferable to use fish instead of meat?

Questions

1. How do finfish differ from shellfish? Name several examples of each.

2. Define fillet and fish steak and drawn, dressed, and round fish.

3. How does cured fish differ from frozen fish?

4. How will you recognize quality in fresh fish? Canned fish?

5. What nutrients are contributed by fish? What do they do for you?

6. What are the principles of fish cookery? Upon what are they based?

7. What should you consider when selecting a method for cooking fish?

8. What methods are used to cook fish?

9. How is fresh, frozen, canned, and cooked fish stored?

10. What kinds of convenience seafood items are available? How will you decide whether to use a convenience or a home-prepared item?

Chapter
14
Vegetables

Words for Thought

Carbohydrate
a building block of food which includes sugars, starches, and cellulose. The sugar and starch provide energy for the body.

Cellulose
a carbohydrate substance which forms the structure of plants. It cannot be digested by the body but serves as a natural laxative.

Chlorophyll
the green coloring substance of plants.

Dehydrate
a method of preserving food by removing most of the water from it. The food is usually dried by heated air in a mechanical dryer.

Gourmet
an expert in the field of cookery

Au gratin
baked in an oven with a top crust of bread crumbs and cheese.

Two million years ago people roamed the earth and ate fruits, roots, and berries; these were their first foods. People's wanderings became seasonal, according to the growth of the plants. They realized that the seeds on the ground grew into edible plants.

Have you eaten leaves, stems, flowers, fruits, seeds, tubers, and roots? You have, if you have eaten a variety of vegetables. Study the chart on pages 244 – 247 to see which parts of the plant you do eat. The word vegetable refers to the plant or its parts eaten with the main portion of the meal.

In this chapter you will learn there is more than one way to cook and serve the large variety of vegetables, and that they add nutrients, eye appeal, and a bright note to any meal.

Classes of Vegetables

It is convenient to think of the many varieties of vegetables in classes or groups. They are often grouped according to the parts of the plant from which they come, their flavor, nutrient content, or color.

Parts of Plant

Vegetables can be most easily classified according to the parts of the plant from which they come such as seeds, leaves, tubers, roots, flowers, bulbs, and fruits. You will find the vegetables classified according to the parts of the plant they represent in the chart shown on pages 244 – 247.

Flavor Classification

According to flavor, vegetables are grouped as either mild or strong. The strong-flavored vegetables include those with a cabbage-like flavor such as brussels sprouts, turnips, and cauliflower, and those with an onion-like flavor such as leeks and garlic. Most other vegetables are considered mild in flavor.

Nutrient Classification

Some vegetables have a high water content while others are high in starch. It is the part of the plant from which the vegetable comes that will influence its nutrient value. The fruits, stems, flowers, and leaves are usually high in water content. Vegetables from these plant parts such as tomato, celery, broccoli, and lettuce have a high water content and are referred to as the juicy or succulent vegetables. The tubers, bulbs, roots, and seeds are usually high in the carbohydrate starch. Vegetables from these parts of the plant such as potato, sweet potato, lima beans, and corn are often referred to as the starchy vegetables.

On the next four pages you will see pictures of a great variety of vegetables. Check to see which ones of these you know. Which ones have you eaten?

Common Vegetables Classified as Parts of Plants

Bulbs

Chives

Onions

Garlic

Leeks

Shallots

Fruits

Cucumbers

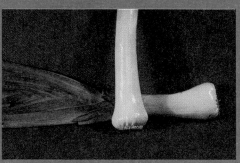

Eggplant

Tomatoes

Okra

Pepper

Squash

Flowers

Artichoke (French/Globe)

Cauliflower

Broccoli

Roots

Beets

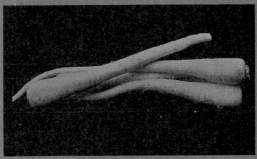

Parsnips

Sweet Potatoes

Turnip

Radishes

Rutabaga

Salsify

Carrots

Leaves

Brussels Sprouts

Cabbage

Chinese Cabbage

Chard

Collard Greens

Dandelion Greens

Endive

Kale

Lettuce

Mustard Greens

Spinach

Watercress

Tubers

Artichoke (Jerusalem)

Potato

Stems

Celery

Asparagus

Kohlrabi

Seeds

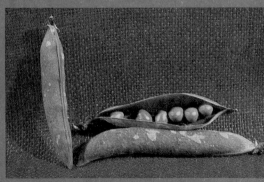

Peas

Beans, green and mature

247

Corn

Color Classification

The color of a vegetable may also be a clue to its nutrient value. The leafy green and yellow vegetables are grouped together because they contain a yellow substance called carotene. Your body can change carotene into vitamin A. In some vegetables the deep green color hides or masks the yellor color of carotene. These various classes of vegetables will help you to select a pleasing variety for your meals. A good rule to follow is to select no more than one vegetable from the same group for the same meal. All groups of vegetables usually can be purchased in more than one form.

Forms of Vegetables

Because of modern transportation and refrigeration some fresh vegetables are available throughout the year. You may buy fresh carrots, lettuce, potatoes, and onions any time of the year. Other vegetables such as lima beans, corn, peas, and asparagus may be available in the fresh form only part of the year. You may purchase these seasonal vegetables throughout the year in other forms such as canned, frozen, or dried. Vegetables in all forms will contribute to your appearance and health through the nutrients they provide.

Nutrient Contributions

Vegetables are especially rich in vitamins and minerals and it is for this reason that they should be included in your meals.

Vitamins

Vitamins are made in the green leaves of plants. The green color of vegetables is due to the presence of chlorophyll.

The leafy green and deep yellow vegetables are excellent sources of *vitamin A*. You will recall that these vegetables contain carotene (a yellow substance) which can be converted into vitamin A. The deeper the yellow and the darker the green of the vegetable, the higher the vitamin A content. Dark green vegetables such as broccoli and spinach and deep yellow vegetables such as carrots and sweet potatoes are abundant sources of carotene. When carotene is converted into vitamin A, it serves the same purpose as the vitamin A found in milk. Do you remember that vitamin A is needed to help your eyes adjust quickly to light or dark, to help you grow, and to add a glow and softness to your hair and skin?

Leafy green vegetables are also good sources of *vitamin C.* Most vegetables contain vitamin C but some are richer sources of it than others. Broccoli, green peppers, tomatoes, and raw cabbage are important sources of vitamin C.

In addition to vitamins A and C, vegetables contain fair amounts of the *B vitamins.* However, seed vegetables, lima beans and peas for example, are good sources of vitamin B.

Minerals

The leafy green vegetables are doubly good since they are not only rich in vitamins but they are also excellent sources of the minerals *calcium* and *iron.*

Carbohydrates

Cellulose, starch, and sugar are the carbohydrates in vegetables. The carbohydrate content of most vegetables is low except in the seeds such as beans, corn, and in tubers, which are good sources of starch. The skin and pulp of vegetables contribute cellulose for body regularity. The sweet flavor of young corn and peas and sweet potatoes is due to their sugar content. As these vegetables mature the sugar is changed into starch and no longer has a sweet flavor.

Vegetables as a rule are low in calories, but vegetables which are rich in starch will also supply more calories than those low in starch. The nutrient content of vegetables can be your clue to their caloric values. Vegetables are considered lower in calories than most other food groups; the vegetables with a high water content supply fewer calories than the vegetables with a high starch content.

Protein

Most vegetables contain only small amounts of incomplete protein. Dried peas and beans (legumes) contain important amounts of protein even though it is incomplete. The incomplete protein should be supplemented with animal protein to provide the missing amino acids.

The vitamins and minerals which vegetables provide make great contributions to your health, vitality, and appearance. It is important to know how to cook vegetables so that they will keep their bright color and nutrients.

Principles of Cookery

Along with valuable nutrients, vegetables will add glamour to your meals when you treat them properly. Their color, flavor, and texture add a pleasing contrast to the other foods of the meal. Careless cooking will make vegetables drab and lifeless, and their important vitamins and minerals will be lost.

Several changes take place when vegetables are cooked. The cellulose structure will soften and the vegetable becomes less crisp. The starch will absorb water, swell, and become more soluble. There are changes in color and flavor, and some nutrients dissolve into the cooking liquid. The principles of vegetable cookery are designed to protect color, flavor, and texture, and to preserve nutrients. The amount of water to be used and the cooking time are important considerations.

Amount of Water

Some of the nutrients in vegetables are soluble in water and seep out into the cooking liquid. The B vitamins, vitamin C, and minerals dissolve in water. When you cook vegetables in small amounts of water or with no added water (baking), the loss of soluble nutrients is reduced. So that vegetables can be cooked in small amounts of water, the pan is covered to prevent scorching and loss of water due to evaporation.

Strong-flavored vegetables, such as onions and cabbage, may be cooked in larger amounts of water, enough to cover the vegetable, so that the flavor will become milder. However, more of the soluble nutrients will be lost in the larger amount of water.

Length of Cooking Time

There are several ways in which the length of cooking time will influence vegetables. You will recall that some vitamins are easily destroyed by heat and overcooking. To avoid nutrient loss, vegetables should be cooked only until they are fork tender and still slightly crisp.

Potatoes cooked in too much water are unappetizing and have lost much of their nutrient value.

250

Overcooking causes the bright colors of vegetables to become drab, and can cause an unpleasant flavor to develop in cabbage-flavored vegetables. The strong flavor of cabbage- and onion-flavored vegetables is influenced more by overcooking than by the quantity of water used. Overcooked vegetables lose their texture and shape and become mushy.

Well-cooked vegetables retain their color, flavor, and texture as well as their nutrients. There are several ways to cook vegetables so they will retain their bright color, delicious flavor, and nutrients.

This broccoli is mushy, shapeless, and has poor color because it has been overcooked.

Methods of Cookery

Vegetables can be boiled, steamed, baked, or panned. They can be cooked in a microwave oven. The color, texture, flavor, and nutrients will be kept, and the vegetables will cook in less time than on top of the range. Vegetables can be cooked covered in the oven with other parts of a meal so that energy is conserved.

Fresh Vegetables

Boiling is suitable for all vegetables and is the method used most often. The vegetable is added to a small amount of boiling water and covered. The water is quickly returned to a boil, and the heat is reduced so that the water simmers gently. To protect the color of bright green vegetables (chlorophyll), cook them without a cover for the first few minutes. Baking soda should not be used to preserve the green color since it will destroy vitamins. Vegetables should be cooked only until they are fork tender.

Frozen Vegetables

Frozen vegetables are placed into boiling water while still frozen. Frozen vegetables will cook in a shorter time than fresh vegetables because they have been scalded in preparation for freezing.

Some vegetables can be *baked* in their skins. Vegetables such as potato and squash are washed thoroughly and placed directly on the oven rack or in a shallow pan and baked until tender. Baking is a way to preserve water-soluble nutrients.

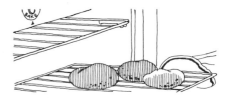

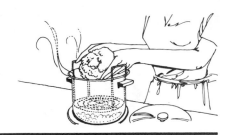

Mild-flavored vegetables may be *steamed*. The steamer consists of a pan in which to boil water and a basket to hold the food. The vegetable is steamed over rapidly boiling water.

Vegetables, potatoes, for example, may be *fried plain* or *dipped in batter or crumbs* and then fried. (Eggplant is prepared in this way.) They are fried in hot fat but not smoking-hot fat. They may be fried in shallow fat or in deep fat. *French frying* is cooking in fat deep enough to cover the vegetable.

Vegetables cook very quickly when *pressure-cooked*. Carefully follow the directions which come with the pressure pan. Vegetables cooked in a pressure cooker usually have a good color and flavor because of the short cooking time. Be careful not to overcook them.

To *stir-fry, pan*, or *braise* vegetables place 15-30 milliliters (1-2 tablespoons) of fat in a skillet or pan. Melt the fat and add broken or cut vegetables. Cover the pan and cook the vegetable over low heat for a short time. The cooked vegetable will be slightly crisp.

To *broil* raw vegetables, such as tomato or eggplant or cooked vegetables, brush them with fat or oil.

Canned Vegetables

Canned vegetables are cooked during canning and require only heating. Some of the water-soluble nutrients are dissolved into the liquid. The amount of liquid is usually more than is served with the vegetable.

You will benefit from all of the dissolved nutrients if you first drain the liquid from the vegetable and heat it in an uncovered pan to evaporate the excess water. When only about one-third of the liquid remains, add the vegetable and heat to serving temperature. In this way, the liquid can be served with the vegetable.

Dried Vegetables

Dried vegetables or legumes such as mature beans and peas require soaking before cooking. They may be covered with boiling water or they may be boiled for two minutes and allowed to soak for about an hour. Or they may be soaked in cold water for several hours. Cook dried vegetables in the liquid which remains after soaking to avoid loss of soluble nutrients. For dehydrated or instantized dry vegetables, follow the directions on the package.

Uses of Vegetables

Vegetables are most commonly served as an accompaniment to a meat or a main dish. Two or more vegetables are chosen to enhance and complement the main dish. They add contrast in color, texture, flavor, size, and shape as well as nutrients to any meal. Once in a while they may even appear at breakfast as a vegetable juice or as potatoes with the meat or egg. They are served as appetizers, soups, salads, side dishes, and casseroles. They may appear as garnishes to add glamour to other foods.

Vegetables are a nutritious contrast to any meal.

Selection and Buying

A large variety of vegetables is displayed in modern food markets. You may purchase them fresh, canned, frozen, and dried or dehydrated. You need to know the signs of quality so that you can select vegetables which will best serve your purpose.

Fresh Vegetables

You can judge the freshness of a vegetable by its crispness, color, firmness, and soundness, that is, the absence of bruises

and decay. Fresh vegetables are crisp not wilted, firm not soft, and free of bruises. They have a characteristic bright color but are not overripe.

The size of the vegetable does not necessarily influence quality. Small carrots and tomatoes can be as fresh as the larger ones. Fresh vegetables are of the best quality when they are in season. The crispness, firmness, soundness, and bright color are good general clues that will help you select good-quality, fresh vegetables.

Canned Vegetables

The information on the labels will be your best guide to the quality of canned vegetables. Vegetables which have been canned according to United States government standards may have a grade on the label. The grade may be listed as a letter or a descriptive word. The quality grades of canned vegetables set by the United States Department of Agriculture are Grade A or Fancy, Grade B or Extra Standard, Grade C or Standard, and Grade D or Substandard.

Some canned vegetables may carry a brand name on the label to indicate the quality of the vegetable. A manufacturer may pack several grades of a vegetable and use a different brand name for each to indicate its quality. Your experience with brand labels will be your only clue to the selection of brands which are best for your purposes.

When buying canned vegetables, consider can sizes so that you will choose the size best suited for the purpose intended. Of the cans listed, the 303 can is the principal can size for vegetables.

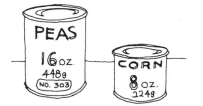

Most vegetables are sold in large and small size cans.

227 g (8 oz)	#303—454 g (1 lb)	#2½—822 g (29 oz)
250 mL (1 c)	500 mL (2 c)	875 mL (3½ c)
2 servings	4 servings	7 servings
		(for pumpkin, spinach, sauerkraut, tomato)

Frozen Vegetables

Frozen vegetables may or may not be graded. The information on the labels is your best guide to quality. Purchase only solidly frozen vegetables. Vegetables once thawed deteriorate in quality.

Dried Vegetables

Again, the information on the labels is your clue to quality of dried or dehydrated vegetables. It is not only important to select good quality vegetables, but it is also important to preserve their quality during home storage.

Care and Storage

You probably will not shop daily for your supply of vegetables; therefore you will need to store vegetables until they are used. It is important to preserve the quality of a vegetable during storage. With improper storage there will be loss of flavor, crispness, color, and nutrients. Good vegetable products cannot be prepared from poor quality vegetables. The method for storing will vary with the form of vegetable.

Fresh Vegetables

Most fresh vegetables are stored in the refrigerator compartment specially designed for this purpose. Before placing vegetables in the refrigerator, examine them carefully, remove any imperfect leaves, and wash to remove dirt and spray. When storage space in the vegetable crisper is limited, vegetables should be stored in a plastic bag or a covered container in the refrigerator. Several hours of proper refrigeration can restore crispness in vegetables to be eaten raw.

Tubers and root vegetables such as potatoes, onions, and turnips may be stored in a cool—7 to 10°C (45 to 50°F)—dry, dark place. Other root vegetables such as carrots and beets maintain their quality best when stored in the refrigerator.

During prolonged and improper storage vitamin C is lost and the color, flavor, and texture of the vegetable deteriorates. Most vegetables are at their peak of quality at the time they are harvested.

Canned Vegetables

Canned vegetables are stored at room temperature or in a cool, dry place. They will keep for a long period, but plan to use them within a year. There is some loss of nutrients and quality in canned vegetables when they are stored for a longer period of time.

Frozen Vegetables

Frozen foods keep best when they are stored at $-18°C$ ($0°F$) or below. They should be placed into the freezer or frozen food compartment immediately and kept there until they are cooked. Any vegetable which has thawed should be used immediately.

Dried Vegetables

Dried and dehydrated vegetables may be kept at room temperature on shelves. Opened packages should be tightly sealed or the contents transferred to a tightly closed container to prevent bugs or insects from reaching the vegetable.

The form of the vegetable determines the best storage method. The fresh and frozen vegetables are the most perishable and require refrigerator and freezer storage to retain their quality and to prevent spoilage, which wastes money. Frozen, canned, and dehydrated vegetables not only preserve quality but add to the convenience of using vegetables.

Convenience in Vegetables

Canned and dried vegetables have been with us for some time. The frozen, dehydrated instantized, and prepared vegetable products are rather recent developments that contribute to the convenience of vegetable use. Convenience foods are those which have been partially or completely prepared when you buy them. They eliminate the washing, peeling, chopping, cutting, shredding, shelling, straining, and simmering which are involved in vegetable preparation. Today, vegetable convenience items include prewashed vegetables and salad greens, shredded cabbage and tossed salad vegetables, washed and bagged carrots and spinach, and cut vegetables.

A long list of canned vegetable items is available but the frozen vegetable product list is even longer. It ranges from frozen vegetables, soups, boil-in-bag vegetables, vegetables in a butter or a special sauce, and prepared gourmet vegetable specialties such as spinach soufflé and artichoke hearts in lemon-butter sauce. Frozen potato products include grated potato patties, precooked french fries, hash brown potatoes ready-to-fry, and baked stuffed potatoes that need only to be heated for a relatively short time.

Dried beans and peas have been favorites for many years. Modern processing has added dehydrated vegetables to the large assortment of canned and frozen products. Dehydrated vegetables are used in dried soup mixes; dried processed potatoes, onions, and parsley are also popular. Dehydrated processed potato products include flaked potatoes, scalloped potatoes, hash browned, and au gratin potatoes.

As with other convenience items with which you are familiar, these require less time and energy, and in many cases cost more than a similar home-prepared product. Again you become the judge as to how good they are. Do their quality, color, flavor, texture, and nutrient values meet with your standards? How important is the time and energy they require? Would you use the same amount of time and energy by simplifying your menu? One- or two-dish meals may include nutritious foods which require only a few cooking procedures.

Convenience results from built-in pre-preparation but also from using cooking methods that require less supervision or pot-watching; from one- and two-dish meals; oven meals; broiler and pressure cooker meals; proper use of equipment and appliances; and good work habits.

However, convenience products serve many useful purposes and it is you who will determine how they will serve you. These decisions are yours to make in terms of your goals and needs.

Main Ideas

Vegetables, the edible parts of plants, are usually accompaniments to a main dish. However, they may be grouped in meals so that they become the main dishes themselves. They are especially rich in vitamins and minerals. The variety of vegetables is tremendous, and because of their many colors, shapes, flavors, and textures they are a valuable addition to any meal.

The acceptance of vegetables is directly related to the degree of success with which their original flavors, colors, and textures have been kept after the vegetables have been prepared. The degree to which the flavors, colors, and textures have been retained is also a good indication of the nutritive value which has been kept.

Today the market offers a wide variety of forms of vegetables. There are fresh, frozen, canned, freeze-dried, and dried or dehydrated vegetables which represent products from all over the world. The wide variety satisfies the many personal preferences that people have.

Activities

1. Browse through cookbooks and list different methods for preparing potatoes. How many of these have you tried?

2. Visit a local food market and list the fresh vegetables for sale. Record all available information concerning the price, grade, size, etc. How would you rate their quality and freshness? Why?

3. Examine the canned and frozen vegetable departments of a market. Which vegetables were available? What information was listed on the labels? How did the costs compare with those available in the fresh form? How did the nutrient value of canned and frozen vegetables compare to that of the fresh vegetable?

4. Examine magazines and note how vegetables are used and arranged to make attractive meals. Which vegetables are being promoted? Which recipes are available?

5. In what ways has your understanding and acceptance of vegetables changed? Why?

6. Select a green vegetable. Boil it in 125 milliliters (½ cup) of water; then in water to cover it; with and without a lid; only until fork tender; and then for thirty minutes. Compare the color, flavor, and texture. Write the directions you would recommend for boiling green vegetables.

7. Select a vegetable which can be purchased in several forms. Prepare each form by the recommended directions. Compare the flavor, color, texture, general appearance, time involved, and cost per serving. What influence does form have on characteristics, the time involved, and cost?

8. Select a vegetable. Prepare it in a way that appeals to you. Describe the method you used.

Questions

1. Name the various classifications used for vegetables and give two examples for each.

2. What nutrients are contributed by vegetables? What do these nutrients contribute to your diet?

3. What is carotene? Why is this substance important to you?

4. What nutrients are found in large amounts in dark green and yellow vegetables?

5. In what ways do vegetables add attractiveness to meals?

6. What changes take place when vegetables are cooked?

7. What are the principles or rules for cooking vegetables so that nutrients, color, flavor, and texture will be preserved?

8. What water-soluble nutrients are found in vegetables?

9. What occurs when vegetables are overcooked?

10. What methods would you use to cook each of the following: potatoes, spinach, cabbage, frozen corn, canned peas? Why?

11. How are vegetables used in meals?

12. What are the signs or clues to quality when selecting fresh, canned, and frozen vegetables?

13. Give three popular can sizes used for vegetables and the number of servings from each.

14. Describe the proper storage of fresh tomatoes, canned asparagus, frozen broccoli, and dried beans.

15. What is the place of convenience vegetable products in daily meals? How will they differ from homemade vegetable products?

Soups

Words for Thought

Bouillon
a clear soup made from beef or chicken.

Bisque
a rich cream soup made from fish, shellfish, or vegetable.

Chowder
a soup using fish, seafood, or vegetable such as clam or corn chowder.

Consommé
a clear soup usually made from a combination of veal, chicken, and vegetable.

Crouton
toasted buttered cubes of bread used as a garnish or topping.

Purée
the strained thick pulp and juice of vegetable or fruit. Also to force food through a sieve or colander to separate the pulp and juices.

Stock
the liquid in which meat, poultry, fish, or vegetables were cooked.

Soup-making is an art even older than the art of cookery. It began when prehistoric people placed whatever animal flesh they could find into a kettle and cooked it over an open fire. It was probably by accident that they discovered certain vegetables and herbs which made the soup taste better. The French are famous for their always simmering soup kettle filled with meat bones, herbs, and vegetable trimmings. As the story goes, the word restaurant originated in sixteenth-century France when a chef painted the name *Restaurant* over the door to advertise the soup being served.

Soups may be eaten chilled such as shrimp bisque and Vichyssoise, or steaming hot such as chili and minestrone. They may be rich in meats and hearty with vegetables, noodles, rice, or barley. There are soups that are appropriate for any season or meal. Soup may be used to begin a meal, or may be served as the main dish, almost a meal in itself.

Kinds of Soup

Most soups fall into two general groups: stock and milk. The soup made with stock may be clear such as bouillon and consommé, or it may have vegetables, rice, or noodles added. Chicken noodle, vegetable beef, and French onion are popular meat-stock soups. Cream of tomato, New England clam chowder, and oyster stew are popular milk-base soups.

Stock Soups

You can make flavorful soup stock from less tender meats such as the leg and neck sections. Bones and meat from beef and chicken are most commonly used for stock. Veal lacks flavor and is usually combined with other meats. Lamb and fish stocks have distinct flavors and are used only when these flavors are wanted. The meat is not browned for light stock but it is browned to make brown stock.

When bones and meat trimmings are simmered, the flavorings are extracted into the cooking liquid and stock is produced. The stock may be strained and clarified or cleared to remove any solid materials. The clarified broth is known as bouillon or consommé. Bouillon is made from meat broth while consommé is made from meat and vegetables.

The broth or soup in which meats were cooked will gel when cooled. Can you explain why this can happen? Some of the protein in connective tissues of less tender meats can be converted to gelatin when cooked in moist heat. Meat stock will contain some of this gelatin and will tend to jell when cooled. Concentrated meat broths from beef and chicken are used to form a jellied soup which is served as an appetizer.

Milk Soups

Cream soups are popular milk-base soups. A cream sauce made from milk thickened with flour to which strained (puréed) vegetables or seafoods are added forms a cream soup. Bisques are rich cream soups made with cream.

Most chowders and stews are soups made with unthickened milk and the fish or vegetables or a combination of the two are in small pieces. Some chowders, however, do not use milk; instead they are made with tomato and water. Stews and chowders are similar, except stews have fewer ingredients combined in the milk than chowders.

Nutrient Contributions

The nutrient values of soups are determined by the foods used to make the soup. Clear soups or broths will contain only dissolved flavoring substances or extractions from the meat and have little nutrient value. Such soups are valued for their flavor and are used as appetizers. You can increase the nutrient value of a broth by adding vegetables, meats, or noodles. What nutrients would these foods contribute to the soup? The vegetable would provide vitamins; the meat, protein; and the noodles would add energy. Hearty soups are made from stock to which other foods have been added.

Milk-base soups contribute the nutrients found in milk. Can you name the nutrient values of milk? The calcium, vitamins, and protein of milk make these soups nutritious. You may get part of your daily milk requirement from the milk in cream soups. The vegetables and seafoods used in milk- and cream-type soups will contribute important nutrients to your daily needs. You will need to know the ingredients or foods used to make the soup before you can judge the nutrients contributed. Soups can be made easily when you follow the principles of soup-making.

The foods which you have prepared up to now were treated so the flavors and nutrients remained within the food. When making soup, you will want the food flavors and nutrients to dissolve into the soup.

Stock-base Soups

Good stock is important to soup-making. Meats and vegetables are cut into small pieces for soup, and bones are broken or cracked so that a large surface area of the food comes in contact with the water. The nutrients and flavorings will dissolve in the cooking liquid giving you a flavorful and nutritious soup. You must protect the dissolved nutrients by allowing the water to simmer but not boil. Here is how to make good soup stock.

1. Use bones and less tender meats from the leg (shin), neck, or oxtail. One-third bone to about two-thirds meat is a good proportion for soup. Crack the bone and cut the meat and vegetables if used. The meat may be browned for brown stock.

2. Use a large kettle with a tight-fitting lid. Add water to cover the meat.

3. Use a long, slow cooking process to extract the flavors. The water should simmer but not boil.

After the simmering is completed, the soup is strained to separate the broth from the solid materials and is stored in the refrigerator in a covered container. The layer of fat which collects on top may be removed before the soup is used.

If you wish to clarify the broth, add a slightly beaten egg white and pieces of egg shell to the broth after it is heated to a boil. The egg protein will coagulate in the hot broth and trap any solid particles. The broth is strained to remove the coagulated egg.

Meat left from making soup is nutritious. It may be cut and served in the soup or used in other dishes calling for cooked meat.

Milk-base Soups

The milk-base soups may or may not be thickened. Cream soups are made with thickened milk while chowders or stews call for unthickened milk. The chief ingredients of milk-base soups are milk, other foods such as vegetables or seafoods, and at times a thickener such as flour.

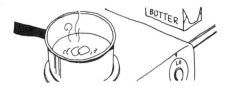

The principles of milk, vegetable, and starch cookery apply to cream soups. Remember that: (1) milk requires a low temperature to prevent scorching; (2) vegetables should be cooked in small amounts of water until fork tender to protect their nutrients; and (3) starch grains need to be separated with cold liquid or melted fat to prevent lumping.

The white sauce determines the quality of a cream soup. It is made with milk, flour, fat, and salt.

1. Melt the fat over low heat. Butter and margarine are most often used because their flavor is preferred.

2. Then, blend the flour with the melted fat to prevent lumping. Cook the mixture over low heat until bubbly to prevent a raw-starch flavor.

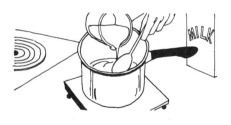

3. Remove the cooked fat and flour mixture from the range so that the milk can be quickly and easily blended.

4. Finally, cook the milk mixture over low heat with constant stirring until it reaches a boil and is thickened.

Uses of Soups

Soups can serve a double purpose. Their flavor and aroma will stimulate your appetite; the variety of foods from which they are made will provide wholesome nourishment. In your meals, you may use soups as an appetizer or as a beginning to your meal. At other times, you may use them as the main part of a meal.

Thin, clear soups are used as appetizers and are a good way to begin a meal. Their purpose is to stimulate the appetite for the meal which follows. Stock soups such as broth, bouillon, consommé, or jellied soups are popular appetizers. A hearty stock soup with vegetables, meat, or cereal products such as rice or noodles is used as a main dish. Chowders, gumbos, stews, and cream soups can be a meal in themselves.

Select the soup appropriate for the rest of your meal. If your meal is rich and heavy, select a thin, clear soup that will rouse your appetite. When you use the soup as a meal in itself or when the foods to follow are light, choose a rich and hearty soup. For soup at its best, serve hot soups very hot, and cold soups very cold.

Cream soups and white sauces are often used as an ingredient in casseroles, creamed foods, croquettes, and scalloped dishes. Clear stock soups can be used as the liquid for a gravy or a casserole.

Soups are served with crackers, croutons (toasted bread cubes), bread sticks, or melba toast. You can add eye appeal and a decorative touch to soups with garnishes (colorful bits of food) such as grated cheese; chopped hard-cooked egg; thinly sliced olives, lemon, or radishes; and crisp bacon curls. Soup as an appetizer or a main dish can make a meal more attractive and enjoyable; as an ingredient, it contributes to the convenience of meal preparation.

Soups can be made more decorative and unusual when they are topped with a garnish of your choice.

Convenience in Soups

Canned soups are a very familiar item and we often forget that they are a convenience product. Most canned soups are condensed which means that part of the water has been removed. When you prepare them, all you need to do is add an equal amount of water and heat to serving temperature. Some canned soups are not condensed and require no added water; they need only to be heated for serving. The label will indicate the type of soup in the can. Many varieties of canned stock- or milk-base soups are available.

Frozen soups and dehydrated soups are more recent developments. Frozen soups are condensed and must be kept frozen until you are ready to use them. You will add an equal amount of liquid (milk or water) to them just as you did to the canned soup.

All of the water has been removed from a dehydrated soup and all that remains is a dry powder-like mixture. It is easily and quickly reconstituted with the addition of water or milk and is heated to blend the flavors. Both stock-base and milk-base soups are available. They keep well on the shelf in their original containers.

The dehydrated instant soups eliminate the top-of-range heating and require only the addition of boiling water. They include a variety of stock-base and milk-base soups packaged in individual servings. The instant soup mix may be added as a seasoning to gravies, sauces, vegetables, and meat dishes.

Meat extracts compressed into cubes are another type of dehydrated soup. These cubes are commonly referred to as bouillon cubes and come in flavors of beef or chicken or vegetable. When they are dissolved in hot liquid, they usually make 250 mL (1 c) of broth. They keep well and are a convenience item to be used in a variety of ways. In addition to their use as a broth, they can be used as a base for a hearty soup or to add flavor to sauces, gravies, and casseroles, and even to other soups. Because of their flavor, they are often used as an ingredient in a variety of main-dish foods.

In this age of convenience, soup-making convenience is also available if you wish to make homemade soups. Ready-to-use fresh soup vegetables may be purchased in transparent bags. Using them will save you preparation time and the trouble of buying several different vegetables. Prepare homemade chili and vegetables soups in quantities larger than your immediate need and freeze them for later use. However, freezing will lessen the thickening ability of starch or flour and permit separation of homemade cream-base soups.

Home-prepared soups may require long, slow cooking or constant supervision. The convenience item can save time and be prepared with a minimum of supervision. You will need to read labels carefully so that you will purchase the kind of soup best suited for your purpose. However, a well-prepared homemade soup can be superior to the convenience item both in flavor and nutrient values.

Convenience soups may be used as an ingredient in the preparation of other foods. Condensed soups may be used in sauces, casseroles, or gravies. The condensed cream soups can replace a cream sauce or a white sauce in a recipe. Canned and convenience soup items can be blended, mixed, or matched to provide a variety of new flavor combinations and a variety of new uses. Your only limitation will be your own creative ability. Soups, as with all convenience items, may require less time and effort in making a variety of new dishes, but only if they are chosen carefully and used correctly.

Main Ideas

Soups are classified as stock soups and milk-base soups. The nutrient value of any soup depends on the ingredients it contains. While some soups are hearty enough to be used as the main dish, they are often served as accompaniments to a meal or used as an ingredient in preparing some other dish. They are conveniently available in dehydrated cubes, powdered mixes, and in liquid forms which may or may not need additional liquid added to them.

Activities

1. Examine the labels of canned, frozen, and dehydrated soups and see what information is given. How will this information aid you in selecting soups?

2. Compare the cost per serving of the same soup in its canned, frozen, and dehydrated forms. Why do you think there are cost differences?

3. Visit a meat market and identify the cuts of meat which are suitable for soup-making. How did they compare in cost? Which of these would make the most flavorful soup at the lowest cost?

4. Browse through magazines and collect and mount pictures which show the different ways in which soups can be used in meals. What creative ideas do you have for using or serving soups? For garnishing soups?

5. Select meat for use in soup-making. Prepare a meat stock. Use the stock to prepare vegetable or noodle soup or a soup or your choice. Serve the soup to your family in some attractive way. How was it accepted by you and your family? Describe your project and list what you learned from it?

6. Prepare a vegetable for use in a cream soup; prepare a cream sauce; combine the two to form a cream soup. Evaluate the cream sauce separately, and then the completed soup. Serve the soup in a creative way to your family. Describe your project and report the results.

7. Prepare and serve a jellied soup. Were you and your family pleased with the results?

8. Compare the nutrient values of cream and stock soups. Are soups nutritious? Do all soups provide the same nutrients? How do you account for the differences?

Questions

1. What are the two general types of soups? Give four examples of each.

2. How will you determine which soup to serve?

3. How is soup stock made?

4. In what ways do stock soups differ from milk soups?

5. What nutrients are contributed by soups?

6. What principles are involved in soup-making?

7. How is a cream soup made? How can you prevent lumping?

8. How does the preparation of meat or vegetable for soup differ from their preparation for use in a meal?

9. What are the uses of soups in meals? What soups are best for each use? Why?

10. Define the following: broth, soup, bouillon, bisque, chowder, consommé.

Chapter
16

Salads

Words for Thought

Emulsion
a thin film of a substance (such as egg protein) surrounding tiny droplets of a liquid (as an oil) so that they do not separate.

Marinate
to allow foods to stand in dressing or an oil and acid (vinegar, lemon juice) mixture to absorb flavors.

Succulent
a term which means juicy and is often used to describe juicy fruits and vegetables.

Accompaniment
something (such as a food item) that goes along with another.

Even though Caesar never knew the Caesar salad which bears his name, the Romans are given credit for inventing the salad. As the story goes, Roman emperors were served greens on gold plates. The Italians and Greeks mixed the greens with oils and herbs and this custom spread to Spain and France. The French and Spanish introduced salad to America. The merits of salads were recognized by German doctors who in 1758 prescribed different salads for each type of illness. In America, salads have gradually gained popularity and have developed into many specialty items. There are salads for every

269

Gelatin can be used for the body of a salad. Fruit, vegetables, or other foods can be added for variety of texture, flavor, and color.

This gelatin salad with cottage cheese and crisp vegetables is a complement to a light supper or lunch.

occasion. You will learn about the different types of salads and salad dressings and about their preparation and use.

Parts of a Salad

Have you ever tried to define a salad? As you just read, in the days of the Romans and Greeks salads were made from leafy green vegetables. These salads were similar to our lettuce or cabbage salads. You may also make salads from leafy greens and seasonings, but at times you might use the leafy greens as a base upon which to arrange other foods such as fruits or vegetables. The food or combination of food placed on top of the leafy greens which makes up the largest part of the salad is referred to as the body of the salad. To give additional flavor, you may add a salad dressing. Salads, like a triangle, consist of three parts: the base, body, and dressing.

Many different greens may be used for the base of a salad. Lettuce is most often used, but you can use endive, escarole, or watercress. Check the pictures on page 271 to see how many greens can be used in salads. Fruits, vegetables, meats, fish, poultry, cheese, eggs, and macaroni are examples of foods which are used in the main part or body of the salad. The dressing, the third part of a salad, may be French, mayonnaise, or cooked. Or you may prefer to flavor your salad with seasonings, vinegar, and oil. Salads are made from many different foods and they can be grouped into several types.

Types of Salads

Salads may be grouped according to the foods from which they are made or according to the way they are used in a meal. According to the foods which compose salads, they may be grouped as green salads, vegetable, fruit, meat, poultry, fish, egg, and gelatin salads.

Salads are also easily and conveniently grouped according to the way they are used in meals. They are used as accompaniments, main dishes, appetizers, desserts, and garnishes.

Accompaniment Salads

Salads are most frequently used as an accompaniment to the main course: the meat, poultry, fish, or casserole. These are

270

Salad Greens

Bibb Lettuce

Butterhead or Boston Lettuce

Iceberg Lettuce

Leaf Lettuce

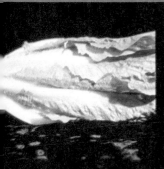

Romaine

Chinese Cabbage

Green Cabbage

Red Cabbage

Curly Endive

Belgian Endive

Escarole

Parsley

Spinach

Swiss Chard

Watercress

Chives

Main-dish salads are suitable for lunch or supper. This salad of seafood is satisfying and delicious.

Appetizer salads are less hearty than main-dish or accompaniment salads. Since they are used only to rouse the appetite rather than satisfy it, they should be served in small quantities.

A salad of a combination of fresh fruits and cottage cheese makes an attractive, sweet dessert.

light, small salads that stimulate the appetite. Salad greens, tart fruits, and combinations of raw vegetables as a tossed salad are examples.

You may prefer to use raw fruits and vegetables in your salads because of their crisp texture. However, cooked or canned fruits and vegetables offer variety and make suitable accompaniment salads. Gelatin salads with fruits or vegetables added are other possibilities.

Main-Dish Salads

The hearty salads are used as the main dish of a lunch or a supper. They are usually made from foods such as cooked or canned meat, poultry, fish, eggs, or cheese. Cottage, feta, cheddar, Parmesan, and Swiss cheeses are popular for salads. Hearty salads can also be made with kidney beans, potatoes, rice, or macaroni.

A less hearty salad such as tossed salad can be served as a main dish if thin slices of meat, poultry, or cheese are added. These foods will make your salad substantial and satisfying. Main-dish salads are, as a rule, larger in size than accompaniment salads.

Appetizer Salads

Appetizer salads are served at the beginning of a meal. Their purpose is to stimulate the appetite. They are light, small salads. You may use tart fruit, salad greens, and seafoods with a tangy sauce for appetizer salads.

Dessert Salads

Dessert salads are a colorful and attractive ending for meals. Fruits, gelatin, and frozen salads are suitable desserts. Canned, frozen, or fresh fruit attractively arranged and framed by crisp greens can be a picture-pretty dessert. Gelatin and frozen salads with a whipped cream base make an elaborate dessert salad. Dessert salads are sweet rather than tart so that they satisfy the appetite.

272

Garnish Salads

Small colorful salads are used as a garnish for a meat or a main dish. They add attractiveness or eye appeal to meals. Vegetables in interesting shapes such as wedges, rings, curls, and strips are used as garnishes. Small servings of fresh fruits, spiced or pickled fruits and vegetables add variety.

The role of a salad in a meal will help you to determine which ingredients to include, the size of the salad, and how hearty or light it should be. The salad also has an important role in helping to provide your nutrient needs.

Nutrient Contributions

The nutrients contributed by salads are determined by the foods used to make them. The fresh fruits and vegetables are important sources of vitamins, minerals, and cellulose. The dark leafy greens are especially helpful in meeting your needs for iron and vitamins A and C. When you make whole salads from greens, the salad can be counted as one serving of a leafy vegetable. The green leaf that you use as a base for a salad is too small to be counted as one serving of a leafy green.

Other foods used in salads include meat, fish, poultry, cheese, and egg. These foods are rich sources of complete proteins. Nuts and mature beans contribute incomplete proteins and add to your protein needs.

When compared with other foods, the caloric value of salads, in general, is low. The starchy vegetables such as potato and mature beans and cereal products such as macaroni are higher in caloric values than fruit and succulent vegetables. Potato and macaroni salads will contain starch and contribute to your energy needs.

The type and quantity of salad dressing will also influence the caloric value of your salads. The fat or the cream in the salad dressing is rich in calories. Some dressings, cooked salad dressing, for example, contain very little fat and are lower in calories than mayonnaise which contains more fat. You will find the nutrient values of other foods used in salads in the food nutrient chart located on pages 388 and 389.

Salads not only provide appetizing and interesting ways to serve fresh fruits and vegetables but contribute important nutrients and add crispness to your meals. These nutrient values should be preserved.

Depending on the main dish, garnish salads may be hearty or light. They should be nutritious, small, and colorful.

Principles of Salad Making

The principles of salad preparation are designed to help you protect the freshness, the nutrient values, the colorfulness, and the attractiveness of salads.

Protecting Salad Freshness

The freshness of fruits and vegetables will influence the texture, color, and flavor of salads. Fresh fruits and vegetables are crisp, have a bright color, and a pleasing flavor. When freshness is lost, they become limp, dull in color, and may become tasteless. You will best protect the freshness of fruits and vegetables by storing them in the covered vegetable compartment of the refrigerator. Salad greens begin to wilt or lose their crispness soon after the dressing is added. This is because dressing tends to draw out the juices from the fruits and vegetables. For this reason, you usually add the dressing just before serving the salad. However, the flavor of a few salads such as potato, meat, or fish will improve if they are mixed with salad dressing an hour before you serve them. This is called marinating the salad. For gelatin and fruit salads it may be better to pass the dressing at the table so that individuals can help themselves.

Protecting Salad Nutrients

You can protect the nutrient values of salads through proper storage, preparation, and use. Salad materials, especially salad greens, are perishable and should be used soon after purchase. Some nutrients are lost during prolonged storage. When cut surfaces of fruits and vegetables are exposed to air for long periods, there is some loss of vitamin C. Cut fruits and vegetables prepared in advance will retain their nutrients better when stored in a covered container. Wilted vegetables have smaller amounts of vitamins than fresh vegetables.

Protecting Salad Attractiveness

The bright color and crispness of fresh fruits and vegetables contribute to the attractiveness of salads, but you can enhance the beauty of these foods by arranging them attractively to form the salad. You become the artist when you make the best possible use of the natural color and shape of the vegetable, fruit, and other salad foods. You can create pleasing salad combinations when you include contrasts in color, texture, form, and shape. The color combination within a salad should be chosen with the same care that you select the colors for your clothes.

Salad ingredients may be cut to a size convenient for eating, but not so small that they cannot be distinguished. Salad materials should be arranged simply. Avoid the fixed look. Simple and natural arrangements are the most attractive and are difficult to improve upon. You should use a large enough plate so the salad does not extend over the edge. The salad should be framed by the plate.

You will be able to create more attractive salads when all salad materials are well drained. Excessive moisture on salad ingredients will dilute the salad dressing and cause an unattractive watery appearance. For a pleasing blend of flavors, use strong-flavored foods in small amounts. Protect the beauty of your salad by handling the ingredients gently to avoid bruising. Use citrus fruit juices such as lemon to prevent the browning of cut fresh fruits such as banana and peach. Remember, a clean, crisp, cool salad is an attractive salad and is a salad at its best. Well-chosen ingredients become your first step toward making fresh, nutritious, and attractive salads.

Selecting Salad Vegetables

A salad can be only as good as the materials from which it is made. When you shop for salad vegetables, select only top-quality vegetables that are sound, crisp, and firm. Poor-quality vegetables have lost their crispness, much of their flavor, and most of their nutrient values.

Salad greens are very perishable. Buy them only in quantities that you can use while they are fresh. Many salad greens are prepackaged in transparent wraps. Examine the package carefully and make sure that you can see the quality of the vegetable. All leafy greens should be crisp with a bright green rather than a yellow color.

Storing Salad Vegetables

After you have purchased high-quality, fresh salad vegetables and greens, preserve their quality by proper storage. The soil in which greens are grown may cling to the leaves and stems. Wash the greens in cold water to remove the soil, drain them thoroughly on paper toweling, and place them in a vegetable crisper, a lettuce keeper, or in a transparent bag for storage in the refrigerator. All washed vegetables should be well drained before they are stored in order to avoid spoilage by excess water. Handle greens and all other vegetables gently to avoid bruising.

Salad Dressings

The three basic types of salad dressings are French, mayonnaise, and cooked. The kind of salad dressing you use with a salad is your personal preference. However, some salad dressings seem to blend well with certain kinds of salad materials. Some popular salad and dressing combinations are French dressing with tossed salad, mayonnaise with potato or macaroni salad, and cooked dressing with fruit salad. Any one of these three basic dressings is suitable for most salads.

French Dressing

French dressing can be made easily at home. You only need to blend the proper proportion of vinegar, salad oil, and seasonings to make a French dressing. You may include the seasonings of your preference when you make French dressing. Homemade French dressing will separate on standing. You will need to blend the ingredients by shaking the dressing before it is used on salads.

Mayonnaise

Mayonnaise is an uncooked dressing prepared from vinegar, salad oil, seasonings, and egg yolk. The yolk will help to form a permanent emulsion so that the dressing will not separate on standing. The yolk, seasonings, and vinegar are beaten until they are blended. The beating is continued as the oil is added very slowly, at first, drop by drop. As the mixture thickens, slowly increase the amount of oil and continue beating until all of the oil is added and the mayonnaise is thick and smooth.

276

Cooked Salad Dressing

Cooked salad dressing resembles mayonnaise. It is thickened with flour or starch, and usually does not contain large amounts of oil or fat.

1. The flour and seasonings are combined by blending.

2. The egg yolk and milk or water are blended in. Then, the vinegar is stirred in gradually.

3. The mixture is cooked over very low heat, with constant stirring until it becomes thickened.

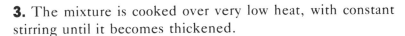

Other ingredients may be added to the basic salad dressings to increase variety. For example, chili sauce, catsup, or Roquefort cheese may be added to French dressing; mayonnaise may be blended with relish, horseradish, peanut butter, or tomato paste; cooked dressing may be combined with cream, fruit juice, or crushed fruit as pineapple. The flavor of the ingredients added to the basic dressing should harmonize with the flavor of the salad. All salad dressings should be stored in a covered container in the refrigerator to keep them fresh and to keep the refrigerator free of odor.

When you do not wish to make a dressing from the basic ingredients, you can use commercially prepared dressings.

Convenience in Salad Making

Many different prepared basic salad dressings and dressings containing special flavors can be purchased ready-to-use. The label on the container will list the ingredients included and is a useful guide for selecting the salad dressing you wish. A mayonnaise dressing is labeled "mayonnaise" to distinguish it from one labeled "salad dressing," a cooked dressing.

If you wish to have only a part in preparing salad dressing, packaged salad dressing mixes are available. The mix usually contains a blend of herbs and seasonings which you combine with oil and vinegar. The prepared mixes permit you to enjoy the flavors of herbs and seasonings which you may not use often and do not wish to purchase individually.

Salad-making convenience items include more than salad dressing. Washed salad greens and shredded cabbage can be purchased in transparent packages. In some food specialty stores you may purchase prepared salads such as gelatin, macaroni, potato, or fish. These salads need only to be served on a base of salad greens to be ready for use on the table.

The newest of convenience salad items are the freeze-dried salad mixes. These were first developed for use on space flights and are now becoming available to the food service industry. The ready-made salad mixes require only the addition of water. They are complete salads, the ingredients and dressing are all-in-one. The freeze-dried salad mixes include ham, tuna, seafood, and egg. These salad mixes keep well and do not require refrigeration until after the salads have been prepared for serving.

The prepared salad mixes and other salad convenience items can be kept on hand to meet emergencies or unexpected arrivals. You need to read labels carefully so that you can select the salad products which will best serve your purpose.

Main Ideas

Salads have three distinct parts: the base, the body, and the dressing. Since there are endless combinations possible for salads, there is always opportunity for being creative. The ingredients to be used in any salad determine whether the salad is to be an accompaniment, main dish, appetizer, dessert, or a garnish. The nutrients in salads depend on the foods in the salads.

Activities

1. Visit a local supermarket and notice the salad greens available. Which are best buys?

2. Browse through magazines and find examples of salads. Explain how each might be used.

3. Select one of your favorite salads. List all of its ingredients. Check to see what nutrients you will receive from the salad.

4. Plan a main-dish salad; list the nutrient values it provides. Select the other foods needed to complete the lunch menu and to supply the other nutrients that you would need. What nutrients will be provided by each food in your menu?

5. Prepare a cooked salad dressing and compare its flavor and texture with a purchased salad dressing which you have at home. Cook rice and cool or cook potatoes in the skins. Prepare the potatoes for use in potato salad or use the cooled rice in a rice salad. Mix one-half of the salad ingredients with the cooked salad dressing you made and the remaining half with the purchased dressing. Judge the two salads for flavor, texture, and acceptability.

6. Select a gelatin salad recipe and prepare it. In what way do you plan to serve the salad? How was the salad accepted by you and your family?

7. Prepare mayonnaise. Evaluate it for texture, flavor, and color. How does it compare with purchased mayonnaise?

8. Make a French dressing from a recipe of your choice. Select a similar French dressing mix and prepare it. Compare the two dressings.

9. What convenience foods, if any, are used in salad making? What are the advantages and disadvantages of their use?

Questions

1. What are the important parts of a salad? What ingredients are used for each?

2. Suggest two ways in which salads may be grouped and give an example of a salad for each type within the two groups.

3. What do salads contribute to menus that cooked vegetables do not contribute?

4. Compare main-dish salads with accompaniment salads?

5. How do dessert salads differ from appetizer salads?

6. What determines the nutrients contributed by salads?

7. Which salad foods will provide vitamins, minerals, and protein?

8. What are the principles of salad preparation?

9. How will you recognize good salad ingredients?

10. What is responsible for the attractiveness of salads?

11. How should salad greens be stored?

12. Compare the three basic salad dressings.

13. What ingredients can be added to the basic salad dressings to change their flavor?

279

Words for Thought

Knead
to manipulate by folding dough forward and rolling it back with the heels of the hands.

Gluten
an elastic substance formed (from the protein in flour) when flour is mixed with water. It gives structure to the baked flour product.

Cut in
to divide finely and distribute a solid fat by cutting with a pastry blender or two knives.

Carbon dioxide
a gas produced by baking powder or soda and an acid, and used to leaven flour mixtures.

Leaven
to make light or to force to rise by producing a gas.

Instantized flour
a granular all-purpose flour that blends easily with liquids.

Dough
a soft mixture of flour and other ingredients ready for baking.

Batter
a thick flour mixture of several ingredients beaten together and used in cookery.

Scones
a rich biscuit dough containing egg and sugar, baked.

Chapter
17
Quick Breads

The story of bread reveals the tradition of many lands. The crude hearth cakes of primitive peoples were carefully fashioned into the delicious hot breads of our day. The colonists were taught by the Indians to parch corn and to make thin corn cakes which were baked before an open fire. Hunters took the corn cakes on long journeys, and they soon became known as "journey cakes," and then later as "johnny cakes."

The waffle originated in England during the thirteenth century when a crusader accidentally sat on some freshly baked oat cakes. His armor flattened them and left deep imprints.

His wife was so thrilled with the way melted butter remained in the imprints that she ordered him to wear his armor and sit on the cakes each week! The flattened cakes were called "waffre" (flat, honeycomb-like). The Dutch brought waffre or waffle irons to America.

When hunters sat around their camp fires and fried fish, their dogs howled; to keep them quiet, they tossed leftover corn cakes to them. In this way the cakes became known as "hush puppies."

Crumpets and muffins came to us from England. Hot biscuits and spoonbread were served daily on southern plantations. Waffles, scones, popovers, muffins, and other breads have added variety to our daily bread. These delicious hot breads are known as quick breads because they are made with fast-acting leavening agents such as baking powder or soda rather than with yeast which is slower acting.

As you read this chapter, you will learn of the various types of quick breads, how to prepare and use them, and their nutrient values.

Types of Quick Breads

Quick breads are flour mixtures. They include many different kinds of breads which differ greatly in flavor, size and shape, and general appearance. Some are baked in an oven or on a griddle, and others are deep-fat fried. All of them can be made quickly and served piping hot. They are conveniently grouped according to the thickness of the batter used. Quick breads are of three types: pour batters, drop batters, and soft doughs. The thickness or stiffness of the dough depends upon the amount of liquid used in relation to the flour. Those with less liquid are stiffer than those with more liquid.

Pour batters are of a thin consistency and you can pour them from the mixing bowl. They may contain the same amount of liquid as flour or slightly less liquid than flour (250 mL (1 c) flour to 250 mL or 185 mL (1 or ¾ c) liquid). Waffles, pancakes, and popovers are examples of quick breads made from pour batters.

Drop batters are fairly thick and need to be scraped from the spoon or the bowl into the baking pan. They usually contain about twice as much flour as liquid (250 mL (1 c) flour to 125 mL (½ c) liquid). Muffins, biscuits, and some quick loaf breads and coffee cakes are examples of quick breads from drop batters.

Soft dough is thick enough to roll and shape by hand. It contains about one-third as much liquid as flour (250 mL (1 c) flour to 80 or 125 mL (⅓ or ½ c) liquid). Biscuits, doughnuts, scones, and some quick coffee cakes are quick breads made from soft doughs.

Quick breads are made quickly and usually baked as soon as mixed. The kind and proportion of ingredients used accounts, in part, for the wide variety of quick breads.

Ingredients Used

All quick breads, regardless of type, contain the basic ingredients of flour, leavening, salt, fat, and liquid. In addition to the basic ingredients in quick breads, egg and sugar are frequently used. Each ingredient contributes a particular characteristic to the bread and has a specific purpose.

The flour contains the materials which form the structure or body of the bread. *All-purpose flour* is used most often for making quick breads. When water is mixed with flour, a substance called *gluten* is formed from the protein of the flour. Gluten gives strength and elasticity to the batter or dough and will retain the air, steam, or carbon dioxide so that the bread can increase in volume. Cornmeal, whole wheat, and other flours are used in some recipes for flavor and variety.

Nonsift and *instantized flours* were developed to eliminate the need for sifting. They will give the best results when they are used with their own special recipes or when you make adjustments in other recipes as directed by the flour manufacturers. Most recipes in cookbooks were developed for use with sifted flour. Incorrect measure results in poor-quality products.

282

Salt in small amounts is used to improve the flavor of quick breads.

Leavening agents enable the quick bread to rise so that it becomes light and porous. *Baking powder* is the most common leavening agent used in quick breads but air, steam, and a combination of soda and acid are sometimes used.

Commercial bakers make selections from a variety of leavening acids, each designed to meet the special needs of packaged mixes and doughs, frozen batters, and a variety of baked products. Some of these acids are fast-acting (react in mixing bowl), others are slow-acting (react in the oven). A double-acting baking powder contains at least one fast-acting and one slow-acting acid ingredient. The double action refers to the release of some carbon dioxide during mixing and the remainder during baking.

All baking powders are made of soda, a dry acidic powder, and cornstarch. The soda of the baking powder will react with the acid ingredient it contains to form carbon dioxide.

Only double-acting baking powder is available for you, as a home baker. It contains two acid-reacting ingredients, a slow- and a fast-acting ingredient. One reacts in the presence of moisture at room temperature in the dough (fast-acting), the other reacts during baking (slow-acting). Some carbon dioxide is released during mixing, but most of it is released after the product is placed in the oven. The double-action baking powder requires both moisture and heat to release completely all of its carbon dioxide.

Baking soda and acid react rapidly at room temperature to produce carbon dioxide. You will need to work quickly when using soda and sour milk or buttermilk so that all of the carbon dioxide is not lost before the product is baked.

Milk is the liquid most often used in quick breads. However, *sour milk* or *buttermilk* is used in some recipes. The milk will dissolve the dry ingredients, salt, sugar, and chemical leaveners. Milk contributes to the flavor and browning quality of bread. You may replace fresh milk with *evaporated* or *dried milk*. You must reconstitute evaporated milk before using it by adding an equal amount of water to it. You may reconstitute dry milk to a liquid by following the directions on the package, or you may add it to the dry ingredients and then add the same amount of water (as milk) to replace the fluid milk.

The fat or shortening gives tenderness to the breads. *Vegetable shortening* and *lard* are bland in flavor, but *margarine* and *butter* contribute a pleasing flavor.

When *eggs* are used in quick breads, they contribute to color, texture, and nutritive values.

The kinds and amounts of ingredients you use will not only influence the character of the breads but also will contribute to the nutrient values of the breads.

Nutrient Contributions

The ingredients you use to make quick breads will determine their nutrient contributions. Flour is a basic ingredient of all quick breads and is the ingredient used in the largest amount. All kinds of flour are rich in starch and will contribute to your energy needs. In addition to starch, whole grain and enriched flours will provide the B vitamins and iron.

Milk and eggs are rich sources of nutrients and, when used in quick breads, will increase the mineral and vitamin content of the bread and provide some complete protein.

The fat and sugar in the bread add to its caloric value, while the salt and leavening make no nutrient contributions.

Quick breads which are made with whole grain or enriched flours contribute vitamins and minerals along with their caloric values.

Uses of Quick Breads

Quick breads are versatile foods and you may use them in several ways.

Griddle cakes and waffles are often served as the main dish of a breakfast or a supper. You may serve them with the traditional syrup and butter, or you may wish to serve them topped with creamed meat or poultry. The quick loaf breads come in many flavors (raisin, nut, banana, and others) and may be used for lunch or party sandwiches.

Muffins and biscuits are popular hot breads that add a special touch to almost any meal. They may be used as the breadstuff to complement the main course of any meal.

Drop biscuits may be used as dumplings for a stew, and rolled biscuits are used as a pastry for a meat pie. They are often used as a garnish or an accompaniment to a main dish.

You may be surprised to learn that quick breads are also served as desserts. Baked sweetened biscuits are used as shortcake, or the sweetened dough may be used as the pastry for cobblers, fruit turnovers, and deep-dish pies. Waffles or pancakes topped with sweetened fruits are also served as desserts.

Regardless of the way in which you choose to use and serve quick breads, you will get the best results when you apply the principles of quick-bread preparation.

Principles and Preparation

Success in the preparation of quick breads depends upon the kind and proportion of ingredients you use and upon the manner in which you combine them. Flour is the chief ingredient in all quick breads. In addition to a high proportion of starch, flour also contains two proteins: *gliadin* and *glutenin*. When you mix flour with water, a substance called gluten is formed from these two proteins. Gluten is an elastic substance which forms a mesh-like structure in the dough or batter that can surround the gases, carbon dioxide, air, or steam, responsible for leavening. The gluten will stretch as the gas expands until the heat of the oven coagulates the gluten, forming a fairly firm, porous structure.

The principles of quick-bread preparation are concerned with gluten formation. When you overmix and handle quick-bread mixtures too much, a large amount of gluten is developed and the breads become tough. Quick breads require little mixing and careful handling to avoid overproduction of gluten. You will use one of two methods to mix quick breads: the muffin method or the biscuit method which is also called the pastry method.

1. You will use the muffin method of mixing for muffins, waffles, griddle cakes, popovers, and for quick fruit and nut breads. The muffin method consists of first sifting the dry ingredients into a mixing bowl.

2. The eggs are beaten until blended in a second bowl; then, milk of room temperature and melted or liquid shortening are added.

3. The liquid ingredients are poured into a well in the center of the dry ingredients. They are mixed only enough to dampen the flour but not enough to make a smooth batter. When you overmix muffins, too much gluten will develop causing toughness and long, narrow tunnels in the muffin.

4. Carefully lift the batter into the muffin pan to avoid extra mixing. Your results will be a perfect muffin, one that is rounded with a golden-brown, pebbly surface.

1. Biscuits can be made quickly and easily. In the biscuit method of combining ingredients, you will sift together the dry ingredients (flour, salt, leavening) into a bowl and cut the solid shortening into the flour mixture.

2. The liquid is then added all at once and the dough is stirred with a fork until all of the flour is moistened.

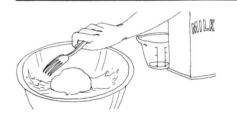

3. The dough is formed into a ball and placed on a lightly floured board. You knead the dough on the board (10 to 12 times) by folding the dough toward you and then giving it a light push with the heels of your hands. Then, rotate the dough a quarter of a turn, and begin to knead it again. During kneading, the ingredients are distributed more evenly and flakiness is developed. Overkneading will develop too much gluten and the biscuits will become tough.

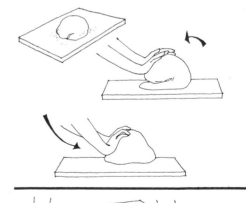

4. Next, roll the biscuit dough (1.2 cm (½ inch) or slightly thicker). Thick biscuits will be crusty on the outside and bread-like in the center; thin ones will be crusty and dry.

5. Dip the biscuit cutter into flour so that it will not stick when it is used in cutting the dough. Cut as many biscuits as possible from the first rolling. Each rerolling develops more gluten, making the biscuits tougher. They are baked on an ungreased sheet. Well-made biscuits have a golden-brown crust, a flat top, and are symmetrical.

Muffins and biscuits and most quick breads are best when they are served soon after baking, but with proper storage their goodness can be retained for some time.

These biscuits are perfect because the dough has been kneaded, rolled, and baked properly.

Care and Storage

Since quick breads lose their freshness rapidly, you should store them in a tightly closed container or sealed in moisture-proof wrap. The texture and flavor of quick breads deteriorate rapidly even under ideal storage conditions.

The freshness of quick breads is better preserved by frozen storage. Breads to be frozen should be packaged in suitable freezer wrap soon after baking. Frozen quick breads are a convenience and need only to be warmed for serving.

Convenience in Quick Breads

A wide variety of convenience quick breads is available: ready-to-serve, frozen, refrigerated, and mixes. Most mixes require only the addition of milk or water; others may include the addition of eggs. The frozen or refrigerated product may require baking or simply heating.

No standards or means for grading convenience quick-bread products have been established. Your only guide to quality and ingredient content is the information listed on the label. You should be familiar with the usual ingredient content of quick breads so that you will be a better judge of the quality of the convenience item. By using a variety of convenience products you will discover those which suit you.

Homemade quick breads are generally prepared in a short time. For this reason there may be little difference between the time required to make the homemade item compared with the time required to make the convenience item.

Convenience quick-bread items usually cost more than the homemade product. The frozen quick breads tend to be more expensive than the dry mixes, while homemade ones are usually the least expensive.

Most quick-bread mixes produce a reasonably acceptable product and can be better than mediocre homemade products. However, when you understand the principles involved in quick-bread preparation, you can often prepare products that are superior to a mix.

You can also prepare your own homemade mix by sifting the dry ingredients and cutting in the shortening. This mix will keep for several weeks at room temperature and several months in the refrigerator. It can be used for biscuits, muffins, waffles, pancakes, and coffee cakes. The home-baked products can also be frozen for later use.

You may want to keep convenience quick-bread mixes on hand for emergencies. In deciding which quick bread convenience item to use, you should consider the quality of the mix, the comparative cost, the time involved, and how it will fit into your situation.

Main Ideas

Quick breads have flour, salt, fat, liquid, and leavening as their basic ingredients. The quality of the quick bread depends upon proper mixing to insure gluten formation, handling, and baking. The nutrient value of any quick bread depends on the ingredients used. Quick breads are made from pour batters, drop batters, and doughs. There are many convenience forms of these breads, ranging from ready-to-eat, frozen pre-prepared, frozen partially-prepared, powdered mixes requiring the addition of both egg and liquid, and powdered mixes requiring only the addition of liquid.

Activities

1. Visit a bakery or the the bakery department of a supermarket and note the different quick breads available. Classify them as ready-to-serve, refrigerated, frozen, and a mix. Read the labels, note the quantity or size of container, and compare the cost.

2. Collect and mount pictures to show the different uses of quick breads in meals.

3. Collect recipes which include unusual ingredients in quick breads, or recipes in which quick breads are used in an unusual way.

4. Prepare homemade biscuits and compare them to a convenience biscuit. Note the cost, texture, flavor, size and shape, and eating quality.

5. Select an unusual recipe for muffins. Prepare and serve them. Decribe the texture, flavor, size and shape. Would you judge them to be of good, fair, or poor quality? Why?

6. Prepare a biscuit dough and use it to prepare a dessert. How did the dessert biscuit dough differ from a biscuit served as a bread?

7. Make a list of your favorite quick breads and compare their nutrient content. What did you find?

Questions

1. List the types of quick breads and give examples of each.

2. Name the ingredients most often used in quick breads and give the purpose of their use in quick breads.

3. What determines the nutrient contribution of quick breads? What nutrients are generally provided by breads?

4. What methods of mixing are used to make quick breads?

5. How does the mixing of muffins differ from the mixing of biscuits?

6. What principles are involved in making quick breads?

7. What is gluten? What is its purpose? What causes toughness in quick breads?

8. What are the different types of leavening agents? How is the action different in each?

9. How are quick breads stored?

Chapter
18

Yeast Breads

Words for Thought

Fermentation
the breaking down of sugar into carbon dioxide and alcohol by yeast.

Proofing
permitting carbon dioxide to develop in yeast dough as the dough doubles in bulk.

Canapés
small pieces of bread or pastry topped with flavorful spreads (meat, fish, poultry, cheese, etc.) served as appetizers.

Gluten
developed with wheat protein and moisture and gives flour the ability to retain leavening gases during baking to yield a light product.

Knead
to manipulate a dough-like mixture with a pressing-pushing motion accompanied with folding and stretching.

Bread has been known as the "staff of life" throughout history because it is one of the most important foods for people. Excavations of primitive life from ten thousand years ago show evidence of crude ovens and forms of bread. The first bread was likely a hard, flat loaf baked on a rock over a fire. The ancient Egyptians were probably the first to make leavened white bread. In the days of the pharaohs bread ovens were located in each hamlet, and people of wealth had their own private bread bakers. In England and European countries, the bread a person ate was a sign of social status.

These breads are now sold in many markets and bakeries.

Every nationality or culture developed its own bread. Vienna bread came from Austria and Italian breads from Italy; Limpa is a bread of Swedish origin and pumpernickel of German origin; the Jewish have Challah, and the French, brioche. Very special and elegant breads were reserved for celebrations. In southern Yugoslavia, no holiday, wedding, or christening was complete without Poteca. Kolache is a bread from Czechoslovakia, and Jule Kage is an interesting Christmas bread from Norway.

The shape of bread varies with the cultural background of the baker. The large round corn-rye is popular in Jewish neighborhoods; Jewish Challah is formed of braided coils; brittle bread sticks come from Italy; Greek kouloura is a ring; French breads are slim and smooth; and German pumpernickel is a dark, long, rectangle. Our American heritage has been enriched by all of these breads.

Classes of Yeast Breads

The wide variety of yeast products can be classified according to the flour used to make them such as whole wheat and rye, or according to their forms or shapes. Yeast products can be conveniently grouped by their basic shape such as loaf breads, rolls, and doughnuts.

Loaf Breads

The loaf breads are the most commonly used yeast products and include the plain breads which are known by their flour content as white, whole wheat, cracked wheat, and rye. Some variations of the basic white bread are raisin, cinnamon, and nut breads. Breads made from sweetened yeast doughs may be fashioned into tea rings and coffee cakes.

Rolls

Small pieces of yeast dough are shaped into rolls. Rolls are made from both plain and sweetened doughs and can be made in a variety of shapes. Rolls made from plain doughs are often used instead of sliced loaf breads.

Sweet yeast doughs are made into many fancy sweet rolls. Other foods such as raisins and fruits, nuts, and spices are often added to sweet roll doughs, and they are frequently frosted or iced. Sweet rolls are popular accompaniments to breakfast or salad lunches.

Deep-fat Fried Bread

The term doughnut refers to dough which has been fried in deep fat. The raised doughnut is made from a yeast dough, and the cake-like doughnut is made without yeast. Doughnuts are most often used as desserts or to replace sweet rolls rather than as substutites for breads.

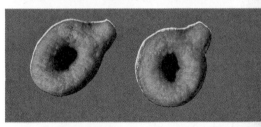

Crullers (Dutch for twisted dough), Nantucket doughnuts (small irregular pieces of dough), and Bismarcks (jelly-filled balls) are other deep-fat fried yeast doughs. You will find that all of these forms of yeast dough are made of the same basic ingredients.

Ingredients Used

Nothing quite measures up to the satisfaction and pride derived from a well-made loaf of fragrant golden-brown bread. This enjoyment and pride can be yours too when you begin by selecting the proper ingredients. The basic ingredients of all yeast doughs are yeast, flour, liquid, and salt; sugar and shortening are often used. Crusty, crisp breads as French or Italian bread are made with only the four basic ingredients, while breads with a soft crust use all of them. The ingredients used will determine the characteristics of the bread.

Flour

Flour is the chief ingredient of yeast breads. You will recall that flour contains two proteins, gliadin and glutenin, which form gluten when liquid is added and the mixture is stirred and kneaded. Gluten gives elasticity to yeast dough and permits it to stretch and retain the leavening gas (carbon dioxide) produced by the yeast. Flours that contain a high percentage of gluten-forming protein are well suited to making yeast breads.

Wheat flour is best for bread-making. The two types of wheat flour are made from *hard* and *soft wheat*. Hard wheat flour contains more gluten-forming protein than soft wheat and is best for yeast doughs. Soft wheat flour is best for quick breads. Hard wheat flour or bread flour is not usually available in local stores. A blend of hard and soft wheat flours called all-purpose flour is most often used in yeast breads. All-purpose flour contains enough protein to make good yeast breads and is soft enough for general home baking. Flour gives structure and body to the bread. It is important for you to buy a flour suitable for yeast doughs and to keep in mind the importance of enriched flour.

Yeast

Yeast is the leavening agent. It is a microscopic plant which can cause fermentation in sugar or flour to form carbon dioxide. The carbon dioxide gas can expand the gluten structure and cause the bread to rise.

Yeast works best at room temperature—27° to 29°C (80° to 85° F)—as it is quickly destroyed at high temperatures; low temperatures slow down yeast activity. All liquid must be cooled down to lukewarm (a drop of liquid feels neither hot nor cold when tested on the inner arm). After the dough is mixed, it is allowed to rise in a warm place.

Yeast is purchased in a dry, granular form or as a compressed cake. The compressed yeast requires refrigeration, but the granular yeast keeps well on the shelf. Granular yeast gives the best results when it is used within the date stamped on the back of the envelope. The directions for its use are also included on the envelope. Both granular and compressed yeast give equally good results.

Liquid

The liquid ingredient of bread is usually milk or water or a combination of the two. Breads made with milk have higher nutrient values, brown better, and have a richer flavor. The liquid provides the moisture needed to develop gluten and to dissolve the dry ingredients.

Salt

Salt improves the flavor of bread and controls the rate of yeast growth. It slows down yeast growth so that fermentation is controlled and the bread texture will be moderately firm. However, too much salt will inhibit the growth of yeast and produce a heavy bread.

Sugar

Breads can be made without sugar, but a small amount of sugar is a ready source of food for yeast and speeds up yeast activity. Avoid using too much sugar because this will slow down yeast action. Sugar helps the crust to brown and can contribute to flavor.

Shortening

Shortening makes the bread more tender and improves its keeping quality. Shortenings and cooking oils are often used and are bland in flavor, but butter or margarine may also be used and will contribute a pleasing flavor.

You will prepare the best breads when you use the proper ingredients and when you understand and follow the principles of yeast-dough preparation.

Principles

The principles of yeast dough preparation are concerned with gluten and carbon dioxide formation. The gluten forms the framework or structure of the dough and expands as carbon dioxide is produced by the yeast.

Gluten Formation

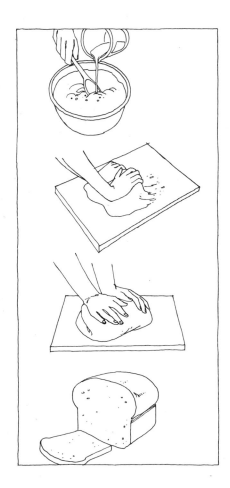

Gluten formation begins when liquid is stirred into the flour. The protein particles of the flour absorb water, swell, and stick together to form gluten. The gluten is further developed by kneading. You will recall that kneading is working the dough by folding it over to the edge nearest you and gently pushing it away from you with the heels of your hands. As you develop the gluten by kneading, it will form an elastic network throughout the dough that can hold or entrap the leavening gas (carbon dioxide).

When you first begin to knead the dough, it may tend to cling to the board; but as you work it, the water will be taken up by the gluten and the dough will become stiffer. The kneading is continued until the dough becomes elastic and satiny smooth with blisters of carbon dioxide showing under the surface. During baking, the gluten network becomes firm and contributes to the shape of the baked bread.

Carbon Dioxide Formation

The production of carbon dioxide by yeast is called *fermentation*. The yeast is able to change sugar into carbon dioxide and alcohol. Even though yeast plants may begin to grow while you mix the dough, most of the carbon dioxide for leavening is formed during the fermentation period. The dough rises as carbon dioxide is produced during fermentation. This process is called *proofing*. After the dough is kneaded sufficiently, place it in a warm spot so that fermentation can occur. Fermentation is continued until the dough has doubled in bulk.

You can help yeast produce carbon dioxide when you measure ingredients accurately and when you are careful to maintain the proper temperature. Too much salt or sugar can interfere with gluten formation; too much flour makes the dough too stiff. Too much heat destroys yeast; too little slows down yeast action.

296

You can help the dough retain carbon dioxide by kneading it sufficiently to develop a gluten that is elastic and strong enough to retain carbon dioxide. When the dough is not kneaded enough, the carbon dioxide is not contained and the bread is heavy and small in volume.

You will want to bake perfect rolls and bread, and you can, when you learn the steps involved in bread preparation.

Preparation

Several steps are required to make the perfect yeast breads. You need to use the right proportion of ingredients and to combine them in the order listed in the recipe. You must knead the dough sufficiently to develop gluten and permit it to ferment properly so that enough carbon dioxide is produced. The dough must be shaped correctly and baked in the right pan at the proper temperature.

There are several ways to mix yeast dough. You may combine the basic ingredients of flour, yeast, salt, and liquid, and usually sugar and fat, by one of three methods: the straight-dough method, sponge-dough method, or the batter or "no-knead" method.

In the straight-dough method, all of the ingredients are combined and the dough is kneaded and set aside to rise (ferment or proof). In the sponge method, the yeast is combined with part of the liquid, flour, and sugar to make a batter. This batter is covered and permitted to rise in a warm place until it becomes light and bubbly. The remaining sugar, salt, shortening, and flour are added to make a stiff dough.

Methods

1. In the straight-dough method, first add salt, sugar, and shortening to scalded milk. Allow to cool.

2. Then, mix one cake of compressed yeast with warm water.

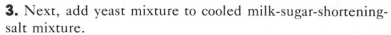

3. Next, add yeast mixture to cooled milk-sugar-shortening-salt mixture.

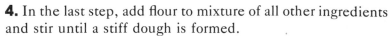

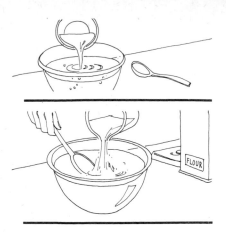

4. In the last step, add flour to mixture of all other ingredients and stir until a stiff dough is formed.

In the batter or "no-knead" method, all of the ingredients are combined but the dough is not kneaded and the texture is not as fine and uniform as in kneaded dough.

The straight-dough method, with a slightly larger quantity of yeast and salt, is sometimes known as the cool-proofed, cool-rise, or quick-action method. This dough can be held overnight in the refrigerator for baking on the following day. The dough retains enough heat so that fermentation (proofing) continues during refrigeration and it is doubled in bulk before the dough becomes chilled.

After the ingredients are mixed, place the dough on a lightly floured board and knead it to develop gluten. During kneading the gluten becomes firmer and more elastic.

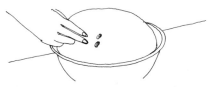

1. Put the kneaded dough or the "no-knead" dough in a warm place—27° to 29°C (80° to 85° F)—to rise or ferment. Allow to rise until the dough is doubled in bulk and an imprint is left when you press the dough with two fingers.

2. Knead the fermented dough gently to distribute the bubbles of gas more evenly. Then shape the dough into the form you desire, either loaves or rolls. The shaped dough is placed into a suitable pan and allowed to rise until double in bulk.

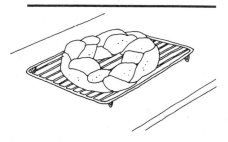

3. Bake the risen, shaped dough in a hot oven—200°C (400°F). The high temperature will kill the yeast and coagulate the protein (gluten) to produce a firm, porous structure. The alcohol produced by the yeast is driven off during baking. The bread will become crusty and golden brown with a superb fragrance! The baked bread will have a hollow sound when you thump it on top. Immediately remove the baked bread or rolls from the pan and place them on a wire rack to cool. If you wish, you may brush the top crust with melted butter or margarine. The crust will be satiny and soft.

Fresh breads not only contribute to eating pleasure but, at the same time, contribute to nutrient needs.

Nutrient Contributions

The nutrient values of breads are influenced by the ingredients used to make them. Flour is the chief ingredient of bread and contributes abundantly to its energy value. If you use enriched and whole wheat flours in yeast breads, they will also provide thiamin or B_1, riboflavin or B_2, niacin, and iron. When milk is used instead of water, it, too, adds to the nutrient value of breads. Milk will make bread an even better food since it is a rich source of calcium, riboflavin, and complete protein. Whole milk will also supply vitamin A. Some yeast doughs include eggs and their nutrient value is further enriched with the nutrients of the eggs.

Yeast breads are a rich source of energy and can make important contributions of vitamins and minerals to meet your daily needs. Bread is a nutritious food with a bland flavor that blends well with many foods. For these reasons, bread continues to be the staff of life and should be included in meals.

Uses of Breads

Ever since civilization began, bread, in some form or other, has occupied an important place at mealtime. Bread is used as a staple or to add festivity to mealtimes. Bread as a staple is served as an accompaniment to main dishes and as a base for some main dishes. Sliced breads and rolls are popular accompaniments to any meal. Bread forms the base of sandwiches which are often accompaniments to soups. Hearty sandwiches are frequently served as the main dish of a meal. Breads, usually toasted, are used as the base for creamed meats, poultry, or seafoods. Rolled yeast dough may be used for meat rolls and meat turnovers which are served as main dishes.

Hot bread or rolls as well as the many special uses of bread contribute to mealtime festivity. Bread is a base for fancy party sandwiches and canapés; rolled yeast dough is a base for pizza. Fancy rolls and tea rings are suitable desserts.

Whether you use breads as a staple or to add festivity to mealtimes and parties you will need to store them properly to retain their freshness.

Storage of Yeast Breads

Yeast breads like quick breads should be stored in a covered container or a breadbox to prevent drying and loss of freshness. It is difficult to retain the freshness of breads with prolonged storage. Storing breads in the refrigerator does not protect the freshness of bread, but will retard spoilage by mold. You will find it most satisfying to use bread soon after it is made. When you have an extra supply of yeast breads, it is best to store them in moisture-vapor-proof wrap in the freezer. Proper storage will add to your enjoyment of yeast breads and the many convenience yeast items make it even easier to enjoy them more often.

Convenience in Yeast Breads

Whole loaves of baked bread followed by sliced bread were among the first convenience bread items. Since then, many new convenience items, both of the quick bread and yeast variety, have been added. They include mixes, frozen, refrigerated, ready-to-serve, and brown-and-serve items. The frozen, refrigerated, and brown-and-serve breads need only to be warmed or baked. The mix for bread contains all of the measured ingredients except the liquid. Adding the liquid to the mix, stirring, and shaping the dough require little time.

There are so many varieties of convenience bread items that it becomes difficult to evaluate their quality, nutrient values, cost, and the savings in time and effort. In order to help you as a consumer, the United States Department of Agriculture has made a study of convenience items and compared them with similar homemade products. They found that the brown-and-serve and the ready-to-serve yeast rolls were the most expensive. Frozen yeast rolls were slightly more expensive than homemade items, but homemade items were still the lowest in cost.

The convenience product will help you to save more time especially when the home-prepared product requires many ingredients and several steps for preparation. When the home product requires few ingredients and is simply mixed, there is little saving of time when you use the convenience product.

Frozen homemade products are also a convenience. Yeast doughs will keep frozen for about six weeks, and frozen baked products for several months. Frozen baked products are more of a convenience than frozen yeast dough which requires thawing, shaping, rising, and baking.

You can also keep prepared yeast dough (covered to prevent drying) in the refrigerator for several days. You then need only to shape the dough and let it rise before baking. Yeast doughs may also be made with instantized yeast which is blended directly with the flour instead of first having to be dissolved in water before blending.

The use of convenience yeast products becomes your choice. When it is important to save time and effort, you may select a convenience yeast product rather than make the dough from the ingredients.

You should check the labels to learn which ingredients were used to make the yeast products. No grades or standards are available to assist you with your selection. You are wise to select yeast products that are made with enriched flour and those which also contain eggs and milk. Which nutrients will these foods add to your breads? From the many kinds of yeast products and convenience items, you will be able to enjoy a variety of yeast products.

Main Ideas

Yeast breads are similar to quick breads in their basic ingredients with the exception that yeast is the leavening agent rather than baking powder or soda. The correct mixing and handling influence bread quality.

Activities

1. Visit a supermarket and list the various types of breads and rolls available. What information is on the labels? How do the breads compare in cost, weight, and nutrient values? Which do you think is the best buy? Why?

2. Visit a bakery and note the breads offered for sale. How do the breads in a bakery compare with those sold in a supermarket as to variety, cost, nutrient values, and labels?

3. Which yeast-dough products are found on refrigerated shelves or in frozen food cabinets, and as dry mixes on shelves? How do these compare in cost, variety, and nutrient values to ready-to-eat loaf breads and rolls? Which of these labels give the most information?

4. Look through magazines and, when possible, find pictures to show unusual uses of yeast breads.

5. Prepare yeast bread using the straight-dough method. Keep a record of the time spent in mixing, kneading, and shaping the dough. Prepare bread from a mix and record time as above. Did the mix save time? Was it more expensive than an equal amount of homemade bread?

6. Prepare refrigerator rolls but save part of the dough in the refrigerator to bake later. Compare the refrigerator rolls with brown-and-serve rolls for flavor, texture, and cost. Bake the remaining refrigerated dough and evaluate it for flavor and texture. Can homemade refrigerated yeast doughs be considered a convenience?

7. Make a sweet yeast dough and use it to make cinnamon rolls. Compare the flavor, texture, cost, and quantity produced with a tube of refrigerated cinnamon rolls. Which did you prefer and why?

8. Which convenience yeast products are used in your home? Why are they used? What nutrients are listed on their nutrition information labels?

Questions

1. What is a convenient classification for yeast breads?

2. Which ingredients are used in yeast breads and what is their purpose?

3. What principles are involved in gluten formation? In carbon dioxide formation?

4. What methods are used to make yeast breads?

5. Describe the steps in making yeast dough.

6. How does the "no-knead method" differ from the straight-dough method?

7. In what ways does "cool-proofed" differ from fermentation? Give the meaning of proofed and fermentation.

8. What is the purpose of gluten in breads?

9. What are the nutrient contributions of bread? Which bread ingredients provide them?

10. How are yeast breads stored?

11. Which convenience bread products are available?

Chapter 19

Beverages

Words for Thought

Caffeine
the chief stimulant in coffee.

Decaffeinated coffee
coffee from which about 95 percent of the caffeine has been removed.

Volatile
evaporates easily by changing into a vapor.

Theobromine
the chief stimulant in cocoa and chocolate.

Steep
to allow a substance to stand in water below the boiling point to extract flavor and color.

Stimulant
any substance (such as a food component) that excites or increases body activity.

Beverages are a part of the American heritage. Our basic beverages of coffee, tea, and cocoa each emerged from a unique historic past, each from a different part of the world.

Coffee, a popular symbol of hospitality, was discovered centuries ago in Abyssinia. A herdsman, tending goats, noticed they were very lively after grazing on shrubs covered with red berries. He gathered some of the berries and presented them to the abbott of a nearby monastery. The berries were dried and boiled. The new dark beverage delighted the abott and his monks. They called it "kaffia" after the name of the bush. The use of coffee spread to Arabia where it was first cultivated and then taken by caravan to Egypt, Syria, and India. Coffee was introduced in Europe about 1500, and by the seventeenth century "coffee houses" were prospering in England and in the American colonies.

A disease of the coffee plant in Ceylon forced the growers to replace coffee with tea. Tea was served with ceremony and glamour for centuries in China and Japan and it came to England about 1666. The London coffee houses, unable to buy coffee, soon became "tea" shops, and the English became known for their afternoon tea. Tea was more popular than coffee in America until the Boston Tea Party, after which coffee became the all-American beverage.

In America, Cortez was the first European to taste chocolate. He learned that cacao beans were used as money by the Indians. The French, Dutch, and Austrians soon began to experiment with the beans. It was announced in a London newspaper in 1657 that a delicious West Indian drink, "jacolatte," was being sold in France. Chocolate houses became favorite social gathering places, and soon chocolate was served in America by the English colonists. Hot chocolate was said to be George Washington's favorite.

Today, along with coffee, tea, and cocoa, we regard milk as a delicious and nutritious beverage, and we can add a number of fruit and vegetable juices to the list. You will make your selection from a wide variety of beverages to suit your mood, the occasion, and the weather.

Coffee beans grow on leafy branches which also produce lovely white blossoms.

Kinds and Selection

When beverages first appeared in Europe and the western civilization, they were prized foods which only the rich could afford. Today, tea, coffee, and cocoa are staple items in nearly every home. Coffee is our most popular beverage, followed by tea, and cocoa. We drink about one-half of the coffee produced in the world.

Coffee

Most of our coffee comes from Brazil. A small amount comes from Latin America, Asia, Mexico, and the East Indies. Several varieties of coffee beans are blended and roasted to develop a special flavor. You will find that many blends of coffee are available and that they are sold under different brand names. You can choose whichever brand you like. Both the kind of coffee beans used and the degree to which they are roasted influence its flavor.

Even though it is possible to buy coffee in the whole bean, you will notice that most of the coffee offered for sale is ground and sealed in vacuum cans. Vacuum-packed coffee will retain its freshness longer than coffee not vacuum packed. During vacuum packing, air is withdrawn and the container sealed. The coffee which you purchase in paper containers will become stale in several days after roasting and grinding. Because ground coffee becomes stale quickly, it is best to purchase it in rather small quantities. Vacuum-packed coffee stays fresh until it is opened, and then, when it is exposed to air, begins to lose some of its freshness.

Coffee comes in four different grinds. The coffee grind you select is determined by the method that you plan to use to prepare the beverage. The regular grind is used for percolator or steeped coffee, drip grind for drip coffee, ADC for automatic drip coffee, and fine grind for vacuum coffee.

A special kind of coffee from which most of the caffeine has been removed before roasting is known as decaffeinated coffee. Instant coffee is a powdered form of coffee that dissolves quickly in either hot or cold water.

Tea

Even though coffee may be a favorite in our country, tea is probably the most popular beverage in the world. It is the national beverage of the Middle East, Asia, and the United Kindgom. Tea is grown in tropical climates; most of it comes from India, Indonesia, Ceylon, and Africa.

The leaf of an evergreen shrub is dried to make tea. The unopened bud near the end of a shoot produces the best tea, and the first two leaves are used for good quality tea. The quality of tea is determined by the size of the leaves, the variety of the plant, the climate, and the curing of the leaves. Green, black, and oolong are the three kinds which are made from the same type of tea leaves. The fresh tea leaves are steamed and dried to make *green tea*. Green tea is fragrant and has an astringent flavor. For *black tea*, the leaves are permitted to wilt, then are rolled, and spread on trays to ferment. During fermentation the enzymes of the tea cause a dark color and a

These tea leaves can be used to make green, black, or oolong tea depending on when they are picked and how they are treated.

mild flavor to develop. Black tea is less fragrant and has a less astringent flavor than green tea. For *oolong tea,* the tea leaves are withered and allowed to ferment slightly. This tea has the combined flavor and color of black and green tea. Oolong tea is usually imported from Formosa. Black tea is used most often in the United States.

The term pekoe often appears on the label of a package of black tea. Pekoe (shorter) or orange pekoe (longer) refers only to the size of the tea leaf and not to its quality or flavor.

Tea may be sold in bulk—114, 227, or 454 g (¼, ½ or 1 lb)—in tea bags, or as instant tea. There are several brands of tea and, as with coffee, you decide which brand you prefer. Some teas may include flavorings such as spices, orange peel, mint, or jasmine. The label will indicate the type, black, green, etc.; the form, bulk, tea bags, etc.; and any flavorings that have been added.

Cocoa

Cocoa and chocolate are made from the beans of the cacao tree which grows near the equator. Most of the cocoa beans come from Latin America and Africa. The imported cocoa beans are processed in the United States.

Chocolate and cocoa are made from the meat of the cocoa bean which is passed through rollers to form a "chocolate liquor." Bitter chocolate or baking chocolate is made from the chocolate liquor, semisweet chocolate has added sugar, and milk and sugar are added to make milk chocolate. Chocolate is sold in squares or bars, small bits or chips, and premelted in individual envelopes.

Cocoa is made by removing some of the cocoa butter as the chocolate liquor is squeezed by a hydraulic press. Dutch processed cocoa is treated with an alkali to make it darker in color and less likely to settle in the cup. The label will be your guide when selecting both chocolate and cocoa.

Both cocoa and chocolate tend to lose flavoring substances once the container is opened. You should purchase cocoa and chocolate in small quantities which you can use within a reasonable period.

Fruit and Vegetable Beverages

Fruit and vegetable juices can be prepared at home, or purchased canned or frozen, or sometimes in a powdered form. As

This bean will be dried and partly fermented before it is used to make cocoa or chocolate.

306

you know, the label is your guide in selecting canned, frozen, or powdered juices. Smaller fruits and vegetables and those less perfect in size and shape are usually used to make juices. Fresh, well-ripened fruits and vegetables will give you the most flavorful juices. The fruit and vegetable juices along with milk are prized for the nutrients they contribute, while coffee and tea lack nutrients.

Nutrient Contributions

Hot tea and coffee have a pleasant flavor and are stimulating and refreshing, but lack nutrient values. You may serve cream or milk and sugar with coffee and tea to increase their caloric value. The quantity of milk added is rather small and cannot be counted as a serving of milk. At times, a small amount of lemon is added to tea to enhance its flavor.

Neither tea nor coffee can replace your need for milk. As a beverage, milk is a superior source of the nutrients which you need for growth and which give vitality and glow to your appearance.

Neither can you afford to crowd out milk with soft and cola-type beverages which provide only calories and no other nutrient values. When you have too many soft drinks and cola-type drinks, it may affect your face and figure. Poor complexions and shapeless figures are the penalties paid for crowding out milk, fruit, and vegetables. Use your imagination to create new and interesting milk and fruit beverages.

Cocoa and chocolate contain small amounts of protein, starch, and minerals but large amounts of fat. The fat in cocoa and chocolate is called cocoa butter. Chocolate is a rich source of energy and gives many calories per pound. Most of the cocoa butter is removed when cocoa is made, leaving it with fewer calories.

The beverages cocoa and chocolate, because of their high milk content, offer you a pleasing way to include a portion of your daily milk. Cocoa and chocolate are considered to be the best hot beverages because of their high milk content. Milk-made beverages are wholesome and can be made in many different flavors. The flavored milk drinks include milk shakes and malted milks which are hearty enough to make a substantial contribution to a meal.

Fruit and vegetable juices, when used as beverages, add contrast to other foods of the meal and are a rich source of

Milk is too important a beverage to be crowded out by other less nutritious beverages which have more calories and may encourage tooth decay and poor skin.

vitamins and minerals. If the juices are diluted with water to make ades, for example, lemonade, the amount of nutrient becomes less concentrated and will contribute little to your nutrient needs. Fruit ades and punches are valued for their refreshing quality and versatility rather than for their nutrient content.

In general, beverages are stimulating and refreshing and contribute little to nutrient values unless they are undiluted fruit and vegetable juices or ones made with milk. Your greatest enjoyment will come from beverages which you learn to prepare using the basic principles of beverage preparation.

Principles

Everyone, including you, wants to make the perfect cup of coffee or brew the perfect pot of tea. The ability to make a good cup of coffee or tea is often regarded as the hallmark of a good cook. All beverages contain flavoring substances which give a desirable and pleasing flavor, and all, except milk and fruit-vegetable juices, contain stimulants (some in larger amounts than others) which can cause a bitter flavor. The principles of beverage preparation are concerned with developing a pleasing flavor and avoiding the extraction of too much stimulant. The way you will apply the principles of beverage preparation will vary with the nature of the beverage. These principles are grouped according to the three basic beverages; coffee, tea, and cocoa.

Coffee Preparation

Caffeine is the chief stimulant in coffee. The flavor substances of coffee are fat-like compounds called cafferol. Other substances called tannins, when dissolved, give coffee its bitter flavor. The perfect cup of coffee has a pleasing flavor without bitterness, is sparkling clear with a rich, dark brown color, and has a pleasing aroma.

The principle of brewing or making coffee requires that the coffee grounds come in contact with water just below the boiling point so that only the soluble flavoring substances can be dissolved without dissolving the tannins. When you allow the water containing the coffee grounds to boil, tannins will also dissolve and give a bitter flavor to the beverage. The length of brewing time will be determined by the method you use to

308

make the coffee. The method or coffee maker may differ due to personal preference or availability, but the principle for brewing coffee is always the same.

The methods for making coffee are known by the type of coffee maker as drip, percolator, vacuum, and steeped.

The *drip method* requires a dripolator which consists of three parts: lower section, filter section, and upper section. You may wish to preheat the lower section by rinsing it with hot water. You will add the measured drip-grind coffee into the filter section which is placed into the lower portion of the dripolator. Replace the top section and pour boiling water into it. Cover and allow to drip. You may remove the filter section with the coffee grounds when dripping is completed.

For the *percolator method*, place the measured amount of cold water into the pot and the regular-grind coffee into the basket. As the water is heated it will be forced through the tube and into the coffee basket. Allow the coffee to perk slowly for six to eight minutes. Remove the basket before serving the coffee.

When you use the *vacuum method*, you will measure cold water into the lower bowl. Assemble the upper part and place the measured amount of drip-grind coffee into it. Place it over the heat until the water rises into the upper bowl. After one to three minutes, remove the coffee maker from the heat to permit the coffee to return to the lower bowl. Remove the top bowl before serving the beverage.

Finally to *steep* or *boil* coffee, you may use any pot or pan with a cover. Measure cold water into the pan and add measured regular-grind coffee. Allow the water to come to a boil and then let it steep for two minutes. Add a small amount of cold water to settle the grounds before pouring the beverage.

The Perfect Cup of Coffee

You can make a perfect cup of coffee by whichever method you use when you: (1) use a clean coffee maker (stains in the pot will ruin the flavor); (2) begin with fresh, cold water for a good-flavored beverage; (3) use fresh coffee (ground coffee loses flavor quickly) of the right grind; (4) measure coffee for desired strength (15 mL (1 T) for each 185 mL (¾ c) water for weak coffee); (30 mL (2 T) for each 185 mL (¾ c) water for strong coffee); and (5) keep coffee warm and serve as soon as possible.

Tea Preparation

Tea leaves are placed in a teapot and then allowed to steep in boiling water which is poured over them.

Tea contains both caffeine and tannins and other flavoring substances. The principle for brewing tea is the same as for brewing coffee; that is, to extract the soluble flavoring substances from the tea leaves without dissolving the tannin which makes the tea bitter. A good cup of tea should be sparkling clear; the color should be amber for black tea, pale greenish-yellow for green tea, and light brownish-green for oolong; and the flavor will be brisk without any bitterness.

When you brew tea, you bring freshly drawn water to a full rolling boil. Use a clean china or pottery teapot and preheat it by filling it with boiling water. Do not put it over direct heat. Pour off the water and add the measured tea leaves—5 mL (1 t) or tea bag for each 250 mL (1 c). Then pour the fresh boiling water over the tea leaves, cover the pot, and let the tea steep three to five minutes. If you use tea leaves, the beverage should be strained into another preheated pot. The tea bags need only to be removed.

310

Cocoa Preparation

Cocoa and chocolate contain starch, cocoa butter, and the stimulant theobromine. Because theobromine is a milder stimulant than caffeine and because only a small amount of cocoa or chocolate is used to make the beverages, they are considered to be wholesome beverages. Principles for preparing cocoa differ from those used for tea and coffee. When you make coffee or tea the soluble substances are extracted into the water; but, when you make hot cocoa, the cocoa or chocolate is combined into the milk.

Because cocoa and chocolate both contain starch, you will need to recall the principles of starch cookery when preparing the hot beverages. The starch grains need to be separated with the sugar or cold liquid to prevent lumping, and the starch needs to be cooked to avoid a raw starch flavor.

When you make cocoa, you use milk and sugar in addition to cocoa, and therefore need to apply the principles of milk cookery. Try to avoid boiling over and scorching by using a low temperature to heat the beverage.

The perfect cup of cocoa will be smooth and well blended with a pleasing chocolate flavor. When you make cocoa, apply these principles of starch cookery.

1. Blend the sugar and cocoa and then stir in the cold water to separate the starch grains. When you use chocolate, the starch particles are already separated by the cocoa butter.

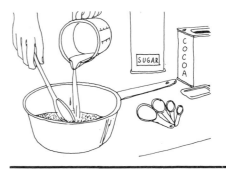

2. Cook the cocoa or chocolate mixture so that a raw starch flavor is avoided; as the starch is heated it will swell and thicken the mixture.

3. Add milk to the cooked chocolate mixture and warm the beverage to serving temperature. At this point, you will apply the principles of milk cookery by using a low heat to prevent scorching and boil-over.

Uses of Beverages

Beverages, like other foods, can serve more than one purpose in our daily eating pattern. You will serve them most often as an accompaniment to a meal, but they can also be used as special refreshments between meals and at parties, and as a flavoring ingredient.

Accompaniment

The basic beverages of coffee, tea, and cocoa are most often used as an accompaniment to a meal. You may serve them hot or cold, along with the main course, with the dessert, or at the end of a meal. On festive and formal occasions, you may choose to serve them in the living room as the conclusion to a meal. Milk, too, can serve a dual purpose; that is, you may serve it as a beverage and at the same time contribute important nutrient values to your meal. It is an important accompaniment to between-meal snacks. Regardless of the ways in which you choose to serve them, beverages are prized for their stimulating and refreshing qualities.

Special Refreshment

All beverages, including fruit and vegetable juices, are served as formal or informal refreshments. The occasion, mood, and weather will help you to determine which beverage to select and how it will be served. On occasions such as teas and receptions, the beverage is the center of interest and other foods are chosen to enhance and accompany the beverage.

The beverage as a special refreshment is very easily included in a simple, friendly gathering or in an elaborate and very formal setting. A good beverage adds something extra to any setting, be it breakfast, an outdoor barbecue, or an elaborate celebration.

A Flavor Ingredient

Cocoa, chocolate, and coffee are used in a variety of ways to add flavor to cakes, pastry, puddings, fancy frozen desserts, and candies. Fruit juices often add flavor to gelatins, puddings, cakes, cookies, and other beverages. Tea is a base for iced beverages to which fruit juices and other flavorings may be added. The color of the tea is usually not affected.

Care and Storage

The flavor and aroma of coffee, tea, cocoa, and chocolate are best retained when stored in air-tight containers; some of the substances which give beverages their flavor and aroma are volatile (can escape into the air).

Once the coffee bean is ground and exposed to air, it loses its flavor and aroma rapidly. When coffee is purchased in paper bags, its flavor and aroma will be retained best when you place it into a metal or glass container with a tight-fitting lid. Vacuum-packed coffee sold in cans will retain the volatile flavors, but once you open the can, they will gradually be lost. It is better not to purchase more ground coffee than you can use in a week because of the loss of flavor and staling which occurs. When you store ground coffee in the refrigerator or freezer, the loss of flavor and aroma will be retarded.

Tea, cocoa, and chocolate retain more of their original aroma and flavor when kept in a tightly closed container. Cocoa and chocolate contain fat and should be stored in a cool place. When chocolate gets warm, cocoa butter will rise to the surface and produce white spots.

As you know, milk retains its flavor and freshness best when stored in the refrigerator. Once you prepare fruit and vegetable juices, you should store them in the refrigerator in covered containers to retain their flavor and vitamin C value. You will recall that vitamin C is easily destroyed by air.

Coffee, tea, cocoa, and chocolate are valued for their flavor. Beverages will be most enjoyable if they have been stored properly. In addition to those which require brewing and preparation, beverages are also available in convenience forms.

Convenience in Beverages

All beverages can be purchased in a convenience form. Instant coffee, tea, and cocoa are available and require only the addition of a liquid. Instant coffee is a powdered form of coffee that dissolves quickly in water. Freeze-dried coffee is another form that requires only the addition of water.

It may surprise you to know that instant coffee is less expensive per serving than regular coffee. This is due to the fact that less green coffee is needed for the instant coffee than for regular roasted coffee. Because instant coffee is very light and takes up less space than regular coffee, it can be transported for less which reduces the cost of the beverage to the consumer. However, you may find the flavor of instant coffee less pleasing than that of regular roasted coffee.

Instant tea is also available. It is widely used for making iced tea because it dissolves quickly in cold water. The flavor of instant tea like that of coffee is not usually as pleasing and full as the beverage brewed from tea leaves. The tea bag eliminates the need to strain tea and is a convenience used by many. Tea is usually more expensive when prepared from a tea bag or instant tea than from tea leaves. Teas, flavored and scented, are higher in cost than unflavored teas.

Instant cocoa or hot chocolate requires only the addition of milk or water to form the beverage. Powdered fruit-flavored beverages and frozen concentrates require only the addition of water, while canned juices are ready for immediate use. Nonfat dry milk is another example of an instantized beverage.

Your guide in the selection of convenience beverage items will be the label. You will need to judge whether the convenience item saves enough time and effort to warrant any increase in cost and whether it is of an acceptable quality. Once again, the decision becomes yours. You are the judge, the one who will include the items that best suit your needs.

Main Ideas

In addition to coffee, tea, and cocoa, milk and juices are also basic beverages. There is a variety of each from which to choose and all come in convenience forms. Usually these products are served with meals or snacks, but they are frequently used as flavor ingredients in other foods.

Activities

1. Experiment by making a cocoa mix with cocoa, sugar, nonfat dry milk, and a few grains of salt. Write directions for its use. How do the ingredients of this mix compare with those used in a regular cocoa recipe?

2. Look through recipe books and magazines to find unusual uses for beverages.

3. Visit a supermarket and read the labels on beverage containers. What information is included? How does the information on convenience beverages differ from that found on regular beverage items?

4. Compare the beverage made from green and black tea for color, flavor, and cost. Which did you prefer? Make the same comparison for a variety of available flavored teas. What conclusions did you reach?

5. Prepare and evaluate cocoa using fresh whole milk, skim milk, and dried milk. Compare the flavor, color, and consistency of the beverages. Which did you prefer?

6. Compare brewed coffee with instant coffee and with the variety of flavored coffees available. Compare their flavor, aroma, clarity, and cost. Which did you prefer? Which was the least expensive?

7. Prepare coffee by steeping and then with an available coffee maker. Compare the color, flavor, aroma, and clarity of the beverage from each method.

Questions

1. What forms of tea and coffee can be purchased?

2. Name three types of tea and explain the differences between them.

3. Explain the differences between cocoa and chocolate.

4. What nutrients do beverages contribute?

5. What principles are used to make tea and coffee? Cocoa?

6. What are some values other than nutrients which are derived from beverages?

7. What other uses can be made of beverages besides using them for drinking?

8. How are tea, coffee, and cocoa stored?

9. How do convenience beverage items differ from regular beverage items?

Chapter
20

Fats and Oils

Words for Thought

Polyunsaturated fats
fats which contain fatty acids with several hydrogen atoms missing. They are usually liquid at room temperature as in corn, peanut, cottonseed, and soybean oils.

Saturated fats
fats which contain fatty acids with no missing hydrogen atoms. They are usually solid at room temperature as in butter, margarine, and meat fats.

Hydrogenated
adding hydrogen to unsaturated fatty acids to make them solid. Oils are then changed into solid fats.

Rancid
having an unpleasant, strong flavor such as that which develops in fats.

Fat
a greasy solid at room temperature composed of glycerol and fatty acids.

Oil
a greasy liquid at room temperature consisting of glycerol and fatty acids.

Shortening
usually a solid fat suitable for baking.

It is believed that primitive peoples tamed wild animals for the fat which they provided. Fats have played an important role in the struggle for food. Historically, fats have been a status symbol and have represented wealth and prosperity. The fatted calf was a sign of hospitality and merrymaking. Even today, during war and famine, fats are among the first foods to become scarce; when foods are in surplus, fats are the first to be used extravagantly.

Fat may be the chief nutrient in a food as in butter, margarine, and salad oils; or, it may be included in varying amounts with other nutrients such as in eggs, milk, and lean meats. Fats which are liquid at room temperature are known as oils, and those that are solid are called fats. The terms fat and oil both refer to the same kind of substance and can be identified by their greasy, slippery quality. The point at which a fat changes to an oil is known as the melting point. The melting point varies with each fat. The entire group of fats and fat-like substances are called lipids.

Fats are present in many foods and are often added when other foods are prepared. They are concentrated sources of energy and make other valuable contributions to your diet.

Nutrient Contributions

Fats are one of the nutrients which make up foods. You have learned about your body's need for carbohydrates, protein, vitamins, and minerals. You will find that fats, too, make important contributions to your daily needs. Fats are the richest source of energy.

They provide two and one-fourth times as much energy (calories) as carbohydrates or proteins. Because fats are digested more slowly than carbohydrates and protein, they keep you from getting hungry too quickly.

Your body can convert the fat that you eat into essential substances which it needs. Some of these fat substances are used to build cell walls. Body fat supports and protects the vital organs of your body, and is a reserve supply of energy. The layer of fat under your skin protects your body against excessive heat loss and in this way helps you to maintain a normal body temperature.

Some fats carry with them the fat-soluble vitamins. These vitamins are stable and are not usually lost during cooking. The fats in milk, eggs, butter, and margarine are important sources of vitamins A and D. Other fats contribute vitamin E, found in green, leafy vegetables and fruits, and vitamin K, found in cauliflower, cabbage, and pork liver.

Fats supply another substance called fatty acids. Your body needs them for growth and to prevent skin diseases. Two kinds of fatty acids are found in fats: the saturated and unsaturated. The saturated fatty acids have in their structure all of the hydrogen they need, while some hydrogen is missing from

317

unsaturated fatty acids. One of the unsaturated fatty acids, linoleic, is called the essential fatty acid because your body is unable to make it, and it must be provided by the food you eat. The fats which contain a large portion of saturated fatty acids are solid at room temperature while those which have a large portion of unsaturated fatty acids are liquid at room temperature.

It may be helpful for you to think of fats as being visible and invisible. The visible fats are butter, margarine, meat fats, oils, and cream. The invisible fats make up a part of foods such as eggs, lean meats, cheese, and whole milk. You may not be aware of invisible fats because you do not see them.

Fat in Food

Fats most often make up a part of other foods, but they may also be in a pure form such as salad or cooking oils. Meats contain fat even after you have trimmed away the visible fat. Milk and cheese contain butter fat. The richest sources of fat in your diet are the animal fats (beef fat or suet, lard from pork, and butter), vegetable oils (corn, cotton seed, peanut, olive, soybean), vegetable shortenings, and nuts. The vegetable oils can be hardened by the process of hydrogenation (adding hydrogen to break double bonds) to form vegetable shortenings and margarines.

The fat content of meat, poultry, and fish varies. Pork usually contains more fat than does beef, and fish contains less fat than do either beef or poultry. Fat is found only in the egg yolk. Foods prepared with fats and oils (cakes, cookies, pastries, and potato chips, for example) often contain a high proportion of fat. Fruits, except for avocados, and vegetables contain little fat.

Most of the fats in the diet are triglycerides, that is, are made of glycerol (an alcohol) and three fatty acids. When you fry foods at a high temperature, the glycerol of the fat is decomposed to acrolein which has a very unpleasant odor and irritates the eyes.

The fatty acids may be saturated or unsaturated. The unsaturated fatty acids have some hydrogen missing and then a double bond forms between the carbon atoms. When two or more double bonds are present, the fatty acid is said to be polyunsaturated and is often identified by the letters, PUFA. Animal fats contain more saturated fatty acids, while vegetable fats contain more polyunsaturated fatty acids.

Fat in the Body

When you eat too much fat as well as more calories than your body needs for energy, the excess is stored in special tissues (adipose) and leads to gain in weight. The fat stored in adipose tissues becomes a reserve source of energy.

The fat stored in your body as well as in animals represents the richest supply of reserve energy. Fat is stored at any time more food—carbohydrate, fat, or protein—is consumed than is needed to provide energy for your body. Americans generally obtain nearly one-half of their calories from fats. In order to lower the risks of coronary heart disease and atherosclerosis, the calories from fat should be reduced to 30 percent or less of total daily calories needed.

There is some evidence that eating too much fat can be harmful. When you eat too much of one nutrient or food you crowd out other needed nutrients. Too much fat in your diet can lead to a disease condition as well as cause added weight. Some scientists believe that a large amount of fat and/or calories in your diet can lead to atherosclerosis (thickening of the lining of the arteries) and an accumulation of a fat-like substance called cholesterol.

Atherosclerosis has been found in teen-age boys, is common in men, and may be a problem with women who are past middle age. Coronary heart disease often occurs when circulation in an artery leading to the heart is hindered by deposits or clots of fat.

Fats and cholesterol are identified as "risk factors" of coronary heart disease, a leading cause of death among Americans. You can control your intake of fat by removing visible fat, preparing foods without added fat, and avoiding frequent consumption of fast foods and other fat-rich foods.

Animal products (eggs, butter, lard, and meat) are rich sources of cholesterol, while foods from plants (fruits, vegetables, grains) contain none. Your body can synthesize or make cholesterol and use it to build compounds (bile acids) necessary in the digestion and absorption of fats.

Scientists also think that eating fats with a high proportion of unsaturated fatty acids, that is, polyunsaturated fats, can help to reduce the cholesterol level in the body. But these scientists also say that an excess of unsaturated fats (liquid at room temperature) can cause damage to body tissues.

Your best safeguard is to eat a well-balanced diet including a moderate amount of fat, both saturated and unsaturated. You

should guard against fad diets or diets which completely leave out any one food. A nutritionally adequate diet—one selected from the food groups—and that maintains desirable body weight is suggested for optimum health.

You should remember that fats are the richest sources of energy and that some fats provide you with fat-soluble vitamins and the essential fatty acids.

Kinds of Fat

The common fats used in food preparation are butter, margarine, lard, and vegetable shortenings and oils.

Butter is the fat of cream which is separated by churning. It is an excellent source of vitamin A and is rich in energy. Butter adds a pleasing flavor to other foods.

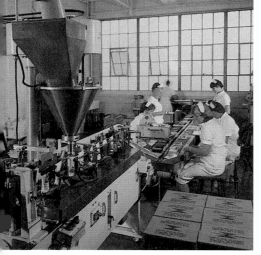

Hardened vegetable oils are churned with milk to produce margarine.

Margarine was developed as a substitute for butter. It is made of vegetable oils (corn, cottonseed, soybean) which have been partially hardened by a process called hydrogenation. The hardened vegetable oils are churned with milk to produce a product that resembles butter in consistency. Most all margarine is fortified with vitamin A and artificially colored. Some margarines also have added vitamin D. Margarine like butter is a rich source of energy and vitamin A.

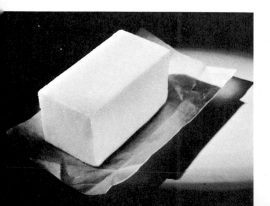

Lard is the fat separated from the fatty tissues of hogs. The fat which lines the abdominal cavity of the animal makes the best quality lard and is known as "leaf" lard. Lard is soft and is bland in flavor. It is prized for its shortening quality. It is a rich source of energy.

320

Vegetable oils are known by the name of the vegetable from which they are made. The commonly used oils are pressed from seeds or nuts such as corn, cottonseed, peanut, soybean, olive, and oil palm. Vegetable oils are sometimes referred to as salad oils.

Vegetable shortenings are made from vegetable oils by the process of hydrogenation. They are firm, plastic fats with a bland flavor. You will use these types of fat in a variety of ways when you prepare foods.

Uses of Fats and Oils

You can use fats and oils for many purposes in cookery. You can use them to add flavor, to prevent foods from sticking, to shorten and make baked products tender, to serve as a cooking medium, and to serve as the chief ingredient of salad dressings. Some fats are suitable for all purposes. Other fats may be used only in a limited number of ways.

Flavor

Fats add flavor and palatability to foods. You may prefer the flavor of butter or margarine for seasoning vegetables and sauces and as a spread for breads. Both butter and margarine will contribute a pleasing flavor to your cookies, cakes, and pastries. However, if you wish, you may sometimes use bacon and other meat drippings to season vegetables. (The flavor of bacon with green beans is popular.) You may also use meat drippings in cookery where their flavor enhances or blends with the food. When you use olive oil, it will contribute a distinctive flavor to salad dressing which is preferred by some. Most other vegetable oils are rather bland and have very little flavor of their own.

Fats can be used to season a variety of foods.

Shortening and Tenderness

In addition to flavor, fats contribute to the shortness or tenderness of baked products. The fat forms layers which separate the starch and gluten particles and in this way helps you to produce a tender product. Lard has a superior shortening value and is often used in making pies. Vegetable shortenings are also suitable for pastry, but butter and margarine have less shortening value. You will need to use special recipes when you make pastry with oil. Quick and yeast breads are made tender with fats and oils.

Plastic fats are important in the aeration of shortened cakes because air beaten into the cake is held in the batter by the fat. Vegetable shortenings are usually preferred to lard for cakes. Chiffon-type cakes require a special recipe and are made with oil. Cake recipes are delicately balanced formulas. You will be most satisfied by using a recipe developed for the shortening you prefer.

Fats help produce a tender and flaky quality in many baked goods.

Frying

You may also use fat as a medium for frying foods. Fat prevents the food from sticking to the pan and helps to distribute the heat. Fried foods become crisp, form an attractive brown crust, and absorb some of the flavor of the fat.

Pan-frying or sautéing is browning food in a small amount of fat.

Deep-fat frying requires a large amount of fat. Fats which have a high smoke point (can be heated to a high temperature without smoking) are best suited for frying. When you permit fats to smoke, they break down chemically to form substances that are irritating to the eyes and nose and have an unpleasant flavor. Use vegetable shortening, lard, and oils for frying; margarine and butter have a low smoke point and decompose quickly at high temperatures.

Deep-fat frying is cooking foods by immersing them completely in hot fat. You will use deep-fat frying for foods such as doughnuts and fritters, french-fried potatoes and onions, breaded or batter dipped poultry, fish, and seafoods.

For french frying you need a deep pan or kettle. A wire basket for holding food in the hot fat is useful. You may also use a deep-fat fryer, with thermostatic temperature controls.

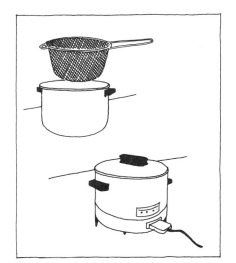

1. You may use all salad oils except olive oil (low smoke point), vegetable shortenings, and high-quality lard for deep-fat frying. You should fill the kettle or fryer one-third to one-half full of fat. The food should be surrounded by fat with room for the fat to bubble over the food.

2. Heat the fat to the temperature listed in the recipe before adding the food. Check the temperature with a thermometer unless you are using an automatic deep fryer. When the fat becomes too hot, the food turns brown and hard on the surface but may not be cooked in the center. It becomes soggy and grease-soaked when the fat is not hot enough.

3. Place a small amount of food (too much food will excessively cool the fat) into the basket and lower it into the fat. When the fat is allowed to become cooled, the food must be cooked longer and will absorb more fat than when the temperature suggested is maintained.

4. Remove the food from the fat and place it on absorbent paper to drain.

Salad Dressings

One of the chief uses of oil in cooking is for making salad dressings. You recall that the oil forms an emulsion in the salad dressing. Usually, oils with a bland or mild flavor are preferable for salad dressing. The consistency of mayonnaise and French dressing depends upon how well the salad oil forms an emulsion. The oil is usually dispersed (broken into small droplets by beating) in a small amount of acid and flavoring materials to form an emulsion.

Some fats and oils are suitable for several uses in cookery; others are best suited for a special purpose. You will need to consider the use for which each is best suited when you make your choice.

Selecting Fats and Oils

There are many fats and oils from which to choose. Your problem in selection will become a little easier when you consider the particular use of each kind of fat. The label will indicate the kind of fat or oil and the ingredients used to make it, but it will give you little information concerning the quality. Your experience with the various kinds will be your best guide. However, grades are indicated for butter and may be used as a guide to quality. Grade AA is the highest, followed by Grades A, B, and C. Good butter has a pleasing flavor and odor, and a smooth, waxy texture. Butter is usually salted unless it is labeled "sweet butter." This indicates that the butter is not salted.

When more than one kind of fat will serve your purpose you will save money by selecting the least expensive fat. Vegetable shortenings and lard usually cost less than margarine, and butter is the most expensive fat. The cost will vary among the various oils, and olive oil is usually the most expensive. Grade and quality will also influence the cost.

Whenever possible, buy a fat that will serve more than one purpose. For example, select a fat suitable both for frying and shortening purposes. It is unnecessary to purchase a wide variety of fats and oils. You need only a well-chosen solid fat suitable for both frying and shortening purposes, a table spread, and perhaps an oil. Fats and oils must be stored properly in order to preserve quality and to prevent any undesirable changes in flavor.

324

Care and Storage

Fats and oils will become rancid (develop an undesirable flavor) when they are exposed to air. You must keep them tightly covered to keep out air and to prevent the absorption of other flavors. All fats can pick up flavors when stored uncovered near fish, onions, and other foods. Vegetable oils and shortenings usually keep well at room temperature. Butter, margarine, and lard require refrigeration.

You will be able to reuse fats which are suited for frying when you handle them properly. Avoid overheating the fat to prevent its decomposition. The use of a thermometer is your only accurate guide to the temperature of the fat. Strain the fat to remove any remaining food particles before storing it. Store the fat in a cold, dark place, in a tightly covered container.

Convenience in Fats

Fats are available in several forms and the convenience comes from the manner in which they are used. Oils can be substituted for melted fat in most recipes unless you prefer the flavor of the melted fat.

Butter and margarine are available in sticks—4 sticks, .45 kilogram (1 pound)—and markings on the wrappers often indicate fractional liter (cup) and milliliter (tablespoon) markings. When precise accuracy in measurement is not essential as in cream sauces, puddings, flavoring, or seasoning food, you may cut the wrapper at the desired mark for an approximate measurement. Also available are butter and margarine which remain soft and easy to spread after refrigeration and which are a convenience.

Since most shortenings are partly precreamed making them softer and easier to measure, you do not need to soften them in preparation for blending with other ingredients.

Fats, except for butter and olive oil, tend to be bland in flavor. Flavored fats have increased the variety of available fats. You are able to purchase butter-flavored oils which will give a rich butter flavor to foods in which they are used. Also available are butter spreads with an added flavor, like honey-butter spread.

You should read labels on fat and oil products carefully so that you know exactly what kind of fat or oil products are available and which ones are most suited to your needs.

Main Ideas

Both fats and oils have a greasy and slippery quality. Although fats and oils are made of the same substance, fats are solid at room temperature and oils are liquid. Some foods are almost pure fat while others contain small amounts of invisible fat. Fats are the richest sources of energy. They are digested slowly, reduce feelings of hunger, offer protection to vital organs, and serve to insulate the body. Some fats also act as carriers for certain vitamins and essential fatty acids. Both fats and oils are subject to absorption of flavors and must be carefully stored.

Activities

1. Read the labels on cooking fat, margarine, and butter. What information is included? What ingredients are used to make them?

2. Read about the process for making margarine and report on it.

3. Some nutrition authorities claim we eat too much fat and especially too much saturated fat, and that we should cut down on our consumption. They also say we should increase our consumption of polyunsaturated fat while cutting down on total fat consumption without eliminating any one type of fat. How can this be done?

4. Make a display of different fats such as lard, oil, and vegetable shortening, and suggest suitable uses for each. Which ones of these contribute polyunsaturated fat? Why is it important to know which ones are polyunsaturated?

5. French fry potatoes in lard, oil, and vegetable shortening. Did any of the fats smoke at the desired temperature? Compare the potatoes for flavor and texture. Which fat did you prefer and why?

6. Make three small recipes of sugar cookies using a different shortening for each (margarine, vegetable shortening, lard). Compare them for texture and flavor. Which did you prefer and why?

7. Make three small recipes of pastry using lard, vegetable shortening, and oil. Compare them for flavor, tenderness, and flakiness. Which do you prefer and why?

8. Consider the three recipes you used in #7. Calculate the cost of each. Would the cost influence your choice of recipe to use? Why? Why not?

Questions

1. What is the difference between fats and oils? Give examples.

2. What nutrients are contributed by fats? Why is each needed?

3. What would happen if fats were completely lacking in the diet?

4. Give examples of visible and invisible fats.

5. Give examples of saturated and unsaturated fats.

6. In what ways is too much fat harmful?

7. In what ways do butter, margarine, lard, and vegetable shortenings differ?

8. What are the characteristics of a fat suitable for deep-fat frying?

9. Give the purpose of the fat for each of the foods listed: cakes, pastry, fried potatoes, cooked green beans, and mayonnaise.

10. What should be considered when fats are selected?

11. How should fats and oils be stored?

Chapter
21
Cakes and Frostings

Words for Thought

Shorten
to make tender with the use of fat or shortening.

Light
delicate, fluffy, and porous; not heavy or dense.

Emulsifier
a substance which improves the texture of a food product by distributing the ingredients evenly throughout the product.

Sponge cake
a delicate cake made without shortening, primarily leavened with air beaten into eggs (egg foam).

Chiffon cake
sponge-like cake containing oil and a high proportion of egg foam.

Frosting
a prepared sugar mixture covering the surface of baked products.

For centuries cakes have continued to be an important part of celebrations from the tiered and beautifully decorated wedding cakes to the birthday cakes studded with blazing candles. Cakes were thought to be fitting foods for the gods.

Have you wondered where and how cakes came into being? About 2800 B.C., a spicy cake similar to our gingerbread was invented in Greece. The Romans served cakes at weddings as we do today. One story tells us that a nun creamed butter, sugar, and eggs to make the first iced layer cake. Until about A.D. 1200, cakes were the shape of large puddings.

The pound cake originated in colonial America and was made from a pound each of sugar, butter, and flour. The chiffon cake, a blend of sponge and butter cakes, is the newest creation. The layer cake has developed into an American specialty and comes in many varieties. Take your choice from layer cakes, sponge and angel cakes, or holiday cakes rich with fruits and nuts.

Cake recipes have been carefully guarded for centuries and passed from generation to generation. But today, recipes for all types of cakes from many other countries can easily be found in many cookbooks.

Types of Cakes

Many cake recipes are available, some which include fats and others which do not. On this general basis, cakes can be classified into two broad groups: cakes with shortening and cakes without shortening. However, solid fats, when used in cakes, are combined differently and give a different cake texture than do liquid fats (oil). Because of this difference in fats, you will find it convenient to classify cakes into three basic types: shortened or butter, sponge or foam, and chiffon.

Shortened or Butter Cakes

The first cakes were made with butter and, therefore, became known as "butter" cakes. Since then, other fats such as margarine and vegetable shortening have been developed and used in cakes. Even today, cakes made with solid fats continue to be called butter cakes whether the fat is butter, margarine, or vegetable shortening.

Shortened or butter cakes are made by one of two methods: the conventional method or the quick method. They have a fine texture, and are light, tender, and moist.

Chiffon Cakes

Chiffon cakes differ from butter cakes in that they are made with oil instead of a solid fat. They have some of the qualities of cakes made without fat even though oil is used. They are made with a large quantity of eggs which gives them the lightness characteristic of sponge cakes; the oil gives them the tenderness of shortened cakes.

Foam or Sponge Cakes

Foam or sponge cakes are made without shortening. They are leavened with the air beaten into the eggs and the steam formed during baking. They have a light, fluffy texture.

Chiffon, foam, and sponge cakes will differ in methods of mixing and the proportion of ingredients used, but many of the same ingredients are used in all three types. Successful cake-making starts with proper ingredients.

Cake Ingredients

Some of the ingredients such as flour, sugar, and eggs are basic and used in all cakes. In addition to these ingredients, shortening, chemical leaveners (baking powder or soda), and liquid are required for butter cakes.

Flour

The flour provides the structure or the framework of a cake and is the ingredient used in the largest quantity. Cake flour and all-purpose flour are used for cakes. Cake flour has a lower gluten content than all-purpose flour. It produces larger, more velvety and delicate cakes than all-purpose flour, but either one will produce good cakes. The recipe will specify which flour you should use. When you want to substitute all-purpose flour in a recipe which calls for cake flour, you must remove 30 mL (2 T) from each .24 L (1 c). It is usually best to use the recipe specially developed for the kind of flour (cake or all-purpose) that you wish to use.

It is possible to make a successful cake without sifting flour when you follow the no-sift directions given for the flour you are using. However, for the most accurate measurements of flour and the lightest and most delicate cakes every time, you should sift the flour.

Sugar

You will recall that sugar gives flavor, improves texture, and helps flour products to brown. The recipe may call for brown or white (granulated) sugar. The sugar should be free of lumps. You may sift granulated white sugar to remove lumps, or roll brown sugar with a rolling pin on waxed paper.

Eggs

Eggs will improve the color and texture of a cake. When you first beat the eggs separately, they will help to make the cake light and fluffy.

Shortening

The term shortening refers to any solid fat, and any good quality solid fat may be used. Most shortenings are bland in flavor except butter and margarine which have a rich, pleasing flavor. The creaming quality of vegetable shortenings is better (due to the emulsifiers which are added) than that of butter. Shortening improves the texture, tenderness, and keeping quality of cakes.

Liquid

The liquid provides moisture and helps to blend the ingredients together. Milk is the most often used liquid; however, some recipes may specify sour milk or buttermilk, water, or fruit juice.

Leavening Agent

Baking powder or soda are the leavening agents used in butter cakes. Sponge cakes are leavened by beating air into the eggs and by the steam produced during baking. The leavening agent causes the cake to rise and become light and porous in texture.

Flavor Ingredients

A variety of ingredients such as spices, extracts (vanilla, etc.), nuts, chocolate, and fruits are used in cakes to produce definite flavors. The flavor ingredients are not classified as basic or essential ingredients, since their only purpose is to contribute flavor.

You should remember that cake recipes are delicately balanced formulas. To bake a good cake, you must not only begin with the proper ingredients, but you must also measure them accurately. When measurements are not accurate or you fail to use the proper ingredients, it is very likely that your cake will flop or be a failure. Also, it is best to have all cake ingredients at room temperature so that they can be well blended and air can be easily incorporated.

You need the proper ingredients and the correct mixing method to bake the perfect cake.

Principles of Mixing

The principles of cake-making are concerned with the influence of ingredients on gluten formation, methods of mixing or combining ingredients, and baking the cake.

Influence of Ingredients on Gluten Formation

The gluten of *flour* forms a network or structure which entraps the leavening gases (air, carbon dioxide, and steam). Cake flour is very finely milled and contains less gluten than all-purpose flour. For these reasons cake flour will produce more tender cakes with a finer and lighter texture. Unlike yeast breads, cake batters are mixed only enough to blend the flour into the other ingredients. Too much mixing will overdevelop the gluten and cause toughness.

Fat and *sugar* tenderize gluten and help to produce a tender cake. However, too much sugar or fat can excessively weaken the gluten structure and produce a heavy, coarse texture, and the cake may fall.

The *liquid* provides the moisture necessary to develop gluten and to produce carbon dioxide from the chemical leavening agent (baking powder or soda). Too much liquid causes a heavy, soggy cake.

The protein of the *egg* adds strength to the gluten framework. In foam-type cakes, the beaten egg incorporates the air which becomes entrapped in the protein of the gluten-egg structure. This air expands when heated and acts as a leavening agent.

Methods of Mixing

The way you combine the ingredients is as important to the success of a cake as the kind and proportion of ingredients you use. Even very slight differences made in the method given in the recipe which you select can lead to failure. The cakes may have coarse, heavy textures and sugary or sticky crusts. The method of mixing depends on the type of cake.

332

The two basic methods for *mixing shortened or butter cakes* are the *conventional method* and the *quick method*. You may find recipes that are variations of these two basic methods. The variation is usually in the way the eggs are added. The sugar and shortening are creamed in the conventional method, and many people think it produces cakes with the lightest and finest texture.

1. To make a cake by the *conventional method*, gradually add sugar to the softened fat and cream it until it is as light and fluffy as whipped cream. Remember that thorough creaming incorporates air bubbles into the fat and sugar mixture giving lightness to the cake.

2. The eggs, whole or yolks, are beaten into the creamed mixture until thoroughly blended.

3. Add the flour, sifted with the baking powder and salt, in four parts. Add it alternately with the milk which you will add in three parts. You should begin with flour and end with flour. After each addition of flour or milk, you stir only until the ingredients are blended.

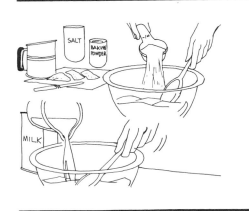

1. Cakes made by the *quick method* are usually made with vegetable shortenings. Sift together all of the dry ingredients including the sugar (flour, baking powder, salt, sugar) into a bowl. Be sure the bowl is big enough.

2. Then, add the plastic fat at room temperature to the sifted dry ingredients and part of the milk (about one-half, usually). The ingredients are beaten vigorously with a spoon or with an electric mixer at low speed for two minutes (300 strokes by hand).

3. Add the remaining liquid and the unbeaten eggs and continue beating for two more minutes.

The *mixing method for foam-type cakes* differs from that for *shortened cakes*. The beating of the egg and folding in of the flour are techniques used to make foam cakes. Foam-type cakes are divided into two groups: sponge cake which contains both the yolk and white, and angel food cake which uses only the white. To make foam-type cakes, you usually separate the white from the yolk.

1. The first step in making a foam-type cake is to sift and measure the flour. Many times, as with angel food cake, a part of the sugar is added to the flour and resifted. This makes it easier to blend the flour into the beaten egg whites.

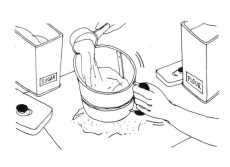

2. Next beat the egg whites until foamy and add the salt and cream of tartar. The beating is continued until the egg whites hold a soft peak. Add the remaining sugar in small portions—30 mL (2 T)—and beat it into the egg whites.

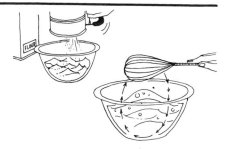

3. A small amount of the flour-sugar mixture—45 mL (3 T)—is sprinkled or sifted over the beaten egg and folded in gently. During folding, the wire whisk follows a circular path over the sides of the bowl, across the bottom, and up and over the top of the mixture. Folding should be done very carefully so that the air bubbles are not broken. Foam cakes are leavened with air which has been beaten into egg whites and with steam which forms during baking.

334

Oil and beaten egg whites are among the ingredients used in *mixing chiffon cakes*. For this reason, they have some of the characteristics of both shortened and foam cakes.

As in the quick method, the dry ingredients, including part of the sugar are sifted into a bowl. The unbeaten egg yolk, liquid, and flavoring are added to the dry ingredients and the mixture is beaten until smooth. Then, as with foam-type cakes, the egg whites and cream of tartar are beaten to form soft peaks. The remaining sugar is added to the whites gradually, and they are beaten until the mixture forms a stiff peak. The egg whites are folded carefully into the yolk-oil-flour mixture. The beaten eggs give lightness to chiffon cakes and the oil adds tenderness.

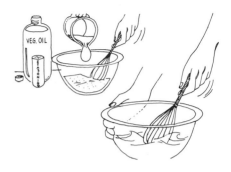

Baking Cakes

Your success in making a cake not only depends upon the ingredients used and the mixing method but also upon the way it is baked. Your recipe will give you the specific directions for the kind and size of pans to use, the oven temperature, and the baking time.

For the best results, select the pan size and shape suggested by your recipe. When you bake cake in pans which are too large, the cake will not brown well; and when the pan is too small, the cake batter may flow over the sides of the pan. Cake pans with a light, dull finish such as aluminum are used successfully for cakes. Dark pans cause a dark heavy crust to form.

You should prepare the pan for the cake batter before you mix the cake. The pans for shortened cakes are prepared by greasing the bottom of the pan and lightly dusting it with flour, or by lining the bottom of the pan with waxed paper cut to fit. Place the pan on a piece of waxed paper, and with the point of the scissors trace the outline of the pan before cutting the paper. The sides of the pan should not be greased. Foam-type cake batter is poured into clean pans which require no further preparation.

The cake batter should be divided evenly when a layer cake is to be baked. The pans are usually filled one-half full. After the batter is in the pan, push the batter from the center to the sides of the pan, leaving a slight depression in the center. In this way, the baked cake will have a slightly rounded top rather than a hump in the center.

Cakes should be baked as quickly as possible after being mixed. Your recipe will give you the oven temperature and baking time. You should place the cake into a preheated oven set for the correct temperature. Too hot an oven will cause peaks and the cake may crack on top. When the oven is too cool, the cake will not rise or brown properly.

Arrange the pans so that the oven heat can circulate freely around the pans. Place the pans so that there is at least 2.5 cm (1 in) of space between the pans and from the sides of the oven. When you use more than one oven rack, never place the pans directly above or below each other.

You can bake shortened cakes fast in a microwave oven. The texture will be all right but the cake will not brown. Electrical units found in some electronic ovens give an uneven browning.

At the end of the minimum baking time given in the recipe, *check* the cake *for doneness*. Notice if the cake is evenly browned and has begun to pull away from the sides of the pan.

1. Lightly touch the center of the cake with your finger tip; if no impression remains, the cake is done.

2. The cake is done when a toothpick inserted in the center of the cake comes out clean. Overbaking will cause a dry, toughened cake.

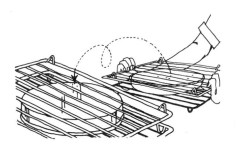

3. After the shortened cake is baked, place it on a wire rack to cool for about ten minutes. Then loosen the edges of the cake with a spatula.

4. Place the cake pan between two cooling racks and invert.

336

5. Carefully remove the cake pan from the cake. Again invert the cake between two racks so that the top of the cake faces you. Remove the top rack and permit the cake to cool before frosting it.

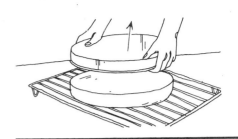

6. You should allow foam and chiffon cakes to remain in the baking pan until they are completely cooled. These cakes are very delicate and may collapse if they are not permitted to remain in an inverted pan until they are cooled and firm.

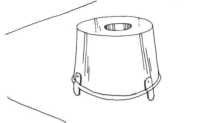

Frostings

Frostings are concentrated sugar mixtures, either cooked or uncooked. They make cakes attractive and help to keep them moist. Most cakes are frosted, but chiffon and foam cakes are sometimes served without frosting.

Cooked Frostings

Cooked frostings are similar to candy but require a shorter cooking period. The principles of cooked frostings deal with the formation of small sugar crystals so that the frosting will have a smooth texture. The sugar mixture must be cooked to the correct temperature (fudge-type, or syrup-type frostings) so that the frosting will be of the proper consistency for spreading and will remain on the cake. A candy thermometer is your best guide to the temperature of cooked sugar mixtures. When you allow the sugar mixture to cook too long, the frosting becomes hard and sugary; when it is not cooked enough, the frosting remains too soft. You must cool fudge-type frostings before they are beaten to avoid the formation of large crystals. After the syrup-type frostings reach the correct temperature and are cooled, you beat the cooled syrup into stiffly beaten egg whites.

The seven-minute frosting is a variation of the syrup-type frosting. The sugar, water, and egg whites are beaten over boiling water until the mixture stands up in peaks. This frosting is called the seven-minute frosting because seven minutes of cooking time are usually required to reach the "peak" stage, or be of the right consistency to spread.

Uncooked Frostings

Uncooked frostings are mixtures of confectioners' (powdered) sugar. The sugar is combined with a liquid and often with margarine or butter. The liquid may be milk, cream, fruit juice, or others. The thickness of an uncooked frosting is determined by the amount of liquid you use. Uncooked frosting containing fat such as butter, margarine, or chocolate remains soft longer than the type made only with liquid. Uncooked frostings will become creamy with vigorous beating.

Cake frostings are not difficult to make when you follow the directions given in the recipe and apply the principles of sugar cookery.

Frosting the Cake

A beautifully frosted cake can be yours when you follow these suggestions. Be sure the cake is cool and brush the loose crumbs from the sides of the cake before you begin to frost it.

1. Place the first layer upside down on the plate. You may arrange narrow strips of waxed paper under the cake edge to keep the plate clean. Place frosting in the center of the layer and spread it evenly to the edge.

2. Arrange top layer, bottom side down, on the frosted layer. Frost sides with a spatula.

3. Place frosting on the top layer, and make swirls with spatula or back of spoon. Remove the paper strips, if you have used them.

You will enjoy your cake even to the last crumb when you store it properly so that it is fresh and moist.

Storage of Cakes

If you plan to use the cake within a short time, store it in a regular cake saver. Should you wish to keep the cake for several days, wrap it gently in foil or transparent wrap and place it in the refrigerator. Cakes with custard or cream fillings should be stored covered in the refrigerator. Cakes may be frozen and stored for later use. Place the cake in the freezer to harden the frosting and then wrap it with moisture-proof paper for storage in the freezer.

Nutrient Contributions

Cakes are usually served at the end of a meal since their sweet flavor and high caloric content will satisfy the appetite. The nutrient value of cakes will vary somewhat with the ingredients used. Cakes made with enriched flour and milk have the added nutrients of flour and milk. However, the quantity of milk or egg you get in a piece of cake is very small and cannot be considered an important source of these foods.

Because of the high proportion of sugar, starch, and fat in shortened cakes, the main contribution of cakes is their calories. Foam cakes, with their much higher proportion of egg, are a somewhat better source of nutrients than shortened cakes. Cake frostings are primarily sugar and contribute only calories. You may eat cakes without frosting and in this way receive fewer calories. Foam or sponge cakes, because they do not contain fat, will contribute fewer calories than shortened or chiffon cakes.

The many convenience cake items make it easy for you to bake a cake quickly, even at a moment's notice.

Convenience

Among the convenience cake items you will find dry cake mixes, ready-to-eat, and frozen products. Shortened cakes are available in an endless variety of flavors. Foam and chiffon cakes are included. Cake frosting convenience comes as a dry mix or in the ready-to-spread form.

Cake mixes are made of the same ingredients basic to all cakes, but in addition may include emulsifiers which contribute to the soft texture of cakes and preservatives which extend the shelf life of the mix. When you use a cake mix, you add the liquid (water or milk) and at times you may add the egg.

Convenience cake items do save time. The ready-to-eat product saves the greatest amount of time, but is usually the most expensive. Some frozen cake products may be more expensive than the ready-to-eat items. A complete cake mix (requiring only the addition of water) and the home-prepared item may cost about the same. Some cake mixes may be less expensive than the home-prepared product. You should compare the cost of convenience cakes with similar home-prepared cakes, and in this way learn which products best fit your food budget.

The quality of cake mixes and other convenience items varies greatly. The label shows the ingredients used but gives no information regarding quality. Here again, it is only through your use of these convenience items that you will be able to judge their quality. It is possible that a mix could result in a better cake than one made by an inexperienced person. The quality of a home-prepared cake will vary with the experience of the person making the cake. An experienced person can produce a cake that is superior to a mix. The quality of the packaged mix, of course, will have its influence.

When you use cake and frosting mixes, you will get the best results when you follow *all* of the instructions on the package. Remember that all cake recipes are balanced formulas; you should not add extra ingredients to cake mixes, except flavor ingredients such as extracts (vanilla, etc.), spices, coconut, or chopped nuts. The creativity and variation which you provide should come from the frosting or filling, the decoration, or the way in which you serve the cake. You may want to experiment and develop special additions of your own.

You can provide homemade convenience cake items for yourself. You may freeze shortened cakes either as a batter or after they have been baked. However, the volume may be slightly less when cake is made from a frozen batter. You may freeze angel food cake batter in the baking pan but not sponge cake batter. Cakes with frosting may be frozen first (prevents frosting from sticking to paper) and then wrapped for freezer storage.

After considering time, cost, quality, and your own personal preferences, you will be ready to select the cake products that fit your circumstances and your plans best. Comparison of the products will be important in making final choices.

Main Ideas

Cakes are classified as butter, sponge or foam, and chiffon. The ingredients vary somewhat with these various types but flour, sugar, and eggs are basic to all. Successful cake baking depends on accurate measurements, proper blending of ingredients, proper pan sizes, accurate baking procedures, and accuracy in testing for a cake's doneness. Convenience forms, readily available in ready-to-eat, frozen, and partially prepared, may vary in quality, size, cost, and ways to be used. Calories are the major contribution of cake to the diet. Frostings are concentrated sugar mixtures which can be easily made from individual ingredients or from the many convenience forms available.

Activities

1. Visit a supermarket and note the convenience frosting items offered. How many dry mixes were available? What information was listed on the label of dry mixes, ready-to-eat, and frozen products?

2. Write a short report on the place of convenience cake items in today's home.

3. Browse through magazines and cookbooks and find unusual uses for cakes and unusual cake recipes. In what ways were these recipes new to you?

4. Find a simple yellow or chocolate cake recipe. Purchase a similar cake mix and prepare the two products. Compare time and cost, flavor, texture, and general appearance of the products. Report your results to the class. Do you think this is a fair comparison? Was the home-prepared cake influenced by your inexperience as a cake baker?

5. Prepare a seven-minute or a fudge frosting for a cake of your choice. Compare it with a similar frosting mix for flavor, texture, cost, and time. Did your experience with frosting influence the quality of the home-prepared item?

6. Find the same cake recipe which can be made by both the conventional and quick methods. Make the cake by each method. Compare time, flavor, and texture of the two products. Which of these methods do you prefer?

7. Design a poster to show the caloric value of cake products and show ways to control their use to avoid a caloric overload. Check the new mixes that come on the market. Test their value and quality.

Questions

1. What are the basic types of cakes?

2. In what ways does the conventional cake method differ from the quick method?

3. In what ways do butter cakes differ from foam cakes?

4. What is the purpose of each of the ingredients used in a shortened cake?

5. In what ways is a chiffon cake similar to a shortened cake? To a foam-type cake?

6. What principles are involved in baking cakes?

7. In what ways is the cake influenced by the method of baking used?

8. What is the proper arrangement of cake pans in an oven when you use only one pan? When you use four pans on two racks?

9. How will you know when a cake is done?

10. What principle of cookery is involved in making a cooked frosting?

11. Besides cooking, what are other differences between cooked and uncooked frostings?

12. Describe the proper way to frost a cake.

13. How are cakes stored?

14. What nutrient values are contributed by cakes?

Chapter
22
Cookies

Words for Thought

Accompaniment
an item that goes with something. In meal service, a food that enhances and harmonizes with another.

Caloric
refers to the calorie or energy value of food.

Extract
a solution of flavor oils in alcohol. It may be a natural or synthetic substance; for example, pure vanilla or imitation vanilla.

Macaroon
a small cake or cookie made with egg foam, sugar, and almond paste, powdered almonds, or coconut.

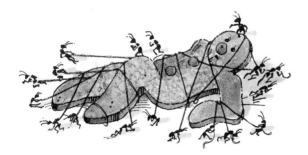

Cookies came to us from many lands. From Finland, came the nut-studded butter strips known as finska kakor (Finnish cakes). The pepparkaror and the sandbakelser (sand tart), a fragile almond-flavored shell, originated in Sweden. The lebkuchen is a famous German honey Christmas cookie, and the springerle and the pfeffernusse are well-known Christmas favorites from Old Germany. From Scotland came the crisp and thick Scotch shortbread with its buttery richness. The Canadian honey drops are soft, brown sugar cookies that are held together in pairs by apricot jam and look like yo-yos. A cream wafer, the pariserwafier, is a butter-rich, creamy-white cookie from France. Very appropriately, from colonial America came the wagon wheel, a very large, flat, chewy molasses cookie which was introduced by the early settlers.

These cookies are only a few of the hundreds which you can make. Cookies come in many flavors, sizes, shapes, and forms. Whether sliced or drop, bar or mix, refrigerator or rolled, they may be grouped into basic types.

Types of Cookies

The stiffness and the method of handling the dough make it convenient to classify cookies into six basic types: drop, bar, rolled, refrigerator, pressed, and molded. The dough for bar cookies and drop cookies is softer than the dough for the other types of cookies.

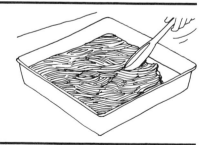

Drop cookie dough is pushed from a spoon onto a cookie sheet. You should allow about 5 centimeters (2 inches) of space between the cookies to keep them from spreading into each other. Use the same amount of dough on the spoon each time so that the cookies will be uniform in size. It is best to use a cool cookie sheet so the dough will not spread before it is placed in the oven.

Bar cookies are made from a soft dough which is spread evenly in a pan and baked. You may cut them into any shape (square, rectangle, triangle) you wish after they are baked. Brownies are probably the most popular bar cookies.

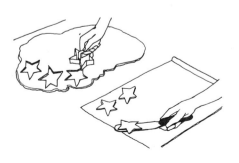

Rolled cookies are made from a stiff dough which has been rolled into a thin sheet. You may cut the rolled dough into various shapes with a cookie cutter. Use only a small amount of flour on the board so that you will not have a hard cookie. You may find it easier to roll cookie dough which has been chilled. Roll only a small amount of cookie dough at a time so that you will avoid overhandling the dough which causes toughness. Leave a small amount of space between the cookies as you place them on the cookie sheet.

For *refrigerator cookies*, a stiff dough is pressed with the hands into a long smooth roll and chilled before baking. The fat in the cookie will harden making it easy to slice the cookies from the roll. If you slice the cookies thinly, they will be crisp and crunchy. The refrigerator cookie dough may be stored in the refrigerator for several days before baking.

Use a rich, stiff dough to make *pressed cookies*. The dough is packed into a cookie press and forced out through cookie discs (cutters) onto an ungreased cookie sheet. The dough will stick to the cookie sheet as you lift the cookie press from it. Leave a small amount of space between the cookies as you squeeze them on to the sheet.

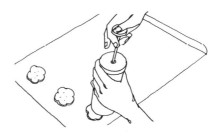

Molded cookies are made from a stiff dough. A small amount of dough is shaped and molded with the fingers to form the desired shape (crescents, rolls, balls, etc.). As you form the molded cookies, space them evenly in rows on the cookie sheet, allowing a small amount of space between cookies.

You will be able to make a wide variety of cookies from the same ingredients you used for cakes.

Principles

Cookie doughs require the same basic ingredients used in cake batters, but the proportion of ingredients is different. You use flour, salt, leavening agents, sugar, shortening, eggs, and liquid to make cookies. Cookies need less liquid and leavening and may need more fat than is used in cakes. Cookies have a crisp texture rather than the light texture of cakes. These ingredients will serve the same purpose in cookies as they did in cakes.

Ingredients in Cookies

All-purpose flour is suitable for all cookies unless cake flour is specified. Flour will provide the structure for the cookie as it does for the cake.

The *fat* or *shortening* is often used to contribute flavor as well as richness to the cookie. Butter or margarine is used to give a pleasing flavor to the cookie. Margarine can usually replace butter in most cookie recipes. Since vegetable shortening is bland, other ingredients are used to provide flavor.

Brown sugar, honey, and molasses are used at times to contribute a special flavor to cookies. Chocolate, spices, coconut, nuts, fruits (usually dried or candied), and extracts are also used for flavor.

Milk is the *liquid* most often used in cookies. It may be sweet milk, sour milk, or buttermilk. Occasionally cream is used for some of the liquid, and at the same time it contributes richness (fat) and a pleasing flavor. Some cookies require no added liquid.

The ingredients used in cookie recipes are usually mixed by methods similar to those used for cakes.

Mixing Cookies

Most cookies are mixed by the conventional method or a slight modification of it. Because a crisp, crunchy, or chewy texture is characteristic of cookies rather than a light delicate texture, cookies require less creaming than cakes. The flour may be added all at once, instead of in four parts, as in cakes. Macaroons, meringues, and kisses do not contain fat and are mixed in much the same way as foam-type cakes.

The following steps will show you how the conventional method can be modified and still produce perfect cookies.

1. Blend the softened shortening, sugar (including molasses or syrup if used), eggs, and melted chocolate (when used) thoroughly.

2. Stir in the liquid and flavoring all at once. (In a few recipes the liquid and flour may be added alternately.)

3. Sift the flour, salt, and leavening (including spices) together and stir them into the shortening-sugar-egg mixture.

Baking Cookies

Baking sheets are best for baking cookies because there are no sides to interfere with the circulation of heat.

The shiny and bright cookie sheet will give your cookies a delicately browned crust. You should not use cake pans because their deep sides will interfere with distribution of heat and the cookies will remain pale.

You may turn a pan with sides upside down and arrange cookies on the bottom of it. The cookie sheet or pan should be about 5 cm (2 in) smaller than the oven to permit circulation of heat around it.

Because most cookies will spread a little, *spacing* is necessary to prevent them from running together. You should arrange cookies on cool baking sheets to avoid excessive spreading. Rolled cookies spread less so spaces between them can be smaller. Drop and refrigerator cookies spread more and require greater space—usually about 5 cm (2 in)—between them. When you arrange cookies, space them evenly and get more cookies on the sheet.

Bake the cookies arranged on a sheet in a preheated oven set at the temperature indicated in your recipe. When you bake one pan of cookies at a time, place it on a rack near the center of the oven.

When you want to bake two pans of cookies at the same time, place the oven racks so that the oven is divided into thirds. During the last few minutes of baking, you may need to change the cookie sheets from one rack to the other so that the cookies will be browned evenly.

You should check for *doneness* of cookies when the minimum baking time is up. The cookie should be set so that when you touch it lightly with your finger, almost no imprint will re-

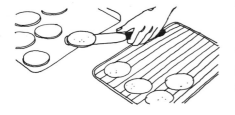

main. Be careful that you do not underbake or overbake cookies. Overbaking will cause cookies to dry out and become too dark; underbaking will leave the cookies doughy and pale. Properly baked cookies are delicately browned.

You should remove cookies from the sheet as soon as you take them from the oven. As the cookie cools it becomes hardened, sticks to the pan, and may break as you remove it. Use a wide spatula to remove the warm cookies onto a cooling rack.

You can preserve the characteristic flavor and texture of the cookies you bake by storing them properly.

Storing Cookies

To keep the perfect eating quality of your cookies, store them in covered containers. Bar and drop cookies are made from soft dough and usually will have a soft texture. Cookies made from stiff dough, such as rolled and refrigerator ones, are crisp. In order that soft cookies remain soft, and crisp cookies remain crisp, store each separately in the proper containers.

Soft cookies keep best in airtight containers. A slice of fresh bread or slices of apple or orange in the jar with the soft cookies will help to keep them moist. The fruit will need to be changed frequently. Crisp cookies should be kept in a can or container with a loose cover.

When you open a package of ready-to-eat cookies, you can retain their texture and flavor by folding the protective wrap tightly around the remaining cookies. You can store bought cookies in covered containers as you do home-baked cookies.

Whether cookies are homemade or bought, their nutrient value depends on the ingredients used.

Nutrient Contributions

Flour, sugar, and fat are the ingredients that you will use in the largest amounts in cookies. Their chief contribution is in calories or energy. Because all other ingredients are used in rather small amounts, you can count on cookies to contribute only to your caloric or energy needs. You need to include milk, fruits, cereals, and meats in your daily eating pattern to meet your needs for vitamins, minerals, and protein.

Uses of Cookies

Like cakes, cookies are served as the dessert at the end of a meal. Because cookies are rich in calories, they will satisfy your appetite, and, if you eat them before meals, they may crowd out other needed foods.

You may wish to serve cookies as an accompaniment to fruit and ice cream desserts. Dainty, colorful cookies are served at afternoon teas and receptions, and are excellent party foods. Cookies are easily packed and carried in both school and picnic lunches. For the unexpected moment or occasion, a wide variety of convenience cookie items is always available.

Convenience in Cookies

Cookie convenience comes in several forms: (1) ready-to-eat, (2) refrigerated or frozen, and (3) as a mix. All of these are on standby reserve, ready to serve on a moment's notice. Cookie mixes come in several varieties and usually require only the addition of the liquid and sometimes an egg. To some cookie mixes you may add flavor ingredients such as coconut, nuts, and extracts. For best results, follow the directions on the package and display your creative ability in shaping and decorating the cookies. You can throw cookie formulas out of balance when you add any extra amounts of basic ingredients such as flour, sugar, and shortening.

Cookie doughs from the refrigerated case require only to be shaped (cut or sliced, spread in pan) and baked. The ready-to-eat cookies are found in all grocery stores, delicatessens, and bakeries. They are ready for immediate use without any further preparation.

The advantage in the use of these products may come from the time saved, but you should consider which of these items are really good buys in terms of your needs and which are luxury items.

You can create "cookie convenience" by preparing a double batch or recipe of cookies, part for immediate use and the rest to be frozen for later use. Homemade convenience comes from home-prepared cookie mixes and refrigerated cookie doughs.

As with most other convenience products, no clue to quality is given on the label. The reputation of the manufacturer and your experience with convenience items will be your best guides in their selection.

Main Ideas

Cookies are grouped into six types: drop, bar, rolled, refrigerator, pressed, and molded. The basic ingredients used—flour, salt, leavening, sugar, shortening, and egg—serve the same purpose in cookies as they do in cakes. Cookies contain less liquid and leavening but may have more fat. Most cookies are mixed by the conventional method except those having beaten egg white which require the foam-cake method of mixing. The type of pan, oven position, and oven temperature, as well as the way in which the cookies are stored, influence the quality of the final product. Cookies primarily contribute calories to the diet. They are available in convenience forms of ready-to-eat, refrigerated, and various dry mixes.

Activities

1. Visit a supermarket and observe the kinds of cookie items sold. Which of these would you judge to be the best buys? Why? Which of the ingredients listed on the labels would you classify as emulsifiers or preservatives?

2. In what ways could the nutritional value of cookies be improved? Find a food table and note the nutrient value for the cookies listed. Which ingredients are chiefly responsible for the caloric value of cookies?

3. Find a cookie recipe using the conventional method and another recipe using the foam or sponge method. In what ways do these recipes differ? In what ways are they alike?

4. Find a recipe for each of the six basic types of cookies. In what ways do the recipes differ?

5. Bake a batch of brownie mix and a batch of home-prepared brownies. Compare them for quantity (weigh each batch), cost, time, flavor, and texture. Which product will serve your home needs best? Why?

6. Make a sugar cookie dough. Divide the dough into three portions. Shape one portion into a roll and refrigerate until it is firm enough to slice; chill the second portion before rolling; and roll the third portion immediately. Which cookie dough was easiest to roll? Which was easiest to shape? Which method for shaping sugar cookies do you recommend and why?

7. Prepare a foam-type cookie such as macaroons or kisses. Were you satisfied with the results? If you were not satisfied, analyze your mistakes. Try again.

Questions

1. What are the basic ingredients used in cookies? What is the purpose of each?

2. In what ways are the principles of cake preparation similar to the principles of cookie preparation?

3. What methods are used to mix cookies? How do they differ from those used for cakes?

4. What baking techniques will insure perfect cookies?

5. Why are most cookies spaced apart on the cookie sheet?

6. When are cookies done?

7. What are the results of overbaking or underbaking cookies?

8. How are cookies stored?

9. What is the chief nutrient contributed by cookies?

10. What convenience cookie items are available? How will you judge which of these are best for your needs?

Chapter
23
Pastry

Words for Thought

Flaky
separated or broken into thin layers.

Crisp
brittle, breaks with a snap.

Pastry
a rich crust.

Flute
to crimp or twist edge of pastry with fingers to form decorative edge.

Meringue
a beaten egg white and sugar mixture.

Cut in
to distribute solid fat into dry ingredients by cutting with two knives or with pastry blades or blender.

Would you believe that pie is as American as the Fourth of July? Pumpkin pies were first made by the wives of the pioneers who filled hollowed out pumpkins with milk and baked them in front of the open fire. Later spices were added to these early pumpkin mixtures and they were baked in pans. Still later, about 1790, pumpkin fillings were baked in pastry-lined pans. As the variety of foods increased in the new world, so did the kinds of pies.

However, legend tells us that pies originated in ancient Greece, spread to Rome, and later to Europe. In England, "pyes" were baked in deep pans called "coffins." The shallow, round pie pan was an American invention so that the pie would serve a number of people. Pie is an American favorite, especially apple pie, and then cherry. Today, a flaky, tender pastry is the hallmark of every good cook.

Kinds of Pastry

Just mention the word pastry and to most of us that means pie. Actually, the term pastry refers to a large variety of baked products made from doughs rich in fat. It includes cream puffs, puff pastry, Danish and French pastries, rich yeast and cake-type sweet rolls as well as the favorite, pies.

Plain or puff pastry may be used for pies, but plain pastry is used most often. It has a golden brown, flaky (blistered) surface and is tender. Puff pastry is extra rich and extra flaky and is used for special pies or fancy tarts.

Pastry that is both tender and flaky is preferred by almost everyone rather than the smooth compact pastry. Because plain pastry is most often used for pies, and flakiness and tenderness are the signs of good pastry, you will want to learn how to make the perfect pastry.

Light, fragile puff pastry filled with fruit and cream adds a delicious finish to a light meal.

Pastry Ingredients

You need only four ingredients to make good pastry: flour, fat, salt, and liquid.

All-purpose flour is usually used. The gluten of the flour will form the framework or structure of the pastry.

Firm fats such as *lard* and *vegetable shortening* are most frequently used to make pastry. *Butter* and *margarine* produce a less tender pastry than other fats and are not usually used for pastry. The firm fat will produce flaky pastry, while the oils which are liquid in nature will make a mealy pastry. Because lard is a soft fat it has more shortening power than vegetable fats, and will produce a more tender pastry. Oils will give a very tender, mealy pastry that is not flaky. For each 250 mL (1 c) of flour, you will use 80 mL (⅓ c) vegetable shortening and only 60 mL (¼ c) of lard or oil.

Use only a small amount of *water*, about 30 mL (2 T), for each 250 mL (1 c) of flour. Water is an important ingredient because it provides the moisture needed to develop gluten.

Salt contributes to the flavor of pastry and has no influence on flakiness or tenderness.

The kind and proportion of ingredients you use and the manner in which you mix and handle the dough will determine the success of your pastry.

Principles of Making Pastry

The principles of making pastry are concerned with the influence of ingredients on gluten formation, methods of mixing and handling the dough, and baking.

Influence of Ingredients on Gluten Formation

The gluten of the *flour* forms the structure or network. The entrapped air and moisture will expand during baking giving a blistered effect which is characteristic of flaky pastry. Too much flour will produce a tough pastry.

The *fat* coats the particles of flour and separates the gluten strands and in this way shortens or makes the pastry tender. Solid fats are cut into the flour to form many particles so that the gluten strands will be separated. Because oils are liquid, the gluten is separated into very short strands making the pastry grainy or mealy. For this reason, oil pastry is tender and crumbly or mealy rather than flaky.

Too little shortening causes a tough pastry because the gluten is not separated into short strands. Too much shortening weakens gluten strands. The pastry is fragile and crumbly.

The *liquid*, which is usually water, moistens the flour particles so that gluten can be developed. When too much water is used, the pastry will be tough; when not enough water is used, the pastry will be dry, crumbly, and difficult to roll.

Methods of Mixing and Handling

The way you mix and handle the dough will determine the success or failure of your pastry. You will have a more tender pastry when the ingredients are at room temperature rather than when they are cold. You should combine the ingredients, and mix them gently so that you will not overdevelop the gluten which causes the pastry to become tough.

Several methods can be used to combine the pastry ingredients. You will recall that plain pastry is most often used for pies. It can be made by any one of three methods: (1) the conventional method; (2) the hot water method; and (3) the stir-and-roll or oil method.

The conventional method will give you a crisp, tender, flaky pastry and is often preferred. You, too, can make a perfect flaky pastry when you learn the techniques of the conventional method.

1. To make pastry by the *conventional method,* measure the sifted flour into a bowl and stir in the salt. Add the shortening to the flour and cut it in with a pastry blender until the pieces of shortening are the size of small peas. When you do not have a pastry blender, you may cut in the shortening with two table knives. Make sure that the fat is evenly distributed throughout the flour so that the gluten strands will be shortened and the pastry tender.

2. Sprinkle the water, 15 mL (1 T) at a time, over different parts of the flour mixture. Mix lightly with a fork. Do not overstir or you will cause too much gluten to develop. You need only to moisten the flour so that the dough will form a loose ball. You should always remember that too much water makes the pastry tough; too little makes it crumble.

The *conventional paste method* differs from the method just described only in the way the water is added. First, remove 30 mL (2 T) of flour from the 250 mL (1 c) of flour used in the recipe. Mix the flour which you removed with all of the water specified by the recipe to make a paste. Add the salt to the remaining flour and cut in the fat. Pour all of the flour paste over the fat-flour mixture and stir it in thoroughly.

1. Instead of cold water as in the conventional method, boiling water is used in the *hot-water method*. Pour a measured amount of boiling water over the shortening and whip it in with a fork. This will form a fluffy, creamed mixture.

2. Add all of the measured flour and salt into the shortening-water mixture and stir until blended. Do not overmix. Hot-water pastry is tender but tends to be mealy and less flaky than conventional pastry.

Oil pastry is mealy rather than flaky. Place the measured flour and salt into the mixing bowl as you did for the conventional method. Next, add the measured oil and liquid all at once and stir gently with a fork until blended. The pastry will be moist but not sticky.

If you prefer a tender, flaky pastry you should use the conventional method; if you prefer a tender, grainy pastry use the hot-water or oil method. Regardless of the method you choose, the rolling and handling of the pastry will be the same for one- and two-crust pies, or tarts.

In *rolling pastry*, roll only enough for one crust at a time. Handle the pastry as little as possible to avoid toughening it. It is easy to work too much flour into pastry when you roll it on a floured board or cloth. This toughens the pastry. You will find it easy to roll pastry without flour between two pieces of waxed paper. Your paper will not slide if you first wipe the counter with a damp cloth and place the paper on that spot. The paper will also help you to lift the pastry into the pie pan without tearing it.

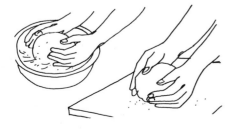

1. After you finish mixing the pastry, gather the dough into a ball with your fingers so that the bowl will be clean. With both hands, press the dough into a firm ball.

2. Place the dough on a piece of waxed paper, and flatten the ball gently with the palm of one hand. Cover the dough with a second piece of waxed paper. In this way you can roll the dough without adding more flour which will toughen the pastry. Your paper will not slide if you wipe the area on which you will roll the pastry with a damp cloth.

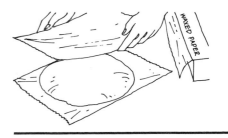

3. Begin rolling from the center of the pastry toward the edge and lift the rolling pin as it comes to the outer edge so your pastry will be of uniform thickness. Repeat rolling from the center in all directions to form a circle.

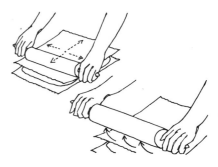

4. Roll gently so that the paper will not wrinkle. Should your paper wrinkle, gently peel it off and smooth it out. Continue to roll until your pastry is 3 mm (⅛ in) thick and is 2.5 cm (1 in) larger than the inverted pie pan.

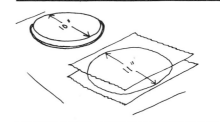

5. Remove the top piece of paper. Lift the pastry by the bottom paper and center the pastry (paper side up) over the pan.

Carefully peel back the waxed paper.

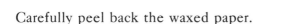

6. With your fingers carefully fit the pastry into the bottom and sides of the pan so that no air bubbles remain between the pastry and the pan. Be careful that you do not stretch the pastry as this will cause it to shrink during baking.

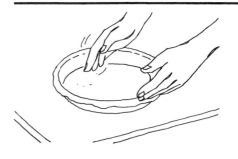

357

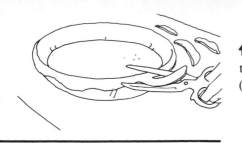

1. For a *one-crust pie* in which the filling and pastry are baked together, trim the overhanging pastry edge so that it is 1.2 cm (½ in) larger than the pie pan.

2. Fold the extra pastry back and under to form a high edge.

3. Flute the edge of the pastry with your fingertips. This will help to retain the filling and give an attractive edge to your pie.

4. You are now ready to fill the shell with a filling which is baked together with the shell (custard, pumpkin, etc.).

1. Use a baked pie shell to hold fillings which are cooked separately and added later as cream, chiffon, etc. After you flute the pastry edge, hook the points of the fluted edge under the pan rim to minimize shrinkage during baking.

2. Prick the bottom and sides of the pastry thoroughly with the tines of a fork to prevent puffing during baking. Should your pastry puff up during baking, prick the pastry again in a few places while it is in the oven to permit the expanding air to escape. Bake the shell until golden brown, following the directions of your recipe.

1. For a *two-crust pie*, divide the dough into two balls. Roll out the dough for the bottom crust in the same way as for a one-crust pie. Trim the overhanging pastry at the edge of the pan with scissors.

Roll the pastry (between waxed paper) for the top crust so that it is 2.5 cm (1 in) larger than the pan. Measure by holding the pie pan over the rolled pastry.

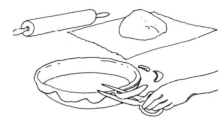

2. Add the filling to the pastry-lined pan.

3. Moisten the edge of the bottom pastry with water. This will help to seal the edges of the pastry so that juices will not be forced out into the oven.

Remove the top piece of paper and lift the rolled upper crust by the remaining layer of paper and center the crust over the top of the filling with the paper side facing you. Remove the paper and trim the edge 1.2 cm (½ in) larger than the pan.

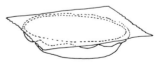

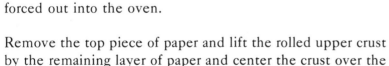

4. Fold the extra edge of the top pastry under the edge of the lower pastry. Seal the edge by pressing with your fingers on the edge of the pie pan. Flute the edge as for a one-crust pie.

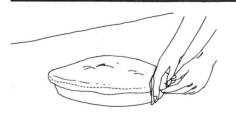

5. Then, cut several slits near the center of the top pastry to allow steam to escape during baking. This will keep the top pastry from rising in the center to form a hump.

6. You may cover the fluted edge with a 3.75 cm (1½ in) strip of foil to prevent overbrowning.

Pie shells and one-crust or two-crust pies are baked in a preheated oven.

Baking Pastry

When you need only one oven rack, place it near the center of the oven to bake pies and pastry shells. When you need two oven racks, arrange them so that the oven is divided into thirds and arrange the pie pans to allow the heat to circulate (see cake pan arrangements, Chapter 21, page 336). Follow the directions given in your recipe for oven temperature and baking time.

As you rolled the pastry, the gluten and particles of fat were flattened to form layers of gluten, fat, and entrapped air. The entrapped air and the steam formed during baking force the layers apart and give your pastry a flaky texture.

Good pastry is evenly browned with a blistered surface and is crisp and tender.

Uses of Pastry

There are three general ways to use pastry: (1) as a dessert; (2) as an accompaniment to other foods; and (3) as an ingredient of main dishes.

Dessert Pastry

Pastry in several forms is used as a dessert. Pies, either one-crust or two-crust, are very popular desserts.

Fruit pies are often made with two crusts and sometimes the top crust is a lattice top. To make a lattice top the rolled pastry is cut into strips with a knife and placed across the top of the filling to form square or diamond shapes.

The thickened fruit may be placed into a deep dish and covered with a pastry to make a deep-dish pie. All kinds of fruits whether they are frozen, fresh, canned, or dried may be used for pie. You will find pie recipes which were developed for each of the many kinds and forms of fruits.

Custard pies are made of a milk and egg mixture which is baked together with the pastry. Pumpkin and pecan are examples of custard-type pies.

A *cream pie* is filled with a pudding mixture thickened with starch. Cream pies come in many flavors, and fruits, nuts, and coconut can be used to add interest and variety to the pie. (You will learn to make puddings in the next chapter.) Cream pies are topped with a soft or whipped cream topping. Follow the principles of starch cookery when you prepare both thickened fruit and pudding pie fillings.

Chiffon pie fillings are cooked gelatin mixtures made fluffy with beaten egg whites. They are poured into a baked pie shell and chilled until set.

Tarts are actually miniature or individual pies. They may be filled with any filling commonly used in a regular size pie. Pecan, chocolate, lemon, and cherry are favorite tarts.

Turnovers are squares of pastry which have a filling placed on one half and the other half folded over; then the edges are sealed. Like all pastry, turnovers are baked until delicately browned.

Pies and pastries are appropriate desserts for meals that are not overly rich in calories.

Accompaniment Pastry

Pastry may be cut into strips or fancy shapes and sprinkled with cheese and paprika to use as an accompaniment for soups or salads. Pastry pieces may be sprinkled with a sugar-cinnamon mixture or spread lightly with jelly or jam to use as an accompaniment to a fruit or sherbet dessert.

Pastry as a Main-Dish Ingredient

Meat, poultry, fish, seafood pies, and quiche are main-dish foods around which the rest of the meal is planned. The meat, poultry, or fish may be combined with vegetables in a sauce or a gravy. This mixture may be baked in a pastry-lined pan with a top crust or covered only with a top crust baked with the mixture. Instead of a solid crust, fancy pastry shapes may be used to decorate the pie or casserole main dishes. The meat, poultry, or fish pies are filling and satisfying main dishes. The nutrients contributed by the various forms of pastry will depend on the ingredients used to make them.

Nutrient Contributions

All pastries contain a high proportion of fat and therefore are rich in energy and calories. Pastry fillings contain sugar which adds to their caloric contribution. Pastries make it very easy to overload your meals with more calories than you may need. You should always remember that calories which you do not use up in your work and play will be stored as body fat and thus add to your weight.

There will be some vitamin and mineral values from custard and fruit fillings, but these do not replace your need for milk and fruit. The amount of milk or fruit in a piece of pie is small and cannot be counted as a serving of these foods. The main-dish meat-vegetable pies will contribute some protein, B vitamins, and mineral values.

A good rule to remember is never to serve more than one calorie-rich food in a meal. Because of their high caloric value, pastry desserts should be served with a light meal. If the starch, fat, or sugar value of your meal is small, pastry may be served. For example, pastries are suitable desserts for most salad or soup lunches. Pastry should be used in moderation and reserved for those times when you may need to increase the caloric value of the meal or foods served.

Storage of Pastry

Store unused chiffon, custard, and meat-type pies in the refrigerator to prevent spoilage. Fillings containing milk, eggs, or meats, including poultry and fish, spoil quickly unless they are refrigerated.

Fruit pies, tarts, and turnovers keep satisfactorily for a day, but the quality is best when you eat them the same day they are made. You may freeze both unbaked and baked pies after wrapping them in suitable freezer wrap. Frozen baked pies are best when you reheat them for serving; however, the pastry of the frozen baked pie may not be as crisp as when freshly baked.

Baked and unbaked pie shells can be satisfactorily stored in the refrigerator for several days or in the freezer for future use. You should reheat the baked shells for a few minutes to restore their crispness. In addition to these home-frozen products, many convenience pastry items are available for your immediate use, especially when your time is limited.

A special pastry dessert is created by using a convenience pudding and a pastry mix.

Convenience in Pastry Items

You will find that convenience in pastries comes in several forms. You may select from mixes or frozen, canned, and ready-to-eat convenience items. Pastries come as a dry mix or a compressed stick to which you need only add water or as a frozen pie shell or as a crumb crust each in its own pan ready for use. Some dry pie mixes come two packages in the same box, one with the crumb crust, the other with the filling.

You will find a variety of dry pie filling mixes for cream or custard pies and canned pudding and fruit fillings for other pies. The dry filling mix requires the addition of liquid and some need to be heated to a boil. The canned pie fillings require only to be put into the pie shell.

You can choose from a variety of frozen fruit and custard pies ready for the oven. Also included are oven-ready frozen turnovers. If you wish, you may select a frozen baked pie that needs only to be warmed or a frozen cream pie ready to be served. You may make your selection from a host of bakery pies—cream, fruit, and chiffon. In addition to the convenience dessert pies, you will find ready-for-the-oven frozen meat, poultry, and fish pies for the main course of a meal.

Without a doubt convenience pastry items will save you time. The frozen and ready-to-eat ones will save the most time. Convenience pastry items tend to be more expensive than the home-prepared ones. Frozen and ready-to-eat pies are more expensive than the mix, and complete mixes are more expensive than homemade pies.

The convenience item may not measure up to a well-prepared home product. The finished convenience product may not give the satisfaction derived from a pie made from individual ingredients. The convenience item can guarantee success and an acceptable product.

You need to rely on your own judgment and experience when it comes to selecting convenience pastry items. The list of ingredients on the label and the manufacturer's reputation will be your only guides.

You can create your own homemade convenience with pastry items. You can prepare your own pastry mix from flour, salt, and shortening, and store it in a covered container in a cool place. You then need only to add water when you are ready to bake a pie.

You can freeze homemade pies before or after baking. The quality of the frozen unbaked pie tends to be better because the bottom crust of frozen baked pies may become soggy. You may freeze chiffon pies, but custard and cream pies tend to separate, and pie meringues may become toughened.

You will recall that pastry shells may be frozen either baked or unbaked. Rolled circles of pastry can be separated with paper, stacked and frozen in a suitable container or freezer wrap. Homemade and purchased convenience pastry items save time and energy but the homemade ones may cost less than the purchased convenience products.

Main Ideas

Pastries have a proportionately higher fat to flour content than either cakes or cookies. The quality of any pastry depends on the accurate proportion of flour to fat to liquid, and the skillful mixing and handling of the dough. The method used in making pastry determines its general texture. Pastry products are available in frozen, dry mix, and ready-to-eat convenience forms. While convenience forms may save time and energy they generally are more expensive than homemade ones.

Activities

1. Visit a supermarket and note the kinds of convenience pastry items offered for sale. Would any of these fit into a low-cost food budget? What did you consider in making your decision?

2. What information not provided on labels of convenience pastry products would be helpful to you as a consumer?

3. Find a recipe for puff pastry and for plain pastry. How do they differ? In what ways are they similar? What nutrients are contributed by each?

4. Prepare three small recipes of pastry using the conventional method. Use a different fat in each. Compare them for flavor, texture, flakiness, and tenderness.

5. Prepare a small recipe of pastry using the hot-water method, conventional-paste, and oil method. Compare their flavor, texture, flakiness, and tenderness.

6. Bake a two-crust pie with a fruit filling of your choice. Use the pastry method you prefer. Evaluate it for flavor, tenderness, texture, appearance, and general acceptability. Serve it to your family. How did your evaluation compare with theirs? What suggestions do you have for improvement the next time you bake this pie?

Questions

1. Define the term pastry.

2. What two types of pastry are used for pies? In what ways do they differ?

3. What are the basic pastry ingredients? What is the purpose of each in pastry?

4. What ingredients influence gluten formation in pastry?

5. How does the method of mixing influence pastry?

6. How does baking influence pastry? What happens during baking?

7. Compare the conventional, conventional-paste, hot-water, and oil or stir-and-roll methods.

8. Describe the way pastry should be rolled to give an even thickness to a circle of pastry.

9. What are the advantages of using waxed paper for rolling pastry? How is the paper kept from slipping during rolling?

10. In what ways does the making of a two-crust pie differ from a one-crust pie?

11. What is the difference in the pastry used for a custard pie and a cream pie?

12. Why are slits placed in the top pastry of a two-crust pie?

13. Why should a pastry shell be pricked before baking?

14. How are fruit, chiffon, custard, and meat pies stored for a day or two?

15. Which pastry items can be frozen for later use?

16. What nutrients are contributed by pastry?

17. What are the uses of pastry in meals?

Chapter
24
Desserts

Words for Thought

Compote
fruits stewed in a syrup and served as
a dessert.

Blanc mange
a milk dessert thickened usually with
cornstarch. Blanc mange (French for
white food) and cornstarch pudding
are used interchangeably.

Scald
to heat milk to just below the boiling
point. Also to dip food into boiling
water.

Dessert dumpling
a pastry or rich biscuit dough
surrounding sweetened fruit and
baked.

Cobbler
thickened, sweetened fruit covered
with pastry or drop biscuits and
baked.

Parfait
a frozen dessert made of beaten egg
whites, whipped cream, and desired
flavorings.

Mousse
a frozen dessert consisting of
sweetened whipped cream, flavoring
(often fruit), and small amount of
gelatin.

The custom of serving food after the table was cleared,
"deserted," gave rise to the dessert course of today. Fruits
are commonly served as desserts in Europe, but they follow a
rich sweet food. Here the sweet is the dessert and is served as
the last course of a meal.

As with other foods, many "sweets" came to us from other
lands. French meringues, Italian soufflés, German tortes, and
British steamed puddings are examples of European desserts
which have become a part of our culture. An early dessert not
too different from our sno-cones was served in the days of

Julius Caesar. Snow flavored with fruit juices was a Roman dessert delicacy. Runners delivered snow from high mountain tops to make this fruit-flavored frozen dessert. King Charles I of England was so fond of "cream ice" that he hired a French chef to prepare it for him and rewarded the chef with a pension. The cream ice was brought to the new world by Virginia Cavaliers. It was Dolley Madison who served the frozen dessert at the White House and called it ice cream. Since her day, ice cream has developed into a truly American dessert, along with fruit cobblers and shortcakes.

Desserts may be as simple as whole strawberries on stems dipped into confectioner's sugar, as fancy as a mousse in a party mold, or as elegant as a Vienna nut torte. Desserts may be simply and conveniently classified according to the chief ingredient from which they are made and by the special preparation methods used to make them.

Types of Desserts

Desserts, whether plain or fancy, add a touch of sweetness to the end of your meals. You have already learned how to make pies, cakes, and cookies in earlier chapters of this book. Included here are the other types of desserts which can be conveniently classified as fruit, milk, gelatin, cake-biscuit-pastry, and frozen desserts.

Fruit Desserts

Fruits are colorful and flavorful desserts which are easy on calorie counters. Besides being low in calories, fruits are rich sources of vitamins. Fresh, frozen, canned, or dried fruits can be served for dessert.

Fresh fruits are the easiest of all desserts to prepare. You need only to wash, drain or dry, and chill the fruit. A basket heaped with colorful fruit is both decorative and tempting and offers a variety for selection.

You may arrange fresh whole fruits or quarters, sections, and slices (cored but not peeled) of fresh fruits on a tray with cubes and wedges of cheese for a simple but satisfying dessert. Popular fruit and cheese partners include apples and Camembert, pears and cream cheese, Tokay grapes and cheddar cheese.

You may arrange large pieces of fruit and small whole fruits on salad greens for an attractive dessert salad.

Melon halves, sliced peaches and cream, and banana and raspberries garnished with whipped cream are popular fruit-in-season desserts. Fruit also can be used as a topping for puddings and custards.

You may wish to prepare a combination of fruits and cut them in a variety of shapes (lightly sweetened, if desired) and chilled to make a delightful fruit cup dessert.

Fruit ambrosia is another dessert which can be made with any fruit you have on hand. You need only to sprinkle the fresh fruit slices with confectioner's sugar and chill. Just before serving, top the fruit with coconut to complete the ambrosia.

369

Fresh fruit may be served warm as well as cold. You may cook fresh fruits to make a sauce (rhubarb, peach, apple) and bake whole or sliced fruits. Apples stuffed with raisins, cinnamon, and brown sugar head the list of baked fruits.

A soufflé, as pictured on the left, broiled grapefruit or banana, and fruit whip (fruit pulp folded into egg whites) are other interesting desserts for you to try.

Canned fruits require no preparation and, when chilled, are refreshing desserts. *Frozen fruits* must be defrosted before serving. Their texture will be best if you serve them while a few ice crystals remain. You can demonstrate your creative talents by serving canned and frozen fruits attractively.

Dried fruits may be served alone or as a dessert ingredient. You can make an attractive fruit compote (fruits stewed in syrup) by combining several cooked dried fruits. You can also make fruit whips, either baked or unbaked, from a variety of cooked dried fruits.

Milk Desserts

Milk is the chief ingredient in milk desserts which can be classified into two general groups: puddings and custards. Puddings are thickened with starch, and custards with egg. Because of their high milk content, you can count puddings and custards as contributing to your daily milk needs.

Puddings are often known by the starch ingredient used to thicken them such as cornstarch, tapioca, and rice puddings. Cornstarch pudding can be made in several flavors, such as chocolate, coconut, or caramel. It is served alone as a dessert. This pudding may also be a basic ingredient in other desserts such as pie fillings and soufflés. When you prepare puddings, you apply the principles of starch and milk cookery. Do you recall them? You can easily learn to make puddings that are smooth and free of lumps.

1. To make a pudding, mix the sugar, cornstarch, and salt until well blended. In this way you separate the starch granules so they will not lump.

2. Stir in a small amount of cold milk to make a smooth paste. Then stir in the remainder of the milk. The cold milk helps to further separate the starch grains.

3. Cook the pudding mixture over medium heat, stirring constantly until the mixture boils. Allow the pudding to boil for one minute to cook the starch and avoid a raw starch flavor. Can you see a reason for cooking pudding on medium to low heat? Is it because milk scorches easily?

4. When the pudding is cooked, remove it from the range and stir in the flavor extract.

5. You may cover the pudding so that a thin skin will not form on top as it cools, or you may pour the pudding into individual dessert dishes and cover them with waxed paper or transparent wrap to prevent the formation of film.

6. For variety, you may add sliced fruit, coconut, nuts, or a whipped topping to your pudding before serving.

Use milk, eggs, sugar, and flavoring to make dessert *custards*. Both types of custards, soft or stirred and baked, are made with the same ingredients. The custards differ in consistency because the method of cooking is different. Soft custards are stirred as they cook over hot water, while baked custards are cooked in the oven without stirring. Soft custards have the consistency of thick cream and can be poured from the container. A baked custard forms a delicate gel and will usually retain its shape when you remove it from the baking dish. Both types of custards are nourishing and easy-to-make desserts.

The principles of egg cookery are applied when you prepare soft or baked custards. To avoid overcoagulation of egg protein, use a low temperature and avoid overcooking.

1. To make a *baked custard*, scald the milk (heat until film begins to form) over low heat. Beat the eggs slightly (enough to blend yolk and white) and add the sugar, salt, and flavoring.

2. Add the scalded milk slowly to the egg-sugar mixture, stirring constantly.

3. Pour the custard mixture into custard cups, add spices such as nutmeg, if you wish, and set the cups in a pan of hot water about 2.5 cm (1 in) deep.

4. Bake the custard in a moderate oven—180°C (350°F)—until a metal knife, inserted at least 2.5 cm (1 in) from edge, comes out clean.

5. A *stirred* or a *soft custard* is mixed in the same way as the baked custard, except it is cooked over hot water, simmering not boiling, or over low heat with constant stirring. Cook a soft custard until it coats a metal spoon. Remove the custard from the heat; place the pan in cold water to avoid overcooking.

An overcooked soft custard will be curdled. If you should overcook a soft custard, you can improve its texture by beating with a rotary beater.

When a baked custard is overcooked, you will see bubbles through the glass cup or dish. It will have a porous texture and liquid will separate from the surface as you dip into it with a spoon.

You can use custards in various ways. You may serve soft custard alone or as a sauce for cakes, steamed puddings, fruits, and gelatin. You can add variety and attractiveness to soft custards with garnishes of fruits, nuts, jelly, coconut, whipped cream, and meringue. Spoonfuls of meringue on a soft custard make a dessert known as floating island.

You can also make baked custards in a variety of flavors such as chocolate, vanilla and other extracts, and coffee. You can make a caramel custard by placing caramelized sugar (sugar heated in a pan) in the bottom of the custard cup before you add the custard mixture. Baked custards may also be removed from the baking dish and served with a fruit sauce.

A custard may be used as a base for a main dish when you leave out the sugar. Quiche is a popular main-dish custard. Foods such as grated cheese, corn, and meats add flavor to main-dish custards. Desserts similar to custards and a variety of others can be made with gelatin.

Gelatin Desserts

Gelatin desserts add color and sparkle to meals. Gelatin is chiefly used to change a liquid into a solid. You will recall that gelatin is an incomplete protein from the connective tissue of animals. The principles involved in making gelatin desserts are the same as those discussed in Chapter 11, page 213, and include, first, mixing unflavored gelatin with cold liquid—water, juices, milk—to soften it. Dissolve the softened gelatin in hot liquid by stirring it until the mixture is clear and no granules of gelatin can be seen. Any remaining liquid is usually added cold. Gelatin mixtures will thicken as they cool. When you wish to add fruits and other foods, the gelatin is cooled to the consistency of thick unbeaten egg whites so that the food will not float or sink to the bottom.

You can make gelatin desserts with either unflavored or flavored gelatin which is a mixture of sugar, gelatin, and flavoring. The principles for the use of flavored gelatin are the same as for unflavored except that it can be dissolved in hot water without first being softened in cold water.

Plain gelatin may be used in a variety of ways. You may serve it sparkling clear with only flavored liquid added, or you may add fruits and nuts when it begins to thicken and before it is poured into molds. Light fluffy desserts can be made from plain gelatins. You can whip gelatin mixtures to about twice their original volume after you first cool them to the consistency of unbeaten egg whites.

Gelatin whips are made from chilled fruit gelatins which have been beaten to the consistency of whipped cream and then chilled until set.

Snows or *sponges* are gelatins to which you add beaten egg whites. You can also make them by adding unbeaten egg whites to the chilled plain gelatin and then whipping the mixture. They are often served with fruit or custard sauces.

Spanish Cream, a gelatin cream, is thickened with gelatin and in this way differs from puddings and custards. You can make a Spanish cream with an egg-yolk custard containing gelatin which you chill until partially set and then fold in beaten egg whites.

You can also make *Bavarian creams* from gelatin creams by folding in whipped cream.

Charlottes are another more elaborate gelatin cream dessert which contain a high proportion of whipped cream and may be molded with ladyfingers or sponge cake. Mousses differ from charlottes in that they are molded but do not have a sponge cake base.

375

Gelatin desserts are often set in fancy molds. They are unmolded for serving. You will be able to unmold gelatin desserts easily when you do the following.

1. First dip the mold into warm water (almost to the top of the mold). Then loosen the edge with a paring knife. (Avoid water that is too hot because it will melt the gelatin.)

2. Place an inverted serving dish on top of the mold and turn the mold upside down. Hold the mold and dish tightly and shake gently to loosen the gelatin from the mold.

3. If the gelatin does not unmold easily, dip the mold in warm water again.

Gelatin desserts add attractiveness to your meals, are easily digestible, and usually contain fewer calories than cakes and pastry desserts.

Cake, Biscuit, and Pastry Desserts

Discussions of cakes, cookies, and pies as desserts have been included in separate chapters. Some of the other desserts which use a cake, biscuit, or pastry base are included here.

In addition to frosted cakes, *cake desserts* come in a great variety of forms such as cake rolls, upside-down cake, cake squares with fruit sauce, and refrigerator cake desserts.

Cake roll is made with a light, delicate sponge cake spread with flavored whipped cream, a pudding, a thickened fruit filling, jelly, or jam, and then rolled.

Upside-down cake is a cake made by first arranging a layer of butter, sugar, and fruit in the bottom of a cake pan or skillet. A cake batter is then poured over the fruit and baked. When you remove the cake from the pan, the arranged fruit is an attractive decoration and no frosting is needed.

Any plain cake can be cut into desired shapes (squares, rectangles, etc.) and served with a fruit or pudding sauce. Here you can display your creative talents by developing an unusual but pleasing combination of shapes and flavors.

Sponge and *angel food cakes* are favorites for *refrigerator-cake desserts*. An angel food cake cut into layers or one from which the center has been carefully removed to form a cavity can be filled and/or spread with flavored whipped cream to give an elaborate and truly beautiful dessert. There are so many wonderful cake desserts that you will want to try them all.

377

A rich biscuit dough or a muffin-like batter can be the base for easy-to-make *biscuit desserts*. You add sugar and sometimes eggs to the basic quick-bread ingredients to make a base for a variety of desserts.

You can use sweetened biscuit dough for fruit *shortcakes*. The baked sweet biscuit is split open, and sweetened fruit is spread on the bottom half and covered with the top half. More fruit is added on top and garnished with whipped cream.

For *dumplings*, cut the dessert biscuit dough into squares. Place sweetened fruit in the center of each square and fold the points of the dough over the fruit pressing them together at the center. Dumplings are served either hot or cold.

A hot thickened fruit filling is poured into a pan or casserole to make *cobblers*. The rolled sweetened biscuit dough may be used as the top pastry, or it can be cut into fancy shapes and arranged on top of the fruit. Cobblers are baked until golden brown, and may be served hot or cold.

You already know how to make the *pastry* desserts: pies, tarts, and turnovers. Cream puffs represent a different kind of pastry from the plain or puff pastry used for pies and other fancy pastry desserts. Eclairs (rectangular shape) and cream puffs (round shape) are small puffed shells made from a soft dough which contains eggs in addition to the basic pastry ingredients of flour, salt, fat, and water. Because cream puff pastry expands so much during baking, the center of the puff

378

is hollow. The water in the cream puff dough changes into steam and along with the expanding trapped air leavens the cream puff. The protein of the egg and flour (gluten) forms the shell of the cream puff.

1. To make cream puffs, you must mix the ingredients— butter or margarine, water, and eggs—in a very special way. Put the water and butter into a saucepan and heat to a rolling boil.

2. Next, add the measured flour all at once to the water-butter mixture and stir vigorously over low heat (about 1 minute) until the ball of dough follows the spoon around the pan.

3. Remove the dough from the range, add one egg at a time, and beat until smooth before adding the next egg.

4. Then, drop the cream puff pastry from a spoon (as you did the drop cookie dough) onto a baking sheet. Bake in a hot oven as directed by your recipe.

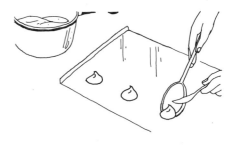

5. After the cream puff is baked and cooled, cut off the top with a sharp knife and fill it with any filling such as whipped cream, pudding, or ice cream. Then replace the top.

Cream puffs are a French delicacy, crisp and hollow, elegant enough for any party. You may dust them with powdered sugar or serve them with a sweet sauce.

Cake, biscuit, and pastry desserts are usually rich and provide you with many calories. They will complement your meals best when you serve them with other foods that are light, that is, low in calories, or low in fat and sugar. In this way, you will not overload your meals with calories. For your heavy meals, you should select a light dessert.

Frozen Desserts

Frozen desserts can be light and refreshing or calorie-rich depending upon the ingredients which they contain. On the basis of the ingredients used to make them, they are grouped as ices, sherbets, ice creams, parfaits, and mousses. *Ices* are made of fruit juices and sugar and are frozen. In addition to fruit juices and sugar, *sherbets* may contain egg whites or gelatin and are frozen. *Ice creams* are made with cream, milk, sugar, and may contain chocolate, fruits, or nuts. French ice cream also contains eggs. *Parfaits* and *mousses* are very rich desserts which are made with sweetened whipped cream and flavoring and frozen without stirring. The mousse may contain some gelatin and the parfait may contain beaten egg whites.

You may make ice cream by using an ice cream freezer in which the mixture is stirred or beaten during freezing or by using the freezing compartment of your refrigerator. Because you cannot stir ice cream as it freezes in the refrigerator tray, you may whip the mixture after it is partially frozen. After you remove the ice cream mixture from the freezer tray, beat it to incorporate air. Then, return the beaten ice cream mixture to the freezer tray and freeze it again.

Beating during freezing breaks up the large ice crystals to give your ice cream a smooth texture. Acceptable ice cream can be made in a refrigerator freezer, but its texture will not be as smooth as that made in an ice cream freezer.

You may serve frozen desserts plain or with a sauce as a sundae. Plain frozen desserts will give you fewer calories, but the nutrients contributed by all desserts will depend upon the ingredients used to make them.

Nutrient Contributions

Except for fruits, most of the desserts which you make will probably contain sugar and many will include fat as well. Both sugars and fats are rich in calories and will increase the caloric value of all foods in which you use them. *Desserts in general will contribute calories for your energy needs, but will add little to your protein, vitamin, and mineral needs unless you include fruit desserts or custards, puddings, and frozen desserts made with milk.* You should look to milk, fruits, vegetables, and cereals for your daily vitamin, mineral, and protein needs.

The many convenience dessert items make it easy to serve desserts often, and, unless you are careful, you can easily overload your meals with calories.

Convenience in Desserts

You will find convenience in all types of desserts. Fruit desserts require no preparation except for washing fresh whole fruit and partially thawing frozen fruits.

You are already familiar with pudding and custard mixes, canned puddings and pie fillings, the pastry, cake, and gelatin mixes, and the convenience whipped toppings. All of these will contribute to the ease with which many delicious desserts can be made.

Your dessert selection can also be made from the wide variety of frozen and ready-to-eat desserts which are ready to serve or may need only to be warmed or baked.

You need to plan your desserts to complement your meals without providing an excess of calories. Use your imagination to create new dessert favorites which best satisfy your needs. Experiment with some of the new convenience items you find in the market. Exchange ideas with friends.

Main Ideas

Desserts are classified according to the ingredients from which they are made and the various methods of preparation. The nutrients contributed by any dessert depend on the ingredients of which it is made. In general, desserts contribute mainly calories except for those which contain significant amounts of fruit or milk.

Activities

1. Use your imagination to create a new dessert from the convenience items available. Prepare and serve it to your family. Would you prepare it again? Give reasons.

2. What home-prepared desserts are not available in a convenience form at your favorite supermarket?

3. Use a food table and list the nutrients and calories you receive from the desserts that you usually eat.

4. Prepare a fruit dessert and serve it as a dinner dessert. Was fruit an appropriate dessert for your meal? Why?

5. Prepare cream puffs and use a pudding filling. Write a lunch menu for which cream puffs would be an appropriate dessert. What did you consider when you planned the menu?

6. Prepare a gelatin whip and select an appropriate meal in your home to serve this dessert.

Questions

1. List the different types of desserts and give examples of each.

2. When would you serve a fruit-cheese tray for dessert?

3. What is a fruit ambrosia, a fruit cup, a fruit whip, a compote?

4. What are the differences between puddings and custards? How do their preparations differ?

5. What causes a watery custard?

6. When are stirred and baked custards done?

7. How are stirred custards served or used?

8. What is gelatin? How is a simple gelatin made?

9. When can gelatin be whipped?

10. What are snows or sponges, Spanish and Bavarian creams, and charlottes? In what ways do they differ?

11. What are cake rolls, cobblers, and dumplings? What do they have in common?

12. In what ways do cream puffs differ from plain pastry?

13. Define sherbet, ice cream, mousse, and parfait.

14. What are two methods for making ice cream?

15. What nutrients are contributed by desserts?

4 The Language of Meals

Chapter 25

Planning Meals

Words for Thought

Nutritional labeling
a label indicating nutritive values in percentages of U.S. RDA (United States Recommended Dietary Allowances).

Recommended Daily Dietary Allowances (RDA)
the daily nutrient allowances for healthy persons (living in U.S.) set by the Food and Nutrition Board of The National Research Council.

Meal patterns
a guide for planning menus.

Generic foods
wholesome foods without store or national brand labels.

Daily Food Guide
a guide which includes the food groups and the amounts of each which individuals should have in their daily diets.

In the preceding chapters you learned about the nutrients contributed by foods. You studied the principles involved in food preparation. You are now ready to plan meals. Attractive, nutritious meals do not just happen. They have to be planned. Several factors are important to remember when planning meals. Personal nutrient needs, and the nutritional needs of those who will eat with you are to be considered.

Other factors that influence the foods you prepare are money, time, energy, and the attractiveness of the meals. Your knowledge and skill in food preparation and the equipment which is available will limit any menus you plan. The importance which you attach to each meal will influence the kind of menu you plan.

In planning you should think of all the meals for a particular day at the same time so that all your nutrient needs will be met. Whether you plan simple meals or elaborate company ones, your first responsibility in meal planning is to make sure that the meals will provide all the needed nutrients.

Kilocalories in Your Meals

You will recall that your body has a very special need for energy just as it has for nutrients. You also know the energy need of your body, and the energy your body obtains from food is measured in kilocalories. The carbohydrates and fats provide most of the body's energy need and protein the remainder of that need. Fats contribute 9 kilocalories per gram, while carbohydrates and protein give 4 kilocalories per gram. The amount of fat, carbohydrate, and protein in a food determines its kilocaloric value. Although some foods are rich sources of fat and other foods are rich sources of carbohydrate or protein, most foods contain varying amounts of each energy nutrient.

This simple rule will help you identify the energy-rich foods. The greasy, fat-crisp, gooey, sticky, or sweet foods contribute many kilocalories (are energy rich), while the juicy, water-crisp foods have few kilocalories.

Your body needs energy (kilocalories) for play and work and for the various reactions taking place within your body's cells. The kilocalories in the meals you eat should equal those required for your daily work and the work of your body's cells. In other words, kilocalories eaten (coming into the body) should equal the kilocalories consumed (spent in work and cellular activity). When you eat more kilocalories than your body uses each day, you will gain weight. When you eat less kilocalories than your body needs each day, you will lose weight. When the kilocalories taken in (eaten) equal those spent, your weight remains constant. You will neither gain nor lose weight.

When the weight you maintain is desirable for your age and height, you have reached a kilocaloric balance. This simply means that you are eating the right amount of food to provide the kilocalories your body needs to function. You are eating the kilocalories to match the energy you spend each day. A gain in weight means you are eating more food than is needed to replace the energy you are spending each day. When this happens, you should take a good look at the foods you are eating and when and how much you are eating. The best place to begin cutting down is with the greasy, gooey, sweet foods. These foods quickly add up to a kilocalorie overload, but contribute very few, if any, of the essential nutrients.

The recommended servings from the food groups provide most of your nutrient needs and give you about 1300 to 1500 kilocalories (depending upon the foods you choose and their methods of preparation). This amount of energy (1300-1500 kcal) is less than your body spends each day and would permit you to lose gradually the unwanted weight gained. When weight loss occurs slowly, your body is given a chance to adjust to the reduced food intake and the weight you lose can be permanent.

Anytime more energy is taken into the body than is spent, the body has no choice other than to store it as fat in adipose tissue. These excess kilocalories that occur day after day allow more and more fat to be stored. This leads to obesity. Individuals weighing about 20 percent above desirable weight are said to be obese. Overweight is a serious health problem in the United States. Obese individuals are found in every age group. Obesity detracts from personal appearance, increases the susceptibility to cardiovascular diseases, complicates other diseases, and shortens the lifespan.

There are no easy solutions to overweight or obesity. Kilocalories in excess of need are the direct cause of gained weight regardless of whatever may be the indirect cause. If miracle diets eliminated weight, there would be no overweight people among us today!

A good weight reduction diet is based on a balanced diet and uses few high-energy foods. You should use cooking techniques which do not add calories such as broil, steam, bake, and boil. You can use large servings of fruits and vegetables to substitute for the decreased intake of energy-rich foods (fat, sugar, dessert).

Nutrients in Your Meals

You recall that foods contain varying amounts of nutrients and that most foods are made of more than one nutrient. You already know that nutrients are the building blocks of food and can be classified into six general groups: carbohydrates, fats, proteins, vitamins, minerals, and water.

The nutrients from food serve your body in three general ways. Carbohydrates and fats supply the energy for your work and play; proteins build and repair your body; and vitamins, minerals, and water regulate and protect your body processes. The table on pages 388-389 will help you to review your need for the various nutrients and the foods in which they are found. However, check Chapters 6 through 14 that present these nutrients in more detail.

You will need all of these nutrients as long as you live. However, during periods of rapid growth, from birth through adolescence to adulthood, you will have a greater need for nutrients so that your body can grow and develop.

Recommended Daily Dietary Allowances

On pages 390-391 you will find the Table of Recommended Daily Dietary Allowances. These allowances are the levels of intake of the essential nutrients which are considered, in the judgment of the Food and Nutrition Board on the basis of available scientific knowledge, to be adequate to meet the known nutritional needs of practically all healthy persons, from infancy through adulthood. There are also estimated safe and adequate intakes for additional selected vitamins and minerals.

RDA are recommendations for the amounts of nutrients that should be eaten daily. Since there are some losses of nutrients which occur during the processing and preparation of food, you must allow for these losses in planning your daily intake of food.

You will find these recommended allowances listed on labels on food packages.

Nutritional Labeling

Nutritional labeling on a food product will tell you the nutritive value of the food. Nutritional labeling was developed by the Food and Drug Administration and the food industry to give you the nutrient content of most foods. It is important for you to have this information. Look at some labels and food products. Near the top of each label locate the section identified as "Nutrition Information."

Nutrients and Food Sources

Nutrient	Food Sources	Body Needs	Nutrient Shortage
Carbohydrates	breads, cereals, spaghetti, macaroni, noodles, potato, lima beans, corn, dried beans and peas, sugar, syrup, jellies, honey	supply energy; supply roughage or cellulose	
Fats	butter, margarine, cream, salad dressings, shortenings, lard, fat of meat; invisible fat in lean meats; egg yolks, cheese	supply energy, essential fatty acids, and fat-soluble vitamins; to protect body organs; to insulate and retain heat	retarded growth; unhealthy skin
Protein	meat, poultry, fish, milk, cheese, dried peas and beans, nuts, breads, cereals	to build and repair body tissues; to build necessary components as enzymes, antibodies	poor growth; weak muscles; shortage of antibodies and enzymes
Minerals Calcium	milk, cheese, ice cream, broccoli, turnip, and mustard greens	bones and teeth; regulate nerve and muscle activity; to clot blood	poor bones and teeth; poor muscles; poor nerve control
Phosphorus	milk, cheese, whole grain cereals and breads; meats; dried beans and peas	bones and teeth; regulate body; cell activity	poor bones and teeth; poor growth
Iodine	seafoods; iodized salt	activity of thyroid gland	goiter
Iron	liver, meats, eggs, whole grain and enriched cereals and breads; dark leafy greens, dried peas, beans, prunes, raisins	for hemoglobin of red blood cells	anemia
Magnesium	whole grains; leafy greens; meat; milk; legumes, nuts	muscle and nerve function; bones, teeth	tremor
Zinc	meats, liver; seafoods; eggs; whole grains; milk	growth, enzymes	retarded growth; impaired sense of taste

Nutrients and Food Sources (continued)

Nutrient	Food Sources	Body Needs	Nutrient Shortage
Vitamins Vitamin A	whole milk, cream, butter, margarine, cheese; dark green and deep yellow vegetables	good skin and mucous membranes, growth, visual purple of eyes	night blindness and eye diseases, poor growth, poor skin condition
Vitamin B$_1$ (thiamin)	enriched or whole grain cereals; pork and other meats, poultry, fish; dried beans and peas	health of nerves, digestive function, helps release energy from carbohydrates, promotes good appetite	fatigue, poor appetite, poor growth, beriberi
Vitamin B$_2$ (riboflavin)	milk, cheese, ice cream; whole grain and enriched cereals; eggs, meat, liver, poultry, fish; dark green vegetables	smooth skin, good eye function; aids body in use of protein and energy foods	poor skin, premature aging, poor vision, poor growth
Vitamin B$_6$ (pyridoxine)	whole grains; meat; fish; potatoes, other vegetables	to utilize amino acids	weight loss; anemia; hyperirritability
Vitamin B$_{12}$	meats, organ meats; fish; poultry; eggs; milk	red blood cell formation; nerve function	pernicious anemia; neurologic degeneration
Folacin	deep-green, leafy vegetables; muscle meats; eggs; whole grains	mature red blood cells	macrocytic anemia
Niacin (part of B com- plex)	enriched and whole grain cereals and breads; milk, cheese, meat, fish, poultry, peanuts	helps body use other nutrients, maintains good nerves and digestion	pellagra, fatigue, poor digestive and nerve function
Vitamin C (ascorbic acid)	oranges, lemons, limes, tomato, strawberries, cantaloupe, dark green leafy vegetables, cabbage, broccoli	helps to firm cementing material of cells and strong blood vessel walls	scurvy, bruise easily, bleeding gums, fatigue
Vitamin D	vitamin-D milk, egg yolks, butter, margarine, fish liver oils	helps body use calcium and phosphorus for strong bones and teeth	rickets, poor bones and teeth

Food And Nutrition Board, National Academy Of Sciences—National Research Council
Recommended Daily Dietary Allowances,[a] Revised 1980
Designed for the maintenance of good nutrition of practically all healthy people in the U.S.A.

	Age (years)	Weight (kg)	Weight (lbs)	Height (cm)	Height (in)	Protein (g)	Fat-Soluble Vitamins			Water-Soluble Vitamins		
							Vitamin A (mg R.E.)[b]	Vitamin D (mg)[c]	Vitamin E (mg α T.E.)[d]	Vitamin C (mg)	Thiamin (mg)	Riboflavin (mg)
Infants	0.0–0.5	6	13	60	24	kg × 2.2	420	10	3	35	0.3	0.4
	0.5–1.0	9	20	71	28	kg × 2.0	400	10	4	35	0.5	0.6
Children	1–3	13	29	90	35	23	400	10	5	45	0.7	0.8
	4–6	20	44	112	44	30	500	10	6	45	0.9	1.0
	7–10	28	62	132	52	34	700	10	7	45	1.2	1.4
Males	11–14	45	99	157	62	45	1000	10	8	50	1.4	1.6
	15–18	66	145	176	69	56	1000	10	10	60	1.4	1.7
	19–22	70	154	177	70	56	1000	7.5	10	60	1.5	.7
	23–50	70	154	178	70	56	1000	5	10	60	1.4	1.6
	51+	70	154	78	70	56	1000	5	10	60	1.2	1.4
Females	11–14	46	101	157	62	46	800	10	8	50	1.1	1.3
	15–18	55	120	163	64	46	800	10	8	60	1.1	1.3
	19–22	55	120	163	64	44	800	7.5	8	60	1.1	1.3
	23–50	55	120	163	64	44	800	5	8	60	1.0	1.2
	51+	55	120	163	64	44	800	5	8	60	1.0	1.2
Pregnant						+30	+200	+5	+2	+20	+0.4	+0.3
Lactating						+20	+400	+5	+3	+40	+0.5	+0.5

a   The allowances are intended to provide for individual variations among most normal persons as they live in the United States under usual environmental stresses. Diets should be based on a variety of common foods in order to provide other nutrients for which human requirements have been less well defined.

b   Retinol equivalents. 1 Retinol equivalent = 1 mg retinol or 6 mg carotene.

c   As cholecalciferol. 10 pg cholecalciferol = 400 I.U. vitamin D.

d   α tocopherol equivalents. 1 mg d-α-tocopherol = 1 αT.E.

Estimated Safe and Adequate Daily Dietary Intakes
of Additional Selected Vitamins and Minerals[a]

	Age (years)	Vitamins			Trace Elements[b]		
		Vitamin K (mg)	Biotin (mg)	Pantothenic Acid (mg)	Copper (mg)	Manganese (mg)	Fluoride (mg)
Infants	0–0.5	12	35	2	0.5–0.7	0.5–0.7	0.1–0.5
	0.5–1	10–20	50	3	0.7–1.0	0.7–1.0	0.2–1.0
Children	1–3	15–30	65	3	1.0–1.5	1.0–1.5	0.5–1.5
and	4–6	20–40	85	3–4	1.5–2.0	1.5–2.0	1.0–2.5
Adolescents	7–10	30–60	120	4–5	2.0–2.5	2.0–3.0	1.5–2.5
	11+	50–100	100–200	4–7	2.0–3.0	2.5–5.0	1.5–2.5
Adults		70–140	100–200	4–7	2.0–3.0	2.5–5.0	1.5–4.0

a   Because there is less information on which to base allowances, these figures are not given in the main table of the RDA and are provided here in the form of ranges of recommended intakes.

The label tells the size and number of servings in the container. Next are listed the number of calories and the amounts of protein, carbohydrate, and fat in one serving. The lower part of the label gives the percentages of the Recommended Daily Dietary Allowances of protein and seven vitamins and

Food And Nutrition Board, National Academy Of Sciences—National Research Council
Recommended Daily Dietary Allowances,[a] Revised 1980
Designed for the maintenance of good nutrition of practically all healthy people in the U.S.A.

| | Water-Soluble Vitamins | | | | Minerals | | | | | |
	Niacin (mg N.E.)[e]	Vitamin B_6 (mg)	Folacin[f] (mg)	Vitamin B12 (mg)	Calcium (mg)	Phosphorus (mg)	Magnesium (mg)	Iron (mg)	Zinc (mg)	Iodine (mg)
Infants	6	0.3	30	0.5[g]	360	240	50	10	3	40
	8	0.6	45	1.5	540	360	70	15	5	50
Children	9	0.9	100	2.0	800	800	150	15	10	70
	11	1.3	200	2.5	800	800	200	10	10	90
	16	1.6	300	3.0	800	800	250	10	10	120
Males	18	1.8	400	3.0	1200	1200	350	18	15	150
	18	2.0	400	3.0	1200	1200	400	18	15	150
	19	2.2	400	3.0	800	800	350	10	15	150
	18	2.2	400	3.0	800	800	350	10	15	150
	16	2.2	400	3.0	800	800	350	10	15	150
Females	15	1.8	400	3.0	1200	1200	300	18	15	150
	14	2.0	400	3.0	1200	1200	300	18	15	150
	14	2.0	400	3.0	800	800	300	18	15	150
	13	2.0	400	3.0	800	800	300	18	15	150
	13	2.0	400	3.0	800	800	300	10	15	150
Pregnant	+2	+0.6	+400	+1.0	+400	+400	+150	h	+5	+25
Lactating	+5	+0.5	+100	+1.0	+400	+400	+150	h	+10	+50

e 1 NE (niacin equivalent) is equal to 1 mg of niacin or 60 mg of dietary tryptophan.

f The folacin allowances refer to dietary sources as determined by *Lactobacillus gaset* assay after treatment with enzymes ("conjugases") to make polyglutanyl forms of the vitamin available to the test organism.

g The RDA for vitamin B12 in infants is based on average concentration of the vitamin in human milk. The allowances after weaning are based on energy intake (as recommended by the American Academy of Pediatrics) and consideration of other factors such as intestinal absorption.

h The increased requirement during pregnancy cannot be met by the iron content of habitual American diets nor by the existing iron stores of many women; therefore the use of 30–60 mg of supplemental iron is recommended. Iron needs during lactation are not substantially different from those of nonpregnant women, but continued supplementation of the mother for 2–3 months after parturition is advisable in order to replenish stores depleted by pregnancy.

Reproduced from: Recommended Dietary Allowances, Ninth Edition, 1980, with the permission of the National Academy of Sciences, Washington, D.C.

Estimated Safe and Adequate Daily Dietary Intakes
of Additional Selected Vitamins and Minerals[a]
Electrolytes

	Age (years)	Chromium (mg)	Selenium (mg)	Molybdenum (mg)	Sodium (mg)	Potassium (mg)	Chloride (mg)
Infants	0–0.5	0.01–0.04	0.01–0.04	0.03–0.06	115–350	350–925	275–700
	0.5–1	0.02–0.06	0.02–0.06	0.04–0.08	250–750	425–1275	400–1200
Children	1–3	0.02–0.08	0.02–0.08	0.05–0.1	325–975	550–1650	500–1500
and	4–6	0.03–0.12	0.03–0.12	0.06–0.15	450–1350	775–2325	700–2100
Adolescents	7–10	0.05–0.2	0.05–0.2	0.1–0.3	600–1800	1000–3000	925–2775
	11+	0.05–0.2	0.05–0.2	0.15–0.5	900–2700	1525–4575	1400–4200
Adults		0.05–0.2	0.05–0.2	0.15–0.5	1100–3300	1875–5625	1700–5100

b Since the toxic levels for many trace elements may by only several times usual intakes, the upper levels for the trace elements given in this table should not be habitually exceeded.

Reproduced from: Recommended Dietary Allowances, Ninth Edition, 1980, with the permission of the National Academy of Sciences, Washington, D.C.

minerals in a serving of the food. The U.S. RDA represent the amounts needed each day by people, plus a margin of safety (30 to 50 percent) to allow for individual differences. To insure enough vitamins, minerals, and protein, the percentages for each food should add up to about 100 percent each day.

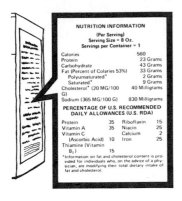

NUTRITION INFORMATION
(Per Serving)
Serving Size = 8 Oz.
Servings per Container = 1

Calories	560
Protein	23 Grams
Carbohydrate	43 Grams
Fat (Percent of Colaries 53%)	33 Grams
Polyunsaturated*	2 Grams
Saturated*	9 Grams
Cholesterol* (20 MG/100 G)	40 Milligrams
Sodium (365 MG/100 G)	830 Milligrams

PERCENTAGE OF U.S. RECOMMENDED
DAILY ALLOWANCES (U.S. RDA)

Protein	35	Riboflavin	15
Vitamin A	35	Niacin	25
Vitamin C		Calcium	2
(Ascorbic Acid)	10	Iron	25
Thiamine (Vitamin			
B_1)	15		

*Information on fat and cholesterol content is provided for individuals who, on the advice of a physician, are modifying their total dietary intake of fat and cholesterol.

NUTRITION INFORMATION
Serving Size = 1/7 of 9" Pie
Servings per Container = 7

Calories	350
Protein	3 Grams
Carbohydrate	51 Grams
Fat	15 Grams

PERCENTAGE OF U.S. RECOMMENDED
DAILY ALLOWANCES (U.S. RDA)

Protein	4
Vitamin A	0
Vitamin C	2
Thiamine	2
Riboflavin	2
Niacin	2
Calcium	0
Iron	2

Look at the label shown here. It shows one serving of the food contains 35 percent of the U.S. RDA for protein, 35 percent of the U.S. RDA for vitamin A, and so on. Some labels will list other vitamins and minerals as well as polyunsaturated and saturated fats, cholesterol, and sodium. Nutrition information is especially helpful to persons on weight reduction, diabetic, and other medical diets.

The nutrition information panel gives you an easy way to learn about the nutritive value of foods. You can compare the information on the labels from different types of foods to determine which nutrients are commonly found in each food, and which ones are particularly good sources of certain vitamins and minerals.

By comparing different kinds of foods, you can learn which foods contribute substantial amounts of nutrients and which ones do not. New food products can be compared with familiar ones to find out whether they are good nutritional buys. Eating a variety of foods each day and using the nutrition information will assure you that you are getting the nutrients needed for a healthful diet.

You will notice that dietary allowances are listed in the preceding table according to age and sex; in this way adjustments in the nutrient allowances are made to meet the demands of the different growth periods. Even though you stop growing at adulthood, your body continues to have a need for all nutrients. You will notice that most of the nutrient values are listed in grams and milligrams (454 grams = 1 pound, and 1 mg = one-thousandth of a gram), and that vitamins A and D are listed in International Units (one I.U. = 0.3 micrograms, or less than one-millionth of a gram). Vitamin A is now also listed in a new unit, the R.E. (retinol equivalent) recommended by the FAO/WHO (Food and Agriculture Organization/ World Health Organization) Expert Committee. A retinol equivalent equals one microgram of retinol.

Generic Foods

In addition to the national or name brands and store brands, you may select foods which are identified only as generic and have no brand names given. The labels are usually black and white and list only the name of the product such as sweet peas, the ingredients, net content, and the name of the manufacturer or distributor. A store may carry between 25 and 50 or more generic items. Popular canned vegetables, fruits, juices and drinks, packaged macaroni and cheese dinners, oil, peanut butter, tomato products, and other items are offered.

Most generic items are displayed together. This may make it more difficult for you to compare prices. Generic items are lower in price than national or store brands. The reduced cost of generic items is due to somewhat lower quality (USDA Grade C and some B), little advertising, inexpensive packaging and labeling, and selection is limited to only one size for each product.

The nutrition information panel on the label will give you the nutritional value of the generic food as it does on brand-name products. You can compare the quality of generic and brand-name products and decide which product best serves your need and represents a good value. Generic food products are wholesome foods.

Meal-Planning Guides

To check the nutrient value of each food and to see that you meet your recommended daily dietary allowance (RDA) for each nutrient is very time-consuming. Nutritionists have set up an easy guide for you to follow when you select your food. This guide is most often called the Daily Food Guide or Food for Fitness.

The Daily Food Guide

Your daily food choices can be listed in five general groups to enable you to make healthful food selections. The five food groups are the Vegetable-Fruit Group; the Bread-Cereal Group; the Milk-Cheese Group; the Meat-Poultry-Fish-Beans-Nuts Group; and the Fats-Sweets Group. The first four of these food groups are rich in nutrients and are referred to as the Daily Food Guide, the Four Food Groups, or the Basic Four. The fifth group includes foods with a high sugar and/or fat content and should only be used in small quantities.

The first group is the Vegetable-Fruit Group. You must be careful to include the dark green leafy or deep yellow vegetables for their rich supply of vitamin A in the form of carotene. You also need to include one serving of foods rich in vitamin C such as citrus fruits (oranges, grapefuit, etc.), cantaloupes, strawberries; or two servings of foods that are fair sources of vitamin C such as raw cabbage, green pepper, tomato, or

Included in the first group of the Daily Food Guide are some vegetables which provide vitamin A as well as some fruits which are rich sources of vitamin C.

asparagus to help meet your daily need for vitamin C. Four or more servings are recommended each day from the Vegetable-Fruit Group (125 mL (½ c) cooked vegetable or fruit, or 1 whole fruit or vegetable such as an apple or potato = 1 serving). Your selection should include a citrus fruit or other fruit or vegetable high in vitamin C and a dark green or deep yellow vegetable for vitamin A, at least every other day. Include any other fruits or vegetables to give you a total of at least four servings. Fruits and vegetables make important contributions of vitamins and minerals and especially vitamins A and C.

The second group is the Bread-Cereal, or Grains Group. All whole grain, enriched, restored, or fortified cereals and breads, macaroni, spaghetti, and noodles are in this group. Rolls, biscuits, muffins, and other quick breads such as waffles and pancakes are included when they are made with enriched flour. To meet the daily requirements you need to select four or more servings each day (1 slice of bread, 185 to 250 mL (¾ to 1 c) of cereal or macaroni product = 1 serving). Cereals and breads are rich in the carbohydrate starch and provide the B vitamins, some iron, and incomplete proteins.

The third group is the Milk-Cheese Group. It includes the various forms of milk and cheese. Milk (whole, skim, nonfat dry, evaporated), chocolate milk, other milk beverages, cheese, and ice cream are included. A portion of your milk requirement can be used to make custards, milk puddings, and cream soups. The table below gives the daily requirements.

Breads and cereals which make up the second group of the Daily Food Guide are an economical and abundant source of carbohydrates.

Whole Milk

Children	Adults
750 mL (3 or more c)	500 mL (2 or more c)
Adolescents	**Pregnant women**
1 L (4 or more c) **Nursing mothers**	750 mL (3 or more c)
1 L (4 or more c)	

The third group includes all forms of milk as well as ice cream and cheese.

The Milk-Cheese Group will provide you with these nutrients: calcium, protein, riboflavin, and other B complex vitamins. You will receive vitamin A from whole milk and vitamin D from milk fortified with vitamin D. Low-fat milk (2 percent) and skim milk may be fortified with vitamins A and D and will give you about one-half the number of calories provided by whole milk.

The fourth group is the Meat-Poultry-Fish-Beans-Nuts Group. It is made up of all kinds of meat including beef, veal, pork, lamb; variety meats such as liver, kidney, heart; poultry and eggs; all fish; and dried beans, peas, and nuts. To help you meet your daily protein requirement, you will select two or more servings (113 g (4 oz) raw meat or 85 g (3 oz) cooked meat = 1 serving) from this group. This group can supply either complete or incomplete protein depending upon which food you select. Meat, poultry, fish, and eggs provide complete protein, while dried peas, beans, and nuts provide incomplete protein. When you choose a food with incomplete protein such as dried peas or beans, include a complete protein food such as milk, cheese, or egg in the same meal. The milk will provide the kind of amino acids which are missing in foods which contain incomplete protein. These foods will also provide the B vitamins and iron. Liver is the richest food source of iron.

The fourth group includes all meat, poultry, and fish as well as eggs, dry beans, peas, and nuts. It supplies both complete and incomplete protein.

The fifth group is the Fats-Sweets Group. You will notice that foods rich in fats and sugars (pastries, cookies, cakes, jellies, etc.) are not included in the Daily Food Guide. These foods are rich in calories, but provide almost no vitamins, minerals, or proteins. They are used to add flavor to other foods such as butter or margarine on vegetables and sugar in puddings and beverages. Foods rich in fats and sugars are considered harmful when they crowd out other needed foods (fruits, vegetables, milk) and when they overload your body with extra calories that cause overweight. Because fats and sugars are so high in calories, it is better to include them in small quantities to complement the Daily Food Guide, rather than to replace foods in the guide.

When you are active, you do need some foods that contain fat and sugar. The Daily Food Guide makes it easy for you to plan meals that include the nutrients you need each day. If you select foods from the Guide for each meal and are careful to include the amounts of food recommended from each group, your nutrient needs will be met. Learn to think of meal planning in terms of the Daily Food Guide.

Foods not included in the Daily Food Guide are a temptation, but add only calories and few nutrients to your diet.

Here are three examples of simple luncheon menus. One is a vegetable plate; one has spaghetti and meatballs as its main dish; the other has pita bread filled with tuna.

Meal Patterns

A meal pattern serves as a blueprint or guide and reminds you to include certain types of foods in your meals. When you do not follow a guide, it is easy to omit certain essential foods such as milk, vegetables, or fruits. Well-planned meals include at least one food from each group of the Daily Food Guide. Your menus will provide calories and protein as well as your vitamin and mineral needs.

No single meal will provide all your nutrient needs, but the meals for an entire day can supply these needs when you plan them well. The following meal patterns will help you choose or plan good meals.

Breakfast Pattern

Fruit (citrus often)
Main Dish (cereal and/or egg, waffles, etc.)
Bread
Milk or Other Beverage

Lunch or Supper Pattern

Main Dish (protein food in casseroles, soups, salads, and sandwiches)
Vegetable and/or Fruit
Bread
Milk or Other Beverage

Dinner Pattern

Main Dish (meat, poultry, fish, or other protein)
Two Vegetables (or vegetable and a fruit)
Salad
Bread
Milk or Other Beverage

When you write menus, list the foods in the order of the meal pattern or the order in which they are served. Capitalize all words except prepositions and conjunctions.

Meatless Meals

We pick and choose our diets from among the many available foods. Everyone needs the same nutrients but can choose them as they like them. Some individuals choose to follow the vegetarian style of eating and prefer meatless meals. The vegetarian diet consists almost entirely of foods of plant origin. Although vegetarianism may be practiced in a variety of forms, there are really only two basic diet patterns—the vegan and the lacto-ovo.

The vegans or pure vegetarians do not eat any animal products. The vegan chooses a diet of legumes, nuts, fruits, vegetables, and grains. The vegan may have some difficulty in getting enough energy (kilocalories) from only foods of plant origin, since these foods are bulky. When the diet is short in kilocalories, the body is forced to use protein for energy rather than for body building and maintenance.

You already know that meats supply complete proteins which contain all of the amino acids your body requires and those which your body cannot make. You also know that plant proteins are incomplete since they lack some of the amino acids your body cannot make, the essential amino acids. When your diet includes foods of animal origin, such as meat, milk, egg, the missing amino acids, which are found in vegetable proteins are easily provided.

The protein content of a pure vegetarian diet can be inadequate in essential amino acids and in the quantity of protein it contributes. Legumes and grains are the chief sources of proteins in the vegetarian diet. Examples of legumes are navy beans, lima beans, kidney beans, pinto beans, soy beans, blackeyed peas, chickpeas or garbanzo beans, and peas.

The legumes are the staple of the vegan diet and help to balance the grain proteins. A carefully chosen combination of legumes, whole grains, nuts, and vegetables can provide a satisfactory intake of protein for the pure vegan.

Another nutrient lacking in the vegan diet is vitamin B_{12} which is found only in foods of animal origin. When soy milk is fortified with vitamin B_{12} and calcium, it becomes a valuable source of these nutrients for vegans.

The vegan or vegetarian must carefully select the foods which contribute good amounts of calcium, riboflavin, and protein—the nutrients usually provided by milk. The vegan food groups are legumes, grains, vegetables, and fruits.

Grains are present in large amounts in the vegan diet. About 625 mL (2½ c) of various grains and 4 slices of bread supply the average vegan's daily need. Seeds and nuts are counted as grains; 250 mL (1 c) of cooked legumes should be included to balance the grain proteins. Vegans also need to include

Legumes are the staple of a vegan diet. However, a combination of legumes, nuts, whole grains, and vegetables must be carefully chosen if there is to be adequate protein in the diet.

generous amounts of fresh, dark green vegetables which provide some iron and calcium. Leafy greens are good sources of riboflavin which is best provided by milk.

Some vegetarians consume only milk with the foods of plant origin and are known as lacto-vegetarians. The lacto-ovo vegetarians do not eat meat, poultry, or fish but they do eat eggs and dairy products. The eggs, milk, and cheese provide the nutrients contributed by meats and which are lacking in foods of plant origin.

An adequate amount of nutrients from vegetarian diets depends upon the combination of foods eaten. The lacto-ovo vegetarians eat some foods from each of the food groups which makes it fairly easy to obtain the nutrients needed by the body.

Because of their bulk, vegetable foods may not provide the energy needed by some individuals, especially children, unless oils and sweeteners are used in food preparation.

When your diet depends upon a limited variety of foods, your body is not provided with the needed nutrients. Your diet must include an adequate amount of food selected from a wide variety of foods. You should remember that no one food has all of the nutrients or the amounts of each nutrient your body needs every day. Balanced selections from the food groups point the way to good health.

The Meals of the Day

Food habits and customs differ with countries and cultures; not all countries serve three meals a day. In some countries it is customary to have 5 or 6 meals a day.

Breakfast

Breakfast is considered the first meal of the day. It breaks the "fast" of the long night. Nutritionists and scientists tell us that breakfast is an important meal. Without breakfast, it is difficult to get the daily nutrient needs. Breakfast skippers are less alert, more subject to illness, and tend to overeat later in the day. This practice often leads to overweight.

A good breakfast includes foods from the Daily Food Guide. A good breakfast should supply from one-fourth to one-third of your total daily nutrients and calories. When you do not include a citrus or a fruit which is high in vitamin C for breakfast, plan to include some other sources of vitamin C in the other meals of the day. When you do not include cereal, use an additional serving of bread and drink a glass of milk for your beverage.

The type of breakfast for you will depend upon your energy needs. (For example, if you are very active, you may prefer a heavy breakfast.) When you include the foods listed in the breakfast pattern, you will have a medium breakfast. You can easily adjust a medium breakfast to meet your individual needs. When energy needs are great, include both cereal and egg and/or additional foods (waffles, pancakes, bacon, sausage) or use larger servings. When energy needs are small, use smaller servings or fewer foods.

Customarily, the variety of foods served for breakfast is smaller than that for other meals. All foods from the Daily Food Guide can be served for breakfast, if you choose. If conventional breakfast foods do not appeal to you, arouse your morning appetite with such unconventional foods as cheeseburgers, chili, pudding, pizza, or soup.

Foods you choose for breakfast should be determined by your energy needs and foods which you choose for other meals of the day. The other meals of the day do not replace your need for breakfast.

Breakfasts start off the day. They can vary greatly to satisfy a wide variety of tastes.

Lunch

In contrast to breakfast, lunch is a moderately heavy meal served at noon; when this same meal is served in the evening, it is then called supper. Lunch and supper are similar meals, and differ only in the time of day they are served.

Your lunch should supply one-third of your nutrient needs. It should not be so heavy that it interferes with your activity the remainder of the day. Use the basic lunch pattern to plan a satisfying and nutritious lunch.

For the lunch main dish, you may choose from among soups, sandwiches, hearty salads, casseroles, or creamed foods. Lunch is usually more satisfying when at least one hot dish is included. It is a good time to serve foods such as egg or vitamin C-rich foods when they have not been included for breakfast.

When you select your lunch from a school cafeteria or pack your lunch, follow the lunch pattern and include foods from the daily guide. Fruits, fresh vegetables, meats, and desserts may be left over from family meals and used creatively for a packed lunch. You can add variety to sandwiches by using different breads as well as different fillings. For a packed lunch, wrap each food in waxed paper or transparent wrap to protect freshness and prevent intermingling of flavors.

Lunches, too, can be light, medium, or heavy depending upon your activity and the foods which you include in your other meals. When you include the foods listed in the lunch pattern you will have a medium lunch. You can adjust the basic lunch pattern to meet your individual needs in the same way as the breakfast pattern, that is, by using additional foods or larger servings. Good lunches, whether purchased, packed, or prepared at home, require careful planning.

Dinner

Dinner is considered to be the largest and most elaborate meal of the day and may be served either at noon or in the evening. During the week, dinner may be served in the evening when all of your family members are at home. On Sundays and holidays, it may be served in the afternoon.

The dinner main dish is usually meat, poultry, or fish, and occasionally a cheese or egg dish. You should choose the other foods in the dinner pattern to enhance and complement the main dish. The other menus for the day are often based on the main dish chosen for dinner. If you plan dinner first, it will be easier to include the foods in breakfast and lunch that will complete your daily nutrient needs.

Although the dinner often consists of one course, the meat, vegetable, and salad, you may have a dessert and at times an appetizer course. The appetizer should probably be light such as a clear soup, tart fruit, or juice.

When you include the foods listed in the dinner pattern, you will have a medium dinner. Dinners, too, may be light, medium, or heavy as the basic pattern is adjusted by adding or subtracting foods or by adjusting portion size.

You will notice that desserts are not included as a part of the meal patterns because they tend to be high in fat and sugar and lack other nutrients. Fruits, custards, and milk puddings are wholesome desserts and contribute to your nutrient needs. Desserts can be used as the additional food, after daily food requirements are met, which provide the energy required for your activity. When you maintain the weight desirable for you, you are doing a good job of matching the food you eat with your energy needs.

A casserole dish of Moussaka along with a green salad, bread sticks, and fresh fruit is a simple, but very nutritious meal.

Main Ideas

Cost, time, energy, skill, and knowledge influence the kinds of meals people plan and prepare. In daily food intake there must be a proper balance of nutrients and kilocalories which are needed to support bodily activity. The number of kilocalories eaten daily should equal the kilocalories consumed in work and body cell activity. Too many kilocalories results in overweight; too few, underweight. Nutrient needs are listed in the RDA table. If planned, meatless meals can satisfy daily nutrient needs.

Nutritional labeling on food products is helpful in making food choices. Generic foods, limited in variety, are usually wholesome but of lower grade and may cost less than name brands but not be comparable in quality.

The Daily Food Guide includes the four nutrient-rich food groups. It is a practical guide to follow in planning daily meals. The food groups are the Vegetable-Fruit Group; the Bread-Cereal, or Grains Group; the Milk-Cheese Group; the Meat-Poultry-Fish-Beans-Nuts Group. Foods rich in fats and sugars comprise the fifth group and may be included when energy expenditure is great.

Activities

1. Examine the generic food section in your supermarket. List the food items available and compare their costs with those of national or name brands and store brands. What can you conclude about food costs? Compare the quality of generic fruit and vegetables with national and store brands of the same foods. List the uses for which generic and brand-name fruits and vegetables are best suited. What did you consider when you decided the use of these products?

2. Plan a meatless meal which will contribute to your nutrient and kilocalorie needs for a full day.

3. Plan a day's food intake for a vegan. What foods contribute to the vegan's protein need? Do these foods provide the needed protein?

4. Keep a record of the food you eat in a day. Check to see if you are getting the nutrients and the kilocalories that you need to support your activity.

5. Plan meals for yourself for a three-day period. Check with the RDA to see if your meals are nutritionally balanced. If you find they are not, rework your plan and check a second time. Analyze where you have made the improvements.

Questions

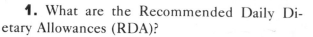

1. What are the Recommended Daily Dietary Allowances (RDA)?

2. Where can you locate the nutrient contributions of specific foods?

3. What is the Daily Food Guide? Of what value is it?

4. What are the foods and the amounts suggested by the Daily Food Guide?

5. What foods can you name that are not included in the Daily Food Guide? Why?

6. What are meal patterns? What is their value? Explain what is suggested in each pattern.

7. Why is breakfast an important meal?

8. How do breakfast, lunch, and dinner meals differ?

9. Defend the statement, "The food groups in the Daily Food Guide do not cut out food favorites."

10. Plan meals for one day. Explain why your plan is a good one from the standpoint of nutrition and interest.

Chapter
26
Influences on Planning

Words for Thought

Menu
a group of foods served as a meal.

Course
foods served at the same time within a meal.

Texture
the way a food feels to the tongue when eaten.

In addition to the meal-planning guides, there are some other factors to help you achieve not only nutritious meals but also attractive meals.

To achieve this goal, you should think about a number of things. You should think about family custom or tradition. There are probably a number of dishes which are especially important to your family. Cost, time, and energy must also be considered. Of course your meals should have variety in color, size and shape, texture, flavor, and temperature of foods.

Family Customs

Your experience with food came from your family meals. Your family food customs or traditions have made certain foods and methods of cooking important to you. These familiar foods continue to give you enjoyment, satisfaction, and a feeling of security. Chicken and potato salad may be the food that some people look forward to. Others may see hush puppies and catfish as their special meal. Still there are others who may enjoy refried beans and enchiladas. As you plan meals you will probably continue to use some of these favorites. When you are away from home and with friends and others who have different family food customs, your experiences with food will broaden. You will come to enjoy many different foods. Some foods from other countries may become as popular with you as those which you are used to. For example, many people enjoy fresh pineapple, shrimp, pizza, spaghetti, fried noodles, tacos, stir-fry vegetables, and barbecued ribs. Family food favorites and new foods will make your meals interesting and a pleasure to prepare.

Cost of Food

Fortunately, the cost of food is not determined by its nutrient value. You can purchase nutritious foods that can be well within your food allowance. Canned vegetables and vegetables in season; nonfat dry milk and margarine; less tender cuts of meat; poultry; and enriched or whole grain breads and cereals to be cooked are examples of foods from each food group which may be not too expensive.

Meats are the most expensive and grains and breads the least expensive. From the meat group, poultry and fish are usually less expensive than meats. Cheese, eggs, and milk are other more economical sources of complete protein.

Your best guide for comparing the cost of food is to determine the cost of each serving. Divide the cost of the food by the number of servings to obtain the cost per serving. For example, when the cost of the food is $3.98 and it serves 4 people ($3.98 divided by 4), the cost per serving becomes $1.00.

Unit pricing is another way to make food cost comparisons. This means the price per kg (lb), gr (oz), L (qt) is listed on the package label or the market shelf. You can easily compare prices. The many different sizes of packages make it difficult for you to compare the price of two or more package sizes of the same product unless a unit price is listed. Some stores list unit prices on easy-to-read colored labels.

It is usually wise to buy a less expensive form of a food if it will serve your purpose. For example, canned tomatoes which are in pieces and vary in size (sometimes marked Grade C) can be made into as flavorful a chili as whole tomatoes, and at a much lower cost. The largest and most perfect foods are apt to be more expensive, but their nutritional value is the same as for the same kind of food of a smaller size.

When you want to spend less money for food, you can reduce the amount of meat you buy and stop buying extras such as potato chips, pretzels, and carbonated beverages. You can choose recipes with less sugar, fat, and egg, and those which have optional ingredients such as mushrooms, toasted almonds, or some other ingredient. Recipes which use canned soups, prepared puddings, or canned onion rings add to the cost of food. Heat-and-serve products, salad dressings, gravy mixes, and foods in pressure cans also add to cost. Why is it not a good idea to cut down on milk, citrus fruits, and the dark green and yellow vegetables? Foods which provide little if any nutrients such as cola beverages and sweets are the truly expensive foods because their return in essential nutrients needed for health is so limited.

Time and Energy

Time, as well as money, is limited. You will be preparing meals each day, but some days you will have more time for food preparation than on others. The time and energy you will have to spend in preparation will be influenced by the foods and the food forms you buy. Some foods such as less tender cuts of meats, yeast breads, and baked beans take more time to prepare than other foods. Raw or fresh foods require less preparation and therefore less time and energy. There may be times when your schedule permits little time for food preparation. If your budget allows, at these times you may decide to use prepared mixes, canned or frozen foods, or heat-and-serve convenience items.

Some methods of food cookery such as broiling and frying require more attention than others, for example, roasting and braising. Small or thin pieces of food cook more quickly than large or thick pieces. Foods such as roasts or casseroles cooked in the oven usually require more time than do many foods cooked on the range surface.

Some foods can be prepared by more than one method. You can choose the method that best fits your time schedule. Drop biscuits, baked potatoes, and strawberry cobbler require less preparation and attention than rolled biscuits, french fries, and strawberry chiffon pie.

Foods which cook slowly and those which require less attention allow you to do other tasks at the same time food is cooking. Mashing potatoes, making gravy or white sauce, and broiling foods are last-minute details which can complicate meal preparation. A menu will be more easily prepared if you include no more than one food which requires any last-minute preparation or attention.

As you plan meals, make your choices from among foods that require different amounts of preparation time and attention. The menus will not only influence the nutrient values provided, but also the time and energy required for preparation of the food.

This meal lacks color (baked white fish, scalloped potatoes, and cauliflower).

Here the same color is repeated too often (white fish, asparagus, green beans, and lime jello).

Variety Adds Attractiveness

Because foods must look good before you are willing to eat them, it is often said that "you eat with your eyes." Pleasing combinations of foods add attractiveness and stimulate your appetite. When you plan or select menus, include a variety of foods that will look attractive together.

Even though you may follow the same meal pattern, you can have variety in meals by varying color, size and shape, texture, flavor, temperature, and methods of cooking.

You may be very aware of color and color combinations in the clothes that you wear. *Color in food* requires the application of these same color principles to the food combinations included in a meal. Contrasting colors add interest and complementary colors enhance the appearance of foods.

You not only want foods to look good together but you want their colors to harmonize with the dishes, place mats or tablecloth, and centerpiece.

In addition to color, the *size and shape* of the foods served can add variety and attractiveness. Repetition of the same shapes is not interesting.

When you serve a combination of foods which are cut into small pieces as in casseroles or stews, serve the accompanying vegetable or salad so that the definite shape and identity of the vegetable or salad ingredients are retained.

Texture in food refers to the way the food feels when you chew it. When you have a variety in the textures, you add a pleasing contrast to a meal. Choose foods which are crisp, crunchy, hard, soft, and tender for additional eating pleasure. Too many foods of the same texture, whether soft or crisp, will detract from your meal.

Contrasts in food flavors add interest to a meal. Avoid serving foods with similar flavors (broccoli, cabbage, brussels sprouts). Also avoid serving too many sweet, sour, or highly seasoned foods at the same time.

Contrasts in food temperatures will also make meals more pleasing. Some foods will be hot, others cold or served at room temperature. Even during the summer months, including at least one hot food makes a meal more acceptable and satisfying. A good rule to follow is to include something hot in a cold meal, and something cold in a hot meal.

You can achieve additional variety in meals by using different *methods of preparation.* Creamed shrimp, creamed potatoes, and creamed peas are all too much the same consistency. They make for an uninteresting meal.

Meals will be more pleasing when there is no excess of carbohydrate, fat, or protein. A *variety of nutrients* makes a meal palatable and nutritionally adequate. Include only one fat-rich or sugar-rich food. You will have a pleasing combination of vegetables if you include a juicy or succulent vegetable, for example, tomato, green beans, or broccoli along with a starchy vegetable such as potato, lima beans, corn, or peas. Cheese, eggs, and meats are excellent protein foods, but choose only one of them for a meal.

Color, flavor, texture, and size and shape, along with a variety in temperature, method of preparation, and nutrient values are all factors which contribute to the enjoyment and attractiveness of meals.

Food away from Home

Work, school, social occasions, celebrations, and vacations may involve foods or meals eaten away from home. All foods consumed including those eaten away from home are a part of your total daily food intake. At anytime food is eaten—home or away—take care to provide the nutrients your body needs

A meal in which colors clash does not look appetizing (salmon, carrots, tomato, and beets).

You may add a garnish to add color and contrast to your meals. You should also arrange food neatly on serving dishes to have it look attractive.

Link sausage, asparagus, french-fried potatoes, carrots, and green beans repeat the long slender shape.

without a calorie overload. The Daily Food Guide and the meal patterns will help you to choose nutrient-rich foods and plan balanced meals.

Foods eaten at school or work replace a meal that might have been eaten at home. Regardless of where a meal is eaten, it should contribute one-third of your daily nutrient and energy needs. Between-meal snacks are not an adequate substitute for any meal. If you want to have some snacks in your pattern of eating, be sure to have them in your total food plan. Foods such as fruit, dessert, sandwiches, and beverages may be saved from your regular meals to eat as snacks. Unless snacks are a part of your daily food plan, they can be sources of unwanted calories and nutrient-poor foods.

Routine activities and social occasions which involve food should be planned as part of a daily pattern of eating. At these times, adjust the foods which you eat at home to include only nutrient-rich foods. Control the size of portions, and eliminate fat-rich or sugar-rich foods to avoid a calorie overload. Fruits and vegetables are not always included abundantly in all away-from-home food functions. When this is the case, include the daily vegetable-fruit allowances in the meals which you do have at home.

With careful planning, you can and should adjust your food intake at home to supplement and enhance the foods you expect to eat away from home. The Daily Food Guide and the meal patterns are valuable guides for choosing those foods to be eaten at home to complement ones to be eaten away from home, and still maintain dietary balance.

Buying Food in Restaurants

Foods away from home often mean buying food or meals in restaurants or fast-food shops. Restaurants may offer a sit-down meal to be selected from a menu. Other restaurants may be cafeteria-style and offer a wide range of food so that you can select the foods appropriate for your need.

A number of table-service restaurants do not include a prepared vegetable, other than potatoes, rice, and salad, as an accompaniment to the main course. A variety of vegetables and fruits is not included. Milk is available at an added cost. When you plan to eat in a restaurant, consider the food choices offered and try to include those foods which are not available at the restaurant in your at-home food plan.

Vegetables which are held for a long time in a steam table will deteriorate in quality. However, quality can be kept if the vegetables are prepared close to the time when they are to be served. Vegetables prepared to order probably will cost more because more time and effort is required.

Fast-food shops offer a limited variety of food. Along with the featured items such as sandwiches, pizza, tacos, burritos, etc., they may offer fries (potato), cole slaw (cabbage), tomato slices, and lettuce at extra cost, along with beverages, and quick shakes.

Nearly all meals which are served in fast-food shops contribute a super abundance of calories. Choose foods with care in order to avoid a calorie overload. A meal which includes a sandwich (hamburger), fries, and a quick shake provides more than half the 2700 calories recommended for the active male adult.

The colas and thick shakes contribute to an abundance of calories with little nutrient value. Quick shakes average about 334 kcal, colas, 111 kcal. Quick shakes are not milk shakes. They usually contain some fat-free milk solids, sweetener, and thickeners.

Typical fast-food meals are usually adequate in protein and rich sources of carbohydrate and fat. Fast-food meals provide some nutrients but often are below one-third of the daily RDA (Recommended Daily Dietary Allowance). Most fast-food meals are deficient in one or more, some in as many as ten essential nutrients. This deficiency is largely due to the omission of fruits, vegetables, and milk. The nutrients most often deficient are vitamin A, folacin, pantothenic acid, iron, and copper. On the other hand, fast foods are likely to be extremely high in sodium, a factor which has to be considered, especially when a sodium-restricted diet is necessary.

On days when you plan to eat in fast-food shops, include the recommendations for milk, vegetables, and fruits in the meals you have at home.

Food for Social Occasions

Foods are frequently a part of social occasions and celebrations. At such times there is usually an abundance of different foods. Again, think about your total daily needs and consume the kind and amount of food that suits your needs. You are not obligated to take large servings. It is quite all right to eat less food than you are served. Concentrate on eating a balanced diet. Rich sauce, gravy, and excess salad dressing may stay on your plate without comment. Desserts and beverages are calorie-rich. You can control the amount you consume. When a calorie problem exists, concentrate on eating fruits and vegetables, and small quantities of other foods.

Carry-away Food

Foods prepared at home to be eaten elsewhere should be planned into your daily food intake. These carry-away foods need not be calorie-rich. Instead they can contribute essential nutrients. Attractively arranged fresh vegetables and fruit trays, well-prepared and arranged vegetable dishes, and vegetable-meat casseroles are welcome additions to pot-luck or covered-dish food service. Covered-dish meals too often include too many desserts. This does not have to be the case.

Home-prepared foods are also a part of packed lunches, picnics, cookouts, camping and bicycling trips.

Safety of Carry-away Food

Regardless of where food is served, it should be wholesome, uncontaminated, well prepared, attractive, and nutritious. Home-prepared foods to be eaten elsewhere must be protected from contamination in order to keep their good eating quality until served. Personal cleanliness, sanitation of food, utensils, and carrying containers are very essential if food-borne illnesses are to be avoided. To guard against possible increased bacterial count during food transport and holding, you should keep a temperature above 60°C (140°F) for hot foods and below 7°C (45°F) for cold foods. Vacuum containers will keep liquid or semiliquid foods hot or cold. Insulated chests will protect hot or cold foods. However, the food has to be thoroughly heated or thoroughly chilled before it is put into an insulated chest or vacuum or thermos container. Ice or reusable cold-pack will help keep foods cold. Failure to keep foods at the proper temperatures can result in illnesses if the food spoils and is eaten.

Carry-away foods should also be chosen on the basis of keeping quality. Foods which have low acid content should not be stored at room temperature. Because they are prone to spoil quickly, it is recommended that milk- and egg-rich foods—creams, custards, cream-filled puffs, meringue pies, and low-acid egg-milk salad dressings—should not be part of the carry-away foods unless the appropriate temperature can be maintained.

Home-prepared carry-away foods, restaurants, and fast-food shops are convenient for food consumption away from home. Whatever the occasion, keep in mind that these foods are a part of your food intake. Plan for them in your total daily food consumption. It is easy to include these types of food without sacrificing nutrients or causing a calorie overload, if you keep in mind the food group recommendations and the basic meal patterns for a day.

Food for Athletes

Some coaches erroneously believe that athletes need a diet different from nonathletes. Athletes require the same balanced meal pattern suggested for the average person, except that the total amount of food eaten may be increased to meet the increased energy expenditure. Your energy expenditure is related to the intensity and duration of activity. When you choose extra calories from a variety of foods in the food groups, they will at the same time contribute additional vitamins and minerals.

There is no evidence to support the belief that a high protein diet, vitamin supplements, or special health foods improve athletic performance or work. Athletes do not need more protein, vitamins, or minerals than other persons of the same age and weight.

The salt used in food preparation or added at the table is adequate for the athlete except during unusually hot weather. The last meal should be eaten at least three hours before the sports event. Nutrition for the athlete is much the same as for all healthy persons—well-balanced meals chosen from a variety of foods in the food groups.

Food and the Life Cycle

Food sustains all of us for today and helps build and maintain our bodies for a lifetime. Nutrition affects each person from the day of birth and even before birth.

Pregnancy

Nutrients for the unborn child's growth and development come from the mother. This means her diet during pregnancy is especially important. The woman who reaches childbearing age well nourished and maintains a good diet during pregnancy is likely to avoid complications and have a healthy baby. Pregnancy can be a problem when the expectant mothers are still adolescents. The teen body must cope with its own growth needs and those of the child it bears. This can lead to complications for the mother and the child. The daily diet during pregnancy should provide generous amounts of nutrients according to the Daily Food Guide. There is a need to cut down on nutrient-poor foods such as sweets, fried foods, and other fats to avoid overweight and to assure nutrient needs.

Infant

Children grow and develop more rapidly during their first two years of life than at any other time. Good nutrition is especially important for mental as well as physical development. Poor nutrition can lead to mental retardation and permanent brain damage. Milk is baby's first food, from bottle or breast. Milk supplies a large portion of nutrients. The pediatrician (children's doctor) gradually adds foods such as cereals, strained fruits, and vegetables to the baby's diet. The balanced diet begun in infancy should continue with progressively larger servings of foods from all of the groups given in the Daily Food Guide as children grow.

Adult

You will never outgrow your need for the nutrients given in the Daily Food Guide. These nutrients give the cells the ability to maintain themselves and slow down aging. As people become older they generally need fewer calories. However, their need for nutrients remains about the same.

Weight Control for All Ages

The requirements given in the Daily Food Guide are an excellent foundation for controlling overweight and a basis for weight reduction. They provide about 1300 calories (most people need more than this) daily depending upon the foods and preparation methods chosen. You know that frying and the addition of cream or sugar increase the original caloric content of food. To control weight at any age requires a balance of energy from food with the energy used as exercise and usual activity. To lose weight, fewer calories must be eaten than those used up. Include some foods from each group of the Daily Food Guide. This will give a feeling of satisfaction until time for the next meal.

Poorly chosen snacks can mean calories and unwanted pounds, while well-chosen ones, planned as a portion of the daily food intake, can provide nutrients and help to control caloric intake.

There is no easy way to weight reduction. The popular or fad diets and miracle foods lack the necessary nutrients and lead to malnutrition. Health does not depend on the nutrients from one or two foods, but on nutrients obtained from foods selected from the food groups.

Main Ideas

The Daily Food Guide is a means of determining what each day's meals should provide so that nutritional requirements of carbohydrates, minerals, protein, fats, and vitamins can be met. Cost, time, and energy must also be considered. Attractive meals reflect variety in color, size and shape of foods, texture, flavor, temperature, cooking methods, and nutrient values.

Activities

1. Keep a list of all the food which you eat for one week and check it with the requirements of the Daily Food Guide. Which requirements were met? Which were not met, if any, and why? What are you willing to do in order to improve your food intake?

2. Plan menus for two days that will provide all of your nutrient requirements. What did you consider when you planned these menus? Check food labels and determine what percentage of the U.S. RDA these foods would provide.

3. Find an article concerning eating habits or nutrition and make a report to your class.

4. From the following list, plan two dinner menus. Plan the quantities needed for each menu to serve five persons.

224 g (½ lb) hamburger	garden lettuce	nonfat dry milk
navy beans	tomato juice	shortening
rice	catsup	baking powder
eggs, 4 only	white bread	vinegar
cabbage	flour	oil
onions	white sugar	salt
apples	brown sugar	pepper

5. List the low- and high-cost foods in the Daily Food Guide. Plan a low-cost and a moderate-cost menu for lunch and dinner.

6. Plan three meals which will provide the nutrients you and your family require. What factors did you consider?

a. Make a time plan for preparing these meals.

b. Prepare and serve the meals and report your results. Were you satisfied with the meals? How could they be improved? Was your time schedule correct?

c. What could you do to adapt these menus so they could be prepared in a limited time?

d. What could you do to reduce the caloric value of these meals so that they would be suitable for anyone needing to lose weight?

Questions

1. What factors should you consider when planning menus?

2. Why are attractive meals of importance? What is responsible for the attractiveness of meals?

3. What nutrients make up foods?

4. What nutrients do you need? Why do you need them?

5. In what three ways does food serve your body? What nutrients are involved in each?

6. How do the nutrient needs of your mother and father differ from your nutrient needs?

7. What are the nutrient values of milk, cereals and breads, meats, and fruits and vegetables?

8. How do time and energy influence meals?

9. Plan a menu which considers all the factors that contribute to the attractiveness of meals.

10. How can you avoid excess carbohydrates and fats?

11. When are fats and sweets considered harmful?

Chapter
27
Preparation and Service

Words for Thought

Flatware
a general term which includes all eating implements and those used to serve foods.

Demitasse
a small cup of strong black coffee usually served in the living room after dinner (after-dinner coffee).

À la mode
a food such as pie or cake topped with ice cream.

Meal service
the style, manner, form, or order in which food is served at the table.

Cover
a place setting on the table for each person. It includes china or dinnerware, flatware, glassware, and place mats or tablecloth.

A memorable occasion includes well-prepared and attractively served food. You now know how to prepare foods and plan menus. The next step is to plan the preparation of the foods in your menu so that they will be ready for service at the desired time. You may still ask how it is possible to have all of the foods done to the peak of perfection, ready to serve at the same time. Your answer is, plan ahead. The preparation of a meal involves following a time schedule as well as the directions of a recipe. Making a plan or schedule is especially important for the begining cook to be successful.

Preparation Time

Meal preparation begins with a menu. Select the recipes you wish to use and note the suggested cooking times and temperatures or heat settings (low, medium, high).

You may want to check again with Chapter 4 on the use of recipes and the definitions of cookery terms. After you read the recipe and make sure that you understand all the terms, you must arrange the activities involved in the menu's preparation in a logical order.

You may divide the foods of a menu into four preparation time zones: (1) foods that can be prepared in advance; (2) foods that require an hour or longer to cook; (3) foods that require less than an hour to cook; and (4) foods that require last-minute preparation.

Certain foods can be prepared in advance. These are foods which maintain good eating quality; that is, do not harden, dry out, or toughen for a period of time. Some may be prepared early in the day or even the day before. Foods that you may prepare in advance include soups, both cream and stock; salads of fish, seafood, poultry, meat, potato, rice, and macaroni; yeast breads and quick breads ready-to-bake; desserts such as cakes, pies, puddings, custards, gelatin, and frozen desserts; sandwich fillings; and iced beverages.

Some foods require an hour or more to cook. *Prepare foods that require the longest cooking time at the beginning of the meal preparation period.* Foods that require an hour or more to cook include stock soups not prepared in advance, casseroles, oven and pot roasts, stews, and braised meats.

Some foods require less than an hour to cook. *Foods that require short cooking periods are prepared closer to the serving time.* Many foods that cook rather quickly have the best flavor and texture when served as soon as they are cooked. You need to arrange the cooking of these foods carefully so that the rest of your meal will be ready to serve when they are done. Foods that you will cook in short periods of time include fried, broiled, and pan-broiled foods; vegetables; egg and cheese dishes; quick breads; and beverages such as coffee, tea, and cocoa.

You must time the last-minute preparations so that you perform them just before you serve the meal. The last-minute items include making gravy, mashing potatoes, toasting bread, browning breads prepared in advance, making tea, pouring milk, and arranging and garnishing foods for serving.

When you divide the preparation of a meal into the four time zones you not only consider the length of cooking time, but you also group the foods into a logical order beginning with the foods which take the longest to cook. Notice how the following menu can be divided into preparation time zones. In addition to the time zones, you should list the actual time at which you will perform each activity.

You must allow time for preparation of the food in addition to the cooking time required. It will be easier for you to judge the peparation time required when you first list all of the steps involved in a recipe. For example, when you prepare scalloped potatoes, you must estimate how long it will take you to make the white sauce (measure ingredients, combine them, and cook the sauce); to pare, slice, and arrange potatoes in a casserole; and cover them with the sauce. If you estimate that it will take fifteen minutes to assemble the dish, you should begin preparing the potatoes fifteen minutes ahead of the time that the dish is to be put into the oven.

You should list even the convenience foods (refrigerated rolls, for example) and any heat-and-serve items in your time

417

Meal Preparation Plan

Menu:
                          Baked Ham
                      Scalloped Potatoes
                   Fresh Asparagus Spears
               Lettuce Salad   French Dressing
                      Crescent Rolls
                  Fresh Strawberry Sundae
                      Coffee   Milk

Serve: 6 P.M.

Preparation Time Zones   Time Schedule

Advance Preparation:

1. Prepare ham for baking	Complete these
2. Wash potatoes	preparations at
3. Wash, trim asparagus, refrigerate	any convenient
4. Wash, cut lettuce into wedges, refrigerate	time in your schedule before
5. Wash, prepare strawberries, refrigerate	4 P.M.
6. Measure coffee into percolator basket	

More Than an Hour to Cook:

1. Set oven to preheat and set table.	4.00 P.M.
2. Place ham into oven	4:10
3. Prepare scalloped potatoes	4:11
Bake scalloped potatoes	4:30
4. Clean up work area	

Less Than an Hour to Cook:

1. Cook asparagus	5:35
2. Prepare coffee in percolator	5:36
3. Shape refrigerated crescent rolls and bake	5:44
4. Select required serving dishes and arrange conveniently near range	

Last-Minute Preparations:

1. Remove butter from refrigerator and pour milk	5:50
2. Arrange lettuce wedges on plates, add dressing	5:52
3. Remove rolls from oven and arrange in napkin-lined bread basket	5:54
4. On serving platter, arrange ham and asparagus	5:55
5. Remove scalloped potatoes from the oven	5:58
6. Serve dinner	6:00 P.M.

plan. A time plan will help you realize the steps involved in meal preparation, develop good work habits, and build self-confidence, in addition to helping you get all the food ready for serving at the same time.

While you are learning to prepare meals, you need a written plan to guide you so you will not forget some preparation procedures or have too many last-minute activities. Even experienced cooks make written time plans when preparing elaborate or special meals. As you gain experience, you too will be able to prepare meals without detailed written plans, but with plans you keep in mind.

The times which you list on your written schedule will depend upon the time you set for serving the meal. You will notice that the time schedule on page 418 not only indicates the time zones but also includes the specific time foods are to be prepared and cooked so that dinner can be served at the desired hour.

You are now ready to serve and eat your meal. Attractive, delicious food is an important part of every meal, but the manner in which you serve it adds to the enjoyment of the occasion.

Table Setting

Mealtime pleasure begins when you serve a well-prepared meal on an attractively set table. Whether you set a table for a family meal or for dinner guests, the principles of table setting are basic and remain the same. They are based upon comfort and convenience. The eating implements are neatly arranged on a table cover.

Table Coverings

Since the table cover provides the background upon which you arrange the china and flatware, you should use clean and wrinkle-free table coverings. Choose a table cover from place mats (cloth, plastic, or paper) or a full-length tablecloth.

Place mats are used without a silence cloth and are placed in the center of the space allowed for each person. Put rectangular mats about 2.5 cm (1 in) from the table edge or even with the table edge, and round mats so that one point of the circle is even with the table edge. Arrange the dishes and flatware on the mat. You may use place mats for family meals and informal guest meals and entertaining.

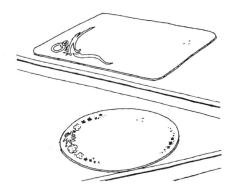

When you use a tablecloth, the hem should be straight and parallel with the floor. The cloth should be centered so the drop or overhang—30 to 38 cm (12 to 15 in)—is even on both sides and ends. A tablecloth without any creases gives the best appearance, but you may use a cloth with a lengthwise center fold (ironed in) which follows the center of the table. It is a good idea to use a silence pad under the tablecloth to protect the table from heat stains.

Place Setting

The place setting for each person is known as the cover. It includes all the flatware, china, glassware, and linen required for one person. Allow 50 to 60 cm (20 to 24 in) of space for each cover. The principles of table setting provide for comfort and convenience. Study the drawing and note the position of each item.

Individual covers are designed for convenience.

1. Place the plate in the center of the cover, or reserve this space for the plate if it is not to be placed immediately. The flatware is placed to the right and left of the plate, or space which has been reserved for the plate. Arrange the flatware in order of use. The flatware to be used first is near the outside of the cover, and that used last is next to the plate.

Arrange the forks to the left of the plate with the tines pointing up. Place the dinner fork and salad fork in order of their use and the dessert fork near the plate. When the salad is eaten as a separate course before the main course, the salad fork is on the outside (left of the dinner fork).

420

2. When salad is to be served with the main part of the meal, the salad fork is placed nearer the plate (right of dinner fork). If you wish, you may use the dinner fork for the salad and eliminate the salad fork.

3. When a knife is not used, you may place the dinner fork at the right of the plate.

4. You should always place the small cocktail fork to the right of the spoons.

5. Place the dinner knife to the right of the plate with the cutting edge facing the plate. The butter spreader or knife is placed across the top of the butter plate with the handle to the right, or along the right side of the plate vertically, never diagonally to detract from your setting.

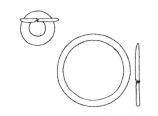

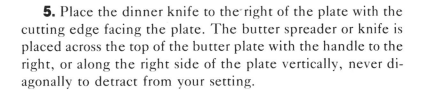

6. Next, arrange the spoons, bowls up, to the right of the dinner knife. Place the teaspoons to the right of the knife, and the soup spoon to the right of the teaspoons.

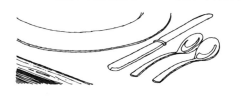

7. Place the folded napkin (folded into a rectangle or square) to the left of the forks, 2.5 cm (1 in) from the table edge, and with the hemmed edges next to the plate and the edge of the table. In this way, you can easily pick up the napkin, unfold it, and place it on your lap.

8. Place the water glass at the tip of the knife, and the milk glass to the right of the water glass and slightly below it. Place the iced beverage glass to the right of the water glass on a plate or a coaster to collect the moisture.

9. At breakfast, place the juice glass to the right of the water glass and a little below it.

10. When you serve juice as an appetizer, the glass is placed on a small plate in the center of the cover.

In the place setting diagram, page 420, you will notice that the cup and saucer are placed to the right of the teaspoons with the cup handle parallel with the table edge. The bread-and-butter plate is at the tip of the dinner fork, and if a salad plate is used, place it to the upper left of the napkin. When you do not use a bread-and-butter plate, the salad plate is placed at the tip of the dinner fork.

Other table accompaniments such as butter, jelly, and relish dishes should be placed so they are within easy reach for passing, and so the table will look balanced.

Place the individual salt and pepper shakers at the top of each cover, or one pair between each of two covers.

You need only to arrange the flatware and dishes required for the meal that you serve. The individual place settings will include only the items which are required for the meal that you are serving. Follow the table-setting principles whenever you set the table, and also when you set trays for tray meals.

The appearance of the table and the food can stimulate your appetite and make mealtime enjoyable. When you plan the setting for a meal, consider what is appropriate and which items look nice together. Your choice of color and pattern or design in table appointments can contribute to the beauty of your table. A well-set table is essential for an attractively served meal.

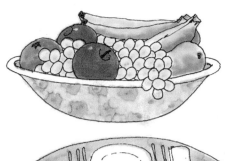

A centerpiece adds beauty and gives color to your table setting. It is often placed near the center of the table, but may be placed at one side or end of the table when convenient.

The centerpiece should harmonize in color with the room, food, and dishes. It should be low enough (about 25 cm (10 in) high) so that you can see each other across the table. Flowers, plants, fruits, fresh vegetables, ornamental glass, pottery, and other household items are often used.

Meal Service

The term meal service refers to the way or manner in which foods are served at the table. The rules of meal service, like the table-setting principles, have evolved through use over a period of time. A simple meal can be special when you serve it beautifully. The way in which you serve a meal should be suited to the menu and table appointments. The meal service should be attractive and convenient. The styles of meal service can be classified as informal and formal.

Informal

When meals are served informally, members of your family or group take part in serving the meal. Informal meals can be served in five ways: plate service, country or family service, modified English, compromise, and buffet service.

You should use *plate service* when you serve the food on individual plates in the kitchen and then set the filled plates on the table before you announce the meal. Plate service is quick and you will have no serving dishes to wash. The plates are most often placed on the dining table, or you may place them on traytables or lap trays, or they can be held on the lap. In any case, each person chooses his or her own plate and then sits where it is most comfortable to handle the plate.

Each person serves himself or herself at the table when country service is used.

Because one person serves the food, modified English service adds some formality to the meal.

Modified English service also requires that one person will serve the dessert.

For *country service* (sometimes called *family service*), place the serving dishes on the table with the serving flatware beside them. The serving dishes are passed at the table so that individuals can serve themselves. Set the individual plates at each cover and the serving dishes on the table before the meal is announced. The dessert is brought to the table at the end of the main course.

For *modified English service* the food is brought to the table in serving dishes. It is served at the table. One person will carve the meat and serve the plates. Place the meat platter above the place setting for the person who is to carve and the vegetable dish usually to that person's right or left. Place the appropriate serving flatware beside each dish. Place the stack of warmed plates in front of the person who is to carve. The main course is served and then a second person at the table may serve the vegetable. As each plate is served, it is passed to the person for whom it was prepared. The first plate is usually passed to the person at the end of the table and then the next plates are passed to people along one side of the table and to those on the other side. When all people at the table have been served, it is all right to begin the meal. One person at the table serves the salad, or it may be in individual portions at each cover before the meal begins. This person may also serve the beverage and the dessert. Other accompaniments of the meal such as rolls, butter, relish, and gravy are passed. One course is served at a time. The table is cleared before the next course is served. This adds dignity and a pleasant note of importance to meal service. The modified English service is sometimes chosen as the service to use when serving special holiday meals or for special kinds of celebrations.

As the name suggests, *compromise service* is a combination of English and formal service. The main course of the meal (meat) is served at the table (as in modified English service), and the remainder of the meal (salad, dessert, etc.) is served in individual portions from the kitchen. The accompaniments (bread, butter, etc.) are passed as in modified English service. The table is cleared and dessert is served in individual portions from the kitchen. The beverage may be served at the table or from the kitchen. Compromise service may be used for any meal, breakfast through dinner, and for family and guest meals. It is an easy way to serve.

For *buffet service,* the food and necessary table appointments (plates, flatware) are attractively arranged on a table or buffet in order of the meal pattern. The guests may help themselves to all of the food, or the person who is entertaining may ask guests to serve the main dish and salad and beverage. The dessert may be served to each guest from the kitchen, or it may be placed on the table after the main course is cleared so that guests may help themselves. When you serve the dessert from the kitchen, you may ask a friend to help you remove the used dishes. When the dessert is served from the table, you may indicate to the guests where to take their dishes that they have used in the first courses of the meal. Then they can go to the table for dessert.

You may seat the guests at tables or provide small tables on which the beverage may be placed. When the meal is eaten from a tray or a plate on the lap, you should plan a menu that can be eaten with a fork and one that can be served on one plate. Foods which can be prepared ahead of time, and those that keep well and stay hot (casseroles, for example) are good choices for buffet meals.

Individual plates for guests and main dishes are usually first in line on a buffet table, and the flatware and napkins, if used on the buffet table, are the last. When guests are to be seated at tables after serving themselves from the buffet table, the flatware is arranged on the tables at which they sit. Tumblers and glasses are better suited for buffet service than goblets.

Buffet service is convenient for entertaining a large number of guests. Since your guests wait on themselves, it gives you more free time with them. In addition, you may use buffet service for all meals including breakfasts, brunches (a combination breakfast and lunch), parties, teas, and receptions. Buffet meals may be elaborate or simple.

Foods which can be eaten neatly and easily and which can be prepared in advance are suitable for buffets.

Formal

Formal service requires the assistance of someone to wait table. It is the most elaborate style of meal service and is sometimes called *Continental* or *Russian service.* It is used for formal luncheons and dinners. Restaurants and hotels often use formal service from the kitchen. Food may be served on individual plates and placed before you. On particularly elaborate occasions the food may be served from serving dishes to the individual guests, or the guests may serve themselves as the person who is serving holds the serving dish.

In strictly formal service, place cards are used and goblets and service plates are required. The service plate is a beautifully decorated large plate. The first-course foods with their underlining plates may be placed on the service plate, but no foods are placed directly upon it. When the service plate is removed, it is replaced with a plate of food for the next course. When the plate for the food course is cleared, it is replaced with the service plate. This procedure is followed until the table is cleared for the dessert course at which time the service plate is no longer required.

During formal service, food does not appear on the table until guests are seated. Because many pieces of flatware are used, dessert flatware is placed before the dessert is served. Finger bowls are used and strong black coffee (demitasse) is served in the living room as a separate and last course.

You probably will not use formal service because it requires someone to wait table. But knowing formal style of service will make you comfortable when you are being served at a banquet or in a formal restaurant.

Selecting the Style of Meal Service

You can select any of the informal styles of meal service for your family meals. Because breakfast and lunch tend to be hurried meals, you may choose to use plate or country service. For dinner and special meals, you may select compromise or modified English service. When you select the style of meal service, be sure that you consider the menu. Simple menus are usually served informally. Elaborate meals are usually served formally. You consider the dining space, available table appointments, time available for serving and eating a meal, number of persons, and the occasion. Select the style of service that can be conveniently and easily performed. It should be one that is most suitable for your situation, and that will contribute the most to a pleasurable meal.

Waiting on Table

When you wait on table, you will leave your napkin at the left of your plate. As the person who is waiting on table you will move quickly and quietly and remain calm even though an emergency may develop. Your responsibility before the meal may be to see that the dining room is comfortable, the table set correctly, and the chairs in place.

Remove dishes and place all foods, except beverages, from the left side with your left hand. The water glass and beverage cup are on the right and you should refill and place them with your right hand from the right side. At times you may serve bread or rolls and desserts.

After the main course, you will first remove all serving dishes. Remove the used plates and flatware from each cover. Remove used dishes and flatware from the left of the person with your left hand.

1. You will be able to clear all of the dishes from one cover at a time when you first remove the dinner plate and flatware with your left hand from the left side. Transfer the dinner plate to your right hand and remove the salad plate with your left hand from the left side. Place the salad plate on the dinner plate in your right hand and next remove the bread-and-butter plate and butter spreader with your left hand. Take the dishes to the kitchen or place them on a portable cart until all the covers are cleared.

2. When you remove extra pieces of flatware or small articles (salt, pepper, etc.), or when you are placing flatware for the next course, use a small tray.

3. Brush crumbs from the table onto a plate with a folded napkin. Crumb each cover from the left side with a folded napkin in your left hand and the small plate in your right hand. Follow the same order around the table as the one used in removing main-course dishes.

4. When you refill glasses, stand to the right of the person and use your right hand. You should not lift the glass from the table, but you may move it to the edge of the table if necessary. Grasp it from the bottom. You will use a napkin in your left hand to catch any drops from the pitcher.

You are now ready to bring in the next course. First place additional flatware, if needed. Then serve the dessert. The dessert course is not usually cleared from the table.

You will offer food from the left side with your left hand when guests serve themselves. Hold the food at a height convenient for each guest. If the dish is hot, place a napkin on your palm to protect it.

All styles of meal service require some waiting on table. Even though the waiting on table may be as limited as in country service, it should be done well.

The variety in the styles of meal service permits you to serve your meals informally or formally. Each, in its own way, can contribute to your pleasure at mealtime. A truly enjoyable atmosphere includes another factor, good table manners. Practicing good table manners is your way of showing consideration for others.

Table Manners

Table manners reflect part of your personality to others and you will want your table manners to reflect nice things about you. As you practice good manners, they become a part of you and you become relaxed and poised at mealtime. Regardless of how food is served, let your good manners show.

Earlier in this chapter, you learned how to set an individual cover on the table. Make sure you know how to use each of the eating implements.

1. Use a *fork* to eat all food served on a plate except finger foods. The fork has three basic uses: to carry food to the mouth, to cut soft foods (waffles, meat loaf, cooked vegetables), and to hold foods when cutting them with a knife. You should hold the fork as you do a pencil, with the tines up when you carry food to the mouth. To cut soft foods with a fork, hold the fork so the tines are turned sideways; after the food is cut, turn the tines upward to carry the bite of food to your mouth. When not in use, place the fork on your plate tines up. At the end of the meal, place the fork across the center of the plate, tines up.

2. You will frequently use the fork when you cut foods with a *knife*. Hold the knife in your right hand so that the handle rests in the palm of your hand and your forefinger is on the back of the knife blade. Hold the fork in your left hand (in the same way as the knife), tines down, and cut only one or two bites of food at a time. Place the knife on the edge of your plate with the blade facing you, transfer the fork to your right hand and with tines up lift the food to your mouth.

3. Perhaps you have seen the fork kept in the left hand after the food was cut, and the food carried to the mouth with the tines down. This is the European or Continental style compared to the American style of tines up. You will use your knife for cutting foods and for spreading butter and jelly when a butter spreader is not provided.

4. At the end of the meal place the knife across the center of the plate with the cutting edge of the blade toward you and the fork beside it, tines up.

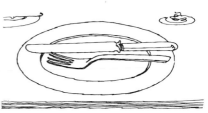

5. Break the slice of bread in half and then break the half to form two pieces. Spread only one-quarter of a slice of bread at a time and break the remaining half of bread when you are ready to eat it. You may butter a whole slice of hot toast and a hot roll may be broken apart and buttered while it is still hot. As you break or butter bread, hold it over the plate to avoid having crumbs on the table. Always keep the buttered roll or bread on your plate, never on the tablecloth. Keep the butter spreader and the knife across the edge of the plate when not in use. Do not use them to help yourself to butter or jelly, but use the provided service flatware (butter knife and jelly spoon).

1. *Spoons* are used for foods that you cannot eat with a fork (soups, milk and cereal, pudding). You use a teaspoon for stirring sugar or cream into a beverage and for tasting beverages. The used teaspoon is placed on the saucer; it never remains in the cup. You also use the teaspoon to eat soft foods. The teaspoon is dipped toward you and the food is eaten from the tip of the spoon.

429

2. *Soup spoons* are larger spoons than teaspoons and are used for eating soup. When eating soup, dip the spoon away from you, fill it about half full, and sip from the side of the spoon. Never lift the soup dish from the plate; you may tip it slightly away from you when it is nearly empty.

You use a *napkin* to protect your clothes, to blot your mouth, and wipe your fingers when soiled at the table. Remove your napkin from the table as others at the table do. Let the napkin unfold as you remove it from the table to your lap. Place a large napkin only half unfolded on your lap, with the fold facing you; a small napkin may be unfolded completely. During the meal, use the napkin inconspicuously when needed. Leave it on your lap until the end of the meal. When you use the napkin for more than one meal, fold it and place it at the left of your plate, otherwise leave it unfolded beside your plate.

In addition to these basic rules for handling eating implements, you may want to check your table courtesy.

Table Courtesy

Table manners can also be called the rules of table courtesy or table etiquette. They represent the rules of eating that have been developed through use over a period of time. These rules are based upon consideration for others before, during, and after the meal.

1. Before you enter the dining area, make sure that you are well groomed and appropriately dressed. You will show your consideration for the person who is entertaining you when you arrive for a meal a few minutes before the scheduled time. When you are unavoidably detained, let it be known that you will be late.

2. You should not go to the table until the meal is announced. Sit down from the left side of your chair. When the chair is properly placed you do not need to move it to seat yourself. It is considered a nice gesture for men and boys to help women and girls be seated.

430

3. You should sit straight (shoulders back) with your arms close to your sides, and feet flat on floor. Keep your hands in your lap when you are not eating. Always keep the free hand in your lap as you eat.

4. Take cues from others at the table as to mealtime procedure. If grace is to be said, all are to remain quiet, and afterward place their napkins on their laps. Remember not to put too much food in your mouth at once. Chew with your mouth closed. Avoid talking with food in your mouth.

5. Take your turn with conversation at the table. Keep it pleasant and include topics which are of general interest to most of the group.

6. Assist with passing food, but do not help yourself first unless the person to whom you are offering the food suggests it. Foods are generally passed to the right.

7. When the meal is ended, place your napkin at the left of your plate and rise from the right side of your chair.

The table manners which you just reviewed are basic to all meals. You will have occasion to use them each day with every meal. Occasionally you will need to know the following rules of eating. Knowing them may avoid embarrassment for you.

Whenever a special accompaniment or a garnish is served with meat (apple rings with roast pork, mint jelly with lamb, raisin sauce with ham), you should place it on your plate with the meat.

A few foods are considered finger foods. Bread, tacos, crackers, most raw fruits, celery, radishes, potato chips, pickles, olives, salted nuts, or cookies may be eaten from your fingers. When you eat corn on the cob, butter small portions at a time and hold it with the fingers of one hand. Chicken should be cut from the bone except in the privacy of your own home or drive-in restaurants.

Bread with gravy and creamed food over toast or biscuits are eaten with a fork, and a knife is used for cutting when necessary. You should eat salads with a fork, but you may use a knife when necessary to cut head lettuce or other salad greens. Cream puffs, eclairs, and ice cream on cake or pie (à la mode) are eaten with a fork.

When you use a spoon to eat fruit with seeds (prunes, canned cherries), remove the seed from your mouth with the

431

tip of your spoon, or, better still, avoid taking the seed into your mouth. Olives or other fresh fruits with seeds are eaten from the fingers and therefore the seed is removed with the fingers. Occasionally a small piece of bone may be taken with fish or chopped meats; you may remove this with your fingers and place it on the edge of your plate.

When you spill water or a beverage, or drop a piece of flatware, make a sincere but brief apology. Offer to help clean it up. The dropped flatware will need to be replaced with clean flatware.

Your study of table manners will help you avoid awkward situations and embarrassing moments. You will be showing your good manners when you are considerate of others, handle eating implements properly, and eat quietly.

Main Ideas

Planned preparation time zones, which allow for foods to be prepared and/or cooked at specific times before a meal is served, increase the possibility for success in the meal's preparation. Advance decisions on table setting, service, and cleanup help to eliminate last-minute crises for those who are entertaining. Knowledge and practice of good manners insure a pleasant time for everyone.

Activities

1. Plan a dinner menu and draw an individual place setting for a guest using graph paper. Indicate the scale which you used for the drawing and explain your place setting in terms of your menu and style of meal service.

2. Collect pictures of table settings and discuss their good and poor features. Can you offer any suggestions for improvement?

3. Which of the styles of meal service is best suited for your family's breakfast, lunch, and dinner?

4. Plan a dinner menu and set the table at school with four place settings for compromise style of service. Discuss the table setting with your class. Ask for class volunteers to sit at the table and demonstrate (without food) how the meal would be served. When should compromise style be used?

5. Ask at home to set the table and select the style of meal service. Direct the service of the meal. Report your results to your class.

432

6. Serve a dinner in your home. Be prepared to explain to the class the style of meal service you used. Describe the tasks you performed.

7. Plan a dinner menu suitable for your family. Divide the preparation of the meal into "time zones" and determine at what times you need to begin the activities so that the meal can be served at your usual dinner hour. Prepare the meal and evaluate your results. How effective was your time plan? Make a report to the class.

Questions

1. What is a meal preparation schedule? How would you develop one?

2. What kinds of food preparation can be done in advance? Which foods require more than an hour to cook? What are last-minute preparations that must be done?

3. Compare formal and informal table service. Describe some situations in which each could be used.

4. Name the informal styles of meal service and explain the differences between them.

5. What is a table setting?

6. Explain the proper way to hold and use a dinner knife, dinner fork, and a teaspoon.

7. What are the rules for the placement of the salad fork? dinner fork?

8. What are the uses of a napkin? How should it be folded? Demonstrate how to fold a napkin.

9. What are the principles of table setting?

10. What is an appropriate centerpiece for a family dinner? What rules govern its height and size?

11. Give the general rules for the arrangement of flatware on the table.

12. What should be considered when selecting a style of meal service?

13. Describe the proper way to wait on table.

14. What are table manners? What is etiquette?

15. List some table manners that will reflect nice things about you.

Words for Thought

Microwave
a form of electromagnetic energy converted to heat when it is absorbed by a food.

Molecule
the smallest particle of a substance that retains the properties of the substance and is composed of one or more atoms.

Atom
the smallest particle of a substance that can exist either alone or in combination.

Volume
the amount, size, quantity, or number of items.

Density
refers to the lightness, firmness, or porous nature of a substance.

Pierce
to force a sharp object (fork, tip of knife) through the surface of a food.

Reconstitute
to restore a dry or concentrated food to its original consistency by adding liquid, usually water.

Transmit
to conduct or allow to pass over or through a substance.

Absorb
to take up or drink in another substance.

Chapter 28

Microwave Cookery

Food requires much less time to cook in a microwave oven than in or on a conventional range. In a regular range the heat from a hot burner or a hot oven is transferred to the food. In microwave cooking the heat is produced directly within the food by microwaves. The microwaves are a form of electromagnetic energy much like that of heat, light, or radio waves. A magnatron tube within the oven produces the microwaves and a stirrer or a fan distributes the microwaves throughout the oven. The microwaves penetrate the food and cause the molecules of the food to vibrate rapidly thus creating heat.

434

Microwave Ovens

Microwave ovens which meet federal standards and are operated according to manufacturer's directions are safe. Each microwave oven comes with a recipe book which includes the same kinds of recipes as other recipe books, but it gives the required microwave cooking time instead of a temperature setting and a time to cook as is done for the conventional oven. Some foods are cooked in several seconds; other foods in a few minutes. The water molecules in the food are agitated at a tremendous rate and heat is generated within the food. Any heat noticed inside the oven or in the baking dish is from the food. 250 mL (1 c) of liquid at room temperature heats in about 1 minute and comes to a boil in about 2 minutes.

The first microwave ovens had a rotating timer and a single power level. All foods were cooked with high power. Foods such as breads, cakes, meats, and casseroles were done but they did not brown as they do in a conventional oven.

Today some ovens combine conventional electric elements and microwave units. This makes it possible to have the advantage of fast cooking and the browning. There are a variety of microwave ovens and ranges from which to choose.

Microwave Oven Features

We now realize high power is not right for all microwave cooking. Microwave power settings are now available on all microwave ovens. You can select the recommended power setting for a particular food by pushing a button, rotating a dial, or selecting a numbered setting. Computerized controls allow a number of processes or operations to be programmed into a complex control system.

In the beginning, time was the only variable in microwave cookery. A number of microwave ovens now come with a temperature probe. The probe is inserted into the food to be cooked and then connected to the electrical system of the oven. The probe senses the internal temperature of the food. When the pre-selected temperature is reached, the microwave power is turned off. Some microwave ovens have a humidity sensor which measures the level of moisture being given off by the food being cooked. Other ovens may have microwaves enter from both sides of the oven cavity giving more cooking area and permitting several foods to be cooked at the same time.

This is one type of microwave oven.

The power shift makes it possible for you to control the speed of microwaves so that foods can be prepared by traditional methods such as simmering or roasting. Here are two rules to follow in order to use a microwave oven properly and efficiently.

1. Read the use and care manual which comes with the microwave oven very carefully to learn how to operate your particular microwave oven.

2. Read the introduction and meal-planning sections of your microwave cookbook. This book will give you suggestions for preparing a variety of foods. You may have other ideas that will increase your use of your microwave oven.

Microwave Cookery Terms

Microwaves give you a new way to cook foods. You should understand the terms which are used to describe the procedure of microwaving. As you understand the meaning of these terms, you will be pleased with the foods you microwave.

Arcing—a spark caused by a discharge of static electricity. This occurs between separated particles of metal (metal trim on dishes or metal twists for plastic bags).

Bursting—refers to a buildup of steam in foods causing the outer surface or skin to break open. This may occur in foods which are enclosed in a skin, membrane, or shell such as fruits, vegetables, poultry, and eggs.

Cooking Time—the time required to heat or cook foods to serving temperature.

Overcooking—foods cooked too long may become dried out, toughened, hard spots may form, and some sauces may separate.

Puncturing—breaking the skin or membrane of foods or a plastic bag or cover to allow steam to escape.

Reheating—bringing cooked food to serving temperature.

Rehydrating—replacing water or liquid removed from food.

Rotating—turning container or a whole food ¼ to ½ turn for more even cooking.

Resting or Standing—the time suggested to allow the heat in the food to spread to the center of the food, either during or after cooking.

Turning—turning over or inverting a food during cooking such as meat.

Trivet—an inverted cover or dish to elevate foods above the cooking liquid (used with meats or poultry).

Undercooking—cooking food to less-than-done stage and using standing time to complete the cooking.

Utensils—any dish or container used to hold food in a microwave oven.

Utensils for Microwaving

Microwaves have a distinct nature. Some materials absorb microwaves, others transfer or reflect them. Foods can absorb microwaves. Foods are cooked by them. The cooking utensils you use should transfer the microwaves to the food. If this does not happen, the food will not be cooked. Because metal utensils reflect microwaves and prevent them from reaching the food, they should not be used. The walls of the oven are metal. They reflect the microwaves toward the oven cavity.

Glass, paper, and some plastics transfer microwaves. China or pottery containers can be used if they have no gold or silver trim, design, or printing anywhere on them. It is best to test any ceramic utensils before using them for microwave cooking. You can easily check the suitability of a utensil by measuring 250 mL (1 c) of water into a glass measuring cup and then placing the cup into the dish, casserole, or other container to be tested in the microwave oven. Heat the oven on full power for 1 minute and 15 seconds. At the end of that time only the water should be warm. The dish should be cool. If the dish is slightly warm or is hot in spots and the water is cool, do not use the container in the microwave oven.

Pictures of some materials and types of utensils and suggested uses in microwave cookery are on the next two pages.

Testing the suitability of a utensil which is to be used in microwave cooking.

437

Glass and glass-ceramic containers, trivets, and covers are used for microwave cooking. Glass and glass-ceramic can withstand high food temperatures and can also be used in a conventional oven. Food may be cooked and served from the container.

Paper serves as a light cover to hold in steam, avoid spatter, and absorb grease. Plastic-coated paper products may be used for juicy foods.

Foam cups and plates are good for thawing and heating foods. Special microwave utensils are used for containers, trivets, and rings. Heavy-duty plastic film serves as an adjustable cover. Puncture holes in plastic bags used in cooking to permit release of steam. Some plastic containers distort with high heat or high-fat foods.

Wood is used for picks or skewers only for short-term heating or cooking, but not for thawing. Wooden spoons are used for stirring. Breads require a short heating period and may be placed in straw baskets in the microwave.

Covers for Microwave Cooking

Foods cooked in a microwave are often covered to retain steam, or to avoid drying or spattering. Porous, light, tight utensil covers may be used. A cover may be used during cooking and standing time.

Paper towels or napkins are porous covers which permit steam to escape. They may be used to warm sandwiches and to cover bacon.

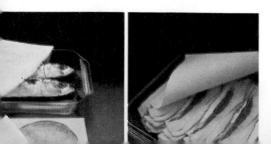

A light cover such as waxed paper holds in steam and may be used to cover meats (poultry, hamburger, roasts) and fruits.

A tight cover holds in steam and is used when vegetables or fish are cooked. A plastic film cover can be turned back slightly or pricked to permit venting (escape of steam). Both cooking and freezer bags hold in steam and moisture. They should be pricked with a knife to allow steam to escape.

Utensil covers hold in steam and are used for vegetables, saucy casseroles, and meat which requires moisture and heat to tenderize.

Selection of Utensils

Utensils or containers can influence the results of microwave cooking. When you select utensils for microwave cookery consider the following points.

1. Material. The material of which the container is made should be sturdy and durable.

2. Shape and design of container. Containers in which meat loaf, casseroles, and quick breads are baked should be round and deep enough to contain the vigorous activity within the food that is being cooked. Deep wells at the sides or ends of utensils (in trays and racks) will catch the drippings which will attract the microwaves and reduce their efficient use. The length of time required to cook the food in such containers will be increased, since the microwaves enter the food from sides, top, and bottom. Therefore these utensils should not be used.

3. Versatile use. Utensils should generally be useful in preparation of several different foods.

4. Easy to handle. The container should be easy to handle when filled with food or when it is hot. The handle on the utensil should make it easy to move the utensil about.

439

5. Microwave label. Look for labels that indicate that the utensil is approved for microwave cooking. Be sure to follow the manufacturer's recommendation for the use of each particular utensil.

Microwave Thermometer

A thermometer is the best way to judge the doneness of meat. Microwave thermometers are now available and can be inserted into the foods to be cooked by microwaves. Most regular cooking thermometers contain mercury which may cause arcing in the microwave oven. Therefore, do not use a regular cooking thermometer in a microwave oven.

Uses of Microwaves

You may use microwaves for cooking, reheating, and defrosting foods. Microwaves produce instant heat within foods but many times this heat may only penetrate a portion of the food. The rest of the food is heated by conduction (heat moves from the outside to the center). Conduction can occur in any of the three uses of microwaves.

Cooking

The heat of cooking changes the flavor, texture, consistency, and appearance of foods. Microwaves produce the desired degree of doneness in quick-cooking foods easily. However, when a food requires a long period of cooking due to its size and density, it may be difficult to control the rate of cooking for the quality of product you want. For some of the long-cooking foods you may prefer to use a conventional range with which it is easier to control the speed of cooking in order to produce the quality of product you want.

Heating

Foods which have been cooked previously become hot but do not change in texture or appearance. You will find microwaves generally satisfactory for heating foods and reconstituting convenience foods. The porous foods (breads, cakes, pastries) and those with a high fat or high sugar content heat through very quickly. Dense foods heat through more slowly

440

than do porous foods. You may need to help distribute the heat throughout dense foods by stirring, rearranging, or allowing such foods to stand for a short time at the end of cooking to permit the heat to move from the outside toward the center of the food. In this way you avoid overcooking the edges.

As you increase the volume or amount of food, the time required to cook or reheat the item also increases. When you use twice as much food, it will take nearly twice as much time to cook that food.

Defrosting

When frozen food is defrosted microwaves change ice to water. The frozen food is defrosted slowly so that the food does not become hot and begin to cook on the outside before the center has thawed. Most microwave ovens have low power settings (10% of total power) to allow quick defrosting. Alternate heating and standing times permit the heat to be conducted to the center of the food without any cooking at the outer edges. Many microwave ovens now include the automatic defrost feature.

Porous items such as breads, cakes, and pastries thaw quickly. Dense items such as meats or casseroles require a longer time for the center to defrost. A standing time is needed to defrost the center without outer-edge cooking. If cooking begins, decrease the microwave time and increase the standing time. A .45 kg (1 lb) portion of ground beef will defrost in about 5 minutes and most of the juices will be retained. Large pieces of meat (over 2.25 kg (5 lb)) require standing time after defrosting to assure even cooking.

The results you want during cooking, heating, or defrosting will determine the time and technique necessary.

Cooking Time

Microwave cookery differs from conventional cookery, which is concerned with temperature and time, in that it is concerned with power level and time. The power level and time which you select control the microwave cooking you do. Although the specific power settings vary among the microwave ovens, they range from high to low. When your microwave oven is set on high, it is using full power or about 650 watts. A medium high setting uses 75 percent of full power; medium setting uses 50 percent of full power; medium low setting uses 30 percent of full power; and low setting uses 10 percent of full power. Microwaves penetrate only to a depth of 2.5 to 3.75 cm (1–1½ in). The distribution of heat toward the center of a large quantity of food is by reflection.

The cooking time which a food will require is determined by the starting temperature, the volume or amount of food, the density, moisture content, fat and sugar contents, and the shape of the food.

Starting Temperature

Foods at room temperature need less cooking time than do those at refrigerator temperature. Those foods which are frozen require the most time. You should remember that the colder the food, the longer it will take to cook or to heat it.

Volume

The larger the size or quantity of food, or the number of food items, the longer will be the cooking, heating, or defrosting time. The time increases in proportion to the number of items (pieces) and the size or volume of the food. Remember that the time of cooking, heating, or defrosting increases as the number of items and size or volume of the food increases.

Density

Internal structure of foods varies according to how many molecules occupy a given space. The more molecules there are per square inch of food, the more dense or compact it is.

Microwaves penetrate dense or solid foods more slowly than they penetrate porous foods. The more solid the food the longer it takes the microwaves to penetrate it. Therefore, the cooking, heating, and defrosting times are increased. Light, porous foods such as cakes, pastries, and breads absorb microwaves faster than do more compact, moist foods of the same weight. They require only a few seconds to heat or to thaw.

Because the density of various foods is different, it is very difficult to state a definite cooking time. Since microwaves penetrate dense food slowly, you may help to distribute the heat within the food by stirring, rearranging, or including a short standing period at the end of cooking. This allows the heat to reach the center of the food. You should consider the density of a food when you estimate the time that is needed to cook the food to the desired doneness.

442

Moisture Content

Water and foods with a high water content require more energy to reach the desired temperature than do similar foods of a lower moisture content. Foods with a high moisture content will take longer to heat than will those of low moisture content. The higher the moisture content, the longer the cooking time will be.

Fat and Sugar

Fat and sugar are heated quickly with microwaves. Foods which contain a high proportion of sugar or fat require less time to heat than do foods without fat or sugar. The frosting on a roll becomes hot before the roll is heated. The side of the meat next to the fat heats more quickly than the side away from the fat. For these reasons you must consider the fat and sugar content of a food when determining the cooking, heating, and defrosting times for it.

Shape of foods

Flat, thin foods heat faster than thick, chunky foods. You should make the pieces of a food as uniform as possible in size and shape. Whenever possible arrange the foods in a circular shape or form them into a rounded shape. Use round-shaped containers whenever possible to avoid overcooking which occurs in the corners of rectangular utensils.

Techniques and Cooking Time

In order to produce quality foods by microwave cookery, you should understand the proper techniques to follow when cooking foods by microwaves. Several of the techniques you will use are the same ones that you use in conventional cooking. Many of these techniques will either speed cooking or promote even cooking. On the next two pages you will see some of the techniques which are used during cooking. These are stirring or rearranging, covering food, or using standing time, which can shorten the cooking time and help you to control the speed of the cooking.

It is important to use these special techniques when doing microwaving in order to achieve the best results in the finished product. Otherwise, you may be disappointed.

Stirring and Rearranging

Stirring is necessary in microwave cooking to redistribute the heat within some foods. Nearly all recipes tell you when and how many times to stir. Stirring or rearranging moves the warmer food from the outside toward the center, and the colder food from the center to the outside. In this way the heat is distributed more evenly. Whole foods such as baked potatoes are easily rearranged during cooking. Whenever it is possible to stir or rearrange the food which is being cooked, you will find that this is a good way to produce foods that are uniformly cooked. If you are using less than full power level, less stirring is necessary. Casseroles, egg dishes, puddings, and sauces are examples of foods which require stirring.

Foods which cannot be stirred are rearranged for even heating. Foods which are cooked covered or at less than full power settings require less rearranging. Whole vegetables, pieces of chicken, and cupcakes are examples of foods which require rearranging.

Turning

Turning is done when foods cannot be stirred or rearranged. Turning over is used for meats and poultry to redistribute the heat within the food. Repositioning or rotating the dish is done by moving the dish a quarter or a one-half turn. Cakes, pies, and soufflés are often repositioned this way. If less than full power level is called for, then less turning or rotating and repositioning are necessary.

Covering

Covering is necessary for many foods to retain steam and to speed cooking. It also helps to prevent dehydration and spattering. You will use a cover on the container to speed cooking, heating, or defrosting of the food. A lid or inverted plate or plastic wrap can be used to provide a tight cover which retains both moisture and heat. Plastic covers, however, should not touch the hot food. Paper napkins and towels provide a loose cover and permit moisture from the food to escape. They are absorbent and can help to avoid spattering food on oven walls. A covering is used during cooking and during standing time. The food continues to cook for a period of time even after removal from the oven.

444

Standing Time

Standing time allows the heat from the outside of the cooked food to reach the center of the food without overcooking the outer edges. You should use standing time to equalize the cooking of dense foods because they retain the heat longer than porous foods do when removed from the oven.

Precautions with Microwaves

Although microwave ovens are designed to be safe and reliable, as with all appliances, you must know how to operate a microwave oven if you are to use it. There are certain precautions or safety tips that you must also know. As you use a microwave oven, put these safety rules into practice.

1. Pierce skins of whole fruits and vegetables such as apples or potatoes before cooking. This permits steam to escape during the cooking and keeps the fruits or vegetables from bursting.

2. Do not cook or reheat eggs in the shell. Always pierce the yolk with the tip of a knife or fork before cooking to avoid bursting. Finely chop cooked eggs before reheating.

3. Pierce or open plastic and other airtight containers before heating to permit the escape of steam during cooking.

4. Liquids should be stirred or poured just before heating to mix in air and avoid eruption in the oven.

5. Extreme overcooking in both conventional and microwave ovens can cause foods to smoke or burn. Should this happen, push the stop button, leave the door closed until the fire is extinguished.

6. Do not use or prepare these items in a microwave oven.

a. Do not pop ordinary popcorn. Special popcorn in bags designed for microwave use is available.

b. Do not use containers with restricted openings such as baby food jars, syrup or catsup bottles. Rapid expansion could cause the container to burst.

c. Metal cookware increases cooking time, decreases microwave efficiency, causes uneven cooking and arcing, and can damage the magnatron tube. Avoid all metal objects such as twists and trims or decorations on cookware.

d. Microwave canning is not recommended. The metal lids reflect microwaves which interferes with uniform heating of the food in jars and leads to food spoilage.

445

e. Newspapers and recycled paper should not be used in a microwave oven. Some printer's inks absorb microwaves and may cause the paper to burn. Recycled paper products may contain small pieces of metal which could cause the paper to catch fire. Paper toweling which is reinforced with synthetic fiber such as nylon could cause the paper to burn.

Cooking Foods Together

When more than one food is to be prepared in the microwave oven, heating time must be carefully considered. Select foods with the same moisture content. Plan to use the same quantity of each food so that all foods can be successfully heated at the same time. If the foods are somewhat different you must consider placement, size and shape, use of cover, and the initial temperature in order to heat such combinations successfully. Here are some suggestions that you can apply when you are trying to heat foods and combinations of foods which vary in quantities or have different moisture contents. Attention to these rules means better results.

1. Placement. Place the foods with the shortest heating time (low moisture, high fat, high sugar) in the center of the container with the smallest parts of the food near the center of the container.

2. Size and shape of portion. Flat and thin foods heat more quickly than chunky, thick foods. Flat, doughnut-shaped foods heat most uniformly. Reduce the size of portions; make two portions of one; change the shape of the food.

3. Cover use. Most foods should be covered to avoid drying. Breaded and crisp products may be left uncovered to avoid sogginess. All foods should stand about 1 minute before removing the cover.

4. Initial temperature. Allow more heating time for refrigerated foods than for room-temperature foods.

5. Additions. To compensate for the somewhat longer cooking time of a particular food, add other foods later in the cooking period. These foods can be added to the plate or container with the food that requires a longer heating time or they can be placed on separate side dishes.

Adjustable shelves are available for microwave ovens. The use of such shelves can make it easier to prepare several foods or to prepare complete meals at one time. This would help to conserve energy.

Adjusting Recipes

It is possible to adapt conventional recipes to microwaving. The same considerations must be made as were made when using recipes from a microwave cookbook. You must consider the nature and density of the food to be prepared (its moisture, fat and sugar content), initial temperature, and volume. Then you must apply the microwaving techniques (stirring, covering, standing time).

When you cook any of your adapted conventional recipes, set the timer for somewhat less than the estimated time you believe is needed. You can always cook a food a few seconds or minutes longer to complete cooking, but you cannot change a food once it has been overcooked. Microwaved foods are generally cooked in about ¼ of the conventional cooking time.

Convenience Foods

Some convenience foods may give instructions for microwave cooking. Follow these directions, but plan to undercook when you prepare the food for the first time. It is always safest to cook the food for a shorter time than that suggested to avoid possible overcooking. Allowing a few extra seconds or minutes can give you a perfectly cooked product. Record this cooking time so that you will have it for future use.

Although all microwave ovens operate on the same basic principles, there are specific individual characteristics for each brand. For this reason, it may be difficult to give one specific optimal cooking time for all brands of microwave ovens.

A number of foods are packaged in materials which are not suitable for microwaving. Foods can be removed from packaging which is not suitable for microwaving and cooked in approved containers. However, if predictions are accurate, more and more foods will be packaged in microwave-approved containers. Read labels on the packages and look for the microwave cooking instructions.

Menu Planning

As with any other menu, menus for microwaving should be nutritious, colorful, and pleasing in texture and flavor. Best results are achieved when you observe the rules of microwave cookery. Energy is also used to the best advantage when rules are followed.

As you prepare various foods by microwave, you will probably develop preferences for certain foods prepared by microwave and others prepared by conventional means. Your preferences can be organized into meals which use both microwave and conventional cookery techniques.

Time is always an important factor in cookery. You have to consider what this means. Microwave cookery is fast. Although several foods may be cooked together in the microwave oven, the heating may not be even. Some foods attract more microwaves than others. Microwave meal preparation in most ovens requires sequential cooking—one food item after the other. Cooking in sequence requires careful planning. You have to consider serving temperature, cooking times, how long foods will remain hot, how easily a particular food reheats, and whether the cooking can be done in this way.

Foods which are usually cooked first include large cuts of meat, casseroles, and foods which have been partially cooked. Small meat items, eggs, vegetables, and sauces are usually cooked near serving time. Breads and foods cooked previously but which have to be reheated before serving are cooked last because they require only a short time.

Complete meals can be prepared easily in the microwave oven when they are well planned. Begin with simple meals, breakfast or lunch. As you gain skill you can plan and prepare more complicated meals.

Care of Microwave Oven

The microwave oven requires little care. Any spatter on the stainless steel sides is easily cleaned with a mild detergent in warm water and a cloth or soft sponge. Abrasives should never be used for cleaning. Cooking vapors and spattered foods do not bake onto the oven surface since the microwave oven interior is never heated like that of the conventional oven.

The glass tray on the oven bottom is easily removed. You wash it in warm water and detergent. The drip tray must be put back in place correctly. Never operate the oven without the drip tray in position.

The use and care manual which the manufacturer supplies will have the best advice for the operation and care of the microwave oven. Proper care means longer service.

Main Ideas

Conventional cooking methods surround the food with heat. Microwave cooking is different. The food absorbs microwaves which generate heat within the food. They are used to cook, reheat, reconstitute, and defrost foods. Time is important in microwave cooking. It is influenced by starting temperature, volume, density, and fat and sugar content of the food. Techniques used in microwave cooking such as covering, stirring, and standing time reduce the time required to cook, heat, or defrost foods.

Activities

1. Prepare the same food in microwave and conventional ovens. Compare the preparation and clean-up times and the quality of the food (color, flavor, texture). What are the advantages of each method?

2. Visit a supermarket and read the labels of convenience foods which require cooking. Are directions given for microwave cooking? If so, what directions are given?

3. Arrange a display of utensils and covers suitable for microwave cookery and give suggestions for their use.

4. Place 80 mL (⅓ c) water, a serving of cake or a roll with frosting, and a small piece of meat with a layer of fat (within or surrounding the meat) in a microwave oven. Heat for 10 seconds and lightly touch the surface of each. Which of these foods felt the warmest? Remove a food as it becomes warmed sufficiently and continue to heat the remaining foods for 10-second intervals until the desired temperature is reached for each food. Which food reached the desired temperature first and which last? Why?

Questions

1. How does microwave cooking differ from conventional cooking?

2. What are the advantages and disadvantages of microwave cooking?

3. What kinds of utensils are used for microwave cooking? Which utensils are not used? Why?

4. What is the nature or character of microwaves?

5. When and why is a cover used in microwave cooking?

6. What should you consider when microwave utensils are selected?

7. Why are special microwave thermometers required?

8. Give examples of microwave uses in preparing foods.

9. What factors influence microwave cooking time?

10. Which characteristics of a food increase microwave cooking time? Which characteristics decrease cooking time?

11. Give examples for the use of the following techniques in microwave cookery. In what ways do these techniques influence microwave cooking?

covering	starting time
rearranging	stirring
rotating	turning

12. List the precautions to be used when cooking with microwaves.

13. Explain the procedure for preparing more than one food in a microwave oven.

14. What must you consider when adjusting conventional recipes to microwave cooking?

15. Compare the care of a microwave oven with that of a conventional oven.

Chapter
29
Foreign Foods

Words for Thought

Food habits
frequently repeated uses and consumption of food.

Culture
a way of life of a group of people, usually of the same nationality, within a specific country or region.

Traditional foods
foods prepared in the same way by each generation and often symbolizing a special event or celebration.

Food products which people eat differ in ingredients, in preparation, and in how they are served and eaten. One diet may be based on beef and potatoes, another on beans and tortillas, and still another on rice and fish or some other combination of foods. Each is capable of contributing to human nutrient needs. Throughout history certain rituals and formalities were established as appropriate practices for the consumption of food. Some people sit on the floor, eat food from their fingers, and smack their lips. Other people serve food from a table, eat from plates with appropriate utensils, and make the least noise.

Food Habits

Your food habits as well as the food habits of people in other parts of the world have been influenced by cultural beliefs and values, religion, climate, regional location, agriculture, technology, and economic status. Consequently, the food habits vary from country to country as well as from region to region within the same country.

The way of life of a group of people (generally of the same nationality) is identified as culture. One culture may think of food only as a way to satisfy hunger, while another culture sees food as a source of pleasure and an opportunity to socialize with family and friends. The family, church, and school pass cultural practices and beliefs on from one generation to the next generation.

Each culture determines its own set of standards and acceptable behavior, and influences the food habits which will be different from those of another culture. Each person selects, uses, and consumes available food within the guidelines of the culture. The past history and present environment of a group influence its food habits and customs.

American Food Patterns

We have a variety of cultural food patterns in the United States. Dishes from these patterns have become popular in the American way of eating. The American diet is a blend of foods from other countries. As new foods gained acceptance, an American version of these foods came to be a part of the American scene. To name a few, Italian spaghetti, Mexican tacos, and French crepes are generally popular foods. The blending of cultures has given us a wide variety of main dishes, breads, soups, salads, and desserts.

Food Preparation

Food preparation methods vary with cultures. Some cultures tend to prepare elaborate meals, others thrive on one-pot meals. Whether the recipe is elaborate or simple, foreign or not, the ingredients (leavening, shortening, eggs, meats, vegetables or fruits, etc.) will serve the same functional purpose. For example, yeast will supply the leavening for the flour mixture in which it is used and shortening will contribute tenderness regardless of the nationality of the recipe. Cultural food

452

recipes will give you new and interesting ways to prepare foods. There is much pleasure and excitement in trying new foods and in learning about the countries and peoples from which they come. The utensils may be different but the general techniques you use in food preparation such as creaming (sugar and shortening), folding in egg foams, and kneading dough are much the same in all cultures.

Dinner is the main meal of the day for most Americans. It is usually served early in the evening and is often considered a social occasion. Lunch is a moderate meal and breakfast the lightest meal for many Americans. In some cultures the noon meal is the main meal of the day. The American breakfast may be considered a heavy meal when compared to the first meal of the day as served in some other countries. The European breakfast is often light and may consist of a bread item and beverage (continental breakfast). Afternoon teas are popular in England.

People from northern and western Europe and the Scandinavian countries were among the first settlers in America and added the pioneer influence to the developing American food culture. The contributions from these countries included characteristic foods, food preparation methods, and styles of food service.

The traditional food habits are promoted from one generation to the next and carry with them strong meanings and feelings which bind families and communities into close units. Here are some cultural food patterns of a number of countries which have become part of the development of the American food heritage.

English

English foods are similar to those served in the United States. The grain products, meats, vegetables, and fruits sold in English markets are also found in American markets.

Grains occupy a prominent place in the English diet. White, whole wheat, and rye breads are served with meals. Scones and biscuits are popular accompaniments for afternoon tea served with hot milk. Oatmeal is served at breakfast, in oaten cakes, or in the evening meal as a porridge. Yorkshire pudding is a popular roast beef accompaniment.

Meats such as beef, lamb, and mutton are roasted, boiled, and sometimes prepared in a meat pie with vegetables. Glandular meats (organs such as liver, kidneys, etc.), bacon, local

453

Steamed plum pudding with hard sauce is an English favorite to be served on festive occasions.

fish (such as cod, trout, herring, etc.), game, and eggs are used. Kidney pie is a favorite. Ham and bacon are broiled while fish are boiled or fried in bacon drippings. Eggs often served in the shell are medium to hard cooked. Stews are frequently prepared with game meats and vegetables.

Potatoes and some other vegetables are usually boiled while cabbage is often cooked with bacon drippings. Popular fruits include berries, cherries, and peaches. Small fruits are often stewed and served as a sauce.

Milk, buttermilk, and cheese often appear in meals. Hot milk is served with cereal and tea, the popular beverage. Cheddar and soft cheeses are often served in the evening meal with biscuits or bread. English foods are substantial and served without sauces. They are seasoned with herbs, spices, salt, and often with bacon drippings.

Breakfast often includes hot cereal, broiled ham or bacon or other local specialties such as kippers. Lunch is served about one o'clock in the afternoon and dinner late in the evening.

French

French cookery is famous for flavorful sauces and soups, crisp-crusted breads, tarts and pastries. Rice and barley are cooked in soups. Poultry, pork, beef, veal, mutton, fresh and saltwater fish, and seafoods are the favored meat items. Eggs and a variety of dried beans and lentils are used.

Meats may be broiled, roasted, fried, boiled, stewed, or prepared in soups. Poultry is sautéd, stewed, or prepared in a soup. The seafoods are boiled, broiled, baked, fried, or cooked in soups.

Artichoke is a popular vegetable. Other vegetables include beets, broccoli, cabbage, carrots, celery, green beans and peas, onions, potatoes, turnips, tomatoes, and salad greens. Potatoes may be boiled, fried, or prepared in soups and stews. Vegetables may be prepared in water and a variety of ways.

The French use a variety of fruits including apples, berries, cherries, grapes, melons, peaches, pears, plums, and citrus. Seasonal fruits are served raw or stewed. Apples may be pressed into cider and grapes into wine.

Boiled cow's milk is used in coffee and chocolate, and served to children. Cow's and goat's milk is made into a variety of cheeses. Cheese is served as snacks or dessert and used in cooking. Little butter is used on bread but is used generously in cooking.

Almost every region of France has its special daubes or casseroles. This is a savory, country-style daube de beouf or beef casserole with vegetables.

In addition to coffee and tea, beer, cider, and wine are popular. Coffee is prepared with chicory and served with hot milk.

Wine is frequently used in food preparation. Popular food seasonings include spices, garlic, parsley, and herbs. A variety of fats are used in food preparation and include butter, lard, pork and poultry fat. Olive oil is used for salads and, at times, for cooking.

The French breakfast is light, consisting of coffee or hot chocolate and a roll, bread, or pastry. The largest meal is served in the middle of the day. Most French people take time for a substantial, leisurely noon meal. Schools and offices are closed from 12 until 2. Some workers may choose a short lunch break (45 minutes) which permits them to work a shorter week. In cities snack shops are available to accommodate the shorter midday meal. Except for Sundays and holidays, prepared desserts are not usually served at noon. Conversation is nearly as essential with meals as is the food.

Choices of desserts and main
entrées from Germany.

Germany

An American favorite, the hot dog or frankfurter, is of German descent, a relative of the German sausage. The hamburger, an American chopped-meat specialty, is said to have
originated in Hamburg, Germany.

Beef, organ meats, veal, pork, sausage, bacon, poultry, and
game are served. Dumplings and noodles are served with
stews. Freshwater fish and shrimp are used. Eggs are used in
noodles, baked products, as a thickening agent, and also as
garnishes for a variety of dishes.

Potatoes are served at most meals. Red and white cabbage
are popular along with broccoli, cauliflower, kohlrabi, carrots,
beets, onions, tomatoes, and lettuce.

Vegetables are not usually served as a separate dish. Cabbage is served cooked, raw, or as sauerkraut. Most other vegetables and greens are frequently cooked with small quantities
of meat. Red cabbage, lettuce, and potatoes are seasoned with

457

bacon and hot vinegar. A variety of fruits—apples, bananas, oranges, peaches, pears, quinces, prunes, grapes, and melons are served as dessert.

A variety of popular dairy products include milk, buttermilk, sour milk, sour cream, cottage cheese, and brick cheeses. Milk is used for cooking rather than as a beverage. Cottage cheese is used in noodle dishes, cake, and strudel. Butter is primarily used for cooking, little is eaten on bread. Jams are the preferred spread on bread.

Tea, coffee, beer, and wine are the popular beverages. Foods may be seasoned with butter, cream, or meat fat. Other seasonings include garlic, onion, paprika, peppers, parsley, horseradish, and caraway seeds.

German meals are substantial and include meat, potatoes, dumplings, cakes or pastries. Beer and white wine are popular with meals. The noon meal is the heaviest, breakfast and the evening meal tend to be light. The Germans begin the day with a breakfast of rolls or bread and coffee, and a few hours later they eat a second breakfast. A midmorning snack and a midafternoon coffee are popular. School children have a sandwich and fruit while working persons have a meat or cheese sandwich and a beverage. The last meal of the day, supper, is light and is served late in the evening.

Italy

Italians use pastas in a variety of shapes with a number of different sauces and cheeses. The pasta makes the meal; wheat, corn, and rice are the major grains. Corn is ground into meal and used as a cooked cereal or in a flour product. The popular flour products are spaghetti, macaroni, pizza, crusty white breads, and whole wheat bread. The cooked pastas are served with sauces and cheese. Breads are served with meals and used to make fried bread dough and stuffings.

The variety of meats served include beef, lamb, veal, pork, poultry, and sausages. Fish and seafoods are popular in southern Italy. Meats are often cut up or ground, then fried, slow-simmered, stewed, or cooked with potatoes. Chicken, veal cutlets, and meat balls are traditional meats. Tomato sauces seasoned with garlic, onion, green pepper, and spices are served with the meat. Dried beans, peas, and lentils are used in thick soups. Eggs may be fried alone or with onion and peppers, served as a plain omelet, an omelet with cheese or mushrooms, or used as a thickener in sauces.

A generous plate of spaghetti topped with a spicy tomato sauce and
served with a crisp green salad and crusty bread is an Italian meal enjoyed
by everyone.

Italians use a variety of vegetables such as tomatoes, green beans, broccoli, cauliflower, celery, eggplant, peppers, radishes, artichoke, and squash. Greens are popular salad items and include dandelion greens, endive, Romaine, scallions, and spinach. Raw greens are served in salads seasoned with oil and wine vinegar. Potatoes are not used commonly. Other vegetables are parboiled and then fried in oil or served with olive oil and vinegar. Tomatoes are cooked into sauces with meat or fish, and are used in soups.

Fresh, dried, or glazed fruits are used. Popular fruits include grapes, plums, peaches, pears, persimmons, quinces, oranges, apples, dates, figs, and raisins. Fruits are served as dessert. Other popular desserts are fancy cakes, ices, and ice creams.

Italians use little milk. Goat's milk is preferred. Milk is the beverage for children. Little butter is used. Coffee and dry wines are the popular beverages. Coffee is served with hot milk and sugar. Espresso, a strong black coffee is a favorite. Wine is used as an adult beverage and in cooking.

Milk is made into cheese. Popular cheeses are Romano, ricotta, mozzarella, Parmesan, and provolone. Italian cheeses are used generously in cooking such as mozzarella and ricotta and cheeses such as Parmesan and Romano grated as seasonings for spaghetti and vegetables.

Italian food tends to be highly seasoned. Fats such as olive oil, cottonseed oil, salt pork, or lard are used to cook meats and to season vegetables. Olive oil is especially popular for cooking meats, preparing vegetables and sauces, and to use in making salads. Other popular seasonings are garlic, onion, pepper, vinegar, parsley, thyme, and cloves.

Italians usually eat a light breakfast, black coffee for adults and milk for children, and bread. Many Italians prefer the heavy meal of the day at noon, others in the evening. A light meal may be cheese, bread, and coffee or wine.

Mexico

Tomatoes, chili peppers, and corn are freely used in Mexican cookery. Mexicans use small amounts of meat in combination with vegetables and many varieties of beans. The popular tamales are made of cornmeal and highly seasoned ground pork rolled in corn husks, and steamed.

Corn is a staple of the diet along with wheat and rice. Corn is being replaced by wheat in the making of tortillas.

Tortillas, garbanzo beans, and gazpacho soup served in handsome Mexican pottery are wonderful to see and marvelous to eat.

Cornmeal gruel served with hot milk is also popular. Rolled oats, when available, and rice are well liked. Macaroni, spaghetti, and some yeast breads are popular.

Chicken and beef are well liked but used sparingly due to their cost. Fish is rarely used. Eggs are used occasionally. Calico or pinto beans are used almost every day. Beans may be cooked with beef, chili peppers, and garlic, or they may be reheated by frying.

Chili peppers and fresh, canned, or dried corn are the chief vegetables. Chili peppers are often dried and ground. Other vegetables include beets, cabbage, peas, potatoes, squash, sweet potatoes, and a variety of tropical greens. Bananas are used frequently and, when available, oranges, apples, and peaches are well liked.

Milk is not generally used, except evaporated milk may be used for infant feeding. Coffee with sugar is a popular beverage. Chili powder is an essential seasoning for almost every dish along with garlic, onion, and salt. Other seasonings include lemon and lime juices, parsley, saffron, mint, cinnamon, and nutmeg.

Breakfast and the evening meal are generally light and include sweet coffee and tortillas (thin, unleavened cakes baked on a hot griddle). The noon meal is the main meal of the day.

Greece

The daily meals of the Greeks are relatively simple while the holidays are festive occasions and call for a variety of delicacies. Wheat, corn, and rice are the staple cereals. White bread from wheat is preferred. Bread is the central part of every meal and is eaten without any spread. Noodles, spaghetti, and macaroni are plain or prepared with tomato and meat sauce. Rice is used. Cornmeal is cooked into a thick gruel.

Lamb is the chief meat. Mutton, goat, pork, and poultry are well liked and some beef is eaten. Meat is often cut into small pieces, browned in fat or oil, and cooked with rice and vegetables. Poultry is often cooked into broth. Fresh, smoked or salted fish and shellfish are used often. The fish may be fried or steamed with vegetables. Egg dishes are popular but not at breakfast. White beans and legumes are used. Soups are prepared from dried beans, onions, celery, and carrots. Legumes are boiled, mashed, and eaten either hot or cold.

Many varieties of vegetables are eaten such as cabbage, cauliflower, eggplant, cucumbers, peppers, zucchini, and salad

462

A colorful Greek salad of spinach, mushrooms, beets, olives, and other vegetables is a nutritious, tasty addition to any meal.

greens. Vegetables may be the main dish. They are cooked until very soft and seasoned with meat broth or tomato, onion, olive oil, and parsley. Fresh vegetables are popular and are combined into a salad or thinly cut raw vegetables with a dressing of olive oil, vinegar, or lemon juice.

Cherries, grapes, peaches, apricots, plums, pears, melons, dates, figs, and raisins are popular. Fresh fruits in season are eaten raw. They are very often eaten for dessert. Grapes may be pressed into wine.

Milk from cows, goats, and sheep is used. Boiled milk is given to children. Adults drink little milk but enjoy fermented milk as yogurt. Cheese is popular, both the soft and mild and the hard and dry cheeses.

Coffee and wine are popular beverages. Coffee similar to the American beverage is served in the morning, while Turkish-style coffee is served with other meals. Some favorite seasonings include olive and seed oils, a variety of herbs, caraway and sesame seeds, and honey.

Meals are family affairs in Greek homes. Bread is considered the main part of the meal and all of the other foods are the accompaniments to the bread.

China

The Chinese try to preserve the original flavor, color, and texture of food. They use the freshest possible foods, and cook them quickly at a high temperature in a small amount of liquid or fat. Vegetables are cooked just before serving and so retain their crispness.

Rice is the staple grain. It appears in almost every meal. Some wheat, barley, millet, and corn may be used. Plain or fried rice is used as the main dish. Millet may be served as a gruel or made into cakes. A steamed bread is eaten at breakfast and noodles are popular.

Small quantities of meat are available. Pork is the favorite meat. Lamb, goat, and poultry are used. The organ meats, skin, and blood of the animals are used. The meat is cut into small, thin slices or cubes, cooked in oil (sesame, peanut) with soybean sauce and a small amount of water. A sweet-sour pork or poultry is popular. Meat cubes are rolled in batter and fried in oil, simmered in a thin sauce made of pineapple, green peppers, brown sugar, vinegar, and seasonings.

Fish and shellfish are popular and are baked with native spices or prepared as a sweet-sour dish. Legumes are used in

A chrysanthemum fire pot filled with simmering broth and surrounded by crisp vegetables and thinly sliced meat to be cooked is the center for this Chinese meal.

place of meat. Soybeans are used as a sauce, as milk for infants, as a cheese, and in other forms.

Chicken, pigeon, and duck eggs are well liked. Eggs may be combined with mushrooms and bean sprouts and served with soy sauce. Chinese egg rolls consist of shrimp or meat and chopped vegetables which have been rolled up in a thin dough, then fried in deep fat.

A variety of vegetables such as carrots, onions, leeks, white turnips, cabbage, corn, green beans, squash, bean and bamboo sprouts, sweet potato, and some weeds are used. Vegetables are cut into uniform small pieces, and cooked briefly in a little oil or water. The vegetables may also be steamed with meat or egg, added to meats, or used in soups.

Fruits are usually eaten raw. Kumquat is a favorite. Pineapple and other fruits are used in food preparation. A small amount of water buffalo milk is used but not cream or butter. Soybean milk is frequently used. Tea is the national beverage and green tea is popular.

Seasonings include soy sauce, sesame seed, salt, garlic, ginger, pepper, and fresh herbs. Peanut oil and lard are used. A dish of plain boiled rice is served for breakfast and with most every meal.

Scandinavian Countries

Scandinavians are famous for the smorgasbord. Their foods not only include fish but also pork and poultry, cream and butter, nuts, a variety of vegetables, and other foods. Their patterns are very similar to those of the northeastern and central United States where the Scandinavian immigrants settled. In contrast to native-born Americans, they use fish, cheese, and dark breads more frequently.

Barley, oats, rye, and wheat are the chief grains. Oatmeal porridge is popular, barley is used in soups. Rye and wheat are made into breads, rolls, and cakes.

Beef, mutton, pork, veal, and poultry are the principal meats. Organ meats and sausages are well liked. Meats may be roasted, stewed, and braised with or without vegetables. Some meats may be smoked or salted.

Fresh and saltwater fish are well liked. They may be smoked, salted, canned, or used fresh. Fish may be broiled, boiled, formed into balls, steamed with vegetables, or prepared into soups. Legumes and beans are prepared into soups. Eggs are used in cooking.

The variety of vegetables include beets, green beans, cabbage, carrots, celery, leeks, peas, potatoes, and greens. Potatoes are used frequently and are boiled, fried, mashed, and cooked with meat or fish. Most other vegetables are boiled, steamed, creamed, or cooked with meat. Lettuce, cucumbers, and tomatoes are eaten raw and used in salads.

Apples, berries, cherries, currants, pears, plums, rhubarb, and dried fruits are used. Seasonal fruits and preserved fruits are served in sauces, puddings, fruit soups, which may be hot or cold, and as fillings for pastry.

Cow's and goat's milk and cream are used. Milk is the beverage for children and is used by adults in coffee. It is also used in cream sauces and in the preparation of porridge, gravies, and desserts. Soft and mild cheeses and the hard and dry varieties are used in cooking. Butter is spread on bread, used in baking and cooking, and to flavor vegetables.

The popular beverages include coffee, tea, and beer. Cocoa may be served as the afternoon beverage. Coffee is served with cream or hot milk. The variety of seasonings include caraway and cardamon seeds, bay leaves, thyme, chives, dill, citron, black pepper, and honey. Butter and salt pork and lard are used in cooking.

An array of dishes from the Scandinavian countries offers variety in color, taste, and texture to please every guest.

Providing Nutrient Needs

As you read the brief descriptions of selected food cultures you noticed that all of these included a variety of foods. These foods contribute to the nutrient needs of all people regardless of their location or culture.

Main Ideas

Food habits are influenced by cultural beliefs and values, religion, climate, location, agriculture, technology, and economic status. The brief description of several cultural food patterns blended into the American food heritage includes those of England, France, Germany, Scandinavia, Italy, Greece, China, and Mexico.

The foods used throughout the world, contribute to the nutrient needs of all people. Recipes from other lands offer an interesting way to use ingredients, while the basic techniques of food preparation remain the same.

Activities

1. Find several bread recipes from two or more countries and compare the ingredients and preparation techniques used. What differences exist in the ingredients and in the methods of preparation?

2. Locate two or more restaurants specializing in cultural foods (such as Italian, Chinese, Mexican, German, French, or others) and compare the foods offered with those offered in an American restaurant serving complete meals. What differences and similarities did you find?

3. Identify fast-food restaurants specializing in cultural foods. Identify the foods and the cultures represented.

4. Select a cultural recipe for meat or a main dish for a lunch or dinner and complete the remainder of the menu with foods that complement this dish. What did you consider as you planned the menu?

5. In this chapter you have had only a glimpse of the many different foods that people eat in various parts of the world. Choose a country you would like to know more about. Find out all you can about the foods and food habits of that country. Make a collection of recipes that you would like to try. Share with other class members.

Questions

1. What contributes to the development of food heritage?

2. What influenced your food habits? The food habits or others?

3. Define culture. What cultural foods are present in America today?

4. Why do food habits differ among countries?

5. Are there any differences in the American breakfast, lunch, and dinner compared to the meals served in other countries? Give some examples.

6. What ingredients and what preparation techniques remain nearly the same in various cultures?

7. What is one of the chief items in a Greek meal?

8. What special technique is characteristic of Chinese cookery?

9. What are the major cereals in Mexican diets?

10. What are tamales?

11. What is meant by the statement "German meals are substantial"?

12. What are 2 vegetables used extensively in Mexican cookery?

Chapter
30
Regional Foods of America

Words for Thought

Food adaptation
adjusting, changing, or fitting a food for a specific use or purpose.

Heritage
customs, practices, rituals, foods passed on through generations.

Regional foods
the typical foods prepared or grown in a specific area of a country.

As the immigrants came to America, they adapted their food patterns to the foods that they found in their new homeland and developed a variety of Americanized foods. The French contributed to the Creole cooking of Louisiana. The Germans developed Pennsylvania Dutch cooking, for example. Each cultural group tended to settle in a specific region or area of America. Thus the groups living in each area tended to develop food combinations and types of cookery based on their cultural food habits and customs which they had brought with them to this new land.

Regional Foods

Each geographic region has its special food patterns. The soft wheat of the South is well suited for the preparation of the hot breads served with almost every meal. The north central plains grow hard wheat from which the flavorful yeast breads are made.

Maine and Idaho are known for their potatoes, Florida and California for citrus fruits, Wisconsin for dairy products, Louisiana for rice, and the coastal states and Alaska for seafoods. From New England come lobsters, codfish cakes, clam chowders, baked beans, pumpkin pies, turkey, and squash. From Hawaii come pineapple and fish. Pennsylvania has its shoofly pie. Texas has its beef and refried beans.

Many of the northern European foods were easily adapted to form the American food patterns since the climatic conditions and crops grown in the New World were similar to those of the settlers' homelands. The food patterns within the United States can be grouped into five regional areas: East Coast, Midwest, West Coast, South, and Southwest.

East Coast

The first Americans, the Indians, made contributions to the American food customs through their use and preparation of corn, fowl, and fish. The Indians taught the people who came from Europe to settle in America to make pudding and johnny cake from cornmeal. Many vegetables of today originated with the Indians, for example, tomatoes, potatoes, squash, pumpkin, wild rice, beans, and cranberries. The Indians also introduced the newcomers to cocoa, herbs, and maple sugar to use as flavorings and seasonings.

The Indians prepared game and fish before an open fire which led the way to the popular New England clam bake. Yellow vegetables such as carrots, turnips, and squash became popular in New England. Some of the early traditions were adopted nationwide such as the Thanksgiving turkey, cranberry sauce, and pumpkin pie.

Midwest

The Midwest includes the shores of the Great Lakes and the fertile lands surrounded by the Mississippi River and its tributaries. The English, German, Scandinavian, Swiss, and other nationalities migrated to this area. Especially Wisconsin, but also Vermont and several other states produce large quantities of dairy products—milk, cream, butter, cheese, and some European-style cheeses. Cattle, fruits, and vegetables abound and fish from the Great Lakes are plentiful.

The Midwest makes a generous contribution to the abundant United States supply of corn and wheat. These grains in turn are made into flour, cereals, and breads; they are used to feed animals which supply meat, milk, and eggs for human needs.

West Coast

The far west provides a bountiful supply of fresh fruits and vegetables; and the coastal areas, fish. The immigrants coming to the west coast from Japan, China, and other far eastern countries contributed an oriental flavor to foods in America. They use a variety of locally grown vegetables and fruits. The short-cooking or stir-frying method of cooking vegetables is a well-known oriental custom. Salads are often featured as the first course of a meal.

South

Corn and rice are popular grains in the South. A variety of vegetables and greens are used, and often are cooked with fatback for a prolonged time and served with the cooking liquid. Canned milks are used frequently since fresh milk is less plentiful. Buttermilk is liked and served when available. Favorite Southern dishes include fried chicken, corn pone, and hominy grits. Sweet potatoes are preferred to white potatoes. Fish and fried shrimp are especially popular along the coast. Nuts, black-eyed peas, and kidney beans are popular. French cookery is found in New Orleans.

Southwest

Spanish and Mexican foods add a hot spicy flavor to the American food heritage. Typical foods include chili, enchiladas, pinto beans, tortillas, tamales, and tacos. Gulf shrimp, crabs, avocados, ripe olives, and almonds are also used. There are green salads, garbanzos and beet salads, and potatoes with sardines. Mangoes, papayas, and pineapples are favorites.

472

Alaska

In Alaska, you would find that the residents enjoy summers in which fruits, vegetables, and flowers grow as they do in the mainland states. The cuisine, or style of preparing and cooking foods, of Alaska is based upon that of the states of the mainland along with their specialty foods. Some Alaskan food specialties include seaweed pickles and jellies made of Balb kelp grown along shores. Their special varieties of cranberries and blueberries are made into relishes, puddings, and ketchup. You would see a variety of wild berries in the fields such as strawberries, red and yellow salmonberries, black and red huckleberries, purple and black gooseberries, juneberries, and yellow cloudberries.

The Alaskans rely on local fish—cod, halibut, herring, and salmon. Salmon is especially liked and is often baked or broiled. A variety of wild game is available in Alaska. You have a choice of wild duck, geese, ptarmigan, mountain goats, rabbits, and beaver. Other relatively large animals contribute to the variety of meat available and include bears, moose, and reindeer. The reindeer is cut into steaks, chops, and roasts, and some of the meat is ground. These meats are prepared in much the same way as beef is prepared.

Sourdough breads were carried into Alaska by gold prospectors. Since breads could not be purchased, the prospectors prepared sourdough breads as they moved from place to place in search of gold. Sourdough breads and pancakes continue to be popular in Alaska along with all kinds of breads, pastries, cakes, and doughnuts.

The traditional Eskimo diet consists of raw fish, seal meat, and hot tea. A unique ice cream is a favorite of the Eskimo. Reindeer fat is finely grated and blended with seal oil and a small amount of water. This foamy, pale mixture is often flavored with wild berries. This Eskimo specialty is considered a delicacy, especially by the children.

Some Eskimos, especially the young, are beginning to show a preference for other foods. They have accepted canned fruits, sugar, and wheat flour.

Hawaii

All of the people who came to live in the fiftieth state—Americans, Filipinos, Chinese, Spanish, Japanese, Koreans, Puerto Ricans, Portuguese, and the native Hawaiians brought

From the Northeast the traditional baked beans and steamed brown bread. From the West a great variety of vegetable, legume, and rice dishes.

Pork chops and baked apples on a bed of sauerkraut (above) from the Midwest. A tempting array of seafood, fruits, and vegetables (below) from Cajun country.

Broiled chicken, bananas, and
Polynesian rice is a special treat
from Hawaii. An attractive vegetable
platter from California. A harvest of
foods from the Southwest.

their own foods, ways of growing, cooking, and eating them. Thus Hawaiian cookery is an adventure in good eating.

There are three major sauces used in Hawaiian cookery: coconut milk from the Polynesians; soy sauce with sugar, wine, oil with garlic, ginger or scallions from the Orientals; sweet-sour flavor from the Chinese and Filipinos.

Poi is a pasty substance made from taro root and is the staple food of Hawaii. Traditionally poi is eaten with the fingers. The consistency of poi is often described as two-finger or three-finger poi which indicates the number of fingers required to carry it to the mouth. Even though the flavor may not be overly inviting, at first, some people learn to enjoy it. Other staple Hawaiian foods include local fish, yams, coconut, bananas, breadfruit, and pineapple. The native diet is relatively simple and includes locally grown foods. Breakfast usually consists of fresh fruit while the afternoon or evening meal is substantial.

The Hawaiian cookout is a festive occasion known as the luau. A barbecued roast suckling pig is the focal point of the celebration which usually includes entertainment as well. The piglets are roasted over an open fire or wrapped in green leaves and placed over hot stones. Pork is preferred and then chicken, while beef and veal are used infrequently.

Meat and fish are often combined in the same dish, for example, laulau. Lomi is a popular salmon dish. Warm-water fish tend to have a very mild flavor and shellfish are considered excellent. Seafood is available in large quantities.

Melons, pomegranates, and other local fruits are served. Pineapples, macadamia nuts and lichee nuts are very popular. Desserts are simple. As a tourist, you would select unusual drinks served in scooped-out pineapples or coconuts. Some beverages and mixed drinks are offered in bowls with gardenias floating in them.

Main Ideas

The regional food patterns developed as cultural groups settled in a specific area of the United States. Each region — the East Coast, Midwest, West Coast, South, Southwest, Alaska, and Hawaii — can be identified with characteristic foods. The regional food patterns of the United States and the American food heritage are the contributions of the first Americans, the Indians, and the immigrants who settled in the United States from other parts of the world.

Activities

1. Plan a dinner menu featuring regional foods. Which regions of the United States were represented?

2. Prepare a report on the food habits of the Eskimos in Alaska.

3. Prepare a menu for a Hawaiian cookout.

4. Give a report on the Hawaiian luau.

Questions

1. What are regional foods? How were they developed?

2. What do you consider to be a typical American food? Why?

3. How do the foods typical of your state differ from those of other states?

4. Identify the origin of the foods characteristic of the: East Coast, Midwest, South, Southwest, and West Coast of the United States.

5. What are the typical foods of Alaska? Of Hawaii?

6. In what ways do the foods of Alaska and Hawaii differ from those of mainland United States? In what ways are they similar?

Suggested Cookbooks

Morrow, Kay. *The New England Cookbook of Fine Old Yankee Recipes.* New York City: Culinary Arts Press, 1936.

Richard, Lena. *New Orleans Cookbook.* Boston: Houghton Mifflin Company, 1940.

The Duchess of Windsor. *Some Favorite Southern Recipes of the Duchess of Windsor.* New York: Charles Scribner's Sons, 1942.

Trahey, Jane. *A Taste of Texas.* New York: Random House, 1949.

Yardley, M. *Hawaii Cooks.* Rutland, VT: Charles E. Tuttle Company, 1970.

5 The Conservation of Food

Chapter 31

Preservation Methods

Words for Thought

Blanch

to precook or preheat in boiling water or steam.

Head space

the free or empty space at the top of a jar or container in which food is packed.

Processing

in canning, to heat foods in containers to sterilize the food and the container.

Seal

to make a container airtight.

Microorganisms

the bacteria, mold, and yeast causing food spoilage and disease.

Pectin

a carbohydrate-like substance found in fruits which helps to jell fruit juices and mixtures of fruits.

With the technology of food preservation as it is today, it is possible to preserve the quality of foods from one harvest time to the next. A wide variety of food is always available in the marketplace. Centuries ago this was not the case. The first foods to be preserved were grains and nuts. They were dried in the sun and air. Later meats and fish were preserved by salting, smoking, and drying. It was not until the nineteenth century that other preservation methods were discovered. The search for these new methods resulted from the great need for a lasting food supply.

Discovery

The need for food was so urgent during the Napoleonic Wars that the French government offered an award of twelve thousand francs to the person who discovered a satisfactory method for preserving foods. M. Nicholas Appert won the award in 1809 and is regarded as the "Father of Canning."

Appert placed hot foods into glass bottles which he sealed with cork, and then heated gradually in a kettle of water for a period of time which varied with the type of food canned. Appert did not know why the canned food kept, but he believed that certain elements in the air caused foods to spoil.

It was Louis Pasteur who discovered that microorganisms—bacteria, mold, and yeast—were present in air, water, soil, and on food and all objects, and that they caused foods to spoil. Pasteur noted that when foods were heated to destroy the spoilage organisms and then sealed tightly to keep out other organisms, the food could be preserved indefinitely.

Peter Durrand of England, in 1810, obtained a patent for preserving foods in glass, pottery, and tin containers. The problem of finding a suitable container for canning was solved by John L. Mason in 1858 when he invented the glass bottle that we call the "mason" jar. Mason jars sealed with a rubber ring and a metal screw-on cap which prevents air from entering and jars having two-piece self-sealing lids with cap and metal screw-on band are used today for home canning.

New Methods

Since the days of Nicholas Appert, several methods have been discovered for preserving food. In addition to freezing and the new methods of drying, foods can be preserved by dehydrofreezing, freeze-drying, and irradiation.

Frozen foods are preserved because they are kept at temperatures too cold for bacterial activity and growth. In dehydrofreezing, fruits and vegetables are dried to about one-half of their original weight and then frozen. This makes them easy to package and freeze. At the present time, dehydrofrozen fruits and vegetables are used by people in institutional food service and by producers of soups and pastries, but eventually they may be available to the homemaker.

During freeze-drying, foods are frozen first and then the water is evaporated while the food remains frozen. Freeze-dried foods are light and porous and about the same size as the original food. You may have eaten freeze-dried fruits in cereals or used freeze-dried coffee. Because freeze-dried foods are light, they are used on space flights and camping trips.

Irradiated foods are sterilized by beta or gamma rays. The rays can pass through the packaging material as well as the food to destroy microorganisms. Irradiated foods do not require refrigeration. The beta rays are produced by an electron accelerator and gamma rays come from radioisotopes. Irradiated bacon has been used by the armed forces. The USDA permits the irradiation of potatoes to control sprouting and of wheat to destroy insects.

In contrast to sun drying which is one of the earliest methods for preserving food, dehydration refers to foods dried by other methods. Foods may be dried by forced dry air, on drums or rollers, such as with mashed potatoes, or on trays such as with pieces of vegetable or fruit, or sprayed into heated cylinders as with instant coffee and nonfat dry milk. Dried and dehydrated foods have a water content so low that microorganisms cannot grow.

Spoilage

The microorganisms responsible for food spoilage are bacteria, mold, and yeast. You can see them under the microscope. Some microorganisms are considered beneficial because they produce desirable changes in food. For example, bacteria are used in the making of buttermilk and sauerkraut. Molds are used in curing cheeses such as Roquefort and Blue cheese. Yeast is used in bread-making. Microorganisms, like any other living organisms, need certain conditions in order to grow. In this case, there are three such conditions: warmth, moisture, and, of course, food. When any of these three elements is restricted or absent, microorganisms cannot grow.

Of the microorganisms, *bacteria* are the most difficult to destroy. There are many kinds of bacteria; some require much higher temperatures to destroy them than others. Different kinds of bacteria are found on the various foods. A few bacteria can grow at refrigerator temperatures, some at temperatures well over 38°C (100°F), but most bacteria grow best at temperatures from 20 to 38°C (68 to 100°F). The various bacteria also have different requirements for moisture, food, and oxygen. Some bacteria, for example, grow without oxygen.

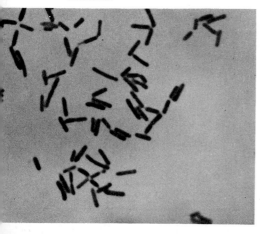

Microscopic view of one type of bacteria.

Mold is a fluffy growth that is often white but some varieties are red, grey, black, orange, or blue-green. Mold grows on many foods such as fruits, breads, meat, and jellies. Some mold even grows at refrigerator temperatures. Most molds are easily destroyed at boiling temperature. They usually grow on the surface and do not produce a harmful substance. A slight growth of mold on the surface can be removed and the remaining food eaten. When the mold growth is very heavy, all of the food may be changed in flavor and should be discarded.

Yeasts usually have only one cell. They are easily destroyed by boiling and most yeasts are destroyed at temperatures below boiling—49 to 60°C (120 to 140°F)—in about fifteen minutes. Yeast is always present in the air and can contaminate food. Bubbles of carbon dioxide form as the yeast grows in food. Fermentation is the process by which yeast changes sugar into carbon dioxide and ethyl alcohol.

In addition to microorganisms, certain *chemical substances called enzymes* produced by the food cells *can cause both desirable and undesirable changes in food.* For example, enzymes are responsible for color, flavor, and texture changes which occur as a food grows and ripens. Enzymes can also produce changes in food during storage. Because of their activity, fruits and vegetables will continue to ripen when stored.

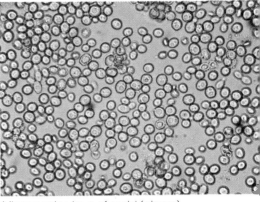

Microscopic views of mold (above) and yeast (below).

Most enzymes act best at room temperature and are easily destroyed by heating foods to the boiling temperature. You will use heat to inactivate the enzymes in the foods when possible and in vegetables before you freeze them. If you do not destroy the enzymes, they will continue to act and cause some fruits to darken and cause undesirable changes in the flavor and texture of vegetables. Enzyme activity in meat during storage is considered beneficial. It may tenderize the meat.

As you learn about the principles of food preservation, you will note that they have been designed to destroy or inactivate spoilage organisms and enzymes and to protect foods from recontamination. When you can foods or freeze foods and when you make jelly, you will be using these principles.

Preserving Foods at Home

Because of the highly specialized and expensive equipment required, not all methods of food preservation are suitable for home use. However, canning, freezing, and jelly-making can be inexpensively and easily done in your own home.

Canning

Canning is preserving foods by using heat to destroy micro-organisms and to inactivate enzymes and then sealing the food in containers. The heat will cook the food and change its flavor and appearance. Fruits, vegetables, and meats are canned.

Canning will not improve the quality of food, but only preserve it. *For good canned products, you should select high-quality foods.* The crisp, young, tender vegetables and mature, ripe fruits give the best canned products. Because changes occur rapidly in the flavor and texture of foods after they are picked, you should can them as quickly as possible.

You will have more attractive canned products when you sort the food to be canned according to size, maturity, and color. The food may be thoroughly cleaned by using a brush to clean large vegetables and fruits, and by placing small ones in a sieve under running water. Some foods are scraped or peeled; peaches and tomatoes are often dipped into boiling water so that you may easily remove the skin. This process is known as blanching. The seeds and cores may be removed. Large pieces may be cut or sliced.

Certain equipment is needed for canning. Much of this equipment is on hand in your kitchen. You need brushes to clean jars and food, knives for peeling and cutting, measuring cups and spoons, and some large kettles for blanching foods. You will also need a canner (large kettle with a rack) for processing acid foods, and a pressure cooker or canner for processing nonacid foods such as vegetables and meats.

You may can foods in either glass or tin containers. Glass jars are used most often for home canning. They do not require a mechanical sealer as do tin cans. Glass jars are suitable for all foods and are reusable until they become cracked or chipped. They are easily sealed with a zinc cap and a rubber ring, or a two-piece metal lid.

When you use tin cans, select those lined with a "C" enamel for corn, and those with an "R" enamel for red fruits and vegetables to protect their color. All other foods are canned in unlined tin cans.

You should inspect the containers and lids. Discard any with cracks, chips, dents, or rust. The containers and lids which you select must be thoroughly washed in hot, soapy water, and then rinsed well.

Two methods used to pack foods into containers are the *hot pack* and the *raw pack* or *cold pack*. The hot-pack method is used most often and is suitable for all foods. Hot foods are placed into hot containers when the hot-pack method is used. First, heat the food for a short time in boiling water (for vegetables) or in a sugar syrup (for fruits). This precooking will remove some of the air from the food tissue and cause it to shrink and pack more evenly in the container. Raw packing is the method of placing raw, prepared (cut, peeled, etc.) foods into containers.

The filled and closed containers are processed either in a boiling-water bath or in a pressure canner. You heat the food and the container at the same time to destroy microorganisms and enzymes.

The boiling-water bath consists of a large kettle, a rack on which the jars are placed, and a lid. The kettle should be deep enough to allow at least 2.5 cm (1 in) of water to cover the tops of the jars. The water is brought to a rolling boil so that the temperature surrounding the jars will be 100°C (212°F)— the temperature of boiling water. You will count processing time when the water reaches a rolling boil.

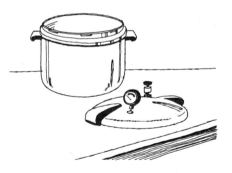

Because the pressure canner or cooker retains steam, temperatures above 100°C (212°F) can be reached. The pressure cooker is essential for processing nonacid foods (vegetables, other than tomato, meats) which require a high temperature to kill microorganisms. You will count processing time after the desired pressure is reached.

Each food has a recommended processing time for the boiling-water bath or the pressure canner (see page 492.) The jars are sealed at the end of the processing time to keep out organisms. The two-piece lids are self-sealing as they cool and are not tightened after processing. The zinc lids need to be tightened completely.

There is a general *canning procedure*. When you know it, you can apply it to the food of your choice. The following step-by-step procedure for canning peaches will show you how easily foods may be canned.

1. Begin by assembling needed equipment and examining the jars to see that there are no nicks or cracks, especially along the sealing edge. Wash the jars and lids in hot soapy water and rinse in hot water. Invert jars on a cloth-lined tray or counter.

2. Sort the peaches according to size and ripeness and wash thoroughly. Remove all decay or bruised spots.

3. Dip the peaches into boiling water for about one minute and then into cold water. The skin will slip off easily.

4. Cut the peach in half, remove the seed, and slip off the skin.

5. Fruits are usually canned in a sugar syrup which should be prepared before fruits are peeled. Most fruits are packed in a medium syrup, 250 mL (1 c) sugar to 500 mL (2 c) water.

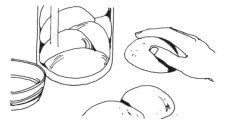

1. For raw pack, place peaches into the jar cut-side down; for hot pack, place the peach halves into boiling syrup for three minutes and then pack them into hot jars cut-side down.

2. Fill the jar to within 1.2 cm (½ in) of the top for most foods. For other foods which are not succulent (corn, peas, lima beans, meats) you need to allow 2.5 cm (1 in) of space (head space).

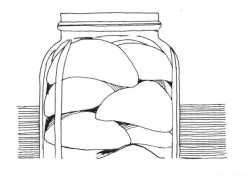

3. Fill the jar with syrup to 1.2 cm (½ in) from the top.

4. Use a table knife or spatula to release the air bubbles that are trapped. Add more syrup, if needed, to bring the level to 1.2 cm (½ in) from the top. Wipe the top of the jar free of syrup and pulp.

5. Place the flat lid with the sealing compound next to the top of the jar and screw the band firmly in place; or place the rubber ring on the sealing shoulder and screw on the zinc cap, then loosen it about a quarter of a turn to permit exhausting of air during processing.

6. Place the jar into a boiling-water-bath canner. Add water to the canner as needed to bring the water level 2.5 or 5 cm (1 or 2 in) over the jar tops. (If desired, a pressure canner may be used as well.)

7. Cover the canner and bring the water to a rolling boil and process for the recommended time listed on page 492. Count processing time after the water reaches a boil.

8. At the end of the processing time, remove the jars from the canner and place them, top-side up, on several thickness of cloth or newspaper to cool. Space the jars 5 to 7.5 cm (2 to 3 in) apart so that they will cool more quickly. Keep them away from a draft.

The canning of vegetables differs only slightly from that of fruits. *Most vegetables are blanched before packing; boiling water is used instead of syrup as the liquid; and they are processed in a pressure canner rather than a boiling-water bath.* To can vegetables, follow the steps given for green beans.

1. To can green beans, wash them thoroughly, trim the ends, remove any strings, and cut or break the beans into pieces— about 2.5 cm (1 in).

2. Put the prepared beans into boiling water and boil for three minutes. The blanching time will vary with the vegetable (see page 492).

3. Place a hot, clean jar on a cloth or paper pad and fill to within 2.5 cm (1 in) of the top.

4. Place 5 mL (1 tsp) of salt in each 1 L (1 qt) of vegetable and add boiling water to within 2.5 cm (1 in) of the top. Wipe the top and threads of the jar and seal it with the lid.

5. Put the jars into a pressure canner containing 5 to 7.5 cm (2 to 3 in) of hot water (or amount recommended by the manufacturer). Adjust the canner lid and turn on the heat.

6. You will usually leave the vent open until steam escapes in a continuous stream (about 10 minutes) and then close it.

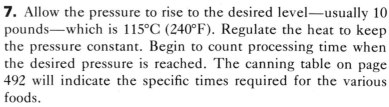

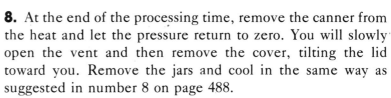

7. Allow the pressure to rise to the desired level—usually 10 pounds—which is 115°C (240°F). Regulate the heat to keep the pressure constant. Begin to count processing time when the desired pressure is reached. The canning table on page 492 will indicate the specific times required for the various foods.

8. At the end of the processing time, remove the canner from the heat and let the pressure return to zero. You will slowly open the vent and then remove the cover, tilting the lid toward you. Remove the jars and cool in the same way as suggested in number 8 on page 488.

9. The next day, after the jars have cooled, test the seal. Press the top of the two-piece lid; if it is flat and does not move, it is sealed. Or if it gives a clear ring when tapped, it is sealed. Place jars with zinc caps on their sides to check for leaks. Should you find a jar not properly sealed, use the contents immediately or recan. Reexamine the container and, if it is defective, you should transfer the food to another container before processing again.

10. You may remove the screw band from the two-piece lids before you store the sealed jars. Wipe the containers to clean them; then label and store them in a cool, dry place. The color of foods in glass containers will be protected when you store them in a dark place.

At times canned fruits may float in the liquid in a jar. This may be caused by too much liquid in proportion to the fruit or by using a too heavy syrup (containing too much sugar). Jars which are not completely filled at the end of processing have been packed too loosely. Raw-packed foods shrink as they are cooked in the container, resulting in a less full container. Precooking foods for hot packing allows the food to shrink before it is packed into jars, assuring full packs for each jar.

The lack of liquid in jars may be due to a tight pack which leaves no room for liquid, or because the jar is sealed so tightly that expanding air cannot escape freely without forcing liquid out. When the pressure fluctuates in a pressure canner, the pressure within the jar also changes, causing liquid to be forced out of the jar.

There may be a change in color, odor, texture, and flavor of canned foods when they spoil. Flat sour is a spoilage caused by bacteria which do not produce a gas. The food has an offensive odor and a sour taste. Bulging ends of cans are caused by microorganisms that produce a gas; when the container is opened, the liquid is usually forced out.

Botulism is a kind of spoilage caused by toxin produced by bacteria (Clostridium botulinum). It is formed in nonacid foods (vegetables, meats) which have not been completely processed due to either a too low temperature—under 115°C (240°F)—or inaccurate timing. No color, flavor, or texture changes are visible in the food. For this reason, *never taste home-canned vegetables and meats until they have been boiled (meats and corn for 20 minutes, other nonacid vegetables for 10 minutes) to destroy any possible toxins.*

You can avoid canned food spoilage if you follow these rules: observe strict cleanliness; follow directions carefully; work quickly so that foods do not stand for some time before processing; and count processing time accurately.

Freezing

Unlike canning, the principles of preserving foods by freezing are based upon the use of very cold temperatures (−18°C (0°F) at least) to prevent the growth of microorganisms and to slow down enzyme activity. As soon as the food begins to thaw, microorganisms and enzymes become active, and the food must be used quickly to avoid spoilage.

All foods except the succulent, crisp foods used raw such as salads or relishes may be frozen. Freezing causes less change in the color, flavor, and texture of foods than canning, and the nutrient values of frozen foods are similar to those of the fresh food.

Use the same care in selecting foods for freezing as for canning. Freezing cannot improve the quality of the food; it can only preserve the quality present in the food at the time it is frozen. Use only foods which are free of decay, spoilage, or bruises, and those which are at the stage of maturity and ripeness most desirable for eating and cooking.

You may freeze meat, fish, poultry, soups, casseroles, stews, yeast and quick breads, cakes, and pastries.

Processing Timetable for Fruits and Vegetables

	Preparation	Boiling Water Bath Minutes	Pressure Canner Minutes	Lbs. Pressure
Fruits				
Apples	Wash, pare, core, cut. Boil 3 to 5 min. in syrup. Pack.	25	10	5
Cherries	Wash, stem, pit. Pack, add syrup.	20	10	5
Grapes	Wash, stem. Pack, add syrup.	15	8	5
Peaches	Peel, pack, add syrup; or boil 3 min. in syrup, pack, add syrup.	25	10	5
Pears	Peel, pack, add syrup; or boil 3 min. in syrup, pack, add syrup.	20	10	5
Plums	Wash, prick skins. Pack, add syrup.	20	10	5
Tomatoes	Scald ½ min., cold dip, peel, core, quarter. Pack.	35	10	5
Tomato Juice	Peel, quarter; simmer until soft. Put through sieve, bring to boil, pour in jars to 6 mm (¼ in) of top.	10	—	—

	Preparation	Boiling Water Bath Minutes	Pts.	Qts.	Lbs. Pressure
Vegetables					
Asparagus	Wash, trim. Pack raw.	—	25	30	10
	For hot pack, boil 3 min. Pack.	—	25	30	10
Beans (string)	Wash, string, cut or whole. Pack.	—	20	25	10
	For hot pack, boil 3 min. Pack.	—	20	25	10
Beets	Wash, boil 15 min., skin. Pack.	—	25	40	10
Carrots	Wash, peel, cut. Pack raw.	—	25	30	10
	For hot pack, bring to boil. Pack.	—	25	30	10
Corn	Cut from cob. Pack raw.	—	55	85	10
	For hot pack, bring to boil. Pack.		55	85	10
Lima beans	Shell. Pack raw and loosely.	—	40	50	10
	For hot pack, bring to boil. Pack.	—	40	50	10
Peas	Shell, wash. Pack raw loosely.	—	40	40	10
	For hot pack, bring to boil. Pack.	—	40	40	10

Adapted from "Home Canning of Fruits and Vegetables," *Home and Garden Bulletin No. 8*, United States Department of Agriculture.

To freeze foods, you will need a freezer and moisture-vapor-proof packaging materials in addition to the usual kitchen equipment. Containers of aluminum, glass, plastic-coated paper, and transparent freezer wraps are suitable for wrapping irregular shaped foods such as meats and baked products for the freezer.

You can easily and quickly prepare fruits for freezing. Fruits may be packed dry, with sugar, or syrup; however, frozen, sweetened fruits usually have a better texture than dry-packed fruits. Small whole fruits (berries, cherries) may be packed dry for use as desired in pies, jellies, and for special diets. You must keep dry-packed fruits at a constant temperature and sealed tightly to avoid excessive dehydration.

The type of syrup and the proportion of sugar used for sugar and syrup pack will vary with the fruit (see page 494). Sugar retards freezing, so the greater the quantity of sugar used, the lower the freezing temperature must be.

When you prepare *fruits for freezing*, they need only to be sorted, washed, hulled, peeled, cored, and cut, if desired. When you pack fruits in syrup, you will prepare the syrup in advance and thoroughly chill it.

Some fruits such as peaches, pears, and apples may darken during frozen storage unless they are treated with ascorbic or citric acid. You will usually use 2.5 mL (½ t) of ascorbic acid for each liter (quart) of syrup.

Illustrations to the right and on page 495 will show you how to pack fruits for freezing, using both sugar and syrup pack.

1. To freeze strawberries (and other fruits) select fresh, ripe fruit free of decay. Wash them gently under running water or with a spray and drain on absorbent paper.

2. Unless you prefer to use whole berries, slice them into a shallow pan. Sprinkle the sugar (185 mL (¾ c) per liter (quart) of berries) over the berries and turn them gently until the sugar dissolves forming a syrup.

493

Food Preparation For Freezing

Fruits	Preparation — Wash Well	Syrup	Sugar
*Apples	Peel, core, slice.	40%	125 mL (½ c)
*Apricots	Cut in halves, pit.	40–50%	125 mL (½ c)
Berries	Sort, wash, drain well.	30–50%	185 mL (¾ c)
Cherries	Sort, wash, pit or leave whole.	40–60%	185 to 250 mL (¾ to 1 c)
*Peaches	Peel, pit, and slice.	30–40%	160 mL (⅔ c)
Pineapple	Peel, core, slice or dice.	40–50%	160 mL (⅔ c)
Plums	Halve and pit.	40–50%	none

Vegetables	Wash, Blanch, Chill in Ice Water	Blanch in Boiling Water
Asparagus	Cut in desired lengths.	2–4 minutes
Beans, string	Cut, or leave whole.	3–4
lima	Shell, sort, wash.	2–3
Broccoli	Peel stock, trim, split lengthwise.	3–5
Carrots	Peel, cut in slices or dice.	3
Cauliflower	Break into flowerlets (2.5 cm (1 in size)).	3–4
Corn	Husk, silk, blanch, cut from cob.	4
Peas	Shell, sort, wash.	1–2

Syrups for Freezing

30%   500 mL (2 c) sugar   1 L (4 c) water = 1.2 L (5 c)
40%   750 mL (3 c) sugar   1 L (4 c) water = 1.3 L (5½ c)
50%   1.18 L (4¾ c) sugar   1 L (4 c) water = 1.6 L (6½ c)
60%   1.75 L (7 c) sugar   1 L (4 c) water = 1.6 L (7¾ c)

Use ascorbic or citric acid to prevent darkening.
Adapted from "Home Freezing of Fruits and Vegetables," *Home and Garden Bulletin No. 10*, United States Department of Agriculture.

3. Carefully pack the sugared berries (including the juice formed) into a carton suitable for freezing. Gently tap the carton to pack the fruit closely, without crushing it, to exclude air. Leave 1.2 cm (½ in) head space to allow for the expansion during freezing.

4. When you use syrup instead of dry sugar, slice the fruit directly into the carton and then add syrup. Allow 2.5 cm (1 in) of head space.

5. Wipe the top of the container with a clean, damp cloth. Seal tightly and label with kind of food, type of pack, and date.

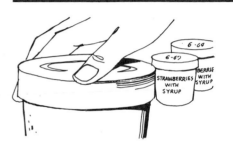

6. Place the labeled carton into the freezer so that the bottom or sides of the carton are in direct contact with the freezing unit. Foods frozen quickly will have better texture than those frozen slowly.

The procedure for preparing *vegetables for freezing* is similar to that used for canning. Most vegetables are blanched for freezing to retard enzyme action and are dry packed. Compare the following steps for freezing green beans with those given earlier for canning and note any differences.

1. Sort the green beans, wash, trim, and cut if desired; blanch for three minutes.

2. After the beans are blanched, remove them from the blanching water and immediately place them in ice water. Chill the beans about the same length of time required to blanch them, or until they feel cold when you bite into one.

3. Spread the chilled beans on a cloth or paper-lined tray to absorb any moisture.

4. Pack the beans into containers (do not add any liquid) and allow 1.2 cm (½ in) head space. The beans may also be packed into plastic bags and tightly closed with a rubber band or a piece of string. Label the carton and place it next to the unit for rapid freezing.

Meat, fish, and poultry require no special preparation for freezing. They should be packaged in the quantity suitable for your use. You may wish to cut them into pieces for serving.

Cut pieces of meat will be easy to separate after they are frozen if you first place a double layer of wrapping material between them before freezing.

Steps in Butcher Wrap

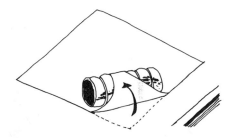

1. Place food diagonally close to one corner of the wrap and fold the corner of the paper over the food.

2. Fold opposite sides of the paper toward the middle so that the paper overlaps.

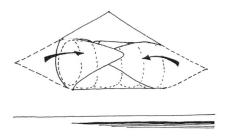

3. Continue rolling the food with the paper to the opposite side and secure the ends of the paper with freezer tape.

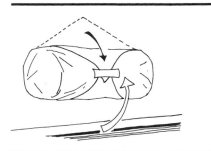

All meats should be wrapped in a moisture-vapor-proof freezer wrap using a butcher or a drugstore wrap. As you wrap the meat, mold and press the paper next to the meat to force out air. Improperly wrapped meats develop freezer burn (drying out) caused by moisture loss.

Steps in Drugstore Wrap

1. Place the food in the center of the paper, bring opposite edges of the paper together.

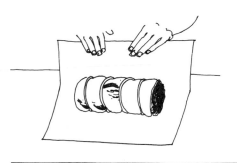

2. Fold down the paper in a series of small folds until it is in direct contact with the food.

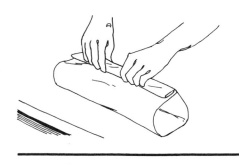

3. Fold the ends to make points, pressing the paper close to the food.

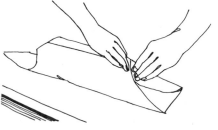

4. Turn the folded ends against the package and seal with freezer tape.

Many other foods can also be frozen. Baked pastry, unfrosted cakes, cookies, breads, and sandwiches may be carefully wrapped for freezing, using either the butcher or drugstore wrap. Frosted cakes and unbaked pies will be more easily wrapped if you freeze them first. Wrap the food carefully and closely to exclude as much air as possible. You may freeze foods such as casseroles and stews in the containers in which they will be heated for serving. By doing this there will be one less pot to wash. Be sure to label all packages and containers with the name of the food and the date.

The *frozen foods storage* conditions are considered to be best when the temperature is kept at −18°C (0°F) or lower. You can maintain a constant temperature by closing the freezer promptly and securely and by putting in no more unfrozen food at one time than is recommended by the manufacturer. When the freezer temperature fluctuates frequently, the foods will thaw and refreeze repeatedly, decreasing the quality of the food.

Some foods will retain their quality for a longer time during frozen storage than others. For example, beef, fish, fruits, vegetables, and cookies can be stored for a year; other foods such as chili con carne and yeast breads for six months; and pies and quick breads for only three months.

Frozen foods are prepared by the same methods used for the fresh food. Most vegetables, except corn on the cob, are cooked without thawing. Frozen fruits are partially thawed and do not require cooking. Meat, poultry, and fish may be cooked after thawing or they may be cooked right from the freezer. Unthawed meat will take longer to cook, however.

Jelly-making

Along with canning and freezing, jelly-making is another form of food preservation which you can easily perform in your kitchen. Jelly is made from the juice of fruit. The principles of food preservation apply to jelly-making. As the fruit juice and sugar are cooked, microorganisms are destroyed, and the resulting jelly is sealed with paraffin (wax) to protect the jelly from any recontamination.

Another principle involved in jelly-making is the formation of a gel. *The jelling quality of fruit juices is determined by the amount of pectin present in the juice.* Some fruits such as grapes, apples, and citrus fruits are good sources of pectin; others, such as pineapple, peaches, and strawberries are low in pectin.

In addition to pectin, acid and sugar are required to make a good gel. Most fruits are somewhat tart and contain acid, but fruits such as bananas and pears are low in acid and are not usually used for jelly. Sugar must be added to all fruit juices to make a good jelly.

The principle of gel formation involves the presence of the right amount of pectin, acid, and sugar, and cooking the juice and sugar mixture to the right stage to form the gel. As the juice and sugar mixture is cooked, water will evaporate and the juice will thicken. The cooking is continued until the juice becomes so thick that two drops will cling to the side of a spoon and drop off as a sheet. When the mixture is cooked to this stage, it will form a firm gel as it cools. The gel formed should be firm enough to retain the shape of the jelly glass but tender enough so that it can be spread easily.

1. The first step in *making jelly* is to extract the juice from the fruit. First wash the fruit thoroughly, remove stems, and cut large fruits into small pieces. Cook the fruit in water (amount stated in your recipe) until it is soft. Place the cooked fruit into a thin cloth bag (muslin), or line a sieve with a thin cloth; let the juice drip into a bowl.

2. Jelly can be made by two methods: with and without pectin. When you make jelly with added pectin, the juice and sugar (185 mL (¾ c) sugar for each 250 mL (1 c) of juice high in pectin) are cooked until a sheet test is evident (2 drops slide together and sheet from a metal spoon). The sheet test is considered reliable, but the thermometer is the most accurate. A gel will form when the sugar and juice are cooked to 104 to 106°C (220 to 222°F).

When added pectin is not used, a longer cooking time is required to reach the gel stage and less jelly is made from an equal amount of juice than when pectin is added. Also, because the quantity of pectin in fruit juices varies greatly, it may be difficult to make a perfect jelly each time without added pectin.

Commercial pectin is available as a powder or a liquid and can also be extracted from apple or citrus peel. The directions for using the commercial pectins may vary slightly. You must follow the directions given with the pectin you are using for combining the juice with the pectin and the sugar.

3. After the sugar is added to the juice, the jelly is cooked at a rolling boil usually for one minute. The use of added pectin makes it possible to prepare a good jelly from all fruits, including those low in pectin.

Whether you prepare jelly with or without added pectin, you will need to wash and sterilize the jelly glasses in boiling water for fifteen minutes and drain them on a tray lined with absorbent paper or a cloth.

4. When the jelly is cooked, remove any scum from the surface with a metal spoon so that your jelly will remain clear.

5. Pour the hot jelly into sterile glasses to within 6 mm (¼ in) of the top.

6. Immediately cover the jelly with melted paraffin which will make a tight seal as it cools. Add the paraffin gently to make a 6 mm (¼ in) layer on the jelly surface.

7. After the jelly has cooled, wipe the glass to remove any jelly on the surface which would attract mold. Cover the glass with a clean lid or foil and label it. Store the jelly in a cool, dry place.

Almost any fruit you like can be preserved in a sugar syrup or made into jelly or marmalade.
Peaches are often sliced or made into a butter or preserves, but they are just as popular when they are served whole and fresh.

You may want to make other spreads such as jams, preserves, conserves, fruit butters, and marmalades. Each of these calls for the jelly-making principles and is made from a different form or portion of the fruit. For example, jam is made from mashed fruit, conserves from a mixture of fruits, and fruit butters from the pulp of the fruit.

Main Ideas

Food spoilage is caused by the growth of microorganisms and by the activity of enzymes. By controlling the environment in which foods are stored, foods can be preserved because the conditions which produce spoilage have been eliminated. If excellent quality is to be retained in foods that are going to be preserved, care must be taken in selecting foods which are of high quality before they are preserved.

Activities

1. Find recipes for jam, conserve, preserve, fruit butter, and marmalade. Note how they differ from a recipe for jelly. Write a definition for each of the above listed spreads.

2. Prepare a display of the different packaging materials suitable for freezing foods and indicate for which each is best suited. Explain why certain packaging materials are more suitable than others for some frozen foods.

3. Visit a supermarket and make a list of the kinds or general groups of frozen foods offered for sale. Which of these could be prepared and frozen at home for a lower cost?

4. Discuss the advantages and disadvantages of a home freezer.

5. Compare the cost and quality of foods canned or frozen at home and those commercially available. Make a report.

501

6. Make jelly with and without pectin and report your results. Which method did you prefer and why?

7. Prepare a bread, pastry, cake, or a casserole suitable for storage, and freeze it. What is the recommended storage life of your product? Make a report to your class and explain how you plan to use the food you prepared.

8. Make a poster to show what causes food spoilage and ways to avoid food spoilage.

Questions

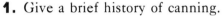

1. Give a brief history of canning.

2. In what ways do freeze-dried foods differ from irradiated foods?

3. Which microorganisms are responsible for food spoilage? How can these be controlled in foods?

4. What are enzymes? Bacteria?

5. Describe the steps in canning and freezing.

6. Define "C" and "R" enamels, raw pack, hot pack, dry pack, and syrup pack.

7. Compare the boiling-water bath and pressure canner methods of processing.

8. What foods make the best canned products? Frozen ones?

9. In what ways does the canning of fruits differ from the canning of vegetables?

10. How does freezing differ from canning and in what ways are the two similar?

11. How do you test the seal of canned food containers?

12. What causes canned food to float? Canned food jars to be only partially filled with food or liquid?

13. Define flat sour, botulism, pectin, and paraffin.

14. What are the storage conditions for frozen foods?

15. What principles are involved in jelly-making?

16. What are signs of spoilage in canned food?

17. What is botulism spoilage?

18. How can spoilage of canned foods be avoided?

19. How can darkening be avoided in frozen peaches?

20. How are meats wrapped or packaged for freezing?

21. How is the quality of frozen food kept in storage?

22. Describe two methods for making jelly.

23. What are the differences between jam, jelly, conserve, and fruit butter? What are preserves and marmalades?

6 Looking Ahead

Chapter
32
Opportunities

Words for Thought

Career

an occupation or a lifetime job.

Vocational training

training or preparation required for a job or profession.

Chef

a chief or head cook; a specialist in preparing and cooking foods.

Dietitian

a college graduate specially trained to deal with food needs of people.

Home economist

a college graduate specializing in home economics.

You have just begun to explore the world of food and the art of cookery. Your study of food has introduced you to the many principles involved in the preparation of the foods basic to your needs.

Your Achievements

You have learned how the American food culture began and how to use foods in a variety of ways. In addition to methods of food preparation and the principles upon which they are based, you have learned to recognize some of the signs of quality in foods and the standards or guides to use in their selection. You have learned to consider your goals, values, and needs when you make your choices among the various forms of food. You realize that foods must be stored properly to retain their attractiveness and eating quality, their color, texture, flavor, and nutrient values.

You have learned which tools are best suited for the various cookery procedures, and understand the cookery terms and abbreviations which enable you to use recipes as your guides in food preparation. You have been shown how to measure ingredients accurately and how to prepare a great variety of food products successfully.

You have learned how to plan, prepare, and serve meals graciously, and how to leave the kitchen and dining areas clean and in order.

You have learned to consider the influence of the various forms of food on cost, time, nutrient value, quality, preparation required, and variety. You now realize that most foods are available in convenience forms which are partly or completely prepared, which can use time and effort to good advantage, and which often cost more than the original food or the ingredients necessary to prepare the food. To use them intelligently, you must consider their quality, cost, and nutrient values as well as the time which is saved through their use.

When you buy convenience foods, you are aware that you also pay for the labor and special packaging used to produce the food. You will be concerned not only with using time well but also with providing good meals.

You are aware that convenience items can be a good investment when you want to save time and energy or make up for your lack of knowledge or skill in preparing a food. You know that too frequent use of the same convenience products can result in uninteresting or monotonous meals, but that when you use them creatively, they can be satisfying.

You also know that the basic principles of food preparation were used when convenience items were processed, and that you will prepare them with greater success when you understand the principles involved.

You learned that foods are made of nutrients and your body has several uses for them which can be classified into three general groups: for growth and repair, you need protein; for energy, you need carbohydrates and fats; and for protection and regulation of your body processes, you need vitamins, minerals, and water. You know that proper storage and preparation techniques are required to retain the nutrient values of the foods you serve.

This has been an overall view of food with a glimpse into the future developments in food and new food sources. The day may come when you will be using algae and protein from plant leaves or petroleum products as ingredients in the foods that you will prepare.

You have accomplished many things in learning to apply the science (principles) and art of cookery to the foods you prepare and serve.

As you know, "practice makes perfect"; this applies to cooking as it does to any other skill. You will want to continue to practice everything you have learned so the principles of cookery will become habits before you forget them. In this way, you too can prepare the foods which can bring you praise and will be enjoyed by all.

Your experience with this food study can lead the way to greater opportunities with food. It does not make you a food expert, but it is a foundation upon which you can build and increase your knowledge about food.

The World of Food

The world of food is exciting, and offers you many opportunities. Food service workers are employed in school lunch, university and college food service, small and large commercial, industrial, and institutional food facilities. Trained and experienced food service employees may be involved in menu planning, food purchasing, standardizing recipes, and training and supervising other workers.

The manager of a small food service facility is responsible for the entire food service operation and the supervision of employees. In a large facility the responsibility may be divided among several persons. The general manager supervises the entire operation. The food production manager plans menus, orders food, selects equipment, and keeps records. The purchasing agent buys the food, equipment, and other supplies needed by the various divisions of the operation. The food cost supervisor studies the menus, estimates the cost per serving, and determines the price for which the food must sell. The food supervisor in each department makes sure the menus are strictly followed, a good quality food is produced, food is ready for service when needed, and supervises the production workers in the unit.

Each year an increasing number of meals are served away from home. All of this food must be produced, processed, and prepared. All of which means many career opportunities for those with an interest in food. If you like good food, have an appreciation of high standards of food production and service, like people and are interested in their health and welfare, you may enjoy a career in food production and service.

Food Service Industry

Many types of food service are designed to meet the needs and desires of those who dine away from home. The food service may be informal or casual as that of the snack bar and drive-in, or formal and elegant as in a fine restaurant. Vending and mobile service are used when distances are great. Foods are prepared in a central kitchen and transported to the mobile or vending service.

Whether you live in a city, town, suburb, or a rural area, you can find many food service jobs.

Food Service Jobs

In City	In Town, Suburb	In Rural Area
hotel, motel	schools	packing, processing
restaurants	stores	plants
nursing homes	drive-ins	roadside stands
catering services	motels	nursing homes
drug stores	processing plants	recreational areas
airline foods		country clubs
child care centers		

The food industry offers a wide variety of jobs which require different skills and training. You can have a successful career in the field of food without a college degree; however, advancement depends upon ability and education.

Summer jobs are available at restaurants, hotels, hospitals, soda fountains, lunch counters, and other establishments. You may get a part-time job which will give you experience and the opportunity to learn about the food service industry.

Some jobs in the industry require no previous training but offer on-the-job training. For example, as a busperson you clear tables and reset them with clean linen and flatware. You may fill water glasses and help keep the dining room clean.

Positions Which May Not Require Previous Training

In Food Preparation

Kitchen Helper
Sandwich-maker
Beverage Worker
Salad-maker
Assistant Cook
Assistant Baker

In Food Service

Busperson
One who waits table
Soda Fountain Worker

In Related Work

Dining Room Head
Porter
Dish Washing Machine Operator

Certain jobs require some previous training. If your school offers a job-training or wage-earning program or has a special food service course, you can easily learn more about food. If you enjoy working with food, this training will prepare you for jobs as a tray-line worker or a food assembler; or if your interest is with food and people, you may work as a counter worker or one who waits table. Other jobs for which you would be prepared are listed below.

Positions for Those with Job-training or Wage-earning Experience

In Food Preparation

Kitchen Helper
Food Assembler
Tray-line Worker
Pantry Worker
Special Kitchen Helper
Formula Room Worker
Caterer's Helper

In Food Service

Dining Room Helper
Counter Worker
Fountain Worker
Snack Bar Worker
One who waits table
Dining Room Head

A kitchen helper proudly displaying a vegetable tray.

As a kitchen helper, you assist the cooks, baker, and chef. You may measure, mix, and prepare salad ingredients.

Vocational or trade school training will give you special knowledge and skills for various positions in the food industry as a chef, pastry cook, butcher, and others listed in the chart below. Trade schools also offer menu planning and dining room service training.

You, as a high school graduate, can begin in the food service industry immediately. You may work as a kitchen worker, counter or fountain worker, or one who waits on table.

In the food service industry, there are also positions which require extensive training and experience.

Positions Which Require Training or Experience

In Food Preparation	In Food Service
Chef	Dining Room Supervisor
Cook	Headperson waiting table
Pastry Chef	Counter Supervisor
Baker	
Pantry Supervisor	**In Related Work**
Kitchen Supervisor	
Meat Cutter	Cashier
	Food Checker
	Purchasing Agent
	Storeroom Supervisor

Junior and community colleges and technical schools offer two-year training programs in quantity food service. These programs will prepare you for supervisory and administrative positions in food service in restaurants, institutions, schools, department stores, and other establishments. You will learn about quantity food preparation and service, nutrition, food purchasing, personnel management, and job analysis. The two-year programs will help you to gain immediate employment and will help you to advance more quickly to better positions as you acquire more experience.

You will need college training to qualify for the top positions in the food industry. As a college graduate, you will earn a Bachelor of Arts or a Bachelor of Science degree in home economics, dietetics, institutional management, or restaurant administration.

With a four-year college degree, you will qualify for positions as assistant manager, manager, food service director, or director of recipe development. Other positions for those with more training are listed in the table on page 511.

A director of recipe development working with one of her staff.

College training can also qualify you as a dietitian or a business home economist. If your interest is to deal directly with people and become personally involved in their food needs, you may choose to be a dietitian.

As a dietitian you will have a college degree with training in the science of nutrition and food management. You may be known as a *nutritionist* or a *nutrition specialist as well as a dietitian*. Dietitians work in hospitals, schools, colleges, and in industrial or commercial organizations. As a dietitian you may be associated with health and welfare agencies, research laboratories, nursing homes, the Peace Corps, Vista, or the World Health Organization.

Many dietitians are employed in food service establishments as well as hospitals. All large restaurant chains, cafeterias, department stores, hotels, and other establishments employ dietitians.

As a *hospital dietitian*, you are responsible for all food served to patients, hospital staff, and visitors. You will plan menus and therapeutic diets, supervise the purchase and preparation of food, and supervise and train dietetic interns. You will meet with doctors and talk to patients. Large hospitals and institutions often employ several dietitians.

511

You may be employed as a *therapeutic dietitian* in a hospital or clinic to plan menus for patients who are unable to eat regular foods. You will plan special diets for those with illnesses such as diabetes or ulcers.

Some dietitians are employed by hospitals, colleges, or universities to instruct others in food and nutrition and dietetics or for research purposes.

As a *research dietitian*, you will conduct experiments or surveys in food and nutrition to learn how food aids in the treatment of disease and helps to maintain good health. You may work as a team member with doctors, nurses, and chemists.

You may prefer to work with food as a *business home economist*. You will need a college degree in home economics. As a business home economist, you may represent the interest of the homemaker to your company, or present the services and products of your company to the homemaker and consumer.

As a business home economist, you may also work in an experimental kitchen and conduct research on food products or develop new products and new recipes for your company.

As an author and TV personality, Julia Child shows her TV viewers how to prepare interesting dishes with a special flair.

You may combine your interest in food with journalism or photography. Home economists design and write labels, recipes, booklets, and news releases for the products of their companies. You may plan and produce textbooks, cookbooks, films, filmstrips, and other educational materials.

Whether you write booklets, scripts for films, or answer letters from homemakers, you must be a writer as well as a food specialist. There is at least one home economist behind every booklet, recipe, or food product; with proper training, you can be that person.

Main Ideas

Your study of food has provided you with information and techniques for your personal use as well as a foundation upon which to build a career in food. Many job opportunities are open in the food service industry. Every job or position requires certain skills and knowledge. The more complex and responsible the job or position, the greater the amount of training and experience that will be required.

Activities

1. Read "Education for 500 Careers" in the Yearbook of Agriculture for 1966 *(Protecting Our Food)*, page 236. Give a report to your class.

2. Read *Exciting Careers for Home Economists* by Lila Spencer, 1967, Julian Messner, division of Simon and Schuster, Inc., 1 West 39th Street, New York, 10018 or *Careers in Home Economics* by Ruth Hoeflin, The Macmillan Co., 1970 or *Home Economics as a Profession*, 2d ed. by Mildred Tate, McGraw-Hill Book Company, New York, 1973.

3. In your school library, locate other books or articles dealing with careers in food. Prepare a written report of your findings.

4. Interview a chef, dietitian, or a home economist for a utility company or a food company and learn about the training and responsibilities of that person. Make a report to your class.

5. Talk to persons who are writers or authors. Find out what their training and experience have been. Learn the kinds of responsibilities which their work requires.

Questions

1. Even though we have convenience foods, why is an understanding of food principles essential today?

2. What do you consider to be your most satisfying achievements in your study of food?

3. What kinds of job opportunities are available in the world of food?

a. Which jobs require college training?

b. What kinds of jobs do not require college training?

4. Other than going to college, how could you obtain training for a job or position in the food service industry?

5. What factors will influence and contribute to your success in the food industry?

6. In what ways can a career in food yield a double benefit to you?

Table of Equivalents

Food	Quantity	Yield
apples	1 medium (150 g)	250 mL (1 c) sliced
bread crumbs	3 to 4 slices bread	250 mL (1 c) dry crumbs
	1 slice bread (25 g)	185 mL ($^3/_4$ c) soft crumbs
cabbage	454 g (1 lb)	1 L (4 c) shredded
cheese	113.5 g ($^1/_4$ lb)	250 mL (1 c) shredded
cherries	947 mL (1 qt)	500 mL (2 c)
crackers, graham	15	250 mL (1 c) fine crumbs
soda	16	250 mL (1 c) coarse crumbs
	22	250 mL (1 c) fine crumbs
cranberries	454 g (1 lb)	750 to 875 mL (3 to 3$^1/_2$ c) sauce
cream, whipping	250 mL (1 c)	500 mL (2 c) whipped
dried raisins, currants	454 g (1 lb)	750 mL (3 c) seedless
		625 mL (2$^1/_2$ c) seeded
dates	454 g (1 lb)	625 mL (2$^1/_2$ c) chopped
dry beans	190 g (1 c)	625 mL (2$^1/_2$ c) cooked
eggs	5 medium	250 mL (1c)
	8 medium egg whites	250 mL (1c)
	12 to 14 medium egg yolks	250 mL (1c)
flour	454 g (1 lb)	1 L (4 c)
lemon	1	30–45 mL (2 to 3 T)
macaroni, spaghetti, noodles	227 g ($^1/_2$ lb)	1 L (4 c) cooked
nuts, peanuts	141.75 g (5 oz)	250 mL (1 c)
pecans, chopped	121 g (4$^1/_4$ oz)	250 mL (1 c)
halves	106.32 g (3$^3/_4$ oz)	250 mL (1 c)
walnuts, chopped	127.58 g (4$^1/_2$ oz)	250 mL (1 c)
halves	99.23 g (3$^1/_2$ oz)	250 mL (1 c)
onion	1 medium	125 mL ($^1/_2$ c)
orange	1	80–125 mL ($^1/_3$ to $^1/_2$ c) juice
rice	250 mL (1 c)	875 mL (3$^1/_2$ c) cooked
rice, precooked	250 mL (1 c)	500 mL (2 c) cooked
sugar, brown	454 g (1 lb)	560 mL (2$^1/_4$ c) firmly packed
confectioners'	454 g (1 lb)	875 mL (3$^1/_2$ c) sifted
granulated	454 g (1 lb)	560 mL (2$^1/_4$ c)

Table of Substitutions

Ingredient	Quantity	Substitute
baking powder	5 mL (1 t) double-acting	7.5 mL (1½ t) phosphate or tartrate or 1.2 mL (¼ t) baking soda plus 125 mL (½ c) buttermilk or sour milk
butter	250 mL (1 c)	250 mL (1 c) margarine 215 to 250 mL (⅞ to 1 c) hydrogenated fat plus 2.5 mL (½ t) salt 215 mL (⅞ c) lard plus 2.5 mL (½ teaspoon) salt
chocolate	1 square (28.35 g) unsweetened	45 mL (3 T) cocoa plus 15 mL (1 T) shortening
cream	250 mL (1 c) coffee cream	45 mL (3 T) butter plus 215 mL (⅞ c) milk
	250 mL (1 c) heavy cream	80 mL (⅓ c) butter plus 185 mL (¾ c) milk
eggs	1 whole egg	2 egg yolks
flour (for thickening)	15 mL (1 T)	7.5 mL (½ T) cornstarch or 10 mL (2 t) quick-cooking tapioca
flour	250 mL (1 c) all purpose	280 mL (1 c plus 2 tablespoons) cake flour
	250 mL (1 c) cake flour	215 mL (⅞ c) all purpose flour
	250 mL (1 c) self-rising	250 mL (1 c) flour, omit baking powder and salt
herbs	15 mL (1 T) fresh	5 mL (1 t) dried
honey	250 mL (1 c)	250–310 mL (1 to 1¼ c) sugar plus 60 mL (¼ c) liquid
milk	250 mL (1 c) fresh whole	250 mL (1 c) reconstituted nonfat dry milk plus 10 mL (2 t) butter
	250 mL (1 c) whole milk	125 mL (½ c) evaporated milk plus 125 mL (½ c) water
	250 mL (1 c) sour milk	15 mL (1 T) lemon juice or vinegar plus sweet milk to make 250 mL (1 c)
yeast	1 cake compressed	1 package or 10 mL (2 t) active dry yeast

Beverages

Cocoa

(See principles page 311)

4 servings

60 mL (¼ c) cocoa
45 mL (3 T) sugar
.6 mL (⅛ t) of salt
125 mL (½ c) boiling water
.75 L (3 c) milk

1. Blend cocoa, sugar, and salt in saucepan.

2. Stir in water gradually.

3. Cook over low heat until mixture is thick and syrupy (3 to 5 minutes).

4. Add milk and continue to heat using low heat, stirring occasionally, until cocoa is steaming hot (do not boil).

5. Remove from heat and beat until frothy to prevent skin from forming on top. Serve immediately.

Coffee

Always use a clean coffee pot and fresh cold water.

Always use right grind for the coffee maker.

Use enough coffee for the desired strength.

15 mL (1 T) coffee to 185 mL (¾ c)
   water for weak coffee
30 mL (2 T) coffee to 185 mL (¾ c)
   water for medium coffee
45 mL (3 T) coffee to 185 mL (¾ c)
   water for strong coffee
(4 servings of moderately strong
   coffee)
90 ml (6 T) coffee
.75 L (3 c) water

Use any of the following three methods commonly used to make coffee.

Drip Method:

(See principles page 309)

1. Place measured drip-grind coffee in coffee basket and fit basket into bottom part of coffee maker.

2. Pour boiling water over ground coffee to 1 L (4 c) mark and cover.

3. Keep coffee maker over low heat as water drips through grounds.

4. Remove basket, cover pot, and serve coffee.

Percolator Method:
(See principles page 309)

1. Measure water into percolator.

2. Place measured regular-grind coffee in coffee basket and insert into percolator and cover.

3. Place over heat and when water begins to percolate, allow coffee to perk slowly for 6 to 8 minutes.

4. Remove basket, cover pot, and serve coffee.

Vacuum Method:
(See principles page 309)

1. Place cold water in lower bowl of coffee maker.

2. Assemble filter in upper bowl and add measured drip-grind coffee.

3. Replace upper bowl into lower bowl of maker.

4. Heat until most of the water rises into upper part. After 1 to 3 minutes, remove from heat. Cover and allow coffee to drain into lower bowl.

5. Remove upper bowl and cover coffee. Serve.

Tea
(see principles page 310)
4 servings

15 mL (3 t) tea or 3 teabags
.75 L (3 c) freshly boiling water

1. Preheat teapot with boiling water and drain after a few minutes.

2. Place measured tea or teabags into hot teapot.

3. Pour measured freshly boiling water over tea and cover pot.

4. Let stand (steep) for 3 to 5 minutes, depending on strength of tea desired.

5. Remove bags or strain tea into another preheated pot.

6. Serve with sugar and milk or lemon.

Breads and Cereals

Breads

Biscuits
(see principles pages 285, 287)
12 large or 24 small biscuits

500 mL (2 c) sifted all-purpose
flour
15 mL (1 T) baking powder
2.5 mL (½ t) salt
60 mL (¼ c) shortening
185 mL (¾ c) milk

Set oven at 230°C (450°F)

1. Sift flour with baking powder and salt into mixing bowl.

2. Cut in shortening with pastry blender or two knives until the particles are fine as cornmeal.

3. Add milk and stir until mixture clings to form a soft puffy dough.

4. Place dough on very lightly floured board or pastry cloth.

5. Rub small amount of flour on palms of hands and knead dough gently 6 to 8 times (too much handling makes biscuits tough).

6. Rub small amount of flour on rolling pin and roll dough 1.25 to 2 cm (12 to 34 in) thick.

7. Cut biscuits close together with a floured biscuit or cookie cutter.

8. Lift biscuits and place on ungreased baking sheet about 2.5 cm (1 in) apart for crusty biscuits and closer together for biscuits with soft sides.

9. Press remaining dough together gently; do not knead; roll; and cut with cutter.

10. Bake at 230°C (450°F) for 12 to 15 minutes, or until golden brown. Serve hot.

If you wish to make a biscuit mixture of drop batter consistency, add 60 mL (¼ c) additional milk to this recipe. Drop the batter by spoonfuls onto a greased baking sheet. These biscuits will have a crisp crust.

Popovers
8 popovers

250 mL (1 c) sifted all-purpose
flour
2.5 mL (½ t) salt
15 mL (1 T) melted shortening or
oil
250 mL (1 c) milk
2 eggs

Set oven at 220°C (425°F)

1. Stir salt into flour in mixing bowl.

2. Add shortening, milk, and eggs; beat until smooth with a rotary beater or mixer on low speed.

3. Fill greased custard cups two-thirds full.

4. Bake at 220°C (425°F) for 40 to 45 minutes.

5. If desired, when popovers are done, slit each popover with the point of a sharp knife to let steam escape. Leave in oven five minutes to dry. Serve hot.

Muffins

(see principles pages 285-286)

12 muffins

500 mL (2 c) sifted all-purpose
    flour
60 mL (1/4 c) sugar
15 mL (1 T) baking powder
2.5 mL (1/2 t) salt
1 egg, beaten
250 mL (1 c) milk
60 mL (1/4 c) cooking oil or melted
    shortening

Set oven at 200°C (400°F)

1. Grease only bottoms of muffin cups, not the sides.

2. Sift flour with sugar, baking powder, and salt into mixing bowl.

3. Stir milk into egg and add shortening.

4. Make a well in center of dry ingredients and add liquid ingredients all at once. Stir only until flour mixture is moist. The batter will be rough-looking and not smooth. Overstirring causes tough muffins with tunnels and peaks.

5. Fill muffin cups two-thirds full.

6. Bake at 200°C (400°F) for 20 to 25 minutes, until golden brown. Serve hot.

Refrigerator Rolls

(see principles page 296)

1¹/₂ dozen

1 package yeast (128 g cake;
    7.5 g dry)
60 mL (1/4 c) warm water
60 mL (1/4 c) sugar
60 mL (1/4 c) shortening
2.5 mL (1/2 t) salt
185 mL (3/4 c) milk, scalded
1 egg
750 to 875 mL (3 to 3¹/₂ c) all
    purpose flour

Set oven at 200°C (400°F).

1. Scald milk; add sugar, shortening, and salt; cool to lukewarm.

2. Crumble or sprinkle yeast into warm water in large mixing bowl; stir to dissolve.

3. Add cooled milk mixture and egg to yeast.

4. Add one-third of the flour and beat until smooth.

5. Add remaining flour gradually to make a soft dough that leaves the sides of the bowl.

6. Place dough onto floured board and knead about 5 minutes, or until dough leaves no impression when pressed with fingers.

7. Place dough into greased bowl and grease the face of the dough.

8. Cover with plastic wrap and place in refrigerator (dough keeps about 4 days in refrigerator).

9. For baking, take dough from refrigerator and shape into rolls.

10. Cover shaped rolls and let rise again in warm place until doubled in bulk, about 2 hours.

11. Bake at 200°C (400°F) for 12 to 15 minutes, until golden brown.

White Bread

(see principles pages 296-298)

1 loaf

250 mL (1 c) milk
1 package yeast (12.8 cake; 7.5 g dry)
60 mL (¼ c) warm water
22.5 mL (1½ T) sugar
2.5 mL (½ t) salt
15 mL (1 T) shortening
750 to 875 mL (3 to 3½ c) flour

Set oven at 200°C (400°F)

1. Scald milk; add salt, sugar, and shortening. Cool to lukewarm.

2. Crumble or sprinkle yeast into warm water in large mixing bowl; stir to dissolve.

3. Stir cooled milk mixture into dissolved yeast.

4. Add about one-third of the flour and beat until smooth.

5. Add remaining flour gradually to make a soft dough which leaves the sides of bowl.

6. Turn out dough onto flour board.

7. With floured hands, knead dough until it is smooth and elastic (springs back when pressed with finger) about 5 to 10 minutes.

8. Lightly grease the mixing bowl, and place kneaded dough in bowl and turn it over to lightly grease the surface.

9. Cover mixing bowl with towel and set in warm place to rise until doubled in bulk, or until a depression remains when dough is pressed with finger.

10. Punch down by inserting fist.

11. Place dough on lightly floured board and shape into loaf (see pictures page 296).

12. Place shaped loaf into greased loaf pan, cover, and let rise until doubled in bulk.

13. Bake at 200°C (400°F) for 40 to 50 minutes or until done (hollow sound results when loaf is tapped with fingers).

14. Remove from pan immediately and place on cooling rack.

When you wish to make the dough one day and bake it another day, follow these steps for cool rising of bread.

1. Follow steps 1 through 7 given above for white bread.

2. After the dough is kneaded in step 7, leave the dough on the board and cover with a plastic wrap and a towel and let rest for 20 minutes.

3. At end of 20 minutes, shape the dough into a loaf (see pictures page 298).

4. Place loaf into greased pan; brush surface of dough with oil or soft shortening; cover loosely with wax paper and plastic wrap.

5. Refrigerate until following day.

6. Remove from refrigerator and uncover; let set for 10 minutes, or while preheating oven.

7. Bake at 200°C (400°F) for 40 to 50 minutes or until done.

Cereals

Examples of Commonly Used Proportions of Cereal to Water

	Amount of Water	Amount of Cereal
Rolled Oats	500 mL (2 c)	250 mL (1 c)
Cream of Wheat	750 mL (3 c)	125 mL (½ c)
Rice	560 mL (2¼ c)	250 mL (1 c)
Macaroni	1.5L (6 c)	250 mL (1 c)

General directions for cooking cereals
(see principles page 120)

1. Because of the great variety of cereals, it is best to following the directions on the package for proportion of cereal to water.

2. Place measured water and salt in saucepan and bring to a boil.

3. Sprinkle cereal slowly into boiling water, stirring constantly.

4. Cook over low heat for time specified on cereal package, or until cereal is tender.

5. Serve immediately, or if necessary cover to prevent drying out of cereal surface.

·Basic Recipes·
Cakes and Frostings

Cakes

Angel Food Cake
(see principles pages 332, 334)
one 25 cm (10 in) tube pan

250 mL (1 c) sifted cake flour
215 mL (³/₄ c plus 2 T) sugar
375 mL (1¹/₂ c) egg whites (12 whites)
7.5 mL (1¹/₂ t) cream of tartar
1.2 mL (¹/₄ t) salt
185 mL (³/₄ c) sugar
7.5 mL (1¹/₂ t) vanilla
2.5 mL (¹/₂ t) almond flavoring

Set oven at 190°C (375°F)

1. Separate eggs and allow to reach room temperature.

2. Sift flour and 215 mL (³/₄ c plus 2 T) onto waxed paper.

3. Combine egg whites, cream of tartar, salt in a large mixing bowl; beat until soft peak is formed when beater is pulled out (use hand beater or medium speed on large mixer).

4. Gradually add second amount of sugar 185 mL (³/₄ c), about 30 mL (2 T) at a time, and beat to blend. Continue beating until meringue holds a stiff peak.

5. Fold in flavoring.

6. Sprinkle flour-sugar mixture, 45 mL (3 T) at a time, over meringue and fold in gently until blended.

7. Carefully pour batter into ungreased 25 cm (10 in) tube pan. Gently pull batter against sides of pan. Carefully draw a spatula through the batter to remove entrapped, large air bubbles.

8. Bake at 190°C (375°F) on lowest rack in oven for 30 to 35 minutes, or until light touch leaves no imprint. Do not underbake.

9. Invert pan over inverted funnel or neck of a bottle and let cake "hang" until cool (about 1 hour).

10. To remove cake, hold a spatula or table knife firmly against sides and encircle pan to loosen cake. Then with short up-and-down strokes loosen cake from tube of pan.

Chiffon Cake

(see principles pages 332, 334-335)

one 22.5 cm (9 in) tube pan or 22.5 x 12.5 x 7.5 cm (9 in x 5 in x 3 in) loaf pan

280 mL (1 c plus 2 T) sifted cake flour
185 mL (3/4 c) sugar
7.5 mL (1 1/2 t) baking powder
2.5 mL (1/2 t) salt
60 mL (1/4 c) salad or cooking oil
2 egg yolks
90 mL (1/4 c plus 2 T) cold water
5 mL (1 t) vanilla
5 mL (1 t) grated lemon rind
125 mL (1/2 c) egg whites (4 whites)
1.2 mL (1/4 t) cream of tartar

Set oven at 160°C (325°F)

1. Sift flour, sugar, baking powder, and salt into bowl.

2. Make a well in dry ingredients and add oil, yolks, water, vanilla, and lemon rind, and beat with spoon until smooth.

3. In another bowl, beat egg whites and cream of tartar at high speed until a stiff peak is formed.

4. Pour egg yolk mixture gradually over beaten whites and fold in gently until blended.

5. Pour into ungreased pan. Bake at 160°C (325°F) for 50 to 55 minutes, or until cake springs back when lightly touched.

6. Invert pan over inverted funnel or neck of a bottle and allow cake to cool (about one hour).

7. To remove cake, first hold a spatula or table knife firmly against sides and encircle pan to loosen cake. Then with short up-and-down strokes loosen cake from tube of pan.

Conventional-Method Cake

(see principles pages 332-333)

two 20 or 22.5 cm (8 or 9 in) layers

560 mL (2 1/4 c) sifted cake flour
2.5 mL (1/2 t) salt
15 mL (3 t) baking powder
125 mL (1/2 c) shortening
250 mL (1 c) sugar
2 eggs
185 mL (3/4 c) milk
5 mL (1 t) vanilla

Set oven at 180°C (350°F)

1. Prepare pans (grease bottom but not sides and dust with flour, or line pan with waxed paper cut to size of pan bottom).

2. Sift flour, baking powder, salt onto waxed paper.

3. Place shortening, sugar, and vanilla into bowl and cream until light and fluffy.

4. Add one egg at a time and beat until light and very fluffy after each addition.

5. Add one-fourth of the sifted dry ingredients and blend.

6. Add one-third of the milk and blend.

7. Continue adding flour in fourths and milk in thirds, alternately, ending with flour.

8. Pour batter into two prepared cake pans and spread toward sides of pan, leaving slightly less batter in center of pan.

9. Bake at 180°C (350°F) 25 to 30 minutes, or until cake springs back when lightly touched.

Quick-Method Cake

(see principles pages 332-334)

**two 20 or 22.5 cm (8 or 9 in) layers
or 32.5 x 22.5 cm (13 in x 9 in)
oblong pan**

560 mL (2¼ c) sifted cake flour
375 mL (1½ c) sugar
15 mL (3 t) baking powder
5 mL (1 t) salt
125 mL (½ c) shortening room
    temperature
250 mL (1 c) milk
7.5 mL (1½ t) vanilla
2 eggs (80 to 125 mL (⅓ to ½ c))

Set oven at 180°C (350°F)

1. Prepare pans (grease bottom but not sides and dust with flour or line pan with waxed paper cut to size of pan bottom).

2. Sift flour, sugar, baking powder, salt into large mixing bowl.

3. Add shortening and about two-thirds of the milk and flavoring.

4. Beat at medium speed with electric mixer or by hand for 300 strokes or 2 minutes.

5. Add remaining milk and eggs, and beat 2 more minutes or 300 strokes by hand.

6. Pour batter into prepared cake pans and spread toward sides of pan, leaving slightly less batter in center of pan.

7. Bake at 180°C (350°F) 30 to 35 minutes for layers, and 40 to 45 minutes for oblong pan.

Frostings

Basic Butter Frosting

**frosts two-layer cake, 20 or 22.5
cm (8 or 9 in)**

80 mL (⅓ c) soft butter or marga-
    rine
750 mL (3 c) confectioners'
    sugar
45 mL (3 T) milk
7.5 mL (1½ t) vanilla

1. Cream butter or margarine in mixing bowl. Stir in one-third of confectioners' sugar.

2. Stir in vanilla, milk, and half of remaining confectioners' sugar.

3. Add remaining confectioners' sugar a little at a time and cream until frosting is creamy and of consistency which will spread easily.

4. Spread immediately on cooled cake (see page 338).

Chocolate Fudge Frosting

frosts two-layer cake, 20 or 22.5 cm (8 or 9 in)

.5 L (2 c) sugar
185 mL (³/₄ c) light cream
57 g (2 squares or 2 oz) unsweet-
    ened chocolate
30 mL (2 T) corn syrup
.6 mL (¹/₈ t) salt
30 mL (2 T) butter or margarine
5 mL (1 t) vanilla extract

1. Combine sugar, cream, chocolate, corn syrup, and salt in a heavy saucepan.

2. Heat slowly, stirring until dissolved.

3. Cook to the soft-ball stage, 110°C (234°F), or until a little dropped in cold water forms a soft ball.

4. Do not stir while cooking. Remove from heat; add butter.

5. Cool to lukewarm, 45°C (110°F).

6. Add vanilla extract. Beat until frosting begins to thicken and loses its gloss. If necessary, thin with a few drops of cream for easy spreading.

7-Minute Frosting

frosts two-layer cake, 20 or 22.5 cm (8 or 9 in)

2 egg whites
375 mL (1¹/₂ c) sugar
1.2 mL (¹/₄ t) cream of tartar or
    15 mL (1 T) light corn syrup
80 mL (¹/₃ c) water
5 mL (1 t) vanilla or flavoring

1. Place enough water into bottom of double boiler so top part will just touch the water; place over heat.

2. Combine all ingredients except vanilla in top of double boiler and stir to blend.

3. Place sugar-egg-white mixture over boiling water in bottom part of double boiler.

4. Make sure the water is boiling gently and beat mixture with rotary beater or electric mixer. Scrape bottom and sides of pan occasionally with rubber scraper.

5. Continue to beat until frosting will stand in stiff peaks as beater is lifted (about 7 minutes). Frosting should be smooth, fluffy, and thick, not foamy or runny.

6. Remove from heat. Add vanilla and beat 1 or 2 minutes longer.

7. Spread on cooled cake immediately (see pages 337-338).

·Basic Recipes·
Cookies

Cocoa Drop Cookies

3¹/₂ dozen

435 mL (1³/₄ c) sifted all-purpose
　flour
2.5 mL (¹/₂ t) soda
2.5 mL (¹/₂ t) salt
125 mL (¹/₂ c) cocoa
125 mL (¹/₂ c) soft shortening
250 mL (1 c) sugar
1 egg
185 mL (³/₄ c) buttermilk or sour
　milk
5 mL (1 t) vanilla
If desired, 250 mL (1 c) chopped
　nuts or 250 mL (1 c) raisins may
　be added with the flour.

Set oven at 200°C (400°F)

1. Sift together flour, soda, salt, cocoa.
2. Blend shortening and sugar, add egg, and mix thoroughly.
3. Stir in milk and vanilla.
4. Add flour mixture and stir until blended.
5. Drop rounded teaspoonful (use back of second spoon or rubber scraper to push dough onto sheet) of dough on ungreased cookie sheet about 5 cm (2 in) apart (see page 344).
6. Bake at 200°C (400°F) for 8 to 10 minutes, or until almost no imprint remains when lightly touched with finger.
7. Remove cookies immediately from sheet by sliding spatula completely under cookie, and then lift to wire cooling rack.

Rolled Sugar Cookies

4 dozen

625 mL (2¹/₂ c) sifted all-purpose
　flour
5 mL (1 t) baking powder
5 mL (1 t) salt
185 mL (³/₄ c) soft shortening (part
　butter or margarine)
250 mL (1 c) sugar
2 eggs
2.5 mL (¹/₂ t) flavoring (vanilla or
　lemon)

Set oven at 200°C (400°F)

1. Sift flour, baking powder, salt onto waxed paper.
2. Place shortening and sugar into bowl and blend.
3. Add eggs and vanilla, and cream until thoroughly blended.
4. Stir in flour mixture until blended.
5. Chill at least 1 hour.
6. Roll on lightly floured board with floured rolling pin until dough is 3 mm (¹/₈ in) thick.
7. Cut cookies with floured cutter (see page 344).
8. Lift cookies with spatula onto ungreased cookie sheet.
9. Bake at 200°C (400°F) 6 to 8 minutes, until lightly browned.
10. Remove cookies immediately by sliding spatula completely under cookie and then lift to cooling rack.

·Basic Recipes·
Desserts

Baked Custard
(see principles pages 370, 372, 374)
6 servings

2 eggs
80 mL (¹/₃ c) sugar
1.2 mL (¹/₄ t) salt
.5 L (2 c) milk, scalded
2.5 mL (¹/₂ t) vanilla

Set oven at 180°C (350°F)

1. Beat egg until well blended but not foamy.
2. Add sugar, salt, vanilla, and stir.
3. Stir scalded milk slowly into egg mixture.
4. Pour into custard cups and fill to about 1.2 cm (¹/₂ in) from top.
5. Place cups in a baking pan; pour hot water into pan up to about 2.5 cm (1 in) from top of cups.
6. Place into oven and bake at 180°C (350°F) for 40 to 50 minutes, or until knife inserted in center of custard comes out clean.
7. Remove cups from water immediately and cool.

Chocolate Blanc Mange (Cornstarch Pudding)
(see principles pages 370-371)
4 to 6 servings

160 mL (²/₃ c) sugar
45 mL (3 T) cornstarch
1.2 mL (¹/₄ t) salt
80 mL (¹/₃ c) cocoa
560 mL (2¹/₄ c) milk

1. Place sugar, cornstarch, salt, and cocoa into a saucepan and stir to blend.
2. Gradually stir in milk.
3. Cook over medium heat, stirring constantly, until mixture boils; let boil for 1 minute.
4. Remove from heat and blend in vanilla.
5. Pour into individual serving dishes and cover with clear wrap to prevent skin from forming on top.
6. When cooled, place into refrigerator.

Cream Puffs

12 large or 24 small puffs

250 mL (1 c) water
125 mL (1/2 c) butter
250 mL (1 c) sifted all-purpose
    flour
4 eggs

Set oven at 220°C (425°F)

1. Place water and butter into pan; heat to a rolling boil.

2. Add the flour all at once and stir in vigorously over low heat until mixture leaves the pan and forms a ball (about 1 minute).

3. Remove from heat.

4. Add one egg at a time and beat in thoroughly until mixture is smooth and glossy.

5. Drop from tablespoon onto ungreased baking sheet 7.5 to 10 cm (3 to 4 in) apart.

6. Bake at 220°C (425°F) for 30 to 35 minutes, or until golden brown and dry.

7. Allow to cool slowly on rack, away from drafts.

8. To fill, cut off tops with sharp knife, scoop out any filaments of soft dough, and fill with desired filling such as sweetened whipped cream or pudding. Replace tops. Dust with confectioners' sugar, if desired, and serve cold.

Note: For small cream puffs drop by small spoonfulls and bake for 20 to 25 minutes.

·Basic Recipes·
Eggs

Hard- and Soft-Cooked Eggs
(see principles pages 161-167)

1 egg for each serving
water to cover eggs
use either cold- or hot-water
   start

General directions for cold-water start:

1. Place eggs in saucepan and add cold water to cover them.

2. Quickly bring water to a boil.

3. Remove pan from heat and cover with lid.

4. Let eggs stand off heat until they are cooked to desired doneness.

    3 to 5 minutes for soft-cooked eggs

    15 to 20 minutes for hard-cooked eggs

5. After cooking, remove soft-cooked eggs immediately from hot water and serve. Cool hard-cooked eggs immediately in cold water to prevent dark ring formation around yolk.

General directions for hot-water start:

1. Allow eggs to reach room temperature.

2. Place water (enough to cover eggs) in saucepan and bring to a boil.

3. With a spoon carefully lower eggs into boiling water.

4. Reduce heat and let eggs stand in simmering water until cooked to desired doneness.

    3 to 5 minutes for soft-cooked eggs

    20 minutes for hard-cooked eggs

5. Remove soft-cooked eggs from water immediately and serve; cool hard-cooked eggs immediately in cold water to prevent dark ring formation around yolk.

Fried Eggs
(see principles pages 161-164)

1 egg for each serving
15 mL (1 T) butter, margarine, or
  bacon fat
salt, pepper as desired

1. Heat a thin layer of fat in skillet until moderately hot (drop of water sprinkled on fat will sputter gently).

2. Break eggs, one at a time, into a custard cup or sauce dish and slip each into heated fat.

3. Reduce heat to low immediately.

4. Cook slowly 3 to 4 minutes, or to desired doneness. If desired, cook top of egg by spooning hot fat over egg or by covering skillet.

5. Sprinkle with salt and pepper to taste, and serve immediately on warmed platter.

Poached Eggs
(see principles pages 161-164)

1 egg for each serving
water to cover egg
5 mL (1 t) salt

1. Fill skillet with hot water to depth of 5 cm (2 in).

2. Add salt and bring to a boil, and then reduce heat to a simmer.

3. Break each egg into a cup or sauce dish and, one at a time, slide the egg toward the side of the pan into the water so the yolk will stay in the center.

4. Cover pan and turn off heat.

5. Let eggs remain in hot water 3 to 5 minutes or until desired degree of doneness is reached.

6. Lift each egg from water with slotted spoon, drain, and serve immediately. Poached eggs can be served plain or on toast.

Scrambled Eggs
(see principles pages 161-164)
4 servings

4 eggs
60 mL (¼ c) milk
1.2 mL (¼ t) salt, and pepper if
  desired
15 mL (1 T) butter, margarine, or
  bacon fat

1. Place eggs, milk, salt, and pepper in mixing bowl and beat with fork or beater until yolks and whites are blended.

2. Place fat in skillet and heat until slightly bubbly, but be careful not to burn.

3. Pour in egg mixture and lower heat. Cook slowly.

4. As mixture thickens on bottom and sides, lift cooked portion with spatula and turn gently. Do not stir, but permit the mixture to thicken in large portions. Do not overcook.

5. When eggs are thickened but still moist and glossy, quickly remove to heated platter and serve.

·Basic Recipes·
Fruits

Apple Sauce
(see principles pages 104-107)
4 to 6 servings

6 medium cooking apples
125 mL (½ c) water
80 mL (⅓ c) sugar, or more if
   desired

1. Wash, pare, quarter, and core apples; place in saucepan.

2. Add water, cover, and simmer over low heat until tender, 15 to 20 minutes.

3. Mash with potato masher or press through coarse sieve.

4. Stir in sugar (sweeten to taste) and heat until sugar dissolves, 1 to 2 minutes.

5. Serve hot or cold, or store in covered jar in refrigerator.

Baked Apples

4 servings

4 baking apples (Rome Beauty,
   Jonathan, Wealthy, etc.)
80 mL (⅓ c) brown or white
   sugar
1.2 mL (¼ t) cinnamon, if desired
5 mL (1 t) butter or margarine
80 mL (⅓ c) water

Set oven at 190°C (375°F)

1. Wash and core apples. Remove by paring a 2.5 cm (1 in) strip of peel around the top of the cored apple, or slit skin around center of each apple with a knife.

2. Place apples close together into baking dish with pared ends up.

3. Fill the center of each apple with sugar or with a sugar-cinnamon mixture.

4. Place 1.2 mL (¼ t) butter or margarine on top of each filled apple.

5. Pour water around apples in baking dish and bake at 190°C (375°F) for 45 minutes, or until apples are tender when tested with a fork.

6. Serve apples warm or cold with syrup which remains in baking dish.

Stewed Dried Fruit

(see principles pages 104-107)

4 servings

227 g (½ lb) or a package of dried fruit
about 60 ml (¼ c) sugar
about 500 mL (2 c) water

Follow directions on package or these general directions for cooking dried fruits:

1. Bulk pack dried fruits are washed before they are used. Packaged fruits usually do not need to be washed; follow washing instructions on package.

2. Place fruit in saucepan and add warm water to 1.2 cm (½ in) above fruit.

3. Bring to a boil and simmer fruit gently until plump and tender, about 15 to 20 minutes.

4. Sweeten to taste at the end of cooking period; remove from heat when sugar is dissolved.

5. Cool and store in a covered jar in refrigerator for several hours to permit the fruit to become plumper and more flavorful before serving.

Stewed Fresh Fruit

(see principles pages 104-107)

6 servings

1 L (4 c) fresh fruit
250 mL (1 c) sugar
250 mL (1 c) water

1. Wash, pare, core, cut, or leave whole (apples, peaches, plums, cherries, etc.).

2. Place sugar and water into saucepan and bring to a boil.

3. Add prepared fresh fruit and simmer until tender and slightly transparent.

4. Serve warm or cold, or store in covered jar in refrigerator.

·Basic Recipes·
Meat, Poultry, Fish

Pan-frying

When fat is allowed to accumulate or a small amount of fat is added, the method of cooking is pan-frying. Thin pieces of tender meat or meat which has been made tender by grinding or cubing, young poultry, and fish are suitable for pan-frying (see pages 223, 237-238).

General directions for pan-frying:
(see principles pages 204)
1. Wipe meat with damp cloth.
2. Place shortening in skillet and melt.
3. Place meat into skillet and brown on both sides. Do not cover.
4. Cook at moderate temperature until done, turning occasionally.
5. Remove to preheated platter and serve immediately.

Broiling

Broiling is used for tender steaks and chops at least 2 cm (¾ in) thick. Tender beef steaks, lamb chops, sliced ham, bacon, and ground beef are suitable for broiling. Fresh pork and veal steaks and chops are not usually broiled since they should be cooked well done; instead they are generally braised. Specific cuts for broiling are listed on page 537.

General directions for broiling meats:
(see principles pages 189-196)
1. Wipe meat with damp cloth.
2. Cut outer edge of fat in several places to prevent curling of meat.
3. Set oven regulator for broiling. The broiler may be preheated, if desired.
4. Place meat on rack of broiler pan.

5. Place the broiler pan in the range so that it is the desired distance from the source of heat. The distance is usually 5 to 7.5 cm (2 to 3 in) for steaks, chops, and patties that are 2 to 2.5 cm (¾ to 1 in) thick; 7.5 to 12.5 cm (3 to 5 in) for cuts which are 2.5 to 5 cm (1 to 2 in) thick.

6. Broil meat until top side is brown, about one-half of the time given in the timetable (meat will be slightly more than half done).

7. Season with salt and pepper, if desired (except ham or bacon).

8. Turn meat with tongs and brown other side.

9. Season with additional salt, if desired; place on preheated platter, and serve immediately.

Pan-broiling

The same tender cuts listed for broiling are suitable for pan-broiling when they are cut 2.5 cm (1 in) or less in thickness.

General directions for pan-broiling meats:
(see principles page 196)

1. Wipe meat with damp cloth.

2. Cut fat around outer edge in several places to prevent curling.

3. Place meat in heavy frying pan or griddle. Do not add fat or water; do not cover. Most meats have enough fat to prevent sticking; however, the frying pan may be lightly brushed with fat for very lean cuts.

4. Pour off fat as it accumulates. If fat is permitted to accumulate, the meat will fry instead of pan-broil.

5. Cook slowly, turning occasionally, to brown meat on both sides. Since meat obtains heat from bottom of pan, turning more than once is required for even cooking.

6. When both sides are browned, remove meat to preheated platter and serve immediately.

Timetable for *Broiling*

Cut	Thickness	Weight	Approx. Total Cooking Time in Minutes	
Beef			*Rare*	*Medium*
Rib or Club Steak	2.5 cm (1 in)	.45 to .68 kg (1 to 1½ lb)	12 to 15	18 to 20
	3.75 cm (1½ in)	.68 to .91 kg (1½ to 2 lb)	20 to 25	25 to 30
	5 cm (2 in)	.91 to 1.13 kg (2 to 2½ lb)	30 to 35	35 to 45
Sirloin Steak	2.5 cm (1 in)	.68 to 1.36 kg (1½ to 3 lb)	15 to 20	20 to 30
	3.75 cm (1½ in)	1.02 to 1.81 kg (2¼ 4 lb)	25 to 35	35 to 45
	5 cm (2 in)	1.36 to 2.27 kg (3 to 5 lb)	30 to 40	45 to 60
Porterhouse Steak	2.5 cm (1 in)	.57 to .91 kg (1¼ to 2 lb)	15 to 20	20 to 30
	3.75 cm (1½ in)	.91 to 1.36 kg (2 to 3 lb)	25 to 35	35 to 45
	5 cm (2 in)	1.13 to 1.58 kg (2½ to 3½ lb)	30 to 40	45 to 60
Delmonico Steak (rib eye)	2.5 cm (1 in)	283.5 to 396.9 g (10 to 14 oz)	18 to 20	20 to 25
	5 cm (2 in)	567 to 680 g (20 to 24 oz)	30 to 40	35 to 45
Tenderloin (Filet Mignon)		113.4 to 226.8 g (4 to 8 oz)	10 to 15	15 to 20
Ground Beef Patties	2.5 cm (1 in) thick by 7.5 cm (3 in)	113.4 g (4 oz)	12 to 15	20 to 25
Pork—Smoked				
Ham Slice	1.25 cm (½ in)	340 to 454 g (¾ to 1 lb)	10 to 12	
	2.5 cm (1 in)		16 to 20	
Canadian-style Bacon (sliced)	.625 cm (¼ in)		6 to 8	
	1.25 cm (½ in)		8 to 10	
Bacon			4 to 5	
Lamb				
Shoulder Chops	2.5 cm (1 in)	141.7 to 226.8 g (5 to 8 oz)	12	
	3.75 cm (1½ in)	226.8 to 283.5 g (8 to 10 oz)	18	
	5 cm (2 in)	283.5 to 454 g (10 to 16 oz)	22	
Rib Chops	2.5 cm (1 in)	85 to 141.75 g (3 to 5 oz)	12	
	3.75 cm (1½ in)	113.4 to 198.5 g (4 to 7 oz)	18	
	5 cm (2 in)	170 to 283.5 g (6 to 10 oz)	22	
Loin Chops	2.5 cm (1 in)	113.4 to 198.5 g (4 to 7 oz)	12	
	3.75 cm (1½ in)	170 to 283.5 g (6 to 10 oz)	18	
	5 cm (2 in)	226.8 to 369.9 g (8 to 14 oz)	22	
Ground Lamb Patties	2.5 cm (1 in thick) by 7.5 cm (3 in)	113.4 g (4 oz)	18	

Roasting

Large tender cuts of beef, veal, lamb, pork, and poultry may be roasted. Specific cuts for roasting are listed in the following timetable.

General directions for roasting meats:
(see principles pages 189-193)

1. Wipe meat with damp cloth and season with salt and pepper, if desired.

2. Place meat fat-side up on shallow roasting pan (standing rib will rest on bones, not in drippings); place meats with no bones on rack in bottom of shallow pan to keep meat out of drippings.

3. Insert meat thermometer in center of thickest muscle of roast and away from bone and fat. Do not cover or add water.

4. Roast meat at 160°C (325°F) until done as desired, using above timetable as a guide for roasting time and internal temperature. Meat thermometer is the most accurate guide to doneness of meats.

5. Remove meat to hot platter and place in warm oven when making gravy.

6. Use drippings to make gravy as in the following recipe.

Gravy from Roast
(see principles pages 119)

500 mL (2 c) water
45 mL (3 T) drippings
45 mL (3 T) flour
salt, pepper as desired

1. Pour off fat drippings from bottom of roasting pan and save.

2. Add 500 mL (2 c) of water to roasting pan to dissolve browned drippings. Pour off and save.

3. Measure 45 mL (3 T) of fat drippings into roasting pan.

4. Add 45 mL (3 T) of flour and blend with fat drippings.

5. Slowly add the dissolved browned drippings from roasting pan.

6. Bring to a boil over low heat, stirring constantly, and cook for 2 or 3 minutes until mixture becomes clear and thickens.

7. Season with salt to taste; pepper if desired.

8. Pour into hot gravy boat and serve with roast.

Timetable for *Roasting Stuffed Chilled Poultry*

Kind of Poultry	Ready-to-Cook Weight kg	lb	Approx. Amount of Stuffing — L	qt	Approx. Total Roasting Time — Hours	
Chicken					160°C (325°F)	200°C (400°F)
Broilers or Fryers	.68 to 1.13	(1½ to 2½)	.24 to .47	(¼ to ½)	1¼ to 2	1 to 2*
Roasters	1.13 to 2.04	(2½ to 4½)	.47 to 1.2	(½ to 1¼)	2 to 3½	1¾ to 3†
Capons	1.81 to 3.63	(2½ to 4½)	1.2 to 1.67	(1¼ to 1¾)	3 to 5	
Ducks	1.36 to 2.27	(3 to 5)	.47 to .95	(½ to 1)	2½ to 3	
Goose	1.81 to 3.63	(4 to 8)	.72 to 1.4	(¾ to 1½)	2¾ to 3½	
	3.63 to 6.35	(8 to 14)	1.4 to 2.4	(1½ to 2½)	3½ to 5	
Turkey						
Fryers or roasters (very young birds)	1.81 to 3.63	(4 to 8)	.95 to 1.9	(1 to 2)	3 to 4½	
Roasters (fully grown young birds)	2.72 to 5.44	(6 to 12)	1.4 to 2.8	(1½ to 3)	3½ to 5	
	5.44 to 6.35	(12 to 14)	2.8 to 3.8	(3 to 4)	5 to 5¾	
	6.35 to 8.16	(14 to 18)	3.8 to 4.7	(4 to 5)	5¾ to 6	
	8.16 to 10.88	(18 to 24)	4.7 to 5.7	(5 to 6)	6 to 6¾	
Halves, quarters, half breasts	1.58 to 2.27	(3½ to 5)	.95 to 1.4	(1 to 1½)	3 to 3½	
	2.27 to 3.63	(5 to 8)	1.4 to 1.9	(1½ to 2)	3½ to 4	
	3.63 to 5.44	(8 to 12)	1.9 to 2.8	(2 to 3)	4 to 5	

*Or roast unstuffed ¾ to 1½ hours.
†Or roast unstuffed 1½ to 2¾ hours.

Based on *Pillsbury Kitchens' Family Cookbook*. Copyright © 1979 by The Pillsbury Company, Minneapolis, Minnesota. Used by permission.

Timetable for *Roasting*

Cut	Approximate Weight	Oven Temperature	Meat Thermometer Reading	Approx. Cooking Time Minutes Per Kg or Lb
Beef				
Standing Rib (7 inch cut)	2.72 to 3.63 kg (6 to 8 lb)	160°C (325°F)	60°C rare (140°F) 70°C medium (160°F) 75°C well (170°F)	23 to 25 27 to 30 32 to 35
Rolled Rib	2.27 to 3.18 kg (5 to 7 lb)	160°C (325°F)	60°C rare (140°F) 70°C medium (160°F) 75°C well (170°F)	32 38 48
Delmonico (Rib Eye)	1.81 to 2.72 kg (4 to 6 lb)	180°C (350°F)	60°C rare (140°F) 70°C medium (160°F) 75°C well (170°F)	18 to 20 20 to 22 22 to 24
Tenderloin	1.81 to 2.72 kg (4 to 6 lb)	230°C (450°F)	60°C rare (140°F) 70°C medium (160°F) 75°C well (170°F)	8 to 10 10 to 12 12 to 15
Rolled Rump (high quality)	1.81 to 2.72 kg (4 to 6 lb)	160°C (325°F)	65 to 75°C (150 to 170°F)	25 to 30
Sirloin Tip (high quality)	1.58 to 1.81 kg (3½ o 4 lb)	160°C (325°F)	65 to 75°C (150 to 170°F)	35 to 40
Beef Loaf		160°C (325°F)	71 to 75°C (160 to 170°F)	30 to 45
Pork—Fresh				
Loin Center	1.36 to 2.27 kg (3 to 5 lb)	160°C (325°F)	85°C (185°F)	35 to 40
Half	2.27 to 3.18 kg (5 to 7 lb)	160°C (325°F)	85°C (185°F)	40 to 45
Ends	.91 to 1.36 kg (2 to 3 lb)	160°C (325°F)	85°C (185°F)	45 to 50
Picnic Shoulder	2.27 to 3.63 kg (5 to 8 lb)	160°C (325°F)	85°C (185°F)	30 to 45
Rolled	1.36 to 2.27 kg (3 to 5 lb)	160°C (325°F)	85°C (185°F)	40 to 45
Cushion-style	1.36 to 2.27 kg (3 to 5 lb)	160°C (325°F)	85°C (185°F)	35 to 40
Boston Butt	1.81 to 2.72 kg (4 to 6 lb)	160°C (325°F)	85°C (185°F)	45 to 50
Leg (fresh ham) Whole (bone in)	4.54 to 6.35 lg (10 to 14 lb)	160°C (325°F)	85°C (185°F)	30 to 35
Spareribs			Cooked well done 1½ to 2½ hours	

(continued)

Based on *Pillsbury Kitchens' Family Cookbook*. Copyright © 1979 by The Pillsbury Company, Minneapolis, Minnesota. Used by permission.

Timetable for *Roasting*

Cut		Approximate Weight	Oven Temperature	Meat Thermometer Reading	Approx. Cooking Time Minutes Per Kg or Lb
Pork—Smoked					
Ham (Cook before eating)	Whole	4.54 to 6.35 kg (10 to 14 lb)	160°C (325°F)	75°C (160°F)	18 to 20
	Half	2.27 to 3.18 kg (5 to 7 lb)	160°C (325°F)	75°C (160°F)	22 to 25
	Shank portion	1.36 to 1.81 kg (3 to 4 lb)	160°C (325°F)	75°C (160°F)	35 to 40
	Butt portion	1.36 to 1.81 kg (3 to 4 lb)	160°C (325°F)	75°C (160°F)	35 to 40
Ham (Fully cooked or canned)	Whole	4.54 to 6.35 kg (10 to 14 lb)	160°C (325°F)	55°C (130°F)	12 to 15
	Half	2.27 to 3.18 kg (5 to 7 lb)	160°C (325°F)	55°C (130°F)	12 to 15
	Picnic Shoulder	2.27 to 3.63 kg (5 to 8 lb)	160°C (325°F)	75°C (170°F)	35
	Shoulder	.91 to 1.81 kg (2 to 4 lb)	160°C (325°F)	75°C (170°F)	35
	Butt	.91 to 1.81 kg (2 to 4 lb)	160°C (325°F)	70°C (160°F)	35 to 40
Lamb					
Leg		2.27 to 3.63 kg (5 to 8 lb)	160°C (325°F)	79 to 80°C (175 to 180°F)	30 to 35
Crown Roast		1.81 to 2.72 kg (4 to 6 lb)	160°C (325°F)	79 to 80°C (175 to 180°F)	40 to 45
Rack		1.81 to 2.27 kg (4 to 5 lb)	160°C (325°F)	79 to 80°C (175 to 180°F)	40 to 45
Shoulder (cushion style)		1.36 to 2.27 kg (3 to 5 lb)	160°C (325°F)	79 to 80°C (175 to 180°F)	30 to 35
Shoulder (rolled)		1.36 to 2.27 kg (3 to 5 lb)	160°C (325°F)	79 to 80°C (175 to 180°F)	30 to 45
Veal					
Leg		2.27 to 3.63 kg (5 to 8 lb)	160°C (325°F)	75°C (170°F)	25 to 35
Loin		1.81 to 2.72 kg (4 to 6 lb)	160°C (325°F)	75°C (170°F)	30 to 35
Rib (rack)		1.36 to 2.27 kg (3 to 5 lb)	160°C (325°F)	75°C (170°F)	30 to 35
Shoulder (rolled)		1.81 to 2.72 kg (4 to 6 lb)	160°C (325°F)	75°C (170°F)	40 to 45

Braising

Braising is suitable for less tender cuts of meat, mature poultry, pork and veal chops, and steaks which need to be cooked well done. Specific cuts are listed in the following timetable for braising.

General directions for braising:
(see principles pages 189-190, 196-204)

1. Wipe meat with damp cloth and trim excess fat from edge.

2. Rub trimmed fat over bottom of warm skillet, or add a small amount of fat when trimmings are not available.

3. Brown meat on one side and turn to brown other side. Season as desired.

4. Pour off any excess fat and cover, or add small amount of water and then cover. Liquid is usually added to less tender cuts but is not usually used for tender cuts such as pork chops or tenderloin which cook quickly.

5. Cook at low temperature (simmer) until tender when tested with fork. Cooking may be continued on top of range or in a slow oven 150°C to 160°C (300°F to 325°F).

6. Gravy may be made from the liquid in the pan, if desired.

Gravy from Braised Meats
(see principles pages 119)

250 mL (1 c) meat broth
60 mL (¼ c) cold water
30 mL (2 T) flour

1. Remove meat to platter and place in warm oven while making gravy.

2. Skim excess fat from meat broth.

3. Pour off broth and measure amount needed and return to kettle.

4. For each cup of medium gravy you will need 250 mL (1 c) broth, 60 mL (¼ c) water, and 30 mL (2 T) flour.

5. Place measured water into jar, add flour on top of water, tighten lid, and shake to form a smooth mixture.

6. Stir flour and water slowly into hot broth. Bring to a boil; cook 1 minute until gravy is clear and thick.

7. Add seasoning to taste and serve.

Timetable for *Braising*

Cut	Approx. Weight or Thickness	Approx. Total Cooking Time
Beef		
Pot-roast	1.36 to 2.27 kg (3 to 5 lb)	3 to 4 hrs
Swiss Steak	3.75 to 6.25 cm (1½ to 2½ in)	2 to 3 hrs
Fricassee	5-cm (2-in) cubes	1½ to 2½ hrs
Beef Birds	1.25 cm × 5 cm × 10 cm (½ in × 2 in × 4 in)	1½ to 2½ hrs
Short Ribs	Pieces: 5 cm × 5 cm × 10 cm (2 in × 2 in × 4 in)	1½ to 2½ hrs
Round Steak	1.8 cm (¾ in)	45 to 60 min
Stuffed Steak	1.25 to 1.8 cm (½ to ¾ in)	1½ hrs
Flank Steak	.68 to .91 kg (1½ to 2 lb)	1½ to 2½ hrs
Pork		
Chops	1.8 to 3.75 cm (¾ to 1½ in)	45 to 60 min
Spareribs	.91 to 1.36 kg (2 to 3 lb)	1½ hrs
Tenderloin, Whole	.34 to .45 kg (¾ to 1 lb)	45 to 60 min
Fillets	1.25 cm (½ in)	30 min
Shoulder Steaks	1.8 cm (¾ in)	45 to 60 min
Lamb		
Shoulder Chops	1.8 to 2.5 cm (¾ to 1 in)	45 to 60 min
Riblets		1½ to 2 hrs
Shanks	.34 to .45 kg (¾ to 1 lb)	1½ to 2 hrs
Cubes	3.75 cm (1½ in)	1½ to 2 hrs
Veal		
Veal Birds	1.25 cm × 5 cm × 10 cm (½ in × 2 in × 4 in)	45 to 60 min
Chops, Steak or Cutlets	1.25 to 1.8 cm (½ to ¾ in)	45 to 60 min
Shoulder Cubes	2.5 to 5 cm (1 to 2 in)	45 to 60 min

Cooking in Liquid (simmering and stewing)

Large less tender cuts and stews are cooked in liquid. This method is used to prepare stock for soups (see pages 261-263). Cuts especially suitable for cooking in liquid are listed in the following timetable.

General directions for cooking meats in liquid, using beef stew as example:

(see principles pages 189-190, 196-204, preparing soup stock pages 261-263)

Beef Stew

4 servings

454 g (1 lb) beef (chuck or bottom round) cut into 2.5 or 5-cm (1 or 2 in) cubes
45 mL (3 T) flour
5 mL (1 t) salt
15 mL (1 T) shortening or drippings
500 mL (2 c) water
4 small whole potatoes
2 carrots, quartered
4 small whole onions
125 mL (½ c) diced celery
15 mL (1 T) flour
60 mL (¼ c) water

1. Blend flour, salt, and pepper, if desired. Spread on waxed paper and roll pieces of meat in seasoned flour.

2. Heat shortening in kettle and brown meat on all sides.

3. Add water, cover, and simmer until meat is almost tender (about 2 hours).

4. If necessary, add more water to replace any that has evaporated.

5. Add vegetables and continue to simmer until vegetables are fork tender.

6. If thicker broth is desired, place 60 mL (¼ c) water into jar, add 15 mL (1 T) flour, cover, and shake to form smooth paste. Slowly stir into stew and boil for 1 minute.

7. Serve on preheated platter.

All fish are tender and are cooked by the same methods used for meats (see principles of fish cookery pages 237-238). The various forms of fish and methods of cooking are listed in the timetable on pages 546-547.

Timetable for *Cooking in Liquid*

Cut	Average Weight or Size	Approx. Total Cooking Time
Beef		
Fresh or Corned Beef	1.8 to 2.7 kg (4 to 6 lb)	3½ to 4½ hrs
Cross-cut Shanks	.34 to .57 kg (¾ to 1¼ lb)	2½ to 3 hrs
Beef for Stew		2½ to 3½ hrs
Pork—Fresh		
Spareribs		2 to 2½ hrs
Hocks		2½ to 3 hrs
Pork—Smoked		
Ham (old style and country cured)		
Large	5.4 to 7.3 kg (12 to 16 lb)	4½ to 5 hrs
Small	4.5 to 5.4 kg (10 to 12 lb)	4½ to 5 hrs
Half	2.3 to 3.6 kg (5 to 8 lb)	3 to 4 hrs
Ham (tendered)		
Shank or Butt Half	2.3 to 3.6 kg (5 to 8 lb)	1¾ to 3½ hrs
Picnic Shoulder	2.3 to 3.6 kg (5 to 8 lb)	3½ to 4 hrs
Shoulder Butt	.91 to 1.81 kg (2 to 4 lb)	1 to 2 hrs
Hocks		2 to 2½ hrs
Lamb		
Lamb for stew	2.5 to 3.75 cm (1 to 1½ in) pieces	1½ to 2 hrs
Veal		
Veal for Stew		2 to 3 hrs.

Timetable for *Cooking Fish and Shellfish*

Method Of Cooking	Product	Market Form*	Approximate Weight Or Thickness	Cooking Temperature	Approximate Total Cooking Time
Baking	Fish	Dressed	1.35 to 1.81 kg (3 to 4 lb)	180°C (350°F)	40 to 60 min
		Pan-dressed	.23 to 145 kg (½ to 1 lb)	180°C (350°F)	25 to 30 min
		Steaks	1.25 to 2.5 cm (½ to 1 in)	180°C (350°F)	25 to 35 min
		Fillets		180°C (350°F)	25 to 35 min
	Clams	Live		230°C (450°F)	15 min
	Lobster	Live	.34 to .45 kg (¾ to 1 lb)	200°C (400°F)	15 to 20 min
			.45 to .68 kg (1 to 1½ lb)	200°C (400°F)	20 to 25 min
	Oysters	Live		230°C (450°F)	15 min
		Shucked		200°C (400°F)	10 min
	Scallops	Shucked		180°C (350°F)	25 to 30 min
	Shrimp	Headless		180°C (350°F)	20 to 25 min
	Spiny lobster	Headless	113 g (4 oz)	230°C (450°F)	20 to 25 min
	tails		227 g (8 oz)	230°C (450°F)	25 to 30 min
Broiling	Fish	Pan-dressed	.23 to .45 kg (½ to 1 lb)		10 to 15 min
		Steaks	1.2 to 2.5 cm (½ to 1 in)		10 to 15 min
		Fillets			10 to 15 min
	Clams	Live			5 to 8 min
	Lobster	Live	.34 to .45 kg (¾ to 1 lb)		10 to 12 min
			.45 to .68 kg (1 to 1½ lb)		12 to 15 min
	Oysters	Live			5 min
		Shucked			5 min
	Scallops	Shucked			8 to 10 min
	Shrimp	Headless			8 to 10 min
	Spiny lobster	Headless	113 g (4 oz)		8 to 10 min
	tails		227 g (8 oz)		10 to 12 min

Cooking in water				
Fish	Pan-dressed	.23 to .45 kg (½ to 1 lb)	Simmer	10 min
	Steaks	1.25 to 2.5 cm (½ to 1 in)	Simmer	10 min
	Fillets		Simmer	10 min
Crabs	Live		Simmer	15 min
Lobster	Live	.34 to .45 kg (¾ to 1 lb)	Simmer	10 to 15 min
	Live	.45 to .68 kg (1 to 1½ lb)	Simmer	15 to 20 min
Scallops	Shucked		Simmer	4 to 5 min
Shrimp	Headless		Simmer	5 min
Spiny lobster	Headless	113 g (4 oz)	Simmer	10 min
tails		227 g (8 oz)	Simmer	15 min

Deep-fat frying				
Fish	Pan-dressed	.23 to .45 kg (½ to 1 lb)	190°C (375°F)	2 to 4 min
	Steaks	1.25 to 2.5 cm (½ to 1 in)	190°C (375°F)	2 to 4 min
	Fillets		190°C (375°F)	1 to 4 min
Clams	Shucked		190°C (375°F)	2 to 3 min
Crabs	Soft-shell	113 g (¼ lb)	190°C (375°F)	3 to 4 min
Lobster	Live	.34 to .45 kg (¾ to 1 lb)	175°C (350°F)	3 to 4 min
	Live	.45 to .68 kg (1 to 1½ lb)	175°C (350°F)	4 to 5 min
Oysters	Shucked		190°C (375°F)	2 min
Scallops	Shucked		180°C (350°F)	3 to 4 min
Shrimp	Headless		180°C (350°F)	2 to 3 min
Spiny lobster	Headless	113 g (4 oz)	180°C (350°F)	3 to 4 min
tails		227 g (8 oz)	180°C (350°F)	4 to 5 min

Based on *Handbook of Food Preparation*, Seventh Edition, 1975, American Home Economics Association, Washington, D.C. pp. 43, 44, 46. Used by permission.

·Basic Recipes·
Pastry

Standard or Cold-Water Pastry
(see principles page 354 –355)

one 22.5 cm (9 in) two-crust pie or two pie shells

500 mL (2 c) sifted all-purpose
    flour
5 mL (1 t) salt
160 mL (²/₃ c) shortening
60 mL (¹/₄ c) water

1. Place flour in mixing bowl and stir in salt.

2. Add shortening and cut in with pastry blender until shortening particles are size of large peas.

3. Sprinkle water, a tablespoon at a time, over flour-shortening mixture and mix lightly with a fork until all flour is moistened.

4. Gather dough with fingers so that it cleans the bowl; press into ball.

5. Roll out between two sheets of waxed paper until .3 cm (¹/₈ in) thick (see pictures page 357).

Hot-Water Pastry
(see principles pages 354, 356)

one 22.5 cm (9 in) two-crust pie or two pie shells

500 mL (2 c) sifted all-purpose
    flour
5 mL (1 t) salt
160 mL (²/₃ c) shortening
60 mL (¹/₄ c) boiling water
15 mL (1 T) milk

1. Put shortening in small mixing bowl. Add boiling water and milk all at once and beat vigorously with fork until creamy and thick.

2. Add flour and salt to shortening-water mixture and stir with fork until flour is moistened forming a stiff dough.

3. Gather dough with fingers so that the bowl is clean; press into ball.

4. Roll between two sheets of waxed paper until .3 cm (¹/₈ in) thick (see pictures page 357).

Stir-N-Roll Pastry
(see principles 354, 356)

one 22.5 cm (9 in) two-crust pie or two shells

500 mL (2 c) sifted all-purpose
    flour
5 mL (1 t) salt
125 mL (¹/₂ c) cooking or salad
    oil
60 mL (¹/₄ c) cold milk

1. Place flour and salt in bowl and mix.

2. Add oil to milk in measuring cup but do not stir.

3. Add oil and milk all at once to the flour mixture.

4. Stir with fork until blended.

5. Gather dough with fingers to clean bowl and then form dough into a ball.

6. Roll between two sheets of waxed paper until .3 cm (¹/₈ in) thick (see pictures page 357).

Apple Pie

one 22.5 cm (9 in) pie

1 pastry recipe for two-crust pie
1.5 L (6 c) pared, sliced apples
185 to 250 mL (³/4 to 1 c) sugar
5 mL (1 t) cinnamon
2.5 mL (¹/2 t) salt
30 mL (2 T) flour
15 mL (1 T) lemon juice
30 mL (2 T) butter

Set oven at 220°C (425°F)

1. Prepare pastry according to selected recipe and line pan with pastry (see pictures, pages 359–360).

2. Add sugar, cinnamon, salt, flour, and lemon juice to sliced apples and mix lightly.

3. Arrange apples in 22.5 cm (9 in) pastry-lined pan. Dot with butter.

4. Roll out top pastry and place over apples (see pictures, pages 359 –360).

5. Seal and flute edge and cover edge with foil (see picture, page 360).

6. Bake at 220°C (425°F) for 50 to 60 minutes, until crust is golden brown and juice bubbles up into slits in top pastry.

Meringue

topping for 22.5 cm (9 in) pie

3 egg whites
1.2 mL (¹/4 t) cream of tartar
90 mL (6 T) sugar
2.5 mL (¹/2 t) vanilla

Set oven at 200°C (400°F)

1. Add cream of tartar to egg whites and beat until soft peak is formed when the beater is lifted.

2. Add sugar, 30 mL (2 T) at a time, and beat it in. Add vanilla and continue beating until meringue will stand in a stiff peak when the beater is slowly lifted.

3. Pile meringue onto hot pie filling, spread evenly to edge of crust to prevent shrinking and weeping. Use back of spoon to swirl or pull up soft points for a decorative meringue.

4. Bake at 200°C (400°F) for 8 to 10 minutes.

Chocolate Cream Pie

one 22.5 cm (9 in) pie

one 22.5 cm (9 in) pie shell,
    baked
2 to 2¹/₂ squares of unsweetened
    chocolate
45 mL (3 T) cornstarch
1.2 mL (¹/₄ t) salt
750 mL (3 c) milk
3 egg yolks, slightly beaten
15 mL (1 T) butter
7.5 mL (1¹/₂ t) vanilla
250 mL (1 c) sugar

1. Prepare one-half of basic pastry recipe for pie shell (see pictures, pages 358–359).

2. Bake pie shell at 230°C (450°F) for 10 to 12 minutes, until golden brown.

3. Place sugar, cornstarch, salt in saucepan and blend thoroughly.

4. Stir the milk in gradually at first to form a smooth paste, then add remaining milk and blend.

5. Add chocolate and cook over medium heat, stirring constantly until mixture thickens and comes to a boil. Boil for 1 minute.

6. Remove from heat. Stir a small amount of the hot mixture into the slightly beaten egg yolks, and then stir the yolk mixture into the rest of the pie filling.

7. Return to heat and boil 1 more minute, stirring constantly.

8. Remove from heat and blend in butter and vanilla.

9. Pour immediately into baked pie shell.

10. Spread meringue lightly on pie filling, sealing to edge of crust to prevent shrinking.

11. Bake until delicately browned at 200°C (400°F) 8 to 10 minutes.

·Basic Recipes·
Salad and Salad Dressings

Tossed Salad

4 servings

1 small head lettuce or 750 mL
  (3 c) assorted greens such as
  leaf, Boston, or iceberg lettuce,
  romaine, curly endive, fresh
  spinach
4 radishes
1 medium tomato
125 mL (1/2 c) celery
1 small green pepper
1 carrot

1. Wash lettuce or salad greens, drain, and chill to crispen.

2. Wash remaining vegetables and drain.

3. Cut each vegetable into different shapes as strips, rings, slices, wedges, or long thin strips to curl. Variety in size and shape adds to the attractiveness of any salad, especially tossed salad.

4. Tear lettuce or other greens into convenient size pieces.

5. Place all prepared vegetables into salad bowl.

6. Add salad dressing such as French dressing, blue cheese, or vinegar and oil, and toss gently with two forks.

7. Serve immediately.

Basic Gelatin Salad

6 servings

1 package flavored gelatin
  (select gelatin flavor to make
  pleasing combination with
  foods you plan to add to it)
250 to 375 mL (1 to 1 1/2 c) drained
  and cut, fresh or canned fruit,
  vegetable or seafood
salad greens

1. Prepare gelatin according to directions on package.

2. Chill and when partially set (consistency of thick egg whites), add prepared fruit, vegetable, or seafood.

3. Place into individual molds and chill until firm.

4. To serve, arrange lettuce or other salad greens on plate.

5. To unmold, loosen gelatin around top of mold with tip of paring knife, and dip mold into hot water for a few seconds (see pictures, page 376).

6. Tap the mold gently against your free hand; invert it over prepared salad greens and let gelatin slide out gently.

Cole Slaw

4 servings

750 mL (3 c) finely shredded
  cabbage
1/2 carrot grated or 60 mL (1/4 c)
  diced green pepper or both
60 mL (1/4 c) cooked salad
  dressing or mayonnaise

1. Wash all vegetables and place into refrigerator to crisp.
2. Shred cabbage and prepare carrot or pepper.
3. Add dressing and mix to coat vegetables.
4. Serve immediately.

Waldorf Salad

4 servings

2 medium size apples
185 mL (3/4 c) diced celery
60 mL (1/4 c) coarsely chopped
  walnuts
45 mL (3 T) cooked salad dressing
  or mayonnaise
4 lettuce cups

1. Wash, quarter, core (do not pare), and cut apples into bite-size cubes.
2. Cut up the celery and chop the nuts.
3. Place all ingredients into salad bowl including salad dressing and toss gently with fork.
4. Arrange on lettuce cups.

French Salad Dressing
(See principles page 276)

makes 250 mL (1 c)

185 mL (3/4 c) salad oil
60 mL (1/4 c) vinegar
5 mL (1 t) paprika
2.5 mL (1/2 t) salt
2.5 mL (1/2 t) dry mustard
.6 mL (1/8 t) pepper

1. Place ingredients in jar with tight-fitting lid and seal tightly.
2. Shake until thoroughly blended.
3. Store in the refrigerator. Shake well again before using.

Cooked Salad Dressing
(see principles page 277)

makes 375 mL (1¹/₂ c)

15 mL (1 T) sugar
30 mL (2 T) flour
5 mL (1 t) salt
5 mL (1 t) dry mustard
1 egg or 2 egg yolks
30 mL (2 T) melted butter
250 mL (1 c) milk
60 mL (¹/₄ c) vinegar

1. Combine dry ingredients in a saucepan.

2. Blend in egg, melted butter, and milk.

3. Gradually stir in vinegar.

4. Cooked over medium heat, stirring constantly, until thickened.

5. Cool. Place in jar, cover, and store in refrigerator.

Mayonnaise
(see principles page 276)

makes 310 mL (1¹/₄ c)

1 egg yolk
2.5 mL (¹/₂ t) salt
2.5 mL (¹/₂ t) sugar
2.5 mL (¹/₂ t) dry mustard
dash white pepper
15 mL (1 T) lemon juice
15 mL (1 T) vinegar
250 mL (1 c) salad oil

1. Place egg yolk, salt, sugar, mustard, and pepper into a deep bowl.

2. Beat with rotary beater or with mixer at low speed to blend.

3. Add lemon juice and vinegar; beat until well blended.

4. Gradually add salad oil, a few drops at a time, until one-third of the oil is used and the mixture is thick.

5. Continue to add the remaining oil, a tablespoon at a time, beating after each addition until oil is blended and the mayonnaise is thick.

6. Pour into jar and store covered in refrigerator.

·Basic Recipes·
Soup

Vegetable Soup
(see principles pages 261-264)

6 servings

1.1 kg (2¹/₂ lb) beef shank
1.5 L (6 c) water
15 mL (1 T) salt
250 mL (1 c) diced celery
125 mL (¹/₂ c) diced onion
1 bay leaf
500 mL (2 c) tomatoes (1 #303 can)
1 340 g (12 oz) can whole kernel corn
500 mL (2 c) cubed potatoes
250 mL (1 c) diced carrots
250 mL (1 c) chopped cabbage, if desired
season to taste

General directions for preparing stock soup using vegetable soup as example:

1. Place into a large kettle the beef shank, salt, celery, onion, bay leaf, and water. Cover and simmer 3 hours, until meat is tender.

2. Remove bones and bay leaf.

3. Skim off fat, or allow stock to cool and refrigerate overnight. Remove solid fat from broth before completing soup.

4. Cut meat taken from bone into small pieces.

5. Add cut meat, tomatoes, corn, potatoes, carrots to stock.

6. Cover and simmer 30 minutes, or until vegetables are tender.

7. Season to taste, and serve as desired.

Tomato Soup
(see principles pages 261, 263–264)

4 servings

500 mL (2 c) tomatoes (1 #303 can)
30 mL (2 T) onion
5 mL (1 t) sugar
¹/₂ bay leaf
2.5 mL (¹/₂ t) celery seed
30 mL (2 T) butter or margarine
45 mL (3 T) flour
5 ml (1 t) salt
500 mL (2 c) milk

General directions for preparing cream soup using tomato soup as example:

1. Place tomatoes, onion, bay leaf, and celery seed into saucepan and simmer 10 minutes.

2. Make white sauce using butter or margarine, flour, salt, and milk. Follow directions for white sauce on page 563.

3. Press tomato mixture through sieve to form purée.

4. Stir hot tomato purée (reheat if necessary) slowly into thickened white sauce. Serve immediately.

·Basic Recipes·
Vegetables

Vegetables should not be overcooked. Too much cooking causes loss of their attractive color, flavor, slightly crisp texture, and nutrient values. The chart on pages 559–561 presents the basic information required to cook fresh vegetables.

Fresh vegetables are cooked in a variety of ways: boiled, steamed, pressure cooked, and baked. They may be cooked alone or with other vegetables. After cooking, they may be mashed, creamed, fried, or seasoned. Boiling is probably the most commonly used method for cooking vegetables.

General directions for boiling frozen vegetables:

1. Read label and use amount of water suggested. Add salt, and heat to a boil.

2. Add frozen vegetables and cover.

3. Bring the water back to a boil quickly, and separate vegetables with a fork for uniform cooking.

4. Lower heat and cook until fork tender. Use suggested time on package as a guide, count time after water begins to boil second time.

5. Season with butter or margarine and serve immediately.

General directions for boiling fresh vegetables:
(see principles pages 250–251)

1. Thoroughly wash the vegetables using a vegetable brush when necessary.

2. Follow the basic preparation suggested in the vegetable chart on pages 559–561.

3. Bring small amount of salted water to boil.

4. Add vegetables, cover, and heat to a gentle boil. The color of green vegetables will be retained better when the cover is left off for the first few minutes of cooking.

5. Cook vegetables only until they are fork tender. Use the time listed in the vegetable chart.

6. Season with butter or margarine and serve immediately.

General directions for heating canned vegetables:
(see principles pages 250–252)

1. Drain liquid into sauce pan (retain vegetables in can); boil quickly to reduce amount to about one-fourth of original volume.

2. Add vegetables and heat quickly but do not boil (canned vegetables are already cooked).

3. Season to taste and serve immediately.

General directions for steaming vegetables:
(see principles page 252)

1. Place water in steamer and bring to a boil.

2. Place vegetable in perforated compartment of steamer and cover.

3. Steam over rapidly boiling water until vegetable is fork tender. See chart pages 559–561.

4. Remove from steamer, season, and serve.

General directions for baking vegetables:
(see principles page 251)

1. Scrub vegetable thoroughly, then wipe dry.

2. Place in a shallow pan or directly on oven rack (as with potato).

3. Bake until fork tender, using vegetable chart, pages 559–561, as a guide for temperature and baking time.

4. Season as desired and serve immediately.

General directions for pressure cooking vegetables:
(see principles page 252)

1. Follow basic preparation listed in vegetable chart, pages 559–561.

2. Pressure cook vegetables at 15 pounds pressure, using directions for your pressure cooker.

3. Time exactly according to the directions given in the chart in order to avoid overcooking.

4. Reduce pressure in cooker as directed.

5. Season as desired and serve immediately.

Vegetable Serving Suggestions

Vegetable	Serving Suggestions
Artichoke, French or Globe	Stuff, marinate, cream; with butter or Hollandaise sauce.
Jerusalem	Buttered, creamed; with lemon juice.
Asparagus	Butter, cream, au gratin; with Hollandaise or cheese sauce.
Beans, Green or Wax	Creamed, au gratin; with almonds, mushrooms.
Beans, Lima, in Pod	Buttered, creamed.
Beets	Glazed; sliced; diced; pickled, hot or cold; sweet-sour.
Broccoli	Buttered; with Hollandaise sauce, grated cheese, buttered crumbs.
Brussels Sprouts	Buttered, creamed; with herb butter, sour cream
Cabbage, Green	Creamed, scalloped, stuffed; with grated cheese, buttered crumbs.
Cabbage, Red	Buttered, creamed, scalloped, au gratin.
Carrots	Glazed, creamed, baked, roasted with meat, sautéed, mashed.
Cauliflower	Buttered, au gratin; with buttered crumbs, grated cheese or Hollandaise sauce.
Celery	Buttered, creamed, braised; with other vegetables.
Corn	On cob, buttered. Whole kernel or cream style, buttered, creamed, scalloped.
Eggplant	Dipped in crumbs, fried; stuffed, scalloped.
Kohlrabi	Buttered, creamed. *(continued)*

Vegetable	Serving Suggestions
Mushrooms	Broil, fry, bake; cream; stuff, serve with other vegetables, meats.
Okra	Boiled, sautéed; with butter, lemon juice. Use with other foods, in casseroles, soups.
Onions, dry	Sautéed, boiled, baked; french-fried; Stuffed, creamed, au gratin.
Parsnips	Buttered, sautéed, mashed.
Peas, Green, in Pod	Buttered, creamed; with herbs, lettuce, chopped onion.
Peas, Black-eyed	Boiled with meat or meat drippings; with other vegetables.
Potatoes White	Baked, sautéed, french-fried; buttered, creamed, au gratin, mashed, in salad.
Sweet	Boiled, baked; candied, buttered, mashed, glazed.
Rutabagas	Buttered, mashed.
Spinach or Greens	Buttered, scalloped; with vinegar, lemon juice, hard-cooked egg; in soufflés.
Squash	
Acorn Hubbard	Buttered, baked, mashed.
Summer (Patty-pan, Yellow Neck) Zucchini (Italian)	Buttered, baked.
Tomatoes	Baked, stewed, broiled, fried, scalloped.
Turnips	Fried, buttered, mashed.

Vegetable Preparation Chart And Timetable*

Vegetable	Amount To Buy For Six	Basic Preparation	Style	Boil	Steam	Pressure Saucepan (15 lb) Pressure	Bake 180°C (350°F)
Artichoke French or Globe	6	Wash thoroughly. Cut off 2.5 cm (1 in) of top, stems, tips of leaves. Remove tough bottom leaves. Dip cut edges in lemon juice.		35–45		10–12	
Jerusalem	.90 kg (2 lb)	Wash, pare, leave whole or slice.		25–35	35		30–60
Asparagus	.68 kg (1½ lb)	Wash, cut off scales, if sandy, and tough part of stalk. Cut into pieces or leave whole.	Whole Tips	10–20 5–15	12–30 7–15	½–1½ ½–2	
Beans, Green or Wax	.68 kg (1½ lb)	Break off ends; leave whole, break into 2.5-cm (1-in) pieces lengthwise.	Whole or Pieces Shredded	15–30 10–20	20–35 15–25	1½–3 1–2	
Beans, Lima, in Pod	1.35 kg (3 lb)	Shell and wash.		20–25	25–35	1–2	
Beets	.68 kg (1½ lb)	Cut off all but 2.5 cm (1 in) of tops and root. Do not pare.	Small, Whole Large, Whole	30–45 45–90	40–60 50–90	5–10 10–18	40–60 40–60
Broccoli	.91 kg (2 lb)	Remove large outside leaves, tough part of stalk. Soak for 10 minutes in cold water, drain.	Split	10–15	15–20	1½–3	
Brussels Sprouts	.57 kg (1¼ lb) or .95 L (1 qt)	Remove wilted outside leaves. Cut off stems. Soak for 10 minutes in cold salt water, drain.		10–20	10–20	1–2	
Cabbage, Green	.68 kg (1½ lb)	Remove wilted outside leaves. Cut into wedges or shred.	Quartered Shredded	10–15 3–10	15 8–12	2–3 ½–1½	
Cabbage, Red	.68 kg (1½ lb)	Same as green cabbage.	Shredded	8–12	10–15	½–1½	

*All times given in minutes.

(continued)

559

Vegetable Preparation Chart And Timetable (Cont'd)*

Vegetable	Amount To Buy For Six	Basic Preparation	Style	Boil	Steam	Pressure Saucepan 15 lb (6.8 kg) Pressure	Bake 180°C (350°F)
Carrots	.57 kg (1¼ lb)	Cut off tops and tips. Scrape or pare. Leave whole, slice, dice or cut into julienne strips.	Young, Whole	15–25	20–30	3–5	35–45
			Sliced	10–20	15–25	1½–3	30–40
			Mature, Whole	20–30	40–50	10–15	60
			Sliced	15–25	25–30	3	
Cauliflower	.90–1.35 kg (2–3 lb) or 1 large head	Remove leaves. Cut off tough part of stem. Leave whole or break into flowerets.	Whole	15–20	25–30	10	
			Floweret	8–15	10–20	1½–3	
Celery	.68 kg (1½ lb)	Cut off leaves and heart. Slice into uniform pieces.		15–18	25–30	2–3	
Corn	.57 kg (1¼ lb) cut or 6 to 12 ears	Remove husks, silk; trim ends. Wash. Leave whole or cut kernels from cob with sharp knife. For cream style, cut only halfway to the cob, then scrape cob with dull edge of knife.	On Cob	5–15	10–15	0–1½	
Eggplant	.68 kg (1½ lb) or 1 medium	Wash, pare only if skin is tough. Slice, dice or leave whole. Dip into lemon juice if pared and not to be used immediately.	Sliced	10–20	15–20		
Kohlrabi	12	Cut off leaves, pare, slice or dice.	Sliced	20–25	30		
Mushrooms	.45 kg (1 lb)	Wash, cut off tips of stems. Leave whole or slice lengthwise.					
Okra	.57 kg (1¼ lb)	Cut off stems. Leave whole or slice.	Sliced	10–15	20	3–4	
Onions (dry)	.68 kg (1½ lb) or 6 medium	Pare. Leave whole, slice or quarter.	Small	15–25	25–35	3–4	50–60
			Large	20–40	35–40	5–8	

Vegetable	Amount	Preparation	Form				
Parsnips	.68 kg (1½ lb) or 6 medium	Pare or scrape. Leave whole or cut into halves, quarters, slices or cubes.	Whole	20–40	30–45	9–10	30–45
			Quartered	10–20	30–40	4–8	
Peas, Green, in Pod	1.36 kg (3 lb)	Shell and wash.		10–20		0–1	
				8–20			
Peas, Black Eyed	.35 kg (¾ lb)	Shell and wash.		30–40			
Potatoes White	1.36 kg (3 lb) or 6 medium	Scrub; leave skins on or pare. Leave whole or cut into pieces, slices, cubes.	Whole	25–40	30–45	8–11	45–60
			Quartered	20–25	20–30	3–5	
Sweet	1.36 kg (3 lb) medium	Scrub; boil in skins, then pare. Or bake in skins.	Whole	25–35	30–35	5–8	30–45
Rutabagas	.68 kg (1½ lb)	Pare; slice, cube or cut into strips.	Diced	20–30	35–40	5–8	5–8
Spinach or Greens	.68 kg (1½ lb)	Wash; remove wilted leaves, tough ribs or stems.		3–10	3–10	5–12	0–1½
Squash **Acorn**	1.4–1.8 kg (3–4 lb)	Wash; cut in half, remove seeds.		15–20	25–40	6–12	40–60
Hubbard	1.4 kg (3 lb)	Pare if skin is tough, remove seeds and fibers, cut into serving pieces.		15–20	25–40	6–12	45–60
Summer (Patty-pan, Yellow Neck)	.9 kg (2 lb)	Remove stem, blossom end, seeds and fibers. Do not peel. Leave whole, slice or dice.	Sliced	10–20	15–20	1½–3	30
Zucchini (Italian)	.9 kg (2 lb)	Remove stem and blossom; slice or cut into pieces.		10–15	12–20	1–2	30
Tomatoes	.9 kg (2 lb)	Peel if desired. Cut out stems; leave whole, quarter or slice.		7–15		½–1	15–30
Turnips	.68 kg (1½ lb) or 4–5 medium	Pare; cut into slices or cubes.	Whole	20–30		8–12	
			Sliced	15–20	20–25	1½	

*All times given in minutes.
Based on *Pillsbury Kitchens' Family Cookbook.* Copyright © 1979 by The Pillsbury Company, Minneapolis, Minnesota. Used by permission.

·Basic Recipes·
White Sauce

Sauces are the special touches that can turn plain and simple foods into something glamorous and distinctive. Sauces for meat and game were an important part of medieval feasts. Today we have sauces for vegetables and desserts as well as for meats. White sauce, also called cream sauce, is the basis for creamed dishes, some casseroles, gravies, and certain special kinds of elaborate sauces. The thick, smooth, and satiny appearance of white sauce accounts for its often being called a cream sauce. The thickness or consistency depends upon the proportion of thickening material to liquid used. White sauces are classified according to their consistency as thin, medium, thick, and very thick. Sauces of different thickness are required for different food products. A thin white sauce is generally used for cream soups, a medium white sauce for creamed dishes, thick sauce for soufflés, and a very thick white sauce for croquettes to blend and hold together the other materials used. The medium white sauce is the one most frequently used.

The basic ingredients of any white sauce, regardless of its thickness, are flour, fat, and liquid. The flour serves as the thickening agent; the liquid, which is usually milk but may be cream or liquid in which vegetables or meats were cooked, contributes flavor. In any white sauce the ratio of flour to fat is always equal. For example, if 15 milliliters (1 tablespoon) of flour is used for a sauce recipe then 15 milliliters (1 tablespoon) of fat is used. The proportion of liquid to fat and flour for each of the types of white sauce is listed in the table which follows.

Proportion of Ingredients for White Sauce *(250 mL (1 c))*

	Margarine Or Butter	Flour	Salt	Milk	Uses
Thin	15 mL (1 T)	15 mL (1 T)	2.5 mL (½ t)	250 mL (1 c)	cream soups
Medium	30 mL (2 T)	30 mL (2 T)	2.5 mL (½ t)	250 mL (1 c)	creamed and scalloped foods, sauces, gravies
Thick	45 mL (3 T)	45 mL (3 T)	2.5 mL (½ t)	250 mL (1 c)	soufflés
Very Thick	60 mL (4 T)	60 mL (4 T)	2.5 mL (½ t)	250 mL (1 c)	croquettes

The perfect white sauce is the start of creamed dishes and many other sauces. Remember these three points for a perfect white sauce:

1. Allow the flour and fat to bubble for about one minute to eliminate a raw, starchy flavor.

2. Remove blended fat and flour from heat when adding milk or other liquid for easy blending.

3. Keep stirring until thickened for a smooth, satiny texture.

General directions for preparing white sauce:
(see principles pages 263–264)

1. Melt butter or margarine over low heat in a sauce pan.

2. Blend in flour and seasonings over low heat, stirring until mixture is smooth and bubbly. Allow to cook for about 1 minute to eliminate a raw, starchy flavor.

3. Remove from heat. Slowly add milk, at first stirring to make a smooth paste. Then stir in remaining milk.

4. Return to heat, stirring constantly. Bring to a boil again and keep stirring until thickened.

5. Cover pan to prevent film formation until sauce is to be used.

·Recipes from Other Countries·

Soups

French Onion Soup

6 servings

80 mL (⅓ c) butter
750 mL (3 c) diced onions
30 mL (2 T) flour
1.67 L (7 c) beef stock
2.5 mL (½ t) black pepper
6 slices French bread, toasted
6 thin slices Swiss cheese
60 mL (4 T) grated Swiss cheese

1. Melt butter, add onions, and sauté over low heat until brown. Stir frequently.

2. Add flour and mix until smooth.

3. Add broth gradually, stirring constantly.

4. Add pepper, cover, cook over low heat for 30 minutes.

5. Place a slice of toasted bread in each soup bowl. Place a cheese slice on top of the bread and pour soup over it.

6. Place under the broiler for 1 minute to melt cheese.

7. Sprinkle with grated cheese and serve.

Carrot Soup from Holland

6-8 servings

1.9 L (2 qt) chicken broth
6 carrots, sliced
250 mL (1 c) celery root, sliced
1 onion, chopped
60 mL (4 T) butter
45 mL (3 T) farina
2.5 mL (½ t) white pepper
dash of nutmeg
30 mL (2 T) chopped parsley

1. In a saucepan, melt butter, add carrots, celery root, onion, and sauté for 15 minutes. Stir often.

2. Add broth, cover, and simmer over low heat for 45 minutes.

3. Purée the soup and vegetables in a blender or force through a sieve.

4. Return the soup to the saucepan. Add the farina, black pepper, and nutmeg. Stir constantly.

5. Simmer over low heat for 20 minutes.

6. Season to taste. Sprinkle each serving with parsley.

Greek Lemon Soup

6-8 servings

.454 kg (1 lb) chicken parts (necks, backs, wings)
2.8 L (3 qt) water
1 stalk celery
1 onion
1 carrot
125 mL (½ c) rice
2 egg yolks
30 mL (2 T) lemon juice
10 mL (2 t) salt

1. Wash chicken and place in saucepan.

2. Add celery, onion, carrot, water. Bring to boil.

3. Skim top with a spoon. Cook over medium heat for 2 hours.

4. Strain and return the stock to saucepan.

5. Rinse rice and add to stock. Cook over low heat for 15 minutes.

6. Beat egg yolks in a bowl. Add lemon juice and salt.

7. Gradually add the stock to the beaten egg yolks. Beat constantly to prevent curdling.

8. Return to saucepan, beating constantly.

9. Heat but do not allow to boil.

10. Serve with a slice of lemon.

Groundnut Soup from Nigeria (Peanut Soup)

4-5 servings

125 mL (½ c) groundnuts (roasted peanuts)
227 g (½ lb) beef chunks or pieces of fish
4 large peppers (hot)
1 small onion
salt and pepper to taste
750 mL (3 c) water

1. Grind or chop fine the roasted groundnuts (peanuts).

2. Grind or chop fine the peppers and onions.

3. Cook the meat or fish in the water to make stock. Allow to simmer until meat is thoroughly cooked.

4. Strain stock.

5. Mix the groundnuts with some of the hot stock into a smooth paste.

6. Add to the rest of the stock and then add the ground or chopped onions and peppers.

7. Cook gently, until the soup is thick.

If you prefer less "hot" soup, reduce the number of peppers in making it.

Note: This soup can also be made by substituting 250 mL (1 c) peanut butter for the peanuts and 500 mL (2 c) tomato juice plus 250 mL (1 c) milk for the meat stock. Mix peanut butter and tomato juice together. Heat. Scald the milk and then add to the hot tomato mixture. Stir well.

Main Dishes

Chicken Paprika from Austria

6-8 servings

1.36 kg (3 lb) frying chicken, cut up
5 mL (1 t) salt
1.25 mL (¼ t) black pepper
30 mL (2 T) butter
2 onions, peeled and thinly
    sliced
10 mL (2 t) sweet paprika
1.25 mL (½ c) sour cream

1. Wash chicken and dry. Sprinkle with salt and pepper.
2. Melt butter in a heavy saucepan. Add onions, paprika, and cook 2 minutes.
3. Add chicken and brown.
4. Cover the pan. Add a little water if the pan becomes dry. Cook 30 minutes.
5. Add sour cream and blend in.
6. Simmer for 15 minutes.

Spaghetti from Italy

4-6 servings

80 mL (⅓ c) olive oil
.227 kg (½ lb) lean, raw pork cut
    into strips
625 mL (2½ c) cooked
    tomatoes
2.5 mL (½ t) salt
1.25 mL (¼ t) crushed red
    pepper
.454 kg (1 lb) spaghetti, cooked
    and drained
grated Parmesan or Romano
    cheese

1. Heat oil in heavy pan and brown pork. Stir in tomatoes, salt, and pepper.
2. Cover and cook over low heat 20 minutes.
3. Pour sauce over spaghetti and toss.
4. Sprinkle with grated cheese.

Sweet-Sour Pork from China

4 servings

.454 kg (1 lb) lean pork
15 mL (1 T) soy sauce
5 mL (1 t) salt
1 egg, slightly beaten
60 mL (¼ c) flour
60 mL (¼ c) cornstarch
cooking oil for deep fat frying

1. Trim fat from pork and cut into 2.5 cm (1 in) cubes.

2. Combine soy sauce and salt. Pour over meat cubes and marinate for 10 minutes.

3. Drain. Coat pork cubes with beaten egg.

4. Stir egg-coated cubes into flour. Be careful to cover each cube evenly.

5. Add cornstarch and stir. If the batter does not cling to the cubes, add a small amount of additional starch.

6. Heat oil to 190°C (375°F) for deep fat frying.

7. Add pork cubes one at a time and fry 5 to 6 minutes until evenly browned.

8. Remove cubes from fat. Drain and keep warm in oven set at 120°C (250°F).

Sweet and Sour Sauce

.227 kg (8 oz) tomato sauce
125 mL (½ c) vinegar
125 mL (½ c) sugar
125 mL (½ c) pineapple juice
45 mL (3 T) cornstarch blended in
    45 mL (3 T) cold water
250 mL (1 c) pineapple tidbits
1 bell pepper cut into 1.5 cm (½ in)
    squares

1. Combine tomato sauce, vinegar, sugar, and pineapple juice. Bring to boil.

2. Slowly stir in the cornstarch mixture. Continue heating until the mixture is thick and clear.

3. Just before serving, add pineapple tidbits and pepper.

4. Add pork cubes and serve.

Salads

Green Salad from France

4-6 servings

1 head romaine lettuce
2 endive
1 head escarole
250 mL (1 c) olive oil
60 mL (¼ c) wine or tarragon
   vinegar
5 mL (1 t) salt
1.25 mL (¼ t) black pepper
1 clove garlic, crushed

1. Combine olive oil, vinegar, salt, pepper, and garlic in a bowl.

2. Beat vigorously, or place ingredients in a jar and shake vigorously.

3. Chill, wash, and drain the salad greens.

4. Tear the lettuce into 5 cm (2 in) pieces.

5. Tear the escarole into small pieces.

6. Cut the endive into 1.25 cm (½ in) pieces.

7. Combine the greens in a salad bowl.

8. Just before serving, add the dressing and toss.

Green Salad from Italy

4-6 servings

250 mL (1 c) chopped green
   pepper
250 mL (1 c) chopped red
   pepper
30 mL (2 T) chopped parsley
125 mL (½ c) chopped fresh
   tomatoes
30 mL (2 T) chopped celery
2 green onions, sliced
6 radishes, chopped
5 mL (1 t) chopped anchovies
45 mL (3 T) capers
1.25 mL (¼ t) salt
1.25 mL (¼ t) black pepper
45 mL (3 T) wine vinegar
1.25 mL (½ c) olive oil

1. Combine the chopped vegetables, anchovies, capers, salt, and pepper in a bowl.

2. Add vinegar. Mix lightly.

3. Add olive oil gradually. Mix thoroughly.

4. Chill.

Cucumber Salad from Turkey

6-8 servings

4 cucumbers
5 mL (1 t) salt
15 mL (1 T) vinegar
1 clove garlic, minced
15 mL (1 T) chopped dill
500 mL (2 c) yogurt
45 mL (3 T) olive oil
15 mL (1 T) chopped mint leaves

1. Peel cucumbers. Cut into quarters lengthwise.

2. Slice into very thin slices. Place in a bowl and sprinkle with salt.

3. Mix together the vinegar, garlic, dill, and yogurt.

4. Pour over the cucumbers and mix well.

5. Sprinkle the olive oil and chopped mint leaves on top of the salad.

6. Serve cool, but do not refrigerate.

Vegetables

Stir-fry Vegetables from China

4 servings

30 mL (2 T) oil
750 mL (3 c) sliced or diagonally
cut vegetables

1. Clean, slice thinly or cut vegetables into strips.

2. Heat oil in large saucepan over medium heat.

3. Add vegetables and salt. Toss vegetables in oil until heated through and crisp tender.

Sweet-sour Red Cabbage from Denmark

6-8 servings

1.36 kg (3 lb) red cabbage
60 mL (¼ c) butter
60 mL (4 T) vinegar
125 mL (½ c) water
30 mL (2 T) currant jelly
15 mL (1 T) sugar
5 mL (1 t) salt

1. Thoroughly wash and drain cabbage. Then cut or shred into thin strips.

2. Melt butter in a deep saucepan. Add cabbage and toss with a large spoon to evenly coat it with butter.

3. Add water and vinegar. Cook on low heat until the cabbage is crisp tender.

4. Add jelly, sugar, and salt. Mix.

5. Cook over low heat to desired tenderness.

This dish may be prepared in advance to permit the blending of flavors. It can be reheated for serving.

Green Beans with Onion from France

4 servings

.454 kg (1 lb) green beans
1 small onion, chopped
45 mL (3 T) butter
salt and pepper to taste
pinch of basil

1. Wash beans. Remove tips and strings.

2. Cook in boiling, salted water for 10 minutes.

3. Sauté onions in half of the butter.

4. Add drained beans and rest of the butter. Sauté until slightly browned.

5. Season with pepper and basil.

Refried Beans from Mexico

6 to 8 servings

.454 kg (1 lb) red or pink beans
1.4 L (6 c) water
375 mL (1½ c) chopped onion
2 cloves garlic
10 mL (2 t) salt
2.5 mL (½ t) ground dried chili
   peppers
125 mL (½ c) lard, bacon drippings, or vegetable oil

1. Clean and wash beans. Place them in a heavy saucepan. Cover with water. Bring to boil.

2. Remove from heat and let beans soak for 1 hour.

3. Drain. Add the 1.4 L (6 c) of water and half of the onion and garlic.

4. Bring to boil, cover loosely. Cook over low heat for 2 hours.

5. Add salt, chili pepper, and 15 mL (1 T) of the fat.

6. Cook 30 minutes or until tender. Mix frequently.

7. Drain any remaining liquid.

8. Mash beans with a potato masher or back of a spoon.

9. In a large skillet, heat the remaining fat, garlic, and onion. Sauté 5 minutes. Stir in the mashed beans.

10. Cook for 10 minutes. Stir frequently.

Desserts

Strawberry-cheese Crepes

6 servings

310 mL (1¹/₄ c) sifted flour
5 mL (1 t) salt
2 eggs, beaten
250 mL (1 c) milk
15 mL (1 T) vegetable oil
60 mL (4 T) butter

1. Combine flour and salt.

2. Gradually add eggs and milk. Beat until mixture is smooth.

3. Add oil and beat 1 minute longer. Chill for 2 hours.

4. Place a small piece of butter in a 15 cm (6 in) frying pan or crepe pan.

When the butter bubbles, place 30 mL (2 T) batter into it. Turn the frying pan or crepe pan from side to side to spread the batter evenly and thinly.

5. Cook over low heat for one minute, then turn over and cook 30 seconds more.

6. Remove carefully to a plate. Repeat the process until all of the batter has been used.

7. The crepes may be spread with jam, jelly, or other fillings and then rolled.

Cheese Filling

6 servings

375 mL (1¹/₂ c) cottage cheese
125 mL (¹/₂ c) brown sugar, packed
10 mL (2 t) vanilla
1.25 mL (¹/₄ t) almond flavoring
250 mL (1 c) thawed, frozen strawberries

1. Mix cottage cheese, brown sugar, vanilla, and almond flavoring.

2. Place some of the cottage cheese mixture on each crepe.

Roll up each crepe and place seam side down on an oven-proof platter.

3. Warm in a preheated oven.

4. Warm the thawed strawberries. Spoon the warm strawberries over the warm crepes and serve.

Strudel from Germany
Pastry

6-8 servings

.227 g (½ lb) (2 sticks) butter
80 mL (⅓ c) sugar
2 egg yolks
5 mL (1 t) vanilla
660 mL (2⅔ c) sifted flour

1. Cream butter. Add sugar and continue to cream until mixture is light.
2. Beat in egg yolks and vanilla.
3. Stir in flour to form a dough.
4. Chill the dough while the filling is being prepared.

Filling

6 apples
125 mL (½ c) sugar
60 mL (¼ c) dry bread crumbs
15 mL (1 T) grated lemon rind
5 mL (1 t) cinnamon
1 egg, beaten

1. Peel apples and slice very thin.
2. Mix sugar, bread crumbs, lemon rind, and cinnamon.
3. Divide the chilled dough into two pieces, one slightly larger than the other.
4. Roll the larger piece into a 30 cm (12 in) square. Place it in a 20 cm (8 in) oiled baking pan.
5. Add the filling and spread over the dough.
6. Roll out the second piece of dough. Cover the filling with this piece of dough. Seal the edges.
7. Brush the top of the dough with the beaten egg.
8. Bake in 200°C (400°F) oven 15 minutes.
9. Reduce the heat to 180°C (350°F) and bake for 30 minutes longer.
10. Cut into squares and serve warm.
11. Sprinkle with powdered sugar, if desired.

Cinnamon Fritters
from Greece

25 fritters

1 package yeast
125 mL (½ c) lukewarm water
125 mL (½ c) scalded milk
1 egg, well beaten
500 mL (2 c) flour
7.5 mL (1½ t) baking powder
1.25 mL (¼ t) salt
5 mL (1 t) cinnamon
.946 L (1 qt) oil for deep-fat frying

1. Sift flour, baking powder, and salt together.

2. Put the yeast and warm water into a medium mixing bowl.

3. Cool milk to lukewarm temperature.

4. Add egg, milk, and flour to the yeast and warm water.

5. Beat until smooth.

6. Cover and let rise in a warm place until double in bulk.

7. Heat oil to 180°C (350°F) in a heavy saucepan.

8. Drop batter by teaspoonful, with aid of a spatula, into the hot fat.

9. Brown fritter on both sides.

10. Remove from fat and drain on absorbent paper.

11. Sprinkle with cinnamon while hot.

12. Serve with hot syrup, if desired.

Syrup

250 mL (1 c) sugar
125 mL (½ c) honey
185 mL (¾ c) water

Make syrup by combining sugar, honey, and water. Boil for 5 minutes.

BUYING GUIDE FOR DAIRY PRODUCTS

Food Item and Form	Market Unit	Approximate Volume per Market Unit	Approximate Weight per Cup	
Butter	1 lb	2 c	224 g	7.9 oz
whipped	1 lb	3 c	152 g	5.4 oz
Cheese				
Cheddar (natural or processed)	1 lb			
grated or chopped		4 c	113 g	4.0 oz
Cheddar or Swiss, sliced	1 lb	8 slices		
cottage	12 oz	1¹/₂ c	236 g	8.3 oz
cream	8 oz	1 c	230 g	8.1 oz
spread	5 oz	¹/₂ c		
Parmesan, grated	3 oz	1 c	92 g	3.3 oz
Cream				
light (table)	¹/₂ pt	1 c	240 g	8.5 oz
heavy (whipping)	¹/₂ pt	1 c	236 g	8.3 oz
whipped		2 c		
sour	¹/₂ pt	1 c	241 g	8.5 oz
half and half (cream and milk), sweet	1 pt	2 c	242 g	8.5 oz
half and half, sour	¹/₂ pt	1 c	242 g	8.5 oz
Milk				
whole or skim	1 qt	4 c	242 g	8.5 oz
buttermilk	1 qt	4 c	242 g	8.5 oz
sweetened condensed	15 oz	1¹/₃ c	306 g	10.8 oz
evaporated, whole or skim	14¹/₂ oz	1²/₃ c	252 g	8.9 oz
reconstituted		3¹/₃ c		
dry, whole	1 lb	3²/₃ c	131 g	4.6 oz
reconstituted		14 c		
dry, nonfat				
instant	9⁵/₈ lb	4 c	75 g	2.6 oz
reconstituted		14 c	242 g	8.5 oz
Milk desserts				
ice cream	1 qt	4 c	142 g	5.0 oz
brick, sliced	1 qt	8 slices		
ice milk	1 qt	4 c	187 g	6.6 oz
sherbet	1 qt	4 c	193 g	6.8 oz
Yogurt	¹/₂ pt	1 c	246 g	8.7 oz

Handbook of Food Preparation, Seventh Edition, 1975, American Home Economics Association, Washington, D.C., p. 30. Used by permission.

BUYING GUIDE FOR FISH AND SHELLFISH

Food Item and Form	Market Unit	Approximate Servings per Market Unit*	Approximate Weight per Cup	
Fish, fresh or frozen				
whole	1 lb	$1^{1}/_{2}$		
chunks	1 lb	3		
dressed	1 lb	$2^{1}/_{3}$		
fillets	1 lb	$3^{1}/_{3}$		
steaks	1 lb	3		
cakes, frozen	1 lb	$5^{1}/_{3}$		
portions, unbreaded, frozen	1 lb	4		
portions, breaded, fried or raw, frozen	1 lb	$5^{1}/_{3}$		
sticks, frozen	1 lb	$5^{1}/_{3}$		
Fish, canned				
gefilte fish	1 lb	3	162 g	5.7 oz
mackerel	15 oz	$4^{1}/_{4}$	182 g	6.4 oz
Maine sardines	12 oz	$3^{3}/_{4}$	160 g	5.6 oz
salmon	1 lb	$4^{1}/_{4}$	168 g	5.9 oz
tuna	7 oz	2	170 g	6.0 oz
Fish, cured				
lox	1 lb	$5^{1}/_{3}$		
salt fish	1 lb	$5^{1}/_{3}$		
smoked fish	1 lb	$3^{1}/_{2}$		
Shellfish				
Clams, fresh or frozen				
in shell (hard)	1 doz	2		
in shell (soft)	1 doz	1		
shucked	1 lb	$2^{1}/_{2}$		
frozen, breaded, raw	1 lb	$4^{1}/_{2}$		
clams, canned, minced	$7^{1}/_{2}$ oz	$2^{1}/_{2}$	158 g	5.6 oz
Crabs, fresh or frozen				
in shell (Blue)	1 lb	$3/_{4}$		
in shell (Dungeness)	1 lb	$1^{1}/_{4}$		
crab meat	1 lb	5	163 g	5.7 oz
crab cakes, frozen	1 lb	5		
crab legs and sections, frozen	1 lb	$2^{1}/_{2}$		
deviled, frozen	1 lb	$5^{1}/_{3}$		
Crab meat, canned	$6^{1}/_{2}$ oz	$1^{3}/_{4}$		
Lobsters, fresh or frozen				
in shell	1 lb	$1^{1}/_{4}$		
meat	1 lb	$4^{3}/_{4}$	154 g	5.4 oz
spiny tails, frozen	1 lb	$2^{2}/_{3}$		
Oysters, fresh or frozen				
in shell	1 doz	2		
shucked	1 lb	2	235 g	8.3 oz
breaded, frozen	1 lb	$4^{2}/_{3}$		
Oysters, canned, whole	5 oz	$1^{2}/_{3}$	156 g	5.5 oz
Scallops, fresh or frozen				
shucked	1 lb	$3^{1}/_{3}$		
breaded, frozen	1 lb	4		
Shrimp, fresh or frozen				
in shell	1 lb	$2^{2}/_{3}$		
raw, peeled	1 lb	$3^{1}/_{3}$		
cooked, peeled, cleaned	1 lb	$5^{1}/_{3}$		
breaded, frozen	1 lb	$4^{1}/_{2}$		
Shrimp, canned	$13^{1}/_{4}$ oz	$4^{1}/_{3}$	129 g	4.6 oz

*One serving equals three ounces of cooked boneless fish or shellfish.
Ibid., pp. 40–41.

BUYING GUIDE FOR MEAT

Food Item and Form	Market Unit	Approximate Volume or Number of Servings per Market Unit*	Approximate Weight per Cup	
Meat, fresh or frozen				
boned or ground meat	1 lb		227 g	8.0 oz
cooked		3 to 4 servings		
diced		1¹/₂ to 2 c	142 g	5.0 oz
meat with minimum amount of bone (steaks, roasts, chops, etc.)	1 lb			
cooked		2 to 3 servings		
diced		1 to 1¹/₂ c	142 g	5.0 oz
meat with large amount of bone (shoulder cuts, short ribs, neck, etc.)	1 lb			
cooked		1 to 2 servings		
diced		1 c	142 g	5.0 oz
Cured and/or smoked				
ham, ground	1 lb		170 g	6.0 oz
cooked, ground		2¹/₂ to 3 servings	109 g	3.8 oz
diced		1¹/₂ to 2 c	147 g	5.2 oz
bacon	1 lb	24 slices		
frankfurters	1 lb	8 to 10 sausages		
luncheon meat, sliced	12 oz	8 slices		
diced			141 g	5.0 oz
Canned				
corned beef	12 oz	4 servings		
ham, smoked	1¹/₂ lb	6 to 8 servings		
diced		3³/₄ to 4¹/₂ c		
luncheon meat	12 oz	4 servings		
sausage, Vienna	4 oz	8 to 10 sausages		
Dried				
chipped beef	4 oz	1²/₃ servings		

*Three ounces of cooked meat is the usual amount for one serving.
Ibid., p. 70.

BUYING GUIDE FOR POULTRY

Food Item and Form	Market Unit	Approximate Volume or Number of Servings per Market Unit*	Approximate Weight per Cup	
Chicken, ready-to-cook				
broiler-fryer	1½ to 3½ lb	2 to 4 servings		
roaster	1 lb	2¼ servings		
Rock Cornish hen	less than 2 lb	1 to 2 servings		
stewing	1 lb			
cooked, boned		2½ servings		
diced		1½ c	136 g	4.8 oz
ground			113 g	4.0 oz
canned, boned	5 to 6 oz	1½ to 2 servings		
Duck, ready-to-cook	1 lb	2 to 2½ servings		
Goose, ready-to-cook	1 lb	2 to 2⅔ servings		
Turkey, ready-to-cook	1 lb			
cooked, boned, diced		1 to 2 servings	133 g	4.7 oz
canned, boned	5 oz	1½ servings		

*Amounts are based on three ounces of cooked poultry meat without bone per serving.
Ibid., p. 78.

BUYING GUIDE FOR EGGS

Food Item and Form	Market Unit	Approximate Volume or Number per Market Unit	Approximate Weight per Cup	
Eggs, whole				
fresh	1 doz	12 eggs	248 g	8.8 oz
extra large	1 doz	3 c		
large	1 doz	2⅓ c		
medium	1 doz	2 c		
small	1 doz	1¾ c		
frozen	1 lb	1⅞ c	248 g	8.8 oz
dried, sifted	1 lb	5¼ c	86 g	3.0 oz
Whites				
fresh	1 doz	12 whites	246 g	8.7 oz
extra large	1 doz	1¾ c		
large	1 doz	1½ c		
medium	1 doz	1⅓ c		
small	1 doz	1¼ c		
frozen	1 lb	1⅞ c	246 g	8.7 oz
dried, sifted	1 lb	5 c	89 g	3.1 oz
Yolks				
fresh	1 doz	12 yolks	233 g	8.2 oz
extra large	1 doz	1 c		
large	1 doz	⅞ c		
medium	1 doz	¾ c		
small	1 doz	⅔ c		
frozen	1 lb	2¼ c	233 g	8.2 oz
dried, sifted	1 lb	5½ c	80 g	2.8 oz

Ibid., p. 34.

BUYING GUIDE FOR VEGETABLES

Food Item and Form	Market Unit	Approximate Volume or Pieces per Market Unit	Approximate Weight per Cup*	
Asparagus, spears				
fresh	1 lb	16 to 20		
cooked		2 c	181 g	6.4 oz
canned	14^1/$_2$ to 16 oz	12 to 18	195 g	6.9 oz
Frozen spears, cuts, and tips	10 oz	2 c	181 g	6.4 oz
Beans, green				
fresh	1 lb	3 c	114 g	4.0 oz
cooked		2^1/$_2$ c	125 g	4.4 oz
frozen	9 oz	1^1/$_2$ c	161 g	5.7 oz
canned	15^1/$_2$ oz	1^3/$_4$ c	135 g	4.8 oz
Beans, kidney, canned	16 to 17 oz	2 c	187 g	6.6 oz
dried	1 lb	2^1/$_2$ c	184 g	6.5 oz
cooked		5^1/$_2$ c	185 g	6.5 oz
Beans, Lima, shelled				
fresh	1 lb	2 c	155 g	5.5 oz
cooked		1^2/$_3$ to 2 c	166 g	5.9 oz
frozen	10 oz	1^3/$_4$ c	173 g	6.1 oz
canned	16 oz	2 c	170 g	6.0 oz
dried	1 lb	2^1/$_2$ c	180 g	6.3 oz
cooked		5^1/$_2$ c	186 g	6.6 oz
Beans, navy, dried	1 lb	2^1/$_3$ c	190 g	6.7 oz
cooked		5^1/$_2$ c	191 g	6.7 oz
Beans, soybeans, dried	1 lb	2 c	210 g	7.4 oz
Beets, without tops				
fresh	1 lb	2 c	145 g	5.1 oz
cooked		2 c	180 g	6.3 oz
canned	16 to 17 oz	2 c	167 g	5.9 oz
Broccoli, fresh, cooked	1 lb	2 c	164 g	5.8 oz
Broccoli, spears, chopped, frozen	10 oz	1^1/$_2$ c	188 g	6.6 oz
Brussels sprouts				
fresh	1 lb	4 c	102 g	3.6 oz
cooked		2^1/$_2$ c	180 g	6.4 oz
frozen	10 oz	18 to 24 sprouts		
Cabbage				
fresh	1 lb			
shredded		3^1/$_2$ to 4^1/$_2$ c	80 g	2.8 oz
cooked		2 c	146 g	5.2 oz
Carrots, without tops				
fresh	1 lb	3 c	130 g	4.6 oz
shredded		2^1/$_2$ c	112 g	4.0 oz
diced			137 g	4.8 oz
cooked		2 to 2^1/$_2$ c	160 g	5.6 oz
frozen	1 lb			
cooked		2^1/$_2$ c	165 g	5.8 oz
canned	16 oz	2 c	159 g	5.6 oz

*Weight per cup is that of food alone without liquid.
Ibid., pp. 86–90.

BUYING GUIDE FOR VEGETABLES (Continued)

Food Item and Form	Market Unit	Approximate Volume or Pieces per Market Unit	Approximate Weight per Cup*	
Cauliflower, fresh	1 lb	1½ c	104 g	3.7 oz
cooked		1½ c	125 g	4.4 oz
frozen	10 oz	2 c	152 g	5.4 oz
cooked		1½ c	179 g	6.3 oz
Celery, fresh	1 lb	2 bunches	121 g	4.3 oz
cooked		2 to 2½ c	153 g	5.4 oz
Corn, fresh ears	1 doz			
cooked		2½ c	165 g	5.8 oz
frozen, cut	10 oz	1¾ c	135 g	4.8 oz
cooked		1½ to 2 c	182 g	6.4 oz
canned, cream style	16 to 17 oz	2 c	249 g	8.8 oz
whole kernel	12 oz	1½ c	169 g	6.0 oz
Eggplant, fresh	1 lb			
diced		2½ c	99 g	3.5 oz
cooked		2½ c	213 g	7.5 oz
Greens, fresh	1 lb		77 g	2.7 oz
cooked		4 to 6 c	190 g	6.7 oz
frozen	10 oz	1½ to 2 c	187 g	6.6 oz
Lentils, dried	1 lb	2¼ c	191 g	6.7 oz
cooked		5 c	202 g	7.1 oz
Lettuce, head	1 lb (about)	6¼ c		
leaf	1 lb	6¼ c		
Romaine	1 lb	6 c		
endive	1 lb (about)	4¼ c		
Mixed vegetables, frozen	10 oz	2 c	182 g	6.4 oz
canned	16 to 17 oz	2 c	179 g	6.3 oz
Mushrooms, fresh, sliced	1 lb	2 to 3 c	68 g	2.4 oz
canned	4 oz	⅔ c	161 g	5.7 oz
Okra, fresh, cooked	1 lb	2¼ c	177 g	6.2 oz
frozen	10 oz	1¼ c	209 g	7.4 oz
canned	15½ oz	1¾ c	171 g	6.0 oz
Onions, fresh	1 lb	3 large		
chopped		2 to 2½ c	135 g	4.8 oz
cooked			197 g	6.9 oz
frozen, chopped	12 oz	3 c		
canned	16 to 17 oz	2 c		
dried			64 g	2.3 oz
Parsnips, fresh	1 lb	4 medium		
cooked		2 c	211 g	7.4 oz
Peas, green, fresh, in pod	1 lb			
shelled		1 c	138 g	4.9 oz
cooked		1 c	163 g	5.7 oz
frozen	10 oz	2 c	156 g	5.5 oz
cooked		2 c	167 g	5.9 oz
canned	1 lb	2 c	168 g	5.9 oz
dried, split	1 lb	2¼ c	200 g	7.1 oz
cooked		5 c	194 g	6.8 oz

BUYING GUIDE FOR VEGETABLES (Continued)

Food Item and Form	Market Unit	Approximate Volume or Pieces per Market Unit	Approximate Weight per Cup*	
Peas, black-eyed, fresh	1 lb		144 g	5.1 oz
cooked		2^1/3 c	162 g	5.7 oz
frozen, cooked	10 oz	1^1/2 c	171 g	6.0 oz
canned	16 to 17 oz	2 c	205 g	7.2 oz
dried, split	1 lb		200 g	7.1 oz
cooked			248 g	8.7 oz
Potatoes, white, fresh	1 lb	3 medium	164 g	5.8 oz
cooked, diced, or sliced		2^1/4 c	163 g	5.7 oz
mashed		1^3/4 c	207 g	7.3 oz
frozen, French fried or puffs	9 oz	3 to 4		
canned, whole	16 to 17 oz	8 to 12	179 g	6.3 oz
dried flakes	6 to 7 oz	4^1/2 c	36 g	1.3 oz
reconstituted		10^3/4 c	212 g	7.5 oz
dried granules	1 lb	2^1/4 c	201 g	7.1 oz
reconstituted		10^1/2 c	212 g	7.5 oz
Pumpkin, fresh, cooked, mashed	1 lb	1 c	247 g	8.7 oz
canned	16 to 17 oz	2 c	244 g	8.6 oz
Radishes, sliced	6 oz	1^1/4 c		
Rutabaga, fresh, cubed	1 lb	2^1/2 c	139 g	4.9 oz
cooked		2 c	163 g	5.7 oz
Sauerkraut, canned	15 to 16 oz	2 c	188 g	6.6 oz
Spinach, fresh	1 lb	4 c	54 g	1.9 oz
cooked		1^1/2 c	200 g	7.1 oz
frozen	10 oz	1^1/2 c	190 g	6.7 oz
canned	15 oz	2 c	221 g	7.8 oz
Squash, winter, fresh	1 lb			
cooked, mashed		1 c	244 g	8.6 oz
frozen	12 oz	1^1/2 c	242 g	8.5 oz
canned	15 to 16 oz	1^3/4 to 2 c		
Squash, summer, fresh	1 lb		136 g	4.8 oz
cooked, mashed		1^2/3 c	238 g	8.4 oz
frozen, sliced	10 oz	1^1/2 c	211 g	7.4 oz
canned	1 lb			
Sweet potatoes, fresh	1 lb	3 medium		
cooked, sliced			232 g	8.2 oz
frozen	12 oz	3 to 4	200 g	7.1 oz
canned	16 to 17 oz	1^3/4 to 2 c	220 g	7.8 oz
dried, flakes	1 lb		115 g	4.1 oz
reconstituted			255 g	9.0 oz
Tomatoes, fresh	1 lb	3 to 4 small	162 g	5.7 oz
cooked		1^1/2 c		
canned, whole	16 oz	2 c	238 g	8.4 oz
sauce	8 oz	1 c	258 g	9.1 oz
Turnips, fresh	1 lb	3 medium	134 g	4.7 oz
cooked		2 c	196 g	6.9 oz

BUYING GUIDE FOR FRUITS

Food Item and Form	Market Unit	Approximate Volume or Pieces per Market Unit	Approximate Weight per Cup*	
Apples				
fresh, whole	1 lb	3 medium		
pared and sliced		2³/₄ c	122 g	4.3 oz
sauce, sweetened (not canned)		1³/₄ c	252 g	8.9 oz
frozen, sliced, sweetened	20 oz	2¹/₂ c	205 g	7.2 oz
canned, sliced	20 oz	2¹/₂ c	204 g	7.5 oz
juice	46 fl oz	5³/₄ c	249 g	8.8 oz
sauce	1 lb	1³/₄ c	259 g	9.1 oz
dried	1 lb	4¹/₃ c	104 g	3.7 oz
cooked		8 c	244 g	8.6 oz
Apricots				
fresh, whole	1 lb	8 to 12	115 g	4.1 oz
sliced or halved		2¹/₂ c	156 g	5.5 oz
canned, whole (medium)	1 lb	8 to 12	225 g	7.9 oz
halved (medium)	1 lb	12 to 20 halves	217 g	7.7 oz
dried	11 oz	2¹/₄ c	150 g	5.3 oz
cooked, fruit and liquid		4¹/₃ c	285 g	10.0 oz
Avocado				
fresh	1 lb			
sliced, diced, wedges		2¹/₂ c	142 g	5.0 oz
Bananas				
fresh, whole	1 lb	3 to 4		
sliced		2 c	142 g	5.0 oz
mashed		1¹/₃ c	232 g	8.2 oz
dried	1 lb	4¹/₂ c	100 g	3.5 oz
Blueberries				
fresh	1 lb	2 c	146 g	5.2 oz
frozen	10 oz	1¹/₂ c	161 g	5.7 oz
canned	14 oz	1¹/₂ c	170 g	6.0 oz
Cherries				
fresh, red, pitted	1 lb	2¹/₃ c	154 g	5.4 oz
frozen, red, tart, pitted	20 oz	2 c	242 g	8.5 oz
canned, red, tart, pitted	1 lb	1¹/₂ c	177 g	6.2 oz
sweet, unpitted	1 lb	1³/₄ c	177 g	6.2 oz
Cranberries				
fresh, uncooked	1 lb	4 c	151 g	5.3 oz
sauce		4 c	215 g	7.6 oz
canned, sauce	1 lb	1²/₃ c	278 g	9.8 oz
juice	1 qt	4 c	250 g	8.8 oz
Currants				
dried	1 lb	3¹/₄ c	140 g	4.9 oz
Dates				
dried, whole	1 lb	60 dates		
pitted, cut	1 lb	2¹/₂ c	178 g	6.3 oz
Figs				
fresh	1 lb	12 medium		
canned	1 lb	12 to 16 figs	230 g	8.1 oz
dried, whole	1 lb	44 figs		
cut fine		2²/₃ c	168 g	5.9 oz

*Weight per cup is that of food alone without liquid, unless otherwise noted.
Ibid., pp. 53–56.

Food Item and Form	Market Unit	Approximate Volume or Pieces per Market Unit	Approximate Weight per Cup*	
Fruit juice				
frozen	6 fl oz	$3/4$ c		
canned	46 fl oz	$5^3/4$ c	247 g	8.7 oz
Fruits				
mixed, frozen	12 oz	$1^1/3$ c		
canned, cocktail or salad	17 oz	2 c	229 g	8.1 oz
Grapefruit				
fresh	1 lb	1 medium		
sections		1 c	194 g	6.8 oz
frozen, sections	$13^1/2$ oz	$1^1/2$ c	219 g	7.7 oz
canned, sections	16 oz	2 c	241 g	8.5 oz
Grapes, fresh				
seeded	1 lb	2 c	184 g	6.5 oz
seedless	1 lb	$2^1/2$ c	169 g	6.0 oz
Lemons				
fresh	3 lb	1 doz		
juice		2 c	247 g	8.7 oz
frozen, juice	6 fl oz	$3/4$ c	283 g	10.0 oz
canned, juice	8 fl oz	1 c	245 g	8.6 oz
Melon				
frozen, balls	12 oz	$1^1/2$ c	231 g	8.2 oz
Oranges				
fresh	6 lb	1 doz		
diced or sectioned		12 c	214 g	7.5 oz
juice		4 c	247 g	8.7 oz
frozen, juice, reconstituted	6 fl oz	3 c	268 g	9.5 oz
canned, juice	46 fl oz	$5^3/4$ c	247 g	8.7 oz
canned, mandarin, fruit and juice	11 oz	$1^1/4$ c	250 g	8.8 oz
Peaches				
fresh	1 lb	4 medium		
sliced		2 c	177 g	6.2 oz
frozen, slices and juice	10 oz	$1^1/8$ c	251 g	8.8 oz
canned, halves	1 lb	6 to 10 halves	224 g	7.9 oz
slices	1 lb	2 c	218 g	7.7 oz
dried	1 lb	3 c	160 g	5.6 oz
cooked		6 c	244 g	8.6 oz
Pears				
fresh	1 lb	4 medium		
sliced		$2^1/8$ c	213 g	7.5 oz
canned, halves	1 lb	6 to 10 halves	227 g	8.0 oz
Pineapple				
fresh	2 lb	1 medium		
cubed		3 c	146 g	5.2 oz
frozen, chunks	$13^1/2$ oz	$1^1/2$ c	204 g	7.2 oz
canned, chunks, tidbits	29 oz	$3^3/4$ c	198 g	7.0 oz
crushed	29 oz	$3^3/4$ c	260 g	9.2 oz
sliced	20 oz	10 slices	208 g	7.3 oz
juice	46 fl oz	$5^3/4$ c		

Food Item and Form	Market Unit	Approximate Volume or Pieces per Market Unit	Approximate Weight per Cup*	
Plums				
fresh	1 lb	8 to 20 plums		
halved		2 c	185 g	6.5 oz
canned, whole	1 lb	10 to 14 plums	223 g	7.9 oz
Prunes				
canned	1 lb	10 to 14 prunes	196 g	6.9 oz
dried, whole	1 lb	2$\frac{1}{2}$ c	176 g	6.2 oz
cooked		4 to 4$\frac{1}{2}$ c	229 g	8.1 oz
pitted	1 lb	2$\frac{1}{4}$ c	162 g	5.7 oz
cooked		4 to 4$\frac{1}{2}$ c	210 g	7.4 oz
Raisins				
seeded, whole	1 lb	3$\frac{1}{4}$ c	142 g	5.0 oz
chopped		2$\frac{1}{2}$ c	182 g	6.4 oz
seedless, whole	1 lb	2$\frac{3}{4}$ c	146 g	5.2 oz
cooked		2$\frac{3}{4}$ c	183 g	6.5 oz
chopped		2 c	189 g	6.7 oz
Rhubarb				
fresh	1 lb	4 to 8 pieces		
cut			122 g	4.3 oz
cooked		2 c	242 g	8.5 oz
frozen, sliced	12 oz	1$\frac{1}{2}$ c	168 g	5.9 oz
Strawberries				
fresh, whole	1$\frac{1}{2}$ lb	4 c	144 g	5.1 oz
sliced		4 c	148 g	5.2 oz
frozen, whole	1 lb	1$\frac{1}{3}$ c	204 g	7.2 oz
sliced or halved	10 oz	1 c	235 g	8.3 oz

BUYING GUIDE FOR SWEETENING AGENTS

Food Item and Form	Market Unit	Approximate Volume per Market Unit	Approximate Weight per Cup	
Sugar				
brown (packed)				
light	1 lb	2^1/4 c	200 g	7.1 oz
dark	1 lb	2^1/4 c	200 g	7.1 oz
granulated	1 lb	3 c	152 g	5.4 oz
cane or beet, granulated	5 lb	11^1/4 c	200 g	7.1 oz
superfine	2 lb	4^2/3 c	196 g	6.9 oz
confectioner's, unsifted	1 lb	3 to 4 c	123 g	4.3 oz
confectioner's, sifted		4^1/2 c	95 g	3.4 oz
Corn syrup, light and dark	16 fl oz	2 c	328 g	11.6 oz
Honey	1 lb	1^1/3 c	332 g	11.7 oz
Maple syrup	12 fl oz	1^1/2 c	312 g	11.0 oz
Molasses, cane	12 fl oz	1^1/2 c	309 g	10.9 oz
Sorghum	1 lb	1^1/3 c	330 g	11.6 oz

Ibid., p. 83

BUYING GUIDE FOR FATS AND OILS

Food Item and Form	Market Unit	Approximate Volume per Market Unit	Approximate Weight per Cup	
Butter (see Dairy Products)				
Oils: corn, cottonseed, olive, peanut, and safflower	1 qt	4 c	210 g	7.4 oz
Margarine	1 lb	2 c	224 g	7.9 oz
whipped	1 lb	3 c	149 g	5.3 oz
Hydrogenated fat	1 lb	2^1/3 c	188 g	6.6 oz
Lard and rendered fat	1 lb	2 c	220 g	7.8 oz
Suet, chopped medium fine	1 lb	3^3/4 c	120 g	4.2 oz

Ibid., p. 37.

BUYING GUIDE FOR CEREALS AND FLOURS

Food Item and Form	Market Unit	Approximate Volume or Pieces per Market Unit	Approximate Weight per Cup	
Cereals				
bulgur	1 lb	2³/₄ c	162 g	5.7 oz
cooked		8 c	230 g	8.1 oz
cornmeal				
white	1 lb	3¹/₂ c	129 g	4.6 oz
yellow	1 lb	3 c	152 g	5.4 oz
cooked		16²/₃ c	238 g	8.4 oz
farina	1 lb	3 c		
cooked		16²/₃ c	238 g	8.4 oz
hominy, whole	1 lb	2¹/₂ c	182 g	6.4 oz
cooked		16²/₃ c		
grits	1 lb	3 c	154 g	5.4 oz
cooked		10 c	236 g	8.3 oz
oats, rolled	1 lb	6¹/₄ c	72 g	2.5 oz
cooked		8 c	240 g	8.5 oz
ready-to-eat				
flaked			32 g	1.1 oz
granulated			87 g	3.1 oz
puffed			23 g	0.8 oz
shredded			37 g	1.3 oz
rice, white, polished				
long grain	1 lb	2¹/₂ c	182 g	6.4 oz
medium grain	1 lb	2¹/₃ c	193 g	6.8 oz
short grain	1 lb	2¹/₄ c	200 g	7.1 oz
cooked		8 c	169 g	6.0 oz
precooked	8 oz		185 g	6.5 oz
prepared		2 c	164 g	5.8 oz
brown	1 lb		185 g	6.5 oz
parboiled	14 oz	2 c	198 g	7.0 oz
soy grits, stirred, low-fat	1 lb	3 c	149 g	5.3 oz
wheat germ	12 oz	3 c	113 g	4.0 oz
whole	2 lb	4¹/₂ c	198 g	7.0 oz
Flours				
corn	2 lb	8 c	116 g	4.1 oz
gluten	2 lb	6¹/₂ c		
sifted			142 g	5.0 oz
rice	2 lb			
sifted		7 c	126 g	4.4 oz
stirred, spooned		5³/₄ c	158 g	5.6 oz
rye	2 lb			
light, sifted		10 c	88 g	3.1 oz
dark, sifted		7 c	127 g	4.5 oz
soy	2 lb			
full-fat, sifted		15 c	60 g	2.1 oz
low-fat		11 c	83 g	2.9 oz
wheat				
all-purpose, sifted	2 lb	8 c	115 g	4.1 oz
unsifted, spooned		7 c	125 g	4.4 oz
instant		7¹/₄ c	129 g	4.6 oz
bread, sifted	2 lb	8 c	112 g	4.0 oz
cake, sifted	2 lb	9¹/₄ c	96 g	3.4 oz
spooned		8¹/₄ c	111 g	3.9 oz
pastry, sifted	2 lb	9 c	100 g	3.5 oz
self-rising, sifted	2 lb	8 c	106 g	3.7 oz
whole-wheat, stirred	2 lb	6²/₃ c	132 g	4.7 oz

BUYING GUIDE FOR CEREALS AND FLOURS (Continued)

Food Item and Form	Market Unit	Approximate Volume or Pieces per Market Unit	Approximate Weight per Cup	
Pasta				
macaroni, 1-inch pieces	1 lb	3³/₄ c	123 g	4.3 oz
cooked		9 c	140 g	4.9 oz
macaroni, shell	1 lb	4 to 5 c	115 g	4.1 oz
cooked		9 c		
noodles, 1-inch pieces	1 lb	6 to 8 c	73 g	2.6 oz
cooked		8 c		
spaghetti, 2-inch pieces	1 lb	4 to 5 c	94 g	3.3 oz
cooked		9 c	160 g	5.6 oz
Starch				
corn, stirred	1 lb	3¹/₂ c	128 g	4.5 oz
potato, stirred	1 lb	3¹/₄ c	142 g	5.0 oz

Ibid., pp. 64–65.

BUYING GUIDE FOR MISCELLANEOUS FOODS

Food Item and Form	Market Unit	Approximate Volume per Market Unit	Approximate Weight per Cup	
Bread, sliced	1 lb	12 to 16 slices		
crumbs, soft		10 c	46 g	1.6 oz
dry	10 oz	2³/₄ c	113 g	3.6 oz
Catsup, tomato	14 oz	1¹/₂ c	273 g	9.6 oz
Chocolate, bitter or semisweet	8 oz	1 c	225 g	7.9 oz
prepared drink		30 c		
Cocoa	8 oz	2 c	112 g	4.0 oz
prepared drink		50 c		
instant	8 oz	1²/₃ c	139 g	4.9 oz
prepared drink		28 c		
Coconut, long thread	1 lb	5²/₃ c	80 g	2.8 oz
canned, moist	1 lb	5 c	85 g	3.0 oz
Coffee	1 lb	5 c	85 g	3.0 oz
brewed		40 to 50 c		
instant	2 oz	1¹/₄ to 1¹/₂ c	38 g	1.4 oz
brewed		60		
Crackers				
graham	1 lb	66		
crumbs		4¹/₃ c	86 g	3.0 oz
soda	1 lb	82		
crumbs		7 c		
soda, crumbs, fine	10 oz	4 c	70 g	2.5 oz
saltines	1 lb	130 to 140		
Gelatin, unflavored, granulated	1 oz	¹/₄ c	150 g	5.3 oz
flavored	3 oz	7 Tbsp	179 g	6.3 oz
prepared		2 c	271 g	9.5 oz

BUYING GUIDE FOR MISCELLANEOUS FOODS (Continued)

Food Item and Form	Market Unit	Approximate Volume Per Market Unit	Approximate Weight per Cup	
Infant foods				
strained and junior (chopped)	$3^1/4$ to $3^1/2$ oz	6 Tbsp		
	$4^1/4$ to $4^3/4$ oz	9 Tbsp		
	$7^1/2$ to 8 oz	15 Tbsp		
juice	4 fl oz	$1/2$ c		
Mayonnaise	1 pt		243 g	8.6 oz
Nuts, shelled				
almonds, blanched	1 lb	3 c	152 g	5.4 oz
filberts, whole	1 lb	$3^1/2$ c	134 g	4.7 oz
peanuts	1 lb	3 c	144 g	5.1 oz
pecans, halved	1 lb	4 c	108 g	3.8 oz
chopped	1 lb	$3^1/2$ to 4 c	118 g	4.2 oz
pistachio	1 lb	$3^1/4$ to 4 c	125 g	4.4 oz
walnuts, Persian, English				
halves	1 lb	$3^1/2$ c	100 g	3.5 oz
chopped	1 lb	$3^1/2$ c	119 g	4.2 oz
Pasta				
macaroni, 1-inch pieces	1 lb	4 to 5 c	123 g	4.3 oz
cooked		9 c	140 g	4.9 oz
macaroni, shell	1 lb	4 to 5 c	115 g	4.1 oz
cooked		9 c		
noodles, 1-inch pieces	1 lb	6 to 8 c	73 g	2.6 oz
cooked		8 c		
spaghetti, 2-inch pieces	1 lb	4 to 5 c	94 g	3.3 oz
cooked		9 c	160 g	5.6 oz
Peanut butter	18 oz	2 c	251 g	8.9 oz
Salad dressing, French	1 pt		248 g	8.8 oz
Salt, free-running	1 lb	$1^1/2$ c	288 g	10.2 oz
Soups, frozen condensed	10 to $10^1/2$ oz	1 to $1^1/2$ c		
ready-to-serve	15 oz	$1^1/2$ to 2 c		
canned, condensed	$10^1/2$ to $11^1/2$ oz	$1^1/4$ c		
prepared		$2^1/2$ c		
ready-to-serve	8 oz	1 c	227 g	8.0 oz
dried	$2^3/4$ oz			
reconstituted		3 c	231 g	8.2 oz
Spices, ground	$1^1/4$ to 4 oz	4 Tbsp		
Tapioca, quick-cooking	8 oz	$1^1/2$ c	152 g	5.4 oz
Tea, leaves	1 lb	$6^1/3$ c	72 g	2.5 oz
brewed		300 c		
instant	$1^1/2$ oz	$1^1/4$ c	34 g	1.2 oz
brewed		64 c		
Water			237 g	8.4 oz

Ibid., pp. 108–109.

BUYING GUIDE FOR LEAVENING AGENTS

Food Item and Form	Market Unit	Approximate Volume per Market Unit	Approximate Weight in Grams per Teaspoon	Approximate Weight in Grams per Tablespoon
Baking powder				
Phosphate	12 oz	$1^2/_3$ c	4.1 g	12.7 g
SAS-Phosphate	14 oz	$2^1/_2$ c	3.2 g	10.2 g
Tartrate	6 oz	$1^1/_4$ c	2.9 g	9.2 g
Baking soda	1 lb	$2^1/_3$ c	4.0 g	12.2 g
Cream of tartar	$1^3/_4$ oz	$5^1/_4$ Tbsp	3.1 g	9.4 g
Yeast				
Active dry	0.28 oz	1 Tbsp	2.5 g	7.5 g
Compressed	0.60 oz	4 tsp	4.2 g	12.8 g

Ibid., p. 67.

Index

Index to Basic Recipes
and Recipes from Other Countries

CDEFGHIJ 085
Printed in the United States of America

Credits